THE WORKS OF EDMUND SPENSER

A Variorum Edition

THE FAERIE QVEENE

BOOK FIVE

LONDON: OXFORD UNIVERSITY PRESS

THE WORKS

OF

EDMUND SPENSER

A Variorum Edition

Volume 5

EDITED BY

EDWIN GREENLAW

CHARLES GROSVENOR OSGOOD

FREDERICK MORGAN PADELFORD

RAY HEFFNER

Baltimore

THE JOHNS HOPKINS PRESS

Copyright 1936, The Johns Hopkins Press

Second printing, 1958
Third printing, 1961
Fourth printing, 1966

PRINTED IN THE UNITED STATES OF AMERICA
LIBRARY OF CONGRESS CATALOG CARD NUMBER: 66-26133

THE FAERIE QVEENE

BOOK FIVE

RAY HEFFNER
Special Editor

Baltimore
THE JOHNS HOPKINS PRESS

The work of the Johns Hopkins Spenser Research Unit in this and the other volumes has been financed wholly from funds granted to the University by the Rockefeller Foundation for aid to research in the Humanities. The Editors wish to thank the Rockefeller Foundation for this generous support. Without it, and without Mrs. Greenlaw's aid in the publication, the Variorum Spenser could not have been begun or carried on.

PREFACE TO VOLUME FIVE

The text is the joint work of Professor Padelford, Dr. James G. McManaway, Dr. Lewis F. Ball, and myself, with the primary responsibility resting on Dr. McManaway; each read a copy of the basic 1596 text, and Dr. McManaway and I both read copies of the 1609 edition. Dr. McManaway collected the variants in the editions later than *1609* and wrote the "Critical Notes on the Text." Professor Roswell G. Ham supplied the corrections from Dryden's copy of the 1679 edition.

In the preparation of the notes for the Commentary, I have had the valuable assistance of Professor Osgood, who not only read the entire MS and proofs, making corrections and additions, but also supplied many of the notes attributed to the editor. Most of the notes appear under his initials (C. G. O.) but some of them are incorporated in notes ascribed to the editor. Professor Padelford, as in Book IV, has assumed the primary responsibility for the Appendices and has read all the proofs, supplying several notes for the Commentary. In the checking of the many references in the Commentary I have had the assistance of Professor Osgood, Dr. McManaway, Dr. Kathrine Koller, Dr. Ball, and Miss Dorothy Mason. Dr. McManaway and Miss Mason also read the proofs, and Mr. William R. Orwen assisted with the "Index of Sources and Analogues."

I acknowledge with thanks the generosity of the following publishers in granting permission to use copyrighted material: Edward Arnold and Company, publishers of Miss Spens' *Spenser's Faerie Queene: An Interpretation*; The University of California Press, publishers of Cory's *Spenser* and of Hughes' *Virgil and Spenser*; Cambridge University Press, publishers of Davis' *Edmund Spenser*; University of Chicago Press, publishers of DeMoss' *Spenser's Twelve Moral Virtues*; Constable and Company, publishers of Miss Warren's edition; F. S. Crofts and Company, publishers of Jones' *A Spenser Handbook*; Houghton Mifflin Company, publishers of Child's edition and Dodge's edition; Kegan Paul, Trench, Trübner and Company, publishers of Dowden's *Transcripts and Studies*; Macmillan Company, publishers of Butcher and Lang's *Odyssey* and Lang, Leaf, and Meyer's *Iliad*; Oxford University Press, publishers of Smith's editions, de Selincourt's introduction to the one-volume Oxford edition, and his *Oxford Lectures on Poetry*; and of Gough's edition of Book V; Princeton University Press, publishers of Lotspeich's *Classical Mythology in the Poetry of Edmund Spenser*; University of Minnesota Press, publishers of Bush's *Mythology and the Renaissance Tradition in English Poetry*;

Blackie and Son, publishers of Blakeney's edition of Book V. I wish to thank also Professor E. B. Fowler for permission to quote from his *Spenser and the System of Courtly Love*, Professor Grierson for permission to quote from his *Cross Currents in English Literature of the Seventeenth Century*, and Professor A. A. Jack for permission to quote from his *Chaucer and Spenser.*

R. H.

BALTIMORE,
    November, 1936.

TABLE OF CONTENTS

THE FIFTH

BOOKE OF THE

FAERIE QVEENE.

Contayning,

THE LEGEND OF ARTEGALL

OR

OF IVSTICE.

SO oft as I with state of present time,
  The image of the antique world compare,
  When as mans age was in his freshest prime,
    And the first blossome of faire vertue bare,
Such oddes I finde twixt those, and these which are,
As that, through long continuance of his course,
Me seemes the world is runne quite out of square,
From the first point of his appointed sourse,
And being once amisse growes daily wourse and wourse.

i

For from the golden age, that first was named,
  It's now at earst become a stonie one;
  And men themselues, the which at first were framed
  Of earthly mould, and form'd of flesh and bone,
  Are now transformed into hardest stone:
  Such as behind their backs (so backward bred)
  Were throwne by *Pyrrha* and *Deucalione*:
  And if then those may any worse be red,
They into that ere long will be degendered.

ii

Let none then blame me, if in discipline iii
  Of vertue and of ciuill vses lore,
  I doe not forme them to the common line
  Of present dayes, which are corrupted sore,
  But to the antique vse, which was of yore,
  When good was onely for it selfe desyred,
  And all men sought their owne, and none no more;
  When Iustice was not for most meed outhyred,
But simple Truth did rayne, and was of all admyred.

For that which all men then did vertue call, iv
  Is now cald vice; and that which vice was hight,
  Is now hight vertue, and so vs'd of all:
  Right now is wrong, and wrong that was is right,
  As all things else in time are chaunged quight.
  Ne wonder; for the heauens reuolution
  Is wandred farre from, where it first was pight,
  And so doe make contrarie constitution
Of all this lower world, toward his dissolution.

For who so list into the heauens looke, v
  And search the courses of the rowling spheares,
  Shall find that from the point, where they first tooke
  Their setting forth, in these few thousand yeares
  They all are wandred much; that plaine appeares.
  For that same golden fleecy Ram, which bore
  Phrixus and *Helle* from their stepdames feares,
  Hath now forgot, where he was plast of yore,
And shouldred hath the Bull, which fayre *Europa* bore.

And eke the Bull hath with his bow-bent horne vi
  So hardly butted those two twinnes of *Ioue*,
  That they haue crusht the Crab, and quite him borne
  Into the great *Nemœan* lions groue.
  So now all range, and doe at randon roue
  Out of their proper places farre away,
  And all this world with them amisse doe moue,
  And all his creatures from their course astray,
Till they arriue at their last ruinous decay.

Ne is that same great glorious lampe of light,
   That doth enlumine all these lesser fyres,
   In better case, ne keepes his course more right,
   But is miscaried with the other Spheres.
   For since the terme of fourteene hundred yeres,
   That learned *Ptolomæe* his hight did take,
   He is declyned from that marke of theirs,
   Nigh thirtie minutes to the Southerne lake;
That makes me feare in time he will vs quite forsake.

And if to those Ægyptian wisards old,
   Which in Star-read were wont haue best insight,
   Faith may be giuen, it is by them told,
   That since the time they first tooke the Sunnes hight,
   Foure times his place he shifted hath in sight,
   And twice hath risen, where he now doth West,
   And wested twice, where he ought rise aright.
   But most is *Mars* amisse of all the rest,
And next to him old *Saturne*, that was wont be best.

For during *Saturnes* ancient raigne it's sayd,
   That all the world with goodnesse did abound:
   All loued vertue, no man was affrayd
   Of force, ne fraud in wight was to be found:
   No warre was knowne, no dreadfull trompets sound,
   Peace vniuersall rayn'd mongst men and beasts,
   And all things freely grew out of the ground:
   Iustice sate high ador'd with solemne feasts,
And to all people did diuide her dred beheasts.

Most sacred vertue she of all the rest,
   Resembling God in his imperiall might;
   Whose soueraine powre is herein most exprest,
   That both to good and bad he dealeth right,
   And all his workes with Iustice hath bedight.
   That powre he also doth to Princes lend,
   And makes them like himselfe in glorious sight,
   To sit in his owne seate, his cause to end,
And rule his people right, as he doth recommend.

Dread Souerayne Goddesse, that doest highest sit
  In seate of iudgement, in th'Almighties stead,
  And with magnificke might and wondrous wit
  Doest to thy people righteous doome aread,
  That furthest Nations filles with awfull dread,
  Pardon the boldnesse of thy basest thrall,
  That dare discourse of so diuine a read,
  As thy great iustice praysed ouer all:
The instrument whereof loe here thy *Artegall*.

Cant. I.

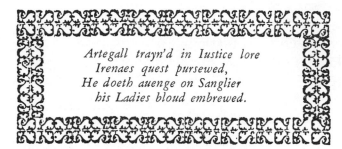

Artegall trayn'd in Iustice lore
Irenaes quest pursewed,
He doeth auenge on Sanglier
his Ladies bloud embrewed.

THough vertue then were held in highest price,   i
   In those old times, of which I doe intreat,
Yet then likewise the wicked seede of vice
Began to spring which shortly grew full great,
And with their boughes the gentle plants did beat.
But euermore some of the vertuous race
Rose vp, inspired with heroicke heat,
   That cropt the branches of the sient base,
And with strong hand their fruitfull rancknes did deface.

Such first was *Bacchus*, that with furious might   ii
   All th'East before vntam'd did ouerronne,
And wrong repressed, and establisht right,
Which lawlesse men had formerly fordonne.
There Iustice first her princely rule begonne.
Next *Hercules* his like ensample shewed,
Who all the West with equall conquest wonne,
   And monstrous tyrants with his club subdewed;
The club of Iustice dread, with kingly powre endewed.

And such was he, of whom I haue to tell,   iii
   The Champion of true Iustice *Artegall*.
Whom (as ye lately mote remember well)
An hard aduenture, which did then befall,
Into redoubted perill forth did call;
That was to succour a distressed Dame,
Whom a strong tyrant did vniustly thrall,
   And from the heritage, which she did clame,
Did with strong hand withhold: *Grantorto* was his name.

Wherefore the Lady, which *Irena* hight,   iv
  Did to the Faery Queene her way addresse,
  To whom complayning her afflicted plight,
  She her besought of gratious redresse.
  That soueraine Queene, that mightie Emperesse,
  Whose glorie is to aide all suppliants pore,
  And of weake Princes to be Patronesse,
  Chose *Artegall* to right her to restore;
For that to her he seem'd best skild in righteous lore.

For *Artegall* in iustice was vpbrought   v
  Euen from the cradle of his infancie,
  And all the depth of rightfull doome was taught
  By faire *Astræa*, with great industrie,
  Whilest here on earth she liued mortallie.
  For till the world from his perfection fell
  Into all filth and foule iniquitie,
  Astræa here mongst earthly men did dwell,
And in the rules of iustice them instructed well.

Whiles through the world she walked in this sort,   vi
  Vpon a day she found this gentle childe,
  Amongst his peres playing his childish sport:
  Whom seeing fit, and with no crime defilde,
  She did allure with gifts and speaches milde,
  To wend with her. So thence him farre she brought
  Into a caue from companie exilde,
  In which she noursled him, till yeares he raught,
And all the discipline of iustice there him taught.

There she him taught to weigh both right and wrong   vii
  In equall ballance with due recompence,
  And equitie to measure out along,
  According to the line of conscience,
  When so it needs with rigour to dispence.
  Of all the which, for want there of mankind,
  She caused him to make experience
  Vpon wyld beasts, which she in woods did find,
With wrongfull powre oppressing others of their kind.

Thus she him trayned, and thus she him taught,   viii
   In all the skill of deeming wrong and right,
   Vntill the ripenesse of mans yeares he raught;
   That euen wilde beasts did feare his awfull sight,
   And men admyr'd his ouerruling might;
   Ne any liu'd on ground, that durst withstand
   His dreadfull heast, much lesse him match in fight,
   Or bide the horror of his wreakfull hand,
When so he list in wrath lift vp his steely brand.

Which steely brand, to make him dreaded more,   ix
   She gaue vnto him, gotten by her slight
   And earnest search, where it was kept in store
   In *Ioues* eternall house, vnwist of wight,
   Since he himselfe it vs'd in that great fight
   Against the *Titans*, that whylome rebelled
   Gainst highest heauen; *Chrysaor* it was hight;
   Chrysaor that all other swords excelled,
Well prou'd in that same day, when *Ioue* those Gyants quelled.

For of most perfect metall it was made,   x
   Tempred with Adamant amongst the same,
   And garnisht all with gold vpon the blade
   In goodly wise, whereof it tooke his name,
   And was of no lesse vertue, then of fame.
   For there no substance was so firme and hard,
   But it would pierce or cleaue, where so it came;
   Ne any armour could his dint out ward,
But wheresoeuer it did light, it throughly shard.

Now when the world with sinne gan to abound,   xi
   Astræa loathing lenger here to space
   Mongst wicked men, in whom no truth she found,
   Return'd to heauen, whence she deriu'd her race;
   Where she hath now an euerlasting place,
   Mongst those twelue signes, which nightly we doe see
   The heauens bright-shining baudricke to enchace;
   And is the *Virgin*, sixt in her degree,
And next her selfe her righteous ballance hanging bee.

But when she parted hence, she left her groome xii
  An yron man, which did on her attend
  Alwayes, to execute her stedfast doome,
  And willed him with *Artegall* to wend,
  And doe what euer thing he did intend.
  His name was *Talus*, made of yron mould,
  Immoueable, resistlesse, without end.
  Who in his hand an yron flale did hould,
With which he thresht out falshood, and did truth vnfould.

He now went with him in this new inquest, xiii
  Him for to aide, if aide he chaunst to neede,
  Against that cruell Tyrant, which opprest
  The faire *Irena* with his foule misdeede,
  And kept the crowne in which she should succeed.
  And now together on their way they bin,
  When as they saw a Squire in squallid weed,
  Lamenting sore his sorowfull sad tyne,
With many bitter teares shed from his blubbred eyne.

To whom as they approched, they espide xiv
  A sorie sight, as euer seene with eye;
  An headlesse Ladie lying him beside,
  In her owne blood all wallow'd wofully,
  That her gay clothes did in discolour die.
  Much was he moued at that ruefull sight;
  And flam'd with zeale of vengeance inwardly,
  He askt, who had that Dame so fouly dight;
Or whether his owne hand, or whether other wight?

Ah woe is me, and well away (quoth hee) xv
  Bursting forth teares, like springs out of a banke,
  That euer I this dismall day did see:
  Full farre was I from thinking such a pranke;
  Yet litle losse it were, and mickle thanke,
  If I should graunt that I haue doen the same,
  That I mote drinke the cup, whereof she dranke:
  But that I should die guiltie of the blame,
The which another did, who now is fled with shame.

Who was it then (sayd *Artegall*) that wrought?   xvi
   And why? doe it declare vnto me trew.
   A knight (said he) if knight he may be thought,
   That did his hand in Ladies bloud embrew,
   And for no cause, but as I shall you shew.
   This day as I in solace sate hereby
   With a fayre loue, whose losse I now do rew,
   There came this knight, hauing in companie
This lucklesse Ladie, which now here doth headlesse lie.

He, whether mine seem'd fayrer in his eye,   xvii
   Or that he wexed weary of his owne,
   Would change with me; but I did it denye;
   So did the Ladies both, as may be knowne,
   But he, whose spirit was with pride vpblowne,
   Would not so rest contented with his right,
   But hauing from his courser her downe throwne,
   Fro me reft mine away by lawlesse might,
And on his steed her set, to beare her out of sight.

Which when his Ladie saw, she follow'd fast,   xviii
   And on him catching hold, gan loud to crie
   Not so to leaue her, nor away to cast,
   But rather of his hand besought to die.
   With that his sword he drew all wrathfully,
   And at one stroke cropt off her head with scorne,
   In that same place, whereas it now doth lie.
   So he my loue away with him hath borne,
And left me here, both his and mine owne loue to morne.

Aread (sayd he) which way then did he make?   xix
   And by what markes may he be knowne againe?
   To hope (quoth he) him soone to ouertake,
   That hence so long departed, is but vaine:
   But yet he pricked ouer yonder plaine,
   And as I marked, bore vpon his shield,
   By which it's easie him to know againe,
   A broken sword within a bloodie field;
Expressing well his nature, which the same did wield.

No sooner sayd, but streight he after sent
  His yron page, who him pursew'd so light,
  As that it seem'd aboue the ground he went:
  For he was swift as swallow in her flight,
  And strong as Lyon in his Lordly might.
  It was not long, before he ouertooke
  Sir *Sanglier*; (so cleeped was that Knight)
  Whom at the first he ghessed by his looke,
And by the other markes, which of his shield he tooke.

He bad him stay, and backe with him retire;
  Who full of scorne to be commaunded so,
  The Lady to alight did eft require,
  Whilest he reformed that vnciuill fo:
  And streight at him with all his force did go.
  Who mou'd no more therewith, then when a rocke
  Is lightly stricken with some stones throw;
  But to him leaping, lent him such a knocke,
That on the ground he layd him like a sencelesse blocke.

But ere he could him selfe recure againe,
  Him in his iron paw he seized had;
  That when he wak't out of his warelesse paine,
  He found him selfe vnwist, so ill bestad,
  That lim he could not wag. Thence he him lad,
  Bound like a beast appointed to the stall:
  The sight whereof the Lady sore adrad,
  And fain'd to fly for feare of being thrall;
But he her quickly stayd, and forst to wend withall.

When to the place they came, where *Artegall*
  By that same carefull Squire did then abide,
  He gently gan him to demaund of all,
  That did betwixt him and that Squire betide.
  Who with sterne countenance and indignant pride
  Did aunswere, that of all he guiltlesse stood,
  And his accuser thereuppon defide:
  For neither he did shed that Ladies bloud,
Nor tooke away his loue, but his owne proper good.

Well did the Squire perceiue him selfe too weake,
  To aunswere his defiaunce in the field,
  And rather chose his challenge off to breake,
  Then to approue his right with speare and shield.
  And rather guilty chose him selfe to yield.
  But *Artegall* by signes perceiuing plaine,
  That he it was not, which that Lady kild,
  But that strange Knight, the fairer loue to gaine,
Did cast about by sleight the truth thereout to straine.

And sayd, Now sure this doubtfull causes right
  Can hardly but by Sacrament be tride,
  Or else by ordele, or by blooddy fight;
  That ill perhaps mote fall to either side.
  But if ye please, that I your cause decide,
  Perhaps I may all further quarrell end,
  So ye will sweare my iudgement to abide.
  Thereto they both did franckly condiscend,
And to his doome with listfull eares did both attend.

Sith then (sayd he) ye both the dead deny,
  And both the liuing Lady claime your right,
  Let both the dead and liuing equally
  Deuided be betwixt you here in sight,
  And each of either take his share aright.
  But looke who does dissent from this my read,
  He for a twelue moneths day shall in despight
  Beare for his penaunce that same Ladies head;
To witnesse to the world, that she by him is dead.

Well pleased with that doome was *Sangliere*,
  And offred streight the Lady to be slaine.
  But that same Squire, to whom she was more dere,
  When as he saw she should be cut in twaine,
  Did yield, she rather should with him remaine
  Aliue, then to him selfe be shared dead;
  And rather then his loue should suffer paine,
  He chose with shame to beare that Ladies head.
True loue despiseth shame, when life is cald in dread.

Whom when so willing *Artegall* perceaued;
  Not so thou Squire, (he sayd) but thine I deeme
  The liuing Lady, which from thee he reaued:
  For worthy thou of her doest rightly seeme.
  And you, Sir Knight, that loue so light esteeme,
  As that ye would for little leaue the same,
  Take here your owne, that doth you best beseeme,
  And with it beare the burden of defame;
Your owne dead Ladies head, to tell abrode your shame.

But *Sangliere* disdained much his doome,
  And sternly gan repine at his beheast;
  Ne would for ought obay, as did become,
  To beare that Ladies head before his breast.
  Vntill that *Talus* had his pride represt,
  And forced him, maulgre, it vp to reare.
  Who when he saw it bootelesse to resist,
  He tooke it vp, and thence with him did beare,
As rated Spaniell takes his burden vp for feare.

Much did that Squire Sir *Artegall* adore,
  For his great iustice, held in high regard;
  And as his Squire him offred euermore
  To serue, for want of other meete reward,
  And wend with him on his aduenture hard.
  But he thereto would by no meanes consent;
  But leauing him forth on his iourney far'd:
  Ne wight with him but onely *Talus* went.
They two enough t'encounter an whole Regiment.

Cant. II.

N Ought is more honorable to a knight,
  Ne better doth beseeme braue cheualry,
Then to defend the feeble in their right,
And wrong redresse in such as wend awry.
Whilome those great Heroes got thereby
Their greatest glory, for their rightfull deedes,
And place deserued with the Gods on hy.
Herein the noblesse of this knight exceedes,
Who now to perils great for iustice sake proceedes.

        i

To which as he now was vppon the way,
  He chaunst to meet a Dwarfe in hasty course;
  Whom he requir'd his forward hast to stay,
  Till he of tidings mote with him discourse.
  Loth was the Dwarfe, yet did he stay perforse,
  And gan of sundry newes his store to tell,
  As to his memory they had recourse:
  But chiefely of the fairest *Florimell*,
How she was found againe, and spousde to *Marinell*.

        ii

For this was *Dony*, *Florimels* owne Dwarfe,
  Whom hauing lost (as ye haue heard whyleare)
  And finding in the way the scattred scarfe,
  The fortune of her life long time did feare.
  But of her health when *Artegall* did heare,
  And safe returne, he was full inly glad,
  And askt him where, and when her bridale cheare
  Should be solemniz'd: for if time he had,
He would be there, and honor to her spousall ad.

        iii

Within three daies (quoth he) as I do here,   iv
  It will be at the Castle of the strond;
  What time if naught me let, I will be there
  To doe her seruice, so as I am bond.
  But in my way a little here beyond
  A cursed cruell Sarazin doth wonne,
  That keepes a Bridges passage by strong hond,
  And many errant Knights hath there fordonne;
That makes all men for feare that passage for to shonne.

What mister wight (quoth he) and how far hence   v
  Is he, that doth to trauellers such harmes?
  He is (said he) a man of great defence;
  Expert in battell and in deedes of armes;
  And more emboldned by the wicked charmes,
  With which his daughter doth him still support;
  Hauing great Lordships got and goodly farmes,
  Through strong oppression of his powre extort;
By which he stil them holds, and keepes with strong effort.

And dayly he his wrongs encreaseth more,   vi
  For neuer wight he lets to passe that way,
  Ouer his Bridge, albee he rich or poore,
  But he him makes his passage-penny pay:
  Else he doth hold him backe or beat away.
  Thereto he hath a groome of euill guize,
  Whose scalp is bare, that bondage doth bewray,
  Which pols and pils the poore in piteous wize;
But he him selfe vppon the rich doth tyrannize.

His name is hight *Pollente*, rightly so   vii
  For that he is so puissant and strong,
  That with his powre he all doth ouergo,
  And makes them subiect to his mighty wrong;
  And some by sleight he eke doth vnderfong.
  For on a Bridge he custometh to fight,
  Which is but narrow, but exceeding long;
  And in the same are many trap fals pight,
Through which the rider downe doth fall through ouersight.

And vnderneath the same a riuer flowes,   viii
  That is both swift and dangerous deepe withall;
  Into the which whom so he ouerthrowes,
  All destitute of helpe doth headlong fall,
  But he him selfe, through practise vsuall,
  Leapes forth into the floud, and there assaies
  His foe confused through his sodaine fall,
  That horse and man he equally dismaies,
And either both them drownes, or trayterously slaies.

Then doth he take the spoile of them at will,   ix
  And to his daughter brings, that dwels thereby:
  Who all that comes doth take, and therewith fill
  The coffers of her wicked threasury;
  Which she with wrongs hath heaped vp so hy,
  That many Princes she in wealth exceedes,
  And purchast all the countrey lying ny
  With the reuenue of her plenteous meedes,
Her name is *Munera*, agreeing with her deedes.

Thereto she is full faire, and rich attired,   x
  With golden hands and siluer feete beside,
  That many Lords haue her to wife desired:
  But she them all despiseth for great pride.
  Now by my life (sayd he) and God to guide,
  None other way will I this day betake,
  But by that Bridge, whereas he doth abide:
  Therefore me thither lead. No more he spake,
But thitherward forthright his ready way did make.

Vnto the place he came within a while,   xi
  Where on the Bridge he ready armed saw
  The Sarazin, awayting for some spoile.
  Who as they to the passage gan to draw,
  A villaine to them came with scull all raw,
  That passage money did of them require,
  According to the custome of their law.
  To whom he aunswerd wroth, Loe there thy hire;
And with that word him strooke, that streight he did expire.

Which when the Pagan saw, he wexed wroth,   xii
  And streight him selfe vnto the fight addrest,
  Ne was Sir *Artegall* behinde: so both
  Together ran with ready speares in rest.
  Right in the midst, whereas they brest to brest
  Should meete, a trap was letten downe to fall
  Into the floud: streight leapt the Carle vnblest,
  Well weening that his foe was falne withall:
But he was well aware, and leapt before his fall.

There being both together in the floud,   xiii
  They each at other tyrannously flew;
  Ne ought the water cooled their whot bloud,
  But rather in them kindled choler new.
  But there the Paynim, who that vse well knew
  To fight in water, great aduantage had,
  That oftentimes him nigh he ouerthrew:
  And eke the courser, whereuppon he rad,
Could swim like to a fish, whiles he his backe bestrad.

Which oddes when as Sir *Artegall* espide,   xiv
  He saw no way, but close with him in hast;
  And to him driuing strongly downe the tide,
  Vppon his iron coller griped fast,
  That with the straint his wesand nigh he brast.
  There they together stroue and struggled long,
  Either the other from his steede to cast;
  Ne euer *Artegall* his griple strong
For any thing wold slacke, but still vppon him hong.

As when a Dolphin and a Sele are met,   xv
  In the wide champian of the Ocean plaine:
  With cruell chaufe their courages they whet,
  The maysterdome of each by force to gaine,
  And dreadfull battaile twixt them do darraine:
  They snuf, they snort, they bounce, they rage, they rore,
  That all the sea disturbed with their traine,
  Doth frie with fome aboue the surges hore.
Such was betwixt these two the troublesome vprore.

So *Artegall* at length him forst forsake　　　　xvi
　　His horses backe, for dread of being drownd,
　　And to his handy swimming him betake.
　　Eftsoones him selfe he from his hold vnbownd,
　　And then no ods at all in him he fownd:
　　For *Artegall* in swimming skilfull was,
　　And durst the depth of any water sownd.
　　So ought each Knight, that vse of perill has,
In swimming be expert through waters force to pas.

Then very doubtfull was the warres euent,　　　　xvii
　　Vncertaine whether had the better side:
　　For both were skild in that experiment,
　　And both in armes well traind and throughly tride.
　　But *Artegall* was better breath'd beside,
　　And towards th'end, grew greater in his might,
　　That his faint foe no longer could abide
　　His puissance, ne beare him selfe vpright,
But from the water to the land betooke his flight.

But *Artegall* pursewd him still so neare,　　　　xviii
　　With bright Chrysaor in his cruell hand,
　　That as his head he gan a litle reare
　　Aboue the brincke, to tread vpon the land,
　　He smote it off, that tumbling on the strand
　　It bit the earth for very fell despight,
　　And gnashed with his teeth, as if he band
　　High God, whose goodnesse he despaired quight,
Or curst the hand, which did that vengeance on him dight.

His corps was carried downe along the Lee,　　　　xix
　　Whose waters with his filthy bloud it stayned:
　　But his blasphemous head, that all might see,
　　He pitcht vpon a pole on high ordayned;
　　Where many years it afterwards remayned,
　　To be a mirrour to all mighty men,
　　In whose right hands great power is contayned,
　　That none of them the feeble ouerren,
But alwaies doe their powre within iust compasse pen.

That done, vnto the Castle he did wend,   xx
  In which the Paynims daughter did abide,
  Guarded of many which did her defend:
  Of whom he entrance sought, but was denide,
  And with reprochfull blasphemy defide,
  Beaten with stones downe from the battilment,
  That he was forced to withdraw aside;
  And bad his seruant *Talus* to inuent
Which way he enter might, without endangerment.

Eftsoones his Page drew to the Castle gate,   xxi
  And with his iron flale at it let flie,
  That all the warders it did sore amate,
  The which erewhile spake so reprochfully,
  And made them stoupe, that looked earst so hie.
  Yet still he bet, and bounst vppon the dore,
  And thundred strokes thereon so hideouslie,
  That all the peece he shaked from the flore,
And filled all the house with feare and great vprore.

With noise whereof the Lady forth appeared   xxii
  Vppon the Castle wall, and when she saw
  The daungerous state, in which she stood, she feared
  The sad effect of her neare ouerthrow;
  And gan entreat that iron man below,
  To cease his outrage, and him faire besought,
  Sith neither force of stones which they did throw,
  Nor powr of charms, which she against him wrought,
Might otherwise preuaile, or make him cease for ought.

But when as yet she saw him to proceede,   xxiii
  Vnmou'd with praiers, or with piteous thought,
  She ment him to corrupt with goodly meede;
  And causde great sackes with endlesse riches fraught,
  Vnto the battilment to be vpbrought,
  And powred forth ouer the Castle wall,
  That she might win some time, though dearly bought
Whilest he to gathering of the gold did fall.
But he was nothing mou'd, nor tempted therewithall.

But still continu'd his assault the more,　　　　　xxiv
　　And layd on load with his huge yron flaile,
　　That at the length he has yrent the dore,
　　And made way for his maister to assaile.
　　Who being entred, nought did then auaile
　　For wight, against his powre them selues to reare:
　　Each one did flie; their hearts began to faile,
　　And hid them selues in corners here and there;
And eke their dame halfe dead did hide her self for feare.

Long they her sought, yet no where could they finde her,　　xxv
　　That sure they ween'd she was escapt away:
　　But *Talus*, that could like a limehound winde her,
　　And all things secrete wisely could bewray,
　　At length found out, whereas she hidden lay
　　Vnder an heape of gold. Thence he her drew
　　By the faire lockes, and fowly did array,
　　Withouten pitty of her goodly hew,
That *Artegall* him selfe her seemelesse plight did rew.

Yet for no pitty would he change the course　　　　xxvi
　　Of Iustice, which in *Talus* hand did lye;
　　Who rudely hayld her forth without remorse,
　　Still holding vp her suppliant hands on hye,
　　And kneeling at his feete submissiuely.
　　But he her suppliant hands, those hands of gold,
　　And eke her feete, those feete of siluer trye,
　　Which sought vnrighteousnesse, and iustice sold,
Chopt off, and nayld on high, that all might them behold.

Her selfe then tooke he by the sclender wast,　　　xxvii
　　In vaine loud crying, and into the flood
　　Ouer the Castle wall adowne her cast,
　　And there her drowned in the durty mud:
　　But the streame washt away her guilty blood.
　　Thereafter all that mucky pelfe he tooke,
　　The spoile of peoples euill gotten good,
　　The which her sire had scrap't by hooke and crooke,
And burning all to ashes, powr'd it downe the brooke.

And lastly all that Castle quite he raced,   xxviii
   Euen from the sole of his foundation,
   And all the hewen stones thereof defaced,
   That there mote be no hope of reparation,
   Nor memory thereof to any nation.
   All which when *Talus* throughly had perfourmed,
   Sir *Artegall* vndid the euill fashion,
   And wicked customes of that Bridge refourmed.
Which done, vnto his former iourney he retourned.

In which they measur'd mickle weary way,   xxix
   Till that at length nigh to the sea they drew;
   By which as they did trauell on a day,
   They saw before them, far as they could vew,
   Full many people gathered in a crew;
   Whose great assembly they did much admire.
   For neuer there the like resort they knew.
   So towardes them they coasted, to enquire
What thing so many nations met, did there desire.

There they beheld a mighty Gyant stand   xxx
   Vpon a rocke, and holding forth on hie
   An huge great paire of ballance in his hand,
   With which he boasted in his surquedrie,
   That all the world he would weigh equallie,
   If ought he had the same to counterpoys.
   For want whereof he weighed vanity,
   And fild his ballaunce full of idle toys:
Yet was admired much of fooles, women, and boys.

He sayd that he would all the earth vptake,   xxxi
   And all the sea, deuided each from either:
   So would he of the fire one ballaunce make,
   And one of th'ayre, without or wind, or wether:
   Then would he ballaunce heauen and hell together,
   And all that did within them all containe;
   Of all whose weight, he would not misse a fether.
   And looke what surplus did of each remaine,
He would to his owne part restore the same againe.

For why, he sayd they all vnequall were, xxxii
  And had encroched vppon others share,
  Like as the sea (which plaine he shewed there)
  Had worne the earth, so did the fire the aire,
  So all the rest did others parts empaire.
  And so were realmes and nations run awry.
  All which he vndertooke for to repaire,
  In sort as they were formed aunciently;
And all things would reduce vnto equality.

Therefore the vulgar did about him flocke, xxxiii
  And cluster thicke vnto his leasings vaine,
  Like foolish flies about an hony crocke,
  In hope by him great benefite to gaine,
  And vncontrolled freedome to obtaine.
  All which when *Artegall* did see, and heare,
  How he mis-led the simple peoples traine,
  In sdeignfull wize he drew vnto him neare,
And thus vnto him spake, without regard or feare.

Thou that presum'st to weigh the world anew, xxxiv
  And all things to an equall to restore,
  In stead of right me seemes great wrong dost shew,
  And far aboue thy forces pitch to sore.
  For ere thou limit what is lesse or more
  In euery thing, thou oughtest first to know,
  What was the poyse of euery part of yore:
  And looke then how much it doth ouerflow,
Or faile thereof, so much is more then iust to trow.

For at the first they all created were xxxv
  In goodly measure, by their Makers might,
  And weighed out in ballaunces so nere,
  That not a dram was missing of their right.
  The earth was in the middle centre pight,
  In which it doth immoueable abide,
  Hemd in with waters like a wall in sight;
  And they with aire, that not a drop can slide:
Al which the heauens containe, and in their courses guide.

Such heauenly iustice doth among them raine,   xxxvi
   That euery one doe know their certaine bound,
   In which they doe these many yeares remaine,
   And mongst them al no change hath yet beene found.
   But if thou now shouldst weigh them new in pound,
   We are not sure they would so long remaine:
   All change is perillous, and all chaunce vnsound.
   Therefore leaue off to weigh them all againe,
Till we may be assur'd they shall their course retaine.

Thou foolishe Elfe (said then the Gyant wroth)   xxxvii
   Seest not, how badly all things present bee,
   And each estate quite out of order goth?
   The sea it selfe doest thou not plainely see
   Encroch vppon the land there vnder thee;
   And th'earth it selfe how daily its increast,
   By all that dying to it turned be?
   Were it not good that wrong were then surceast,
And from the most, that some were giuen to the least?

Therefore I will throw downe these mountaines hie,   xxxviii
   And make them leuell with the lowly plaine:
   These towring rocks, which reach vnto the skie,
   I will thrust downe into the deepest maine,
   And as they were, them equalize againe.
   Tyrants that make men subiect to their law,
   I will suppresse, that they no more may raine;
   And Lordings curbe, that commons ouer-aw;
And all the wealth of rich men to the poore will draw.

Of things vnseene how canst thou deeme aright,   xxxix
   Then answered the righteous *Artegall*,
   Sith thou misdeem'st so much of things in sight?
   What though the sea with waues continuall
   Doe eate the earth, it is no more at all:
   Ne is the earth the lesse, or loseth ought,
   For whatsoeuer from one place doth fall,
   Is with the tide vnto an other brought:
For there is nothing lost, that may be found, if sought.

Likewise the earth is not augmented more,   xl
  By all that dying into it doe fade.
  For of the earth they formed were of yore,
  How euer gay their blossome or their blade
  Doe flourish now, they into dust shall vade.
  What wrong then is it, if that when they die,
  They turne to that, whereof they first were made?
  All in the powre of their great Maker lie:
All creatures must obey the voice of the most hie.

They liue, they die, like as he doth ordaine,   xli
  Ne euer any asketh reason why.
  The hils doe not the lowly dales disdaine;
  The dales doe not the lofty hils enuy.
  He maketh Kings to sit in souerainty;
  He maketh subiects to their powre obay;
  He pulleth downe, he setteth vp on hy;
  He giues to this, from that he takes away.
For all we haue is his: what he list doe, he may.

What euer thing is done, by him is donne,   xlii
  Ne any may his mighty will withstand;
  Ne any may his soueraine power shonne,
  Ne loose that he hath bound with stedfast band.
  In vaine therefore doest thou now take in hand,
  To call to count, or weigh his workes anew,
  Whose counsels depth thou canst not vnderstand,
  Sith of things subiect to thy daily vew
Thou doest not know the causes, nor their courses dew.

For take thy ballaunce, if thou be so wise,   xliii
  And weigh the winde, that vnder heauen doth blow;
  Or weigh the light, that in the East doth rise;
  Or weigh the thought, that from mans mind doth flow.
  But if the weight of these thou canst not show,
  Weigh but one word which from thy lips doth fall.
  For how canst thou those greater secrets know,
  That doest not know the least thing of them all?
Ill can he rule the great, that cannot reach the small.

Therewith the Gyant much abashed sayd;   xliv
  That he of little things made reckoning light,
  Yet the least word that euer could be layd
  Within his ballaunce, he could way aright.
  Which is (sayd he) more heauy then in weight,
  The right or wrong, the false or else the trew?
  He answered, that he would try it streight,
  So he the words into his ballaunce threw,
But streight the winged words out of his ballaunce flew.

Wroth wext he then, and sayd, that words were light,   xlv
  Ne would within his ballaunce well abide.
  But he could iustly weigh the wrong or right.
  Well then, sayd *Artegall*, let it be tride.
  First in one ballance set the true aside.
  He did so first; and then the false he layd
  In th'other scale; but still it downe did slide,
  And by no meane could in the weight be stayd.
For by no meanes the false will with the truth be wayd.

Now take the right likewise, sayd *Artegale*,   xlvi
  And counterpeise the same with so much wrong.
  So first the right he put into one scale;
  And then the Gyant stroue with puissance strong
  To fill the other scale with so much wrong.
  But all the wrongs that he therein could lay,
  Might not it peise; yet did he labour long,
  And swat, and chauf'd, and proued euery way:
Yet all the wrongs could not a litle right downe way.

Which when he saw, he greatly grew in rage,   xlvii
  And almost would his balances haue broken:
  But *Artegall* him fairely gan asswage,
  And said; Be not vpon thy balance wroken:
  For they doe nought but right or wrong betoken;
  But in the mind the doome of right must bee;
  And so likewise of words, the which be spoken,
  The eare must be the ballance, to decree
And iudge, whether with truth or falshood they agree.

But set the truth and set the right aside,   xlviii
   For they with wrong or falshood will not fare;
   And put two wrongs together to be tride,
   Or else two falses, of each equall share;
   And then together doe them both compare.
   For truth is one, and right is euer one.
   So did he, and then plaine it did appeare,
   Whether of them the greater were attone.
But right sate in the middest of the beame alone.

But he the right from thence did thrust away,   xlix
   For it was not the right, which he did seeke;
   But rather stroue extremities to way,
   Th'one to diminish, th'other for to eeke.
   For of the meane he greatly did misleeke.
   Whom when so lewdly minded *Talus* found,
   Approching nigh vnto him cheeke by cheeke,
   He shouldered him from off the higher ground,
And down the rock him throwing, in the sea him dround.

Like as a ship, whom cruell tempest driues   l
   Vpon a rocke with horrible dismay,
   Her shattered ribs in thousand peeces riues,
   And spoyling all her geares and goodly ray,
   Does make her selfe misfortunes piteous pray.
   So downe the cliffe the wretched Gyant tumbled;
   His battred ballances in peeces lay,
   His timbered bones all broken rudely rumbled,
So was the high aspyring with huge ruine humbled.

That when the people, which had there about   li
   Long wayted, saw his sudden desolation,
   They gan to gather in tumultuous rout,
   And mutining, to stirre vp ciuill faction,
   For certaine losse of so great expectation.
   For well they hoped to haue got great good,
   And wondrous riches by his innouation.
   Therefore resoluing to reuenge his blood,
They rose in armes, and all in battell order stood.

Which lawlesse multitude him comming too   lii
   In warlike wise, when *Artegall* did vew,
   He much was troubled, ne wist what to doo.
   For loth he was his noble hands t'embrew
   In the base blood of such a rascall crew;
   And otherwise, if that he should retire,
   He fear'd least they with shame would him pursew.
   Therefore he *Talus* to them sent, t'inquire
The cause of their array, and truce for to desire.

But soone as they him nigh approching spide,   liii
   They gan with all their weapons him assay,
   And rudely stroke at him on euery side:
   Yet nought they could him hurt, ne ought dismay.
   But when at them he with his flaile gan lay,
   He like a swarme of flyes them ouerthrew;
   Ne any of them durst come in his way,
   But here and there before his presence flew,
And hid themselues in holes and bushes from his vew.

As when a Faulcon hath with nimble flight   liv
   Flowne at a flush of Ducks, foreby the brooke,
   The trembling foule dismayd with dreadfull sight
   Of death, the which them almost ouertooke,
   Doe hide themselues from her astonying looke,
   Amongst the flags and couert round about.
   When *Talus* saw they all the field forsooke
   And none appear'd of all that raskall rout,
To *Artegall* he turn'd, and went with him throughout.

Cant. III.

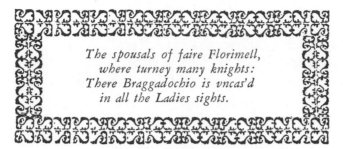

The spousals of faire Florimell,
where turney many knights:
There Braggadochio is vncas'd
in all the Ladies sights.

i

AFter long stormes and tempests ouerblowne,
The sunne at length his ioyous face doth cleare:
So when as fortune all her spight hath showne,
Some blisfull houres at last must needes appeare;
Else should afflicted wights oftimes despeire.
So comes it now to *Florimell* by tourne,
After long sorrowes suffered whyleare,
In which captiu'd she many moneths did mourne,
To tast of ioy, and to wont pleasures to retourne.

ii

Who being freed from *Proteus* cruell band
By *Marinell*, was vnto him affide,
And by him brought againe to Faerie land;
Where he her spous'd, and made his ioyous bride.
The time and place was blazed farre and wide;
And solemne feasts and giusts ordain'd therefore.
To which there did resort from euery side
Of Lords and Ladies infinite great store;
Ne any Knight was absent, that braue courage bore.

iii

To tell the glorie of the feast that day,
The goodly seruice, the deuicefull sights,
The bridegromes state, the brides most rich aray,
The pride of Ladies, and the worth of knights,
The royall banquets, and the rare delights
Were worke fit for an Herauld, not for me:
But for so much as to my lot here lights,
That with this present treatise doth agree,
True vertue to aduance, shall here recounted bee.

When all men had with full satietie   iv
    Of meates and drinkes their appetites suffiz'd,
    To deedes of armes and proofe of cheualrie
    They gan themselues addresse, full rich aguiz'd,
    As each one had his furnitures deuiz'd.
    And first of all issu'd Sir *Marinell*,
    And with him sixe knights more, which enterpriz'd
    To chalenge all in right of *Florimell*,
And to maintaine, that she all others did excell.

The first of them was hight Sir *Orimont*,   v
    A noble Knight, and tride in hard assayes:
    The second had to name Sir *Bellisont*,
    But second vnto none in prowesse prayse;
    The third was *Brunell*, famous in his dayes;
    The fourth *Ecastor*, of exceeding might;
    The fift *Armeddan*, skild in louely layes;
    The sixt was *Lansack*, a redoubted Knight:
All sixe well seene in armes, and prou'd in many a fight.

And them against came all that list to giust,   vi
    From euery coast and countrie vnder sunne:
    None was debard, but all had leaue that lust.
    The trompets sound; then all together ronne.
    Full many deedes of armes that day were donne,
    And many knights vnhorst, and many wounded,
    As fortune fell; yet litle lost or wonne:
    But all that day the greatest prayse redounded
To *Marinell*, whose name the Heralds loud resounded.

The second day, so soone as morrow light   vii
    Appear'd in heauen, into the field they came,
    And there all day continew'd cruell fight,
    With diuers fortune fit for such a game,
    In which all stroue with perill to winne fame.
    Yet whether side was victor, note be ghest:
    But at the last the trompets did proclame
    That *Marinell* that day deserued best.
So they disparted were, and all men went to rest.

The third day came, that should due tryall lend
　　Of all the rest, and then this warlike crew
　　Together met, of all to make an end.
　　There *Marinell* great deeds of armes did shew;
　　And through the thickest like a Lyon flew,
　　Rashing off helmes, and ryuing plates a sonder,
　　That euery one his daunger did eschew.
　　So terribly his dreadfull strokes did thonder,
That all men stood amaz'd, and at his might did wonder.

But what on earth can alwayes happie stand?
　　The greater prowesse greater perils find.
　　So farre he past amongst his enemies band,
　　That they haue him enclosed so behind,
　　As by no meanes he can himselfe outwind.
　　And now perforce they haue him prisoner taken;
　　And now they doe with captiue bands him bind;
　　And now they lead him thence, of all forsaken,
Vnlesse some succour had in time him ouertaken.

It fortun'd whylest they were thus ill beset,
　　Sir *Artegall* into the Tilt-yard came,
　　With *Braggadochio*, whom he lately met
　　Vpon the way, with that his snowy Dame.
　　Where when he vnderstood by common fame,
　　What euill hap to *Marinell* betid,
　　He much was mou'd at so vnworthie shame,
　　And streight that boaster prayd, with whom he rid,
To change his shield with him, to be the better hid.

So forth he went, and soone them ouer hent,
　　Where they were leading *Marinell* away,
　　Whom he assayld with dreadlesse hardiment,
　　And forst the burden of their prize to stay.
　　They were an hundred knights of that array;
　　Of which th'one halfe vpon himselfe did set,
　　Th'other stayd behind to gard the pray.
　　But he ere long the former fiftie bet;
And from th'other fiftie soone the prisoner fet.

So backe he brought Sir *Marinell* againe;   xii
   Whom hauing quickly arm'd againe anew,
   They both together ioyned might and maine,
   To set afresh on all the other crew.
   Whom with sore hauocke soone they ouerthrew,
   And chaced quite out of the field, that none
   Against them durst his head to perill shew.
   So were they left Lords of the field alone:
So *Marinell* by him was rescu'd from his fone.

Which when he had perform'd, then backe againe   xiii
   To *Braggadochio* did his shield restore:
   Who all this while behind him did remaine,
   Keeping there close with him in pretious store
   That his false Ladie, as ye heard afore.
   Then did the trompets sound, and Iudges rose,
   And all these knights, which that day armour bore,
   Came to the open hall, to listen whose
The honour of the prize should be adiudg'd by those.

And thether also came in open sight   xiv
   Fayre *Florimell*, into the common hall,
   To greet his guerdon vnto euery knight,
   And best to him, to whom the best should fall.
   Then for that stranger knight they loud did call,
   To whom that day they should the girlond yield.
   Who came not forth: but for Sir *Artegall*
   Came *Braggadochio*, and did shew his shield,
Which bore the Sunne brode blazed in a golden field.

The sight whereof did all with gladnesse fill: xv
   So vnto him they did addeeme the prise
   Of all that Tryumph. Then the trompets shrill
   Don *Braggadochios* name resounded thrise:
   So courage lent a cloke to cowardise.
   And then to him came fayrest *Florimell*,
   And goodly gan to greet his braue emprise,
   And thousand thankes him yeeld, that had so well
Approu'd that day, that she all others did excell.

To whom the boaster, that all knights did blot,   xvi
   With proud disdaine did scornefull answere make;
   That what he did that day, he did it not
   For her, but for his owne deare Ladies sake,
   Whom on his perill he did vndertake,
   Both her and eke all others to excell:
   And further did vncomely speaches crake.
   Much did his words the gentle Ladie quell,
And turn'd aside for shame to heare, what he did tell.

Then forth he brought his snowy *Florimele*,   xvii
   Whom *Trompart* had in keeping there beside,
   Couered from peoples gazement with a vele.
   Whom when discouered they had throughly eide,
   With great amazement they were stupefide;
   And said, that surely *Florimell* it was,
   Or if it were not *Florimell* so tride,
   That *Florimell* her selfe she then did pas.
So feeble skill of perfect things the vulgar has.

Which when as *Marinell* beheld likewise,   xviii
   He was therewith exceedingly dismayd;
   Ne wist he what to thinke, or to deuise,
   But like as one, whom feends had made affrayd,
   He long astonisht stood, ne ought he sayd,
   Ne ought he did, but with fast fixed eies
   He gazed still vpon that snowy mayd;
   Whom euer as he did the more auize,
The more to be true *Florimell* he did surmize.

As when two sunnes appeare in the azure skye,   xix
   Mounted in *Phœbus* charet fierie bright,
   Both darting forth faire beames to each mans eye,
   And both adorn'd with lampes of flaming light,
   All that behold so strange prodigious sight,
   Not knowing natures worke, nor what to weene,
   Are rapt with wonder, and with rare affright.
   So stood Sir *Marinell*, when he had seene
The semblant of this false by his faire beauties Queene.

All which when *Artegall*, who all this while   xx
  Stood in the preasse close couered, well aduewed,
  And saw that boasters pride and gracelesse guile,
  He could no longer beare, but forth issewed,
  And vnto all himselfe there open shewed,
  And to the boaster said; Thou losell base,
  That hast with borrowed plumes thy selfe endewed,
  And others worth with leasings doest deface,
When they are all restor'd, thou shalt rest in disgrace.

That shield, which thou doest beare, was it indeed,   xxi
  Which this dayes honour sau'd to *Marinell*;
  But not that arme, nor thou the man I reed,
  Which didst that seruice vnto *Florimell*.
  For proofe shew forth thy sword, and let it tell,
  What strokes, what dreadfull stoure it stird this day:
  Or shew the wounds, which vnto thee befell;
  Or shew the sweat, with which thou diddest sway
So sharpe a battell, that so many did dismay.

But this the sword, which wrought those cruell stounds,   xxii
  And this the arme, the which that shield did beare,
  And these the signes, (so shewed forth his wounds)
  By which that glorie gotten doth appeare.
  As for this Ladie, which he sheweth here,
  Is not (I wager) *Florimell* at all;
  But some fayre Franion, fit for such a fere,
  That by misfortune in his hand did fall.
For proofe whereof, he bad them *Florimell* forth call.

So forth the noble Ladie was ybrought,   xxiii
  Adorn'd with honor and all comely grace:
  Whereto her bashfull shamefastnesse ywrought
  A great increase in her faire blushing face;
  As roses did with lillies interlace.
  For of those words, the which that boaster threw,
  She inly yet conceiued great disgrace.
  Whom when as all the people such did vew,
They shouted loud, and signes of gladnesse all did shew.

Then did he set her by that snowy one,
    Like the true saint beside the image set,
    Of both their beauties to make paragone,
    And triall, whether should the honor get.
    Streight way so soone as both together met,
    Th'enchaunted Damzell vanisht into nought:
    Her snowy substance melted as with heat,
    Ne of that goodly hew remayned ought,
But th'emptie girdle, which about her wast was wrought.

As when the daughter of *Thaumantes* faire,
    Hath in a watry cloud displayed wide
    Her goodly bow, which paints the liquid ayre;
    That all men wonder at her colours pride;
    All suddenly, ere one can looke aside,
    The glorious picture vanisheth away,
    Ne any token doth thereof abide:
    So did this Ladies goodly forme decay,
And into nothing goe, ere one could it bewray.

Which when as all that present were, beheld,
    They stricken were with great astonishment,
    And their faint harts with senselesse horrour queld,
    To see the thing, that seem'd so excellent,
    So stolen from their fancies wonderment;
    That what of it became, none vnderstood.
    And *Braggadochio* selfe with dreriment
    So daunted was in his despeyring mood,
That like a lifelesse corse immoueable he stood.

But *Artegall* that golden belt vptooke,
    The which of all her spoyle was onely left;
    Which was not hers, as many it mistooke,
    But *Florimells* owne girdle, from her reft,
    While she was flying, like a weary weft,
    From that foule monster, which did her compell
    To perils great; which he vnbuckling eft,
    Presented to the fayrest *Florimell*;
Who round about her tender wast it fitted well.

Full many Ladies often had assayd,
    About their middles that faire belt to knit;
    And many a one suppos'd to be a mayd:
    Yet it to none of all their loynes would fit,
    Till *Florimell* about her fastned it.
    Such power it had, that to no womans wast
    By any skill or labour it would sit,
    Vnlesse that she were continent and chast,
But it would lose or breake, that many had disgrast.

Whilest thus they busied were bout *Florimell*,
    And boastfull *Braggadochio* to defame,
    Sir *Guyon* as by fortune then befell,
    Forth from the thickest preasse of people came,
    His owne good steed, which he had stolne, to clame;
    And th'one hand seizing on his golden bit,
    With th'other drew his sword: for with the same
    He ment the thiefe there deadly to haue smit:
And had he not bene held, he nought had fayld of it.

Thereof great hurly burly moued was
    Throughout the hall, for that same warlike horse.
    For *Braggadochio* would not let him pas;
    And *Guyon* would him algates haue perforse,
    Or it approue vpon his carrion corse.
    Which troublous stirre when *Artegall* perceiued,
    He nigh them drew to stay th'auengers forse,
    And gan inquire, how was that steed bereaued,
Whether by might extort, or else by slight deceaued.

Who all that piteous storie, which befell
    About that wofull couple, which were slaine,
    And their young bloodie babe to him gan tell;
    With whom whiles he did in the wood remaine,
    His horse purloyned was by subtill traine:
    For which he chalenged the thiefe to fight.
    But he for nought could him thereto constraine.
    For as the death he hated such despight,
And rather had to lose, then trie in armes his right.

Which *Artegall* well hearing, though no more   xxxii
   By law of armes there neede ones right to trie,
   As was the wont of warlike knights of yore,
   Then that his foe should him the field denie,
   Yet further right by tokens to descrie,
   He askt, what priuie tokens he did beare.
   If that (said *Guyon*) may you satisfie,
   Within his mouth a blacke spot doth appeare,
Shapt like a horses shoe, who list to seeke it there.

Whereof to make due tryall, one did take   xxxiii
   The horse in hand, within his mouth to looke:
   But with his heeles so sorely he him strake,
   That all his ribs he quite in peeces broke,
   That neuer word from that day forth he spoke.
   Another that would seeme to haue more wit,
   Him by the bright embrodered hedstall tooke:
   But by the shoulder him so sore he bit,
That he him maymed quite, and all his shoulder split.

Ne he his mouth would open vnto wight,   xxxiv
   Vntill that *Guyon* selfe vnto him spake,
   And called *Brigadore* (so was he hight)
   Whose voice so soone as he did vndertake,
   Eftsoones he stood as still as any stake,
   And suffred all his secret marke to see:
   And when as he him nam'd, for ioy he brake
   His bands, and follow'd him with gladfull glee,
And friskt, and flong aloft, and louted low on knee.

Thereby Sir *Artegall* did plaine areed,   xxxv
   That vnto him the horse belong'd, and sayd;
   Lo there Sir *Guyon*, take to you the steed,
   As he with golden saddle is arayd;
   And let that losell, plainely now displayd,
   Hence fare on foot, till he an horse haue gayned.
   But the proud boaster gan his doome vpbrayd,
   And him reuil'd, and rated, and disdayned,
That iudgement so vniust against him had ordayned.

Much was the knight incenst with his lewd word,   xxxvi
    To haue reuenged that his villeny;
    And thrise did lay his hand vpon his sword,
    To haue him slaine, or dearely doen aby.
    But *Guyon* did his choler pacify,
    Saying, Sir knight, it would dishonour bee
    To you, that are our iudge of equity,
    To wreake your wrath on such a carle as hee:
It's punishment enough, that all his shame doe see.

So did he mitigate Sir *Artegall*,   xxxvii
    But *Talus* by the backe the boaster hent,
    And drawing him out of the open hall,
    Vpon him did inflict this punishment.
    First he his beard did shaue, and fowly shent:
    Then from him reft his shield, and it renuerst,
    And blotted out his armes with falshood blent,
    And himselfe baffuld, and his armes vnherst,
And broke his sword in twaine, and all his armour sperst.

The whiles his guilefull groome was fled away: xxxviii
    But vaine it was to thinke from him to flie.
    Who ouertaking him did disaray,
    And all his face deform'd with infamie,
    And out of court him scourged openly.
    So ought all faytours, that true knighthood shame,
    And armes dishonour with base villanie,
    From all braue knights be banisht with defame:
For oft their lewdnes blotteth good deserts with blame.

Now when these counterfeits were thus vncased   xxxix
    Out of the foreside of their forgerie,
    And in the sight of all men cleane disgraced,
    All gan to iest and gibe full merilie
    At the remembrance of their knauerie.
    Ladies can laugh at Ladies, Knights at Knights,
    To thinke with how great vaunt of brauerie
    He them abused, through his subtill slights,
And what a glorious shew he made in all their sights.

There leaue we them in pleasure and repast,
    Spending their ioyous dayes and gladfull nights,
    And taking vsurie of time forepast,
    With all deare delices and rare delights,
    Fit for such Ladies and such louely knights:
    And turne we here to this faire furrowes end
    Our wearie yokes, to gather fresher sprights,
    That when as time to *Artegall* shall tend,
We on his first aduenture may him forward send.

Cant. IIII.

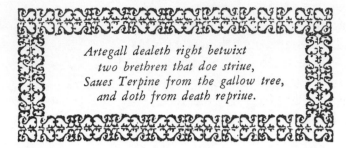

*Artegall dealeth right betwixt
two brethren that doe striue,
Saues Terpine from the gallow tree,
and doth from death repriue.*

W Ho so vpon him selfe will take the skill   i
    True Iustice vnto people to diuide,
Had neede haue mightie hands, for to fulfill
That, which he doth with righteous doome decide,
And for to maister wrong and puissant pride.
For vaine it is to deeme of things aright,
And makes wrong doers iustice to deride,
    Vnlesse it be perform'd with dreadlesse might.
For powre is the right hand of Iustice truely hight.

Therefore whylome to knights of great emprise   ii
    The charge of Iustice giuen was in trust,
That they might execute her iudgements wise,
And with their might beat downe licentious lust,
Which proudly did impugne her sentence iust.
Whereof no brauer president this day
Remaines on earth, preseru'd from yron rust
    Of rude obliuion, and long times decay,
Then this of *Artegall*, which here we haue to say.

Who hauing lately left that louely payre,   iii
    Enlincked fast in wedlockes loyall bond,
Bold *Marinell* with *Florimell* the fayre,
With whom great feast and goodly glee he fond,
Departed from the Castle of the strond,
To follow his aduentures first intent,
Which long agoe he taken had in hond:
    Ne wight with him for his assistance went,
But that great yron groome, his gard and gouernment.

With whom as he did passe by the sea shore, iv
   He chaunst to come, whereas two comely Squires,
   Both brethren, whom one wombe together bore,
   But stirred vp with different desires,
   Together stroue, and kindled wrathfull fires:
   And them beside two seemely damzels stood,
   By all meanes seeking to asswage their ires,
   Now with faire words; but words did little good, (mood.
Now with sharpe threats; but threats the more increast their

And there before them stood a Coffer strong, v
   Fast bound on euery side with iron bands,
   But seeming to haue suffred mickle wrong,
   Either by being wreckt vppon the sands,
   Or being carried farre from forraine lands.
   Seem'd that for it these Squires at ods did fall,
   And bent against them selues their cruell hands.
   But euermore, those Damzels did forestall
Their furious encounter, and their fiercenesse pall.

But firmely fixt they were, with dint of sword, vi
   And battailes doubtfull proofe their rights to try,
   Ne other end their fury would afford,
   But what to them Fortune would iustify.
   So stood they both in readinesse: thereby
   To ioyne the combate with cruell intent;
   When *Artegall* arriuing happily,
   Did stay a while their greedy bickerment,
Till he had questioned the cause of their dissent.

To whom the elder did this aunswere frame; vii
   Then weete ye Sir, that we two brethren be,
   To whom our sire, *Milesio* by name,
   Did equally bequeath his lands in fee,
   Two Ilands, which ye there before you see
   Not farre in sea; of which the one appeares
   But like a little Mount of small degree;
   Yet was as great and wide ere many yeares,
As that same other Isle, that greater bredth now beares.

But tract of time, that all things doth decay,
  And this deuouring Sea, that naught doth spare,
  The most part of my land hath washt away,
  And throwne it vp vnto my brothers share:
  So his encreased, but mine did empaire.
  Before which time I lou'd, as was my lot,
  That further mayd, hight *Philtera* the faire,
  With whom a goodly doure I should haue got,
And should haue ioyned bene to her in wedlocks knot.

Then did my younger brother *Amidas*
  Loue that same other Damzell, *Lucy* bright,
  To whom but little dowre allotted was;
  Her vertue was the dowre, that did delight.
  What better dowre can to a dame be hight?
  But now when *Philtra* saw my lands decay,
  And former liuelod fayle, she left me quight,
  And to my brother did ellope streight way:
Who taking her from me, his owne loue left astray.

She seeing then her selfe forsaken so,
  Through dolorous despaire, which she conceyued,
  Into the Sea her selfe did headlong throw,
  Thinking to haue her griefe by death bereaued.
  But see how much her purpose was deceaued.
  Whilest thus amidst the billowes beating of her
  Twixt life and death, long to and fro she weaued,
  She chaunst vnwares to light vppon this coffer,
Which to her in that daunger hope of life did offer.

The wretched mayd that earst desir'd to die,
  When as the paine of death she tasted had,
  And but halfe seene his vgly visnomie,
  Gan to repent, that she had beene so mad,
  For any death to chaunge life though most bad:
  And catching hold of this Sea-beaten chest,
  The lucky Pylot of her passage sad,
  After long tossing in the seas distrest,
Her weary barke at last vppon mine Isle did rest.

Where I by chaunce then wandring on the shore,   xii
    Did her espy, and through my good endeuour
    From dreadfull mouth of death, which thrcatned sore
    Her to haue swallow'd vp, did helpe to saue her.
    She then in recompence of that great fauour,
    Which I on her bestowed, bestowed on me
    The portion of that good, which Fortune gaue her,
    Together with her selfe in dowry free;
Both goodly portions, but of both the better she.

Yet in this coffer, which she with her brought,   xiii
    Great threasure sithence we did finde contained;
    Which as our owne we tooke, and so it thought.
    But this same other Damzell since hath fained,
    That to her selfe that threasure appertained;
    And that she did transport the same by sea,
    To bring it to hcr husband new ordained,
    But suffred cruell shipwracke by the way.
But whether it be so or no, I can not say.

But whether it indeede be so or no,   xiv
    This doe I say, that what so good or ill
    Or God or Fortune vnto me did throw,
    Not wronging any other by my will,
    I hold mine owne, and so will hold it still.
    And though my land he first did winne away,
    And then my loue (though now it little skill,)
    Yet my good lucke he shall not likewise pray;
But I will it defend, whilst euer that I may.

So hauing sayd, the younger did ensew;   xv
    Full true it is, what so about our land
    My brother here declared hath to you:
    But not for it this ods twixt vs doth stand,
    But for this threasure throwne vppon his strand;
    Which well I proue, as shall appeare by triall,
    To be this maides, with whom I fastned hand,
    Known by good markes, and perfect good espiall,
Therefore it ought be rendred her without deniall.

When they thus ended had, the Knight began;   xvi
   Certes your strife were easie to accord,
   Would ye remit it to some righteous man.
   Vnto your selfe, said they, we giue our word,
   To bide what iudgement ye shall vs afford.
   Then for assuraunce to my doome to stand,
   Vnder my foote let each lay downe his sword,
   And then you shall my sentence vnderstand.
So each of them layd downe his sword out of his hand.

Then *Artegall* thus to the younger sayd;   xvii
   Now tell me *Amidas*, if that ye may,
   Your brothers land the which the sea hath layd
   Vnto your part, and pluckt from his away,
   By what good right doe you withhold this day?
   What other right (quoth he) should you esteeme,
   But that the sea it to my share did lay?
   Your right is good (sayd he) and so I deeme,
That what the sea vnto you sent, your own should seeme.

Then turning to the elder thus he sayd;   xviii
   Now *Bracidas* let this likewise be showne.
   Your brothers threasure, which from him is strayd,
   Being the dowry of his wife well knowne,
   By what right doe you claime to be your owne?
   What other right (quoth he) should you esteeme,
   But that the sea hath it vnto me throwne?
   Your right is good (sayd he) and so I deeme,
That what the sea vnto you sent, your own should seeme.

For equall right in equall things doth stand,   xix
   For what the mighty Sea hath once possest,
   And plucked quite from all possessors hand,
   Whether by rage of waues, that neuer rest,
   Or else by wracke, that wretches hath distrest,
   He may dispose by his imperiall might,
   As thing at randon left, to whom he list.
   So *Amidas*, the land was yours first hight,
And so the threasure yours is *Bracidas* by right.

When he his sentence thus pronounced had,   xx
    Both *Amidas* and *Philtra* were displeased:
    But *Bracidas* and *Lucy* were right glad,
    And on the threasure by that iudgement seased.
    So was their discord by this doome appeased,
    And each one had his right. Then *Artegall*
    When as their sharpe contention he had ceased,
    Departed on his way, as did befall,
To follow his old quest, the which him forth did call.

So as he trauelled vppon the way,   xxi
    He chaunst to come, where happily he spide
    A rout of many people farre away;
    To whom his course he hastily applide,
    To weete the cause of their assemblaunce wide.
    To whom when he approched neare in sight,
    (An vncouth sight) he plainely then describe
    To be a troupe of women warlike dight,
With weapons in their hands, as ready for to fight.

And in the midst of them he saw a Knight,   xxii
    With both his hands behinde him pinnoed hard,
    And round about his necke an halter tight,
    As ready for the gallow tree prepard:
    His face was couered, and his head was bar'd,
    That who he was, vneath was to descry;
    And with full heauy heart with them he far'd,
    Grieu'd to the soule, and groning inwardly,
That he of womens hands so base a death should dy.

But they like tyrants, mercilesse the more,   xxiii
    Reioyced at his miserable case,
    And him reuiled, and reproched sore
    With bitter taunts, and termes of vile disgrace.
    Now when as *Artegall* arriu'd in place,
    Did aske, what cause brought that man to decay,
    They round about him gan to swarme apace,
    Meaning on him their cruell hands to lay,
And to haue wrought vnwares some villanous assay.

But he was soone aware of their ill minde,   xxiv
  And drawing backe deceiued their intent;
  Yet though him selfe did shame on womankinde
  His mighty hand to shend, he *Talus* sent
  To wrecke on them their follies hardyment:
  Who with few sowces of his yron flale,
  Dispersed all their troupe incontinent,
  And sent them home to tell a piteous tale,
Of their vaine prowesse, turned to their proper bale.

But that same wretched man, ordaynd to die,   xxv
  They left behind them, glad to be so quit:
  Him *Talus* tooke out of perplexitie,
  And horrour of fowle death for Knight vnfit,
  Who more then losse of life ydreaded it;
  And him restoring vnto liuing light,
  So brought vnto his Lord, where he did sit,
  Beholding all that womanish weake fight;
Whom soone as he beheld, he knew, and thus behight.

Sir *Terpine*, haplesse man, what make you here?   xxvi
  Or haue you lost your selfe, and your discretion,
  That euer in this wretched case ye were?
  Or haue ye yeelded you to proude oppression
  Of womens powre, that boast of mens subiection?
  Or else what other deadly dismall day
  Is falne on you, by heauens hard direction,
  That ye were runne so fondly far astray,
As for to lead your selfe vnto your owne decay?

Much was the man confounded in his mind,   xxvii
  Partly with shame, and partly with dismay,
  That all astonisht he him selfe did find,
  And little had for his excuse to say,
  But onely thus; Most haplesse well ye may
  Me iustly terme, that to this shame am brought,
  And made the scorne of Knighthod this same day.
  But who can scape, what his owne fate hath wrought?
The worke of heauens will surpasseth humaine thought.

Right true: but faulty men vse oftentimes   xxviii
    To attribute their folly vnto fate,
    And lay on heauen the guilt of their owne crimes.
    But tell, Sir *Terpine*, ne let you amate
    Your misery, how fell ye in this state.
    Then sith ye needs (quoth he) will know my shame,
    And all the ill, which chaunst to me of late,
    I shortly will to you rehearse the same,
In hope ye will not turne misfortune to my blame.

Being desirous (as all Knights are woont)   xxix
    Through hard aduentures deedes of armes to try,
    And after fame and honour for to hunt,
    I heard report that farre abrode did fly,
    That a proud Amazon did late defy
    All the braue Knights, that hold of Maidenhead,
    And vnto them wrought all the villany,
    That she could forge in her malicious head,
Which some hath put to shame, and many done be dead.

The cause, they say, of this her cruell hate,   xxx
    Is for the sake of *Bellodant* the bold,
    To whom she bore most feruent loue of late,
    And wooed him by all the waies she could:
    But when she saw at last, that he ne would
    For ought or nought be wonne vnto her will,
    She turn'd her loue to hatred manifold,
    And for his sake vow'd to doe all the ill
Which she could doe to Knights, which now she doth fulfill.

For all those Knights, the which by force or guile   xxxi
    She doth subdue, she fowly doth entreate.
    First she doth them of warlike armes despoile,
    And cloth in womens weedes: And then with threat
    Doth them compell to worke, to earne their meat,
    To spin, to card, to sew, to wash, to wring;
    Ne doth she giue them other thing to eat,
    But bread and water, or like feeble thing,
Them to disable from reuenge aduenturing.

But if through stout disdaine of manly mind,   xxxii
  Any her proud obseruaunce will withstand,
  Vppon that gibbet, which is there behind,
  She causeth them be hang'd vp out of hand;
  In which condition I right now did stand.
  For being ouercome by her in fight,
  And put to that base seruice of her band,
  I rather chose to die in liues despight,
Then lead that shamefull life, vnworthy of a Knight.

How hight that Amazon (sayd *Artegall*)?   xxxiii
  And where, and how far hence does she abide?
  Her name (quoth he) they *Radigund* doe call,
  A Princesse of great powre, and greater pride,
  And Queene of Amazons, in armes well tride,
  And sundry battels, which she hath atchieued
  With great successe, that her hath glorifide,
  And made her famous, more then is belieued;
Ne would I it haue ween'd, had I not late it prieued.

Now sure (said he) and by the faith that I   xxxiv
  To Maydenhead and noble knighthood owe,
  I will not rest, till I her might doe trie,
  And venge the shame, that she to Knights doth show.
  Therefore Sir *Terpine* from you lightly throw
  This squalid weede, the patterne of dispaire,
  And wend with me, that ye may see and know,
  How Fortune will your ruin'd name repaire,
And knights of Maidenhead, whose praise she would empaire.

With that, like one that hopelesse was repry'ud   xxxv
  From deathes dore, at which he lately lay,
  Those yron fetters, wherewith he was gyu'd,
  The badges of reproch, he threw away,
  And nimbly did him dight to guide the way
  Vnto the dwelling of that Amazone.
  Which was from thence not past a mile or tway:
  A goodly citty and a mighty one,
The which of her owne name she called *Radegone.*

Where they arriuing, by the watchmen were xxxvi
   Descried streight, who all the citty warned,
   How that three warlike persons did appeare,
   Of which the one him seem'd a Knight all armed,
   And th'other two well likely to haue harmed.
   Eftsoones the people all to harnesse ran,
   And like a sort of Bees in clusters swarmed:
   Ere long their Queene her selfe, halfe like a man
Came forth into the rout, and them t'array began.

And now the Knights being arriued neare, xxxvii
   Did beat vppon the gates to enter in,
   And at the Porter, skorning them so few,
   Threw many threats, if they the towne did win,
   To teare his flesh in peeces for his sin.
   Which when as *Radigund* there comming heard,
   Her heart for rage did grate, and teeth did grin:
   She bad that streight the gates should be vnbard,
And to them way to make, with weapons well prepard.

Soone as the gates were open to them set, xxxviii
   They pressed forward, entraunce to haue made.
   But in the middle way they were ymet
   With a sharpe showre of arrowes, which them staid,
   And better bad aduise, ere they assaid
   Vnknowen perill of bold womens pride.
   Then all that rout vppon them rudely laid,
   And heaped strokes so fast on euery side,
And arrowes haild so thicke, that they could not abide.

But *Radigund* her selfe, when she espide xxxix
   Sir *Terpin*, from her direfull doome acquit,
   So cruell doale amongst her maides diuide,
   T'auenge that shame, they did on him commit,
   All sodainely enflam'd with furious fit,
   Like a fell Lionesse at him she flew,
   And on his head-peece him so fiercely smit,
   That to the ground him quite she ouerthrew,
Dismayd so with the stroke, that he no colours knew.

Soone as she saw him on the ground to grouell,   xl
  She lightly to him leapt, and in his necke
  Her proud foote setting, at his head did leuell,
  Weening at once her wrath on him to wreake,
  And his contempt, that did her iudg'ment breake.
  As when a Beare hath seiz'd her cruell clawes
  Vppon the carkasse of some beast too weake,
  Proudly stands ouer, and a while doth pause,
To heare the piteous beast pleading her plaintiffe cause.

Whom when as *Artegall* in that distresse   xli
  By chaunce beheld, he left the bloudy slaughter,
  In which he swam, and ranne to his redresse.
  There her assayling fiercely fresh, he raught her
  Such an huge stroke, that it of sence distraught her:
  And had she not it warded warily,
  It had depriu'd her mother of a daughter.
  Nathlesse for all the powre she did apply,
It made her stagger oft, and stare with ghastly eye.

Like to an Eagle in his kingly pride,   xlii
  Soring through his wide Empire of the aire,
  To weather his brode sailes, by chaunce hath spide
  A Goshauke, which hath seized for her share
  Vppon some fowle, that should her feast prepare;
  With dreadfull force he flies at her byliue,
  That with his souce, which none enduren dare,
  Her from the quarrey he away doth driue,
And from her griping pounce the greedy prey doth riue.

But soone as she her sence recouer'd had,   xliii
  She fiercely towards him her selfe gan dight,
  Through vengeful wrath and sdeignfull pride half mad:
  For neuer had she suffred such despight.
  But ere she could ioyne hand with him to fight,
  Her warlike maides about her flockt so fast,
  That they disparted them, maugre their might,
  And with their troupes did far a sunder cast:
But mongst the rest the fight did vntill euening last.

And euery while that mighty yron man, xliv
    With his strange weapon, neuer wont in warre,
    Them sorely vext, and courst, and ouerran,
    And broke their bowes, and did their shooting marre,
    That none of all the many once did darre
    Him to assault, nor once approach him nie,
    But like a sort of sheepe dispersed farre
    For dread of their deuouring enemie,
Through all the fields and vallies did before him flie.

But when as daies faire shinie-beame, yclowded xlv
    With fearefull shadowes of deformed night,
    Warn'd man and beast in quiet rest be shrowded,
    Bold *Radigund* with sound of trumpe on hight,
    Causd all her people to surcease from fight,
    And gathering them vnto her citties gate,
    Made them all enter in before her sight,
    And all the wounded, and the weake in state,
To be conuayed in, ere she would once retrate.

When thus the field was voided all away, xlvi
    And all things quieted, the Elfin Knight
    Weary of toile and trauell of that day,
    Causd his pauilion to be richly pight
    Before the city gate, in open sight;
    Where he him selfe did rest in safety,
    Together with sir *Terpin* all that night:
    But *Talus* vsde in times of ieopardy
To keepe a nightly watch, for dread of treachery.

But *Radigund* full of heart-gnawing griefe, xlvii
    For the rebuke, which she sustain'd that day,
    Could take no rest, ne would receiue reliefe,
    But tossed in her troublous minde, what way
    She mote reuenge that blot, which on her lay.
    There she resolu'd her selfe in single fight
    To try her Fortune, and his force assay,
    Rather then see her people spoiled quight,
As she had seene that day a disauenterous sight.

She called forth to her a trusty mayd,   xlviii
   Whom she thought fittest for that businesse,
   Her name was *Clarin*, and thus to her sayd;
   Goe damzell quickly, doe thy selfe addresse,
   To doe the message, which I shall expresse.
   Goe thou vnto that stranger Faery Knight,
   Who yeester day droue vs to such distresse,
   Tell, that to morrow I with him wil fight,
And try in equall field, whether hath greater might.

But these conditions doe to him propound,   xlix
   That if I vanquishe him, he shall obay
   My law, and euer to my lore be bound,
   And so will I, if me he vanquish may;
   What euer he shall like to doe or say:
   Goe streight, and take with thee, to witnesse it,
   Sixe of thy fellowes of the best array,
   And beare with you both wine and iuncates fit,
And bid him eate, henceforth he oft shall hungry sit.

The Damzell streight obayd, and putting all   l
   In readinesse, forth to the Towne-gate went,
   Where sounding loud a Trumpet from the wall,
   Vnto those warlike Knights she warning sent.
   Then *Talus* forth issuing from the tent,
   Vnto the wall his way did fearelesse take,
   To weeten what that trumpets sounding ment:
   Where that same Damzell lowdly him bespake,
And shew'd, that with his Lord she would emparlaunce make.

So he them streight conducted to his Lord,   li
   Who, as he could, them goodly well did greete,
   Till they had told their message word by word:
   Which he accepting well, as he could weete,
   Them fairely entertaynd with curt'sies meete,
   And gaue them gifts and things of deare delight.
   So backe againe they homeward turnd their feete.
   But *Artegall* him selfe to rest did dight,
That he mote fresher be against the next daies fight.

Cant. V.

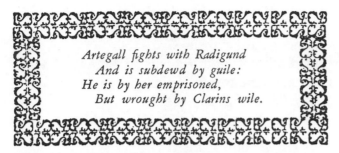

SO soone as day forth dawning from the East,   i
  Nights humid curtaine from the heauens withdrew,
  And earely calling forth both man and beast,
  Comaunded them their daily workes renew,
  These noble warriors, mindefull to pursew
  The last daies purpose of their vowed fight,
  Them selues thereto preparde in order dew;
  The Knight, as best was seeming for a Knight,
And th'Amazon, as best it likt her selfe to dight.

All in a Camis light of purple silke   ii
  Wouen vppon with siluer, subtly wrought,
  And quilted vppon sattin white as milke,
  Trayled with ribbands diuersly distraught
  Like as the workeman had their courses taught;
  Which was short tucked for light motion
  Vp to her ham, but when she list, it raught
  Downe to her lowest heele, and thereuppon
She wore for her defence a mayled habergeon.

And on her legs she painted buskins wore,   iii
  Basted with bends of gold on euery side,
  And mailes betweene, and laced close afore:
  Vppon her thigh her Cemitare was tide,
  With an embrodered belt of mickell pride;
  And on her shoulder hung her shield, bedeckt
  Vppon the bosse with stones, that shined wide,
  As the faire Moone in her most full aspect,
That to the Moone it mote be like in each respect.

So forth she came out of the citty gate,   iv
  With stately port and proud magnificence,
  Guarded with many damzels, that did waite
  Vppon her person for her sure defence,
  Playing on shaumes and trumpets, that from hence
  Their sound did reach vnto the heauens hight.
  So forth into the field she marched thence,
  Where was a rich Pauilion ready pight,
Her to receiue, till time they should begin the fight.

Then forth came *Artegall* out of his tent,   v
  All arm'd to point, and first the Lists did enter:
  Soone after eke came she, with fell intent,
  And countenaunce fierce, as hauing fully bent her,
  That battels vtmost triall to aduenter.
  The Lists were closed fast, to barre the rout
  From rudely pressing to the middle center;
  Which in great heapes them circled all about,
Wayting, how Fortune would resolue that daungerous dout.

The Trumpets sounded, and the field began;   vi
  With bitter strokes it both began, and ended.
  She at the first encounter on him ran
  With furious rage, as if she had intended
  Out of his breast the very heart haue rended:
  But he that had like tempests often tride,
  From that first flaw him selfe right well defended.
  The more she rag'd, the more he did abide;
She hewd, she foynd, she lasht, she laid on euery side.

Yet still her blowes he bore, and her forbore,   vii
  Weening at last to win aduantage new;
  Yet still her crueltie increased more,
  And though powre faild, her courage did accrew,
  Which fayling he gan fiercely her pursew.
  Like as a Smith that to his cunning feat
  The stubborne mettall seeketh to subdew,
  Soone as he feeles it mollifide with heat,
With his great yron sledge doth strongly on it beat.

So did Sir *Artegall* vpon her lay,   viii
   As if she had an yron anduile beene,
   That flakes of fire, bright as the sunny ray,
   Out of her steely armes were flashing seene,
   That all on fire ye would her surely weene.
   But with her shield so well her selfe she warded,
   From the dread daunger of his weapon keene,
   That all that while her life she safely garded:
But he that helpe from her against her will discarded.

For with his trenchant blade at the next blow   ix
   Halfe of her shield he shared quite away,
   That halfe her side it selfe did naked show,
   And thenceforth vnto daunger opened way.
   Much was she moued with the mightie sway
   Of that sad stroke, that halfe enrag'd she grew,
   And like a greedie Beare vnto her pray,
   With her sharpe Cemitare at him she flew,
That glauncing downe his thigh, the purple bloud forth drew.

Thereat she gan to triumph with great boast,   x
   And to vpbrayd that chaunce, which him misfell,
   As if the prize she gotten had almost,
   With spightfull speaches, fitting with her well;
   That his great hart gan inwardly to swell
   With indignation, at her vaunting vaine,
   And at her strooke with puissance fearefull fell;
   Yet with her shield she warded it againe,
That shattered all to peeces round about the plaine.

Hauing her thus disarmed of her shield,   xi
   Vpon her helmet he againe her strooke,
   That downe she fell vpon the grassie field,
   In sencelesse swoune, as if her life forsooke,
   And pangs of death her spirit ouertooke.
   Whom when he saw before his foote prostrated,
   He to her lept with deadly dreadfull looke,
   And her sunshynie helmet soone vnlaced,
Thinking at once both head and helmet to haue raced.

But when as he discouered had her face,   xii
   He saw his senses straunge astonishment,
   A miracle of natures goodly grace,
   In her faire visage voide of ornament,
   But bath'd in bloud and sweat together ment;
   Which in the rudenesse of that euill plight,
   Bewrayd the signes of feature excellent:
   Like as the Moone in foggie winters night,
Doth seeme to be her·selfe, though darkned be her light.

At sight thereof his cruell minded hart   xiii
   Empierced was with pittifull regard,
   That his sharpe sword he threw from him apart,
   Cursing his hand that had that visage mard:
   No hand so cruell, nor no hart so hard,
   But ruth of beautie will it mollifie.
   By this vpstarting from her swoune, she star'd
   A while about her with confused eye;
Like one that from his dreame is waked suddenlye.

Soone as the knight she there by her did spy,   xiv
   Standing with emptie hands all weaponlesse,
   With fresh assault vpon him she did fly,
   And gan renew her former cruelnesse:
   And though he still retyr'd, yet nathelesse
   With huge redoubled strokes she on him layd;
   And more increast her outrage mercilesse,
   The more that he with meeke intreatie prayd,
Her wrathful hand from greedy vengeance to haue stayd.

Like as a Puttocke hauing spyde in sight   xv
   A gentle Faulcon sitting on an hill,
   Whose other wing, now made vnmeete for flight,
   Was lately broken by some fortune ill;
   The foolish Kyte, led with licentious will,
   Doth beat vpon the gentle bird in vaine,
   With many idle stoups her troubling still:
   Euen so did *Radigund* with bootlesse paine
Annoy this noble Knight, and sorely him constraine.

Nought could he do, but shun the dred despight
 Of her fierce wrath, and backward still retyre,
 And with his single shield, well as he might,
 Beare off the burden of her raging yre;
 And euermore he gently did desyre,
 To stay her stroks, and he himselfe would yield:
 Yet nould she hearke, ne let him once respyre,
 Till he to her deliuered had his shield,
And to her mercie him submitted in plaine field.

So was he ouercome, not ouercome,
 But to her yeelded of his owne accord;
 Yet was he iustly damned by the doome
 Of his owne mouth, that spake so warelesse word,
 To be her thrall, and seruice her afford.
 For though that he first victorie obtayned,
 Yet after by abandoning his sword,
 He wilfull lost, that he before attayned.
No fayrer conquest, then that with goodwill is gayned.

Tho with her sword on him she flatling strooke,
 In signe of true subiection to her powre,
 And as her vassall him to thraldome tooke.
 But *Terpine* borne to'a more vnhappy howre,
 As he, on whom the lucklesse starres did lowre,
 She causd to be attacht, and forthwith led
 Vnto the crooke t'abide the balefull stowre,
 From which he lately had through reskew fled:
Where he full shamefully was hanged by the hed.

But when they thought on *Talus* hands to lay,
 He with his yron flaile amongst them thondred,
 That they were fayne to let him scape away,
 Glad from his companie to be so sondred;
 Whose presence all their troups so much encombred
 That th'heapes of those, which he did wound and slay,
 Besides the rest dismayd, might not be nombred:
 Yet all that while he would not once assay,
To reskew his owne Lord, but thought it iust t'obay.

Then tooke the Amazon this noble knight,   xx
　Left to her will by his owne wilfull blame,
　And caused him to be disarmed quight,
　Of all the ornaments of knightly name,
　With which whylome he gotten had great fame:
　In stead whereof she made him to be dight
　In womans weedes, that is to manhood shame,
　And put before his lap a napron white,
In stead of Curiets and bases fit for fight.

So being clad, she brought him from the field,   xxi
　In which he had bene trayned many a day,
　Into a long large chamber, which was sield
　With moniments of many knights decay,
　By her subdewed in victorious fray:
　Amongst the which she causd his warlike armes
　Be hang'd on high, that mote his shame bewray;
　And broke his sword, for feare of further harmes,
With which he wont to stirre vp battailous alarmes.

There entred in, he round about him saw   xxii
　Many braue knights, whose names right well he knew,
　There bound t'obay that Amazons proud law,
　Spinning and carding all in comely rew,
　That his bigge hart loth'd so vncomely vew.
　But they were forst through penurie and pyne,
　To doe those workes, to them appointed dew:
　For nought was giuen them to sup or dyne,
But what their hands could earne by twisting linnen twyne.

Amongst them all she placed him most low,   xxiii
　And in his hand a distaffe to him gaue,
　That he thereon should spin both flax and tow;
　A sordid office for a mind so braue.
　So hard it is to be a womans slaue.
　Yet he it tooke in his owne selfes despight,
　And thereto did himselfe right well behaue,
　Her to obay, sith he his faith had plight,
Her vassall to become, if she him wonne in fight.

Who had him seene, imagine mote thereby,   xxiv
  That whylome hath of *Hercules* bene told,
  How for *Iolas* sake he did apply
  His mightie hands, the distaffe vile to hold,
  For his huge club, which had subdew'd of old
  So many monsters, which the world annoyed;
  His Lyons skin chaungd to a pall of gold,
  In which forgetting warres, he onely ioyed
In combats of sweet loue, and with his mistresse toyed.

Such is the crueltie of womenkynd,   xxv
  When they haue shaken off the shamefast band,
  With which wise Nature did them strongly bynd,
  T'obay the heasts of mans well ruling hand,
  That then all rule and reason they withstand,
  To purchase a licentious libertie.
  But vertuous women wisely vnderstand,
  That they were borne to base humilitie,
Vnlesse the heauens them lift to lawfull soueraintie.

Thus there long while continu'd *Artegall*,   xxvi
  Seruing proud *Radigund* with true subiection;
  How euer it his noble heart did gall,
  T'obay a womans tyrannous direction,
  That might haue had of life or death election:
  But hauing chosen, now he might not chaunge.
  During which time, the warlike Amazon,
  Whose wandring fancie after lust did raunge,
Gan cast a secret liking to this captiue straunge.

Which long concealing in her couert brest,   xxvii
  She chaw'd the cud of louers carefull plight;
  Yet could it not so thoroughly digest,
  Being fast fixed in her wounded spright,
  But it tormented her both day and night:
  Yet would she not thereto yeeld free accord,
  To serue the lowly vassall of her might,
  And of her seruant make her souerayne Lord:
So great her pride, that she such basenesse much abhord.

So much the greater still her anguish grew,
  Through stubborne handling of her loue-sicke hart;
  And still the more she stroue it to subdew,
  The more she still augmented her owne smart,
  And wyder made the wound of th'hidden dart.
  At last when long she struggled had in vaine,
  She gan to stoupe, and her proud mind conuert
  To meeke obeysance of loues mightie raine,
And him entreat for grace, that had procur'd her paine.

Vnto her selfe in secret she did call
  Her nearest handmayd, whom she most did trust,
  And to her said; *Clarinda* whom of all
  I trust a liue, sith I thee fostred first;
  Now is the time, that I vntimely must
  Thereof make tryall, in my greatest need:
  It is so hapned, that the heauens vniust,
  Spighting my happie freedome, haue agreed,
To thrall my looser life, or my last bale to breed.

With that she turn'd her head, as halfe abashed,
  To hide the blush which in her visage rose,
  And through her eyes like sudden lightning flashed,
  Decking her cheeke with a vermilion rose:
  But soone she did her countenance compose,
  And to her turning, thus began againe;
  This griefes deepe wound I would to thee disclose,
  Thereto compelled through hart-murdring paine,
But dread of shame my doubtfull lips doth still restraine.

Ah my deare dread (said then the faithfull Mayd)
  Can dread of ought your dreadlesse hart withhold,
  That many hath with dread of death dismayd,
  And dare euen deathes most dreadfull face behold?
  Say on my souerayne Ladie, and be bold;
  Doth not your handmayds life at your foot lie?
  Therewith much comforted, she gan vnfold
  The cause of her conceiued maladie,
As one that would confesse, yet faine would it denie.

Clarin (sayd she) thou seest yond Fayry Knight,   xxxii
    Whom not my valour, but his owne braue mind
    Subiected hath to my vnequall might;
    What right is it, that he should thraldome find,
    For lending life to me a wretch vnkind;
    That for such good him recompence with ill?
    Therefore I cast, how I may him vnbind,
    And by his freedome get his free goodwill;
Yet so, as bound to me he may continue still.

Bound vnto me, but not with such hard bands   xxxiii
    Of strong compulsion, and streight violence,
    As now in miserable state he stands;
    But with sweet loue and sure beneuolence,
    Voide of malitious mind, or foule offence.
    To which if thou canst win him any way,
    Without discouerie of my thoughts pretence,
    Both goodly meede of him it purchase may,
And eke with gratefull seruice me right well apay.

Which that thou mayst the better bring to pas,   xxxiv
    Loe here this ring, which shall thy warrant bee,
    And token true to old *Eumenias*,
    From time to time, when thou it best shalt see,
    That in and out thou mayst haue passage free.
    Goe now, *Clarinda*, well thy wits aduise,
    And all thy forces gather vnto thee;
    Armies of louely lookes, and speeches wise,
With which thou canst euen *Ioue* himselfe to loue entise.

The trustie Mayd, conceiuing her intent,   xxxv
    Did with sure promise of her good indeuour,
    Giue her great comfort, and some harts content.
    So from her parting, she thenceforth did labour
    By all the meanes she might, to curry fauour
    With th'Elfin Knight, her Ladies best beloued;
    With daily shew of courteous kind behauiour,
    Euen at the markewhite of his hart she roued,
And with wide glauncing words, one day she thus him proued.

Vnhappie Knight, vpon whose hopelesse state
  Fortune enuying good, hath felly frowned,
  And cruell heauens haue heapt an heauy fate;
  I rew that thus thy better dayes are drowned
  In sad despaire, and all thy senses swowned
  In stupid sorow, sith thy iuster merit
  Might else haue with felicitie bene crowned:
  Looke vp at last, and wake thy dulled spirit,
To thinke how this long death thou mightest disinherit.

Much did he maruell at her vncouth speach,
  Whose hidden drift he could not well perceiue;
  And gan to doubt, least she him sought t'appeach
  Of treason, or some guilefull traine did weaue,
  Through which she might his wretched life bereaue.
  Both which to barre, he with this answere met her;
  Faire Damzell, that with ruth (as I perceaue)
  Of my mishaps, art mou'd to wish me better,
For such your kind regard, I can but rest your detter.

Yet weet ye well, that to a courage great
  It is no lesse beseeming well, to beare
  The storme of fortunes frowne, or heauens threat,
  Then in the sunshine of her countenance cleare
  Timely to ioy, and carrie comely cheare.
  For though this cloud haue now me ouercast,
  Yet doe I not of better times despeyre;
  And, though vnlike, they should for euer last,
Yet in my truthes assurance I rest fixed fast.

But what so stonie mind (she then replyde)
  But if in his owne powre occasion lay,
  Would to his hope a windowe open wyde,
  And to his fortunes helpe make readie way?
  Vnworthy sure (quoth he) of better day,
  That will not take the offer of good hope,
  And eke pursew, if he attaine it may.
  Which speaches she applying to the scope
Of her intent, this further purpose to him shope.

Then why doest not, thou ill aduized man,
  Make meanes to win thy libertie forlorne,
  And try if thou by faire entreatie, can
  Moue *Radigund*? who though she still haue worne
  Her dayes in warre, yet (weet thou) was not borne
  Of Beares and Tygres, nor so saluage mynded,
  As that, albe all loue of men she scorne,
  She yet forgets, that she of men was kynded: (blynded.
And sooth oft seene, that proudest harts base loue hath

Certes *Clarinda*, not of cancred will,
  (Sayd he) nor obstinate disdainefull mind,
  I haue forbore this duetie to fulfill:
  For well I may this weene, by that I fynd,
  That she a Queene, and come of Princely kynd,
  Both worthie is for to be sewd vnto,
  Chiefely by him, whose life her law doth bynd,
  And eke of powre her owne doome to vndo,
And als' of princely grace to be inclyn'd thereto.

But want of meanes hath bene mine onely let,
  From seeking fauour, where it doth abound;
  Which if I might by your good office get,
  I to your selfe should rest for euer bound,
  And readie to deserue, what grace I found.
  She feeling him thus bite vpon the bayt,
  Yet doubting least his hold was but vnsound,
  And not well fastened, would not strike him strayt,
But drew him on with hope, fit leasure to awayt.

But foolish Mayd, whyles heedlesse of the hooke,
  She thus oft times was beating off and on,
  Through slipperie footing, fell into the brooke,
  And there was caught to her confusion.
  For seeking thus to salue the Amazon,
  She wounded was with her deceipts owne dart,
  And gan thenceforth to cast affection,
  Conceiued close in her beguiled hart,
To *Artegall*, through pittie of his causelesse smart.

Yet durst she not disclose her fancies wound,
  Ne to himselfe, for doubt of being sdayned,
  Ne yet to any other wight on ground,
  For feare her mistresse shold haue knowledge gayned,
  But to her selfe it secretly retayned,
  Within the closet of her couert brest:
  The more thereby her tender hart was payned.
  Yet to awayt fit time she weened best,
And fairely did dissemble her sad thoughts vnrest.

One day her Ladie, calling her apart,
  Gan to demaund of her some tydings good,
  Touching her loues successe, her lingring smart.
  Therewith she gan at first to change her mood,
  As one adaw'd, and halfe confused stood;
  But quickly she it ouerpast, so soone
  As she her face had wypt, to fresh her blood:
  Tho gan she tell her all, that she had donne,
And all the wayes she sought, his loue for to haue wonne.

But sayd, that he was obstinate and sterne,
  Scorning her offers and conditions vaine;
  Ne would be taught with any termes, to lerne
  So fond a lesson, as to loue againe.
  Die rather would he in penurious paine,
  And his abridged dayes in dolour wast,
  Then his foes loue or liking entertaine:
  His resolution was both first and last,
His bodie was her thrall, his hart was freely plast.

Which when the cruell Amazon perceiued,
  She gan to storme, and rage, and rend her gall,
  For very fell despight, which she conceiued,
  To be so scorned of a base borne thrall,
  Whose life did lie in her least eye-lids fall;
  Of which she vow'd with many a cursed threat,
  That she therefore would him ere long forstall.
  Nathlesse when calmed was her furious heat,
She chang'd that threatfull mood, and mildly gan entreat.

What now is left *Clarinda*? what remaines,   xlviii
   That we may compasse this our enterprize?
   Great shame to lose so long employed paines,
   And greater shame t'abide so great misprize,
   With which he dares our offers thus despize.
   Yet that his guilt the greater may appeare,
   And more my gratious mercie by this wize,
   I will a while with his first folly beare,
Till thou haue tride againe, and tempted him more neare.

Say, and do all, that may thereto preuaile;   xlix
   Leaue nought vnpromist, that may him perswade,
   Life, freedome, grace, and gifts of great auaile,
   With which the Gods themselues are mylder made:
   Thereto adde art, euen womens witty trade,
   The art of mightie words, that men can charme;
   With which in case thou canst him not inuade,
   Let him feele hardnesse of thy heauie arme: (harme.
Who will not stoupe with good, shall be made stoupe with

Some of his diet doe from him withdraw;   l
   For I him find to be too proudly fed.
   Giue him more labour, and with streighter law,
   That he with worke may be forwearied.
   Let him lodge hard, and lie in strawen bed,
   That may pull downe the courage of his pride;
   And lay vpon him, for his greater dread,
   Cold yron chaines, with which let him be tide;
And let, what euer he desires, be him denide.

When thou hast all this doen, then bring me newes   li
   Of his demeane: thenceforth not like a louer,
   But like a rebell stout I will him vse.
   For I resolue this siege not to giue ouer,
   Till I the conquest of my will recouer.
   So she departed, full of griefe and sdaine,
   Which inly did to great impatience moue her.
   But the false mayden shortly turn'd againe
Vnto the prison, where her hart did thrall remaine.

There all her subtill nets she did vnfold,   lii
   And all the engins of her wit display;
   In which she meant him warelesse to enfold,
   And of his innocence to make her pray.
   So cunningly she wrought her crafts assay,
   That both her Ladie, and her selfe withall,
   And eke the knight attonce she did betray:
   But most the knight, whom she with guilefull call
Did cast for to allure, into her trap to fall.

As a bad Nurse, which fayning to receiue   liii
   In her owne mouth the food, ment for her chyld,
   Withholdes it to her selfe, and doeth deceiue
   The infant, so for want of nourture spoyld:
   Euen so *Clarinda* her owne Dame beguyld,
   And turn'd the trust, which was in her affyde,
   To feeding of her priuate fire, which boyld
   Her inward brest, and in her entrayles fryde,
The more that she it sought to couer and to hyde.

For comming to this knight, she purpose fayned,   liv
   How earnest suit she earst for him had made
   Vnto her Queene, his freedome to haue gayned;
   But by no meanes could her thereto perswade:
   But that in stead thereof, she sternely bade
   His miserie to be augmented more,
   And many yron bands on him to lade.
   All which nathlesse she for his loue forbore:
So praying him t'accept her seruice euermore.

And more then that, she promist that she would,   lv
   In case she might finde fauour in his eye,
   Deuize how to enlarge him out of hould.
   The Fayrie glad to gaine his libertie,
   Can yeeld great thankes for such her curtesie,
   And with faire words, fit for the time and place,
   To feede the humour of her maladie,
   Promist, if she would free him from that case,
He wold by all good means he might, deserue such grace.

So daily he faire semblant did her shew,   lvi
  Yet neuer meant he in his noble mind,
  To his owne absent loue to be vntrew:
  Ne euer did deceiptfull *Clarin* find
  In her false hart, his bondage to vnbind;
  But rather how she mote him faster tye.
  Therefore vnto her mistresse most vnkind
  She daily told, her loue he did defye,
And him she told, her Dame his freedome did denye.

Yet thus much friendship she to him did show,   lvii
  That his scarse diet somewhat was amended,
  And his worke lessened, that his loue mote grow:
  Yet to her Dame him still she discommended,
  That she with him mote be the more offended.
  Thus he long while in thraldome there remayned,
  Of both beloued well, but litle frended;
  Vntill his owne true loue his freedome gayned,
Which in an other Canto will be best contayned.

Cant. VI.

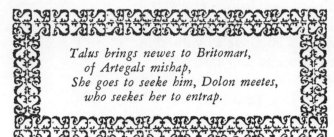

Talus brings newes to Britomart,
of Artegals mishap,
She goes to seeke him, Dolon meetes,
who seekes her to entrap.

SOme men, I wote, will deeme in *Artegall*   i
    Great weaknesse, and report of him much ill,
    For yeelding so himselfe a wretched thrall,
    To th'insolent commaund of womens will;
    That all his former praise doth fowly spill.
    But he the man, that say or doe so dare,
    Be well aduiz'd, that he stand stedfast still:
    For neuer yet was wight so well aware,
But he at first or last was trapt in womens snare.

Yet in the streightnesse of that captiue state,   ii
    This gentle knight himselfe so well behaued,
    That notwithstanding all the subtill bait,
    With which those Amazons his loue still craued,
    To his owne loue his loialtie he saued:
    Whose character in th'Adamantine mould
    Of his true hart so firmely was engraued,
    That no new loues impression euer could
Bereaue it thence: such blot his honour blemish should.

Yet his owne loue, the noble *Britomart*,   iii
    Scarse so conceiued in her iealous thought,
    What time sad tydings of his balefull smart
    In womans bondage, *Talus* to her brought;
    Brought in vntimely houre, ere it was sought.
    For after that the vtmost date, assynde
    For his returne, she waited had for nought,
    She gan to cast in her misdoubtfull mynde
A thousand feares, that loue-sicke fancies faine to fynde.

Sometime she feared, least some hard mishap   iv
  Had him misfalne in his aduenturous quest;
  Sometime least his false foe did him entrap
  In traytrous traine, or had vnwares opprest:
  But most she did her troubled mynd molest,
  And secretly afflict with iealous feare,
  Least some new loue had him from her possest;
  Yet loth she was, since she no ill did heare,
To thinke of him so ill: yet could she not forbeare.

One while she blam'd her selfe; another whyle   v
  She him condemn'd, as trustlesse and vntrew:
  And then, her griefe with errour to beguyle,
  She fayn'd to count the time againe anew,
  As if before she had not counted trew.
  For houres but dayes; for weekes, that passed were,
  She told but moneths, to make them seeme more few:
  Yet when she reckned them, still drawing neare,
Each hour did seeme a moneth, and euery moneth a yeare.

But when as yet she saw him not returne,   vi
  She thought to send some one to seeke him out;
  But none she found so fit to serue that turne,
  As her owne selfe, to ease her selfe of dout.
  Now she deuiz'd amongst the warlike rout
  Of errant Knights, to seeke her errant Knight;
  And then againe resolu'd to hunt him out
  Amongst loose Ladies, lapped in delight:
And then both Knights enuide, and Ladies eke did spight.

One day, when as she long had sought for ease   vii
  In euery place, and euery place thought best,
  Yet found no place, that could her liking please,
  She to a window came, that opened West,
  Towards which coast her loue his way addrest.
  There looking forth, shee in her heart did find
  Many vaine fancies, working her vnrest;
  And sent her winged thoughts, more swift then wind,
To beare vnto her loue the message of her mind.

There as she looked long, at last she spide   viii
  One comming towards her with hasty speede:
  Well weend she then, ere him she plaine descride,
  That it was one sent from her loue indeede.
  Who when he nigh approcht, shee mote arede
  That it was *Talus*, *Artegall* his groome;
  Whereat her heart was fild with hope and drede;
  Ne would she stay, till he in place could come,
But ran to meete him forth, to know his tidings somme.

Euen in the dore him meeting, she begun;   ix
  And where is he thy Lord, and how far hence?
  Declare at once; and hath he lost or wun?
  The yron man, albe he wanted sence
  And sorrowes feeling, yet with conscience
  Of his ill newes, did inly chill and quake,
  And stood still mute, as one in great suspence,
  As if that by his silence he would make
Her rather reade his meaning, then him selfe it spake.

Till she againe thus sayd; *Talus* be bold,   x
  And tell what euer it be, good or bad,
  That from thy tongue thy hearts intent doth hold.
  To whom he thus at length. The tidings sad,
  That I would hide, will needs, I see, be rad.
  My Lord, your loue, by hard mishap doth lie
  In wretched bondage, wofully bestad.
  Ay me (quoth she) what wicked destinie?
And is he vanquisht by his tyrant enemy?

Not by that Tyrant, his intended foe;   xi
  But by a Tyrannesse (he then replide,)
  That him captiued hath in haplesse woe.
  Cease thou bad newes-man, badly doest thou hide
  Thy maisters shame, in harlots bondage tide.
  The rest my selfe too readily can spell.
  With that in rage she turn'd from him aside,
  Forcing in vaine the rest to her to tell,
And to her chamber went like solitary cell.

There she began to make her monefull plaint   xii
  Against her Knight, for being so vntrew;
  And him to touch with falshoods fowle attaint,
  That all his other honour ouerthrew.
  Oft did she blame her selfe, and often rew,
  For yeelding to a straungers loue so light,
  Whose life and manners straunge she neuer knew;
  And euermore she did him sharpely twight
For breach of faith to her, which he had firmely plight.

And then she in her wrathfull will did cast,   xiii
  How to reuenge that blot of honour blent;
  To fight with him, and goodly die her last:
  And then againe she did her selfe torment,
  Inflicting on her selfe his punishment.
  A while she walkt, and chauft; a while she threw
  Her selfe vppon her bed, and did lament:
  Yet did she not lament with loude alew,
As women wont, but with deepe sighes, and singulfs few.

Like as a wayward childe, whose sounder sleepe   xiv
  Is broken with some fearefull dreames affright,
  With froward will doth set him selfe to weepe;
  Ne can be stild for all his nurses might,
  But kicks, and squals, and shriekes for fell despight:
  Now scratching her, and her loose locks misusing;
  Now seeking darkenesse, and now seeking light;
  Then crauing sucke, and then the sucke refusing.
Such was this Ladies fit, in her loues fond accusing.

But when she had with such vnquiet fits   xv
  Her selfe there close afflicted long in vaine,
  Yet found no easement in her troubled wits,
  She vnto *Talus* forth return'd againe,
  By change of place seeking to ease her paine;
  And gan enquire of him, with mylder mood,
  The certaine cause of *Artegals* detaine;
  And what he did, and in what state he stood,
And whether he did woo, or whether he were woo'd.

Ah wellaway (sayd then the yron man,)   xvi
   That he is not the while in state to woo;
   But lies in wretched thraldome, weake and wan,
   Not by strong hand compelled thereunto,
   But his owne doome, that none can now vndoo.
   Sayd I not then (quoth shee) erwhile aright,
   That this is things compacte betwixt you two,
   Me to deceiue of faith vnto me plight,
Since that he was not forst, nor ouercome in fight?

With that he gan at large to her dilate   xvii
   The whole discourse of his captiuance sad,
   In sort as ye haue heard the same of late.
   All which when she with hard enduraunce had
   Heard to the end, she was right sore bestad,
   With sodaine stounds of wrath and griefe attone:
   Ne would abide, till she had aunswere made,
   But streight her selfe did dight, and armor don;
And mounting to her steede, bad *Talus* guide her on.

So forth she rode vppon her ready way,   xviii
   To seeke her Knight, as *Talus* her did guide:
   Sadly she rode, and neuer word did say,
   Nor good nor bad, ne euer lookt aside,
   But still right downe, and in her thought did hide
   The felnesse of her heart, right fully bent
   To fierce auengement of that womans pride,
   Which had her Lord in her base prison pent,
And so great honour with so fowle reproch had blent.

So as she thus melancholicke did ride,   xix
   Chawing the cud of griefe and inward paine,
   She chaunst to meete toward th'euen-tide
   A Knight, that softly paced on the plaine,
   As if him selfe to solace he were faine.
   Well shot in yeares he seem'd, and rather bent
   To peace, then needlesse trouble to constraine,
   As well by view of that his vestiment,
As by his modest semblant, that no euill ment.

He comming neare, gan gently her salute
  With curteous words, in the most comely wize;
  Who though desirous rather to rest mute,
  Then termes to entertaine of common guize,
  Yet rather then she kindnesse would despize,
  She would her selfe displease, so him requite.
  Then gan the other further to deuize
  Of things abrode, as next to hand did light,
And many things demaund, to which she answer'd light.

For little lust had she to talke of ought,
  Or ought to heare, that mote delightfull bee;
  Her minde was whole possessed of one thought,
  That gaue none other place. Which when as hee
  By outward signes, (as well he might) did see,
  He list no lenger to vse lothfull speach,
  But her besought to take it well in gree,
  Sith shady dampe had dimd the heauens reach,
To lodge with him that night, vnles good cause empeach.

The Championesse, now seeing night at dore,
  Was glad to yeeld vnto his good request:
  And with him went without gaine-saying more.
  Not farre away, but little wide by West,
  His dwelling was, to which he him addrest;
  Where soone arriuing they receiued were
  In seemely wise, as them beseemed best:
  For he their host them goodly well did cheare,
And talk't of pleasant things, the night away to weare.

Thus passing th'euening well, till time of rest,
  Then *Britomart* vnto a bowre was brought;
  Where groomes awayted her to haue vndrest.
  But she ne would vndressed be for ought,
  Ne doffe her armes, though he her much besought.
  For she had vow'd, she sayd, not to forgo
  Those warlike weedes, till she reuenge had wrought
  Of a late wrong vppon a mortall foe;
Which she would sure performe, betide her wele or wo.

Which when their Host perceiu'd, right discontent   xxiv
  In minde he grew, for feare least by that art
  He should his purpose misse, which close he ment:
  Yet taking leaue of her, he did depart.
  There all that night remained *Britomart*,
  Restlesse, recomfortlesse, with heart deepe grieued,
  Not suffering the least twinckling sleepe to start
  Into her eye, which th'heart mote haue relieued,
But if the least appear'd, her eyes she streight reprieued.

Ye guilty eyes (sayd she) the which with guyle   xxv
  My heart at first betrayd, will ye betray
  My life now to, for which a little whyle
  Ye will not watch? false watches, wellaway,
  I wote when ye did watch both night and day
  Vnto your losse: and now needes will ye sleepe?
  Now ye haue made my heart to wake alway,
  Now will ye sleepe? ah wake, and rather weepe,
To thinke of your nights want, that should yee waking keepe.

Thus did she watch, and weare the weary night   xxvi
  In waylfull plaints, that none was to appease;
  Now walking soft, now sitting still vpright,
  As sundry chaunge her seemed best to ease.
  Ne lesse did *Talus* suffer sleepe to seaze
  His eye-lids sad, but watcht continually,
  Lying without her dore in great disease;
  Like to a Spaniell wayting carefully
Least any should betray his Lady treacherously.

What time the natiue Belman of the night,   xxvii
  The bird, that warned *Peter* of his fall,
  First rings his siluer Bell t'each sleepy wight,
  That should their mindes vp to deuotion call,
  She heard a wondrous noise below the hall.
  All sodainely the bed, where she should lie,
  By a false trap was let adowne to fall
  Into a lower roome, and by and by
The loft was raysd againe, that no man could it spie.

With sight whereof she was dismayd right sore,   xxviii
  Perceiuing well the treason, which was ment:
  Yet stirred not at all for doubt of more,
  But kept her place with courage confident,
  Wayting what would ensue of that euent.
  It was not long, before she heard the sound
  Of armed men, comming with close intent
  Towards her chamber; at which dreadfull stound
She quickly caught her sword, and shield about her bound.

With that there came vnto her chamber dore   xxix
  Two Knights, all arm'd ready for to fight,
  And after them full many other more,
  A raskall rout, with weapons rudely dight.
  Whom soone as *Talus* spide by glims of night,
  He started vp, there where on ground he lay,
  And in his hand his thresher ready keight.
  They seeing that, let driue at him streight way,
And round about him preace in riotous aray.

But soone as he began to lay about   xxx
  With his rude yron flaile, they gan to flie,
  Both armed Knights, and eke vnarmed rout:
  Yet *Talus* after them apace did plie,
  Where euer in the darke he could them spie;
  That here and there like scattred sheepe they lay.
  Then backe returning, where his Dame did lie,
  He to her told the story of that fray,
And all that treason there intended did bewray.

Wherewith though wondrous wroth, and inly burning,   xxxi
  To be auenged for so fowle a deede,
  Yet being forst to abide the daies returning,
  She there remain'd, but with right wary heede,
  Least any more such practise should proceede.
  Now mote ye know (that which to *Britomart*
  Vnknowen was) whence all this did proceede,
  And for what cause so great mischieuous smart
Was ment to her, that neuer euill ment in hart.

The goodman of this house was *Dolon* hight,   xxxii
   A man of subtill wit and wicked minde,
   That whilome in his youth had bene a Knight,
   And armes had borne, but little good could finde,
   And much lesse honour by that warlike kinde
   Of life: for he was nothing valorous,
   But with slie shiftes and wiles did vnderminde
   All noble Knights, which were aduenturous,
And many brought to shame by treason treacherous.

He had three sonnes, all three like fathers sonnes,   xxxiii
   Like treacherous, like full of fraud and guile,
   Of all that on this earthly compasse wonnes:
   The eldest of the which was slaine erewhile
   By *Artegall*, through his owne guilty wile;
   His name was *Guizor*, whose vntimely fate
   For to auenge, full many treasons vile
   His father *Dolon* had deuiz'd of late
With these his wicked sons, and shewd his cankred hate.

For sure he weend, that this his present guest   xxxiv
   Was *Artegall*, by many tokens plaine;
   But chiefly by that yron page he ghest,
   Which still was wont with *Artegall* remaine;
   And therefore ment him surely to haue slaine.
   But by Gods grace, and her good heedinesse,
   She was preserued from their traytrous traine.
   Thus she all night wore out in watchfulnesse,
Ne suffred slothfull sleepe her eyelids to oppresse.

The morrow next, so soone as dawning houre   xxxv
   Discouered had the light to liuing eye,
   She forth yssew'd out of her loathed bowre,
   With full intent t'auenge that villany,
   On that vilde man, and all his family.
   And comming down to seeke them, where they wond,
   Nor sire, nor sonnes, nor any could she spie:
   Each rowme she sought, but them all empty fond:
They all were fled for feare, but whether, nether kond.

She saw it vaine to make there lenger stay,   xxxvi
   But tooke her steede, and thereon mounting light,
   Gan her addresse vnto her former way.
   She had not rid the mountenance of a flight,
   But that she saw there present in her sight,
   Those two false brethren, on that perillous Bridge,
   On which *Pollente* with *Artegall* did fight.
   Streight was the passage like a ploughed ridge,
That if two met, the one mote needes fall ouer the lidge.

There they did thinke them selues on her to wreake: xxxvii
   Who as she nigh vnto them drew, the one
   These vile reproches gan vnto her speake;
   Thou recreant false traytor, that with lone
   Of armes hast knighthood stolne, yet Knight art none,
   No more shall now the darkenesse of the night
   Defend thee from the vengeance of thy fone,
   But with thy bloud thou shalt appease the spright
Of *Guizor*, by thee slaine, and murdred by thy slight.

Strange were the words in *Britomartis* eare;   xxxviii
   Yet stayd she not for them, but forward fared,
   Till to the perillous Bridge she came, and there
   Talus desir'd, that he might haue prepared
   The way to her, and those two losels scared.
   But she thereat was wroth, that for despight
   The glauncing sparkles through her beuer glared,
   And from her eies did flash out fiery light,
Like coles, that through a siluer Censer sparkle bright.

She stayd not to aduise which way to take;   xxxix
   But putting spurres vnto her fiery beast,
   Thorough the midst of them she way did make.
   The one of them, which most her wrath increast,
   Vppon her speare she bore before her breast,
   Till to the Bridges further end she past,
   Where falling downe, his challenge he releast:
   The other ouer side the Bridge she cast
Into the riuer, where he drunke his deadly last.

As when the flashing Leuin haps to light   xl
  Vppon two stubborne oakes, which stand so neare,
  That way betwixt them none appeares in sight;
  The Engin fiercely flying forth, doth teare
  Th'one from the earth, and through the aire doth beare;
  The other it with force doth ouerthrow,
  Vppon one side, and from his rootes doth reare.
  So did the Championesse those two there strow,
And to their sire their carcasses left to bestow.

Cant. VII.

Britomart comes to Isis Church,
　Where shee strange visions sees:
She fights with Radigund, her slaies,
　And Artegall thence frees.

Ought is on earth more sacred or diuine,   i
　That Gods and men doe equally adore,
Then this same vertue, that doth right define:
For th'heucns themselues, whence mortal men implore
Right in their wrongs, are rul'd by righteous lore
Of highest Ioue, who doth true iustice deale
To his inferiour Gods, and euermore
Therewith containes his heauenly Common-weale:
The skill whereof to Princes hearts he doth reueale.

Well therefore did the antique world inuent,   ii
　That Iustice was a God of soueraine grace,
　And altars vnto him, and temples lent,
　And heauenly honours in the highest place;
　Calling him great *Osyris*, of the race
　Of th'old Ægyptian Kings, that whylome were;
　With fayned colours shading a true case:
　For that *Osyris*, whilest he liued here,
The iustest man aliue, and truest did appeare.

His wife was *Isis*, whom they likewise made   iii
　A Goddesse of great powre and souerainty,
　And in her person cunningly did shade
　That part of Iustice, which is Equity,
　Whereof I haue to treat here presently.
　Vnto whose temple when as *Britomart*
　Arriued, shee with great humility
　Did enter in, ne would that night depart;
But *Talus* mote not be admitted to her part.

There she receiued was in goodly wize   iv
  Of many Priests, which duely did attend
  Vppon the rites and daily sacrifize,
  All clad in linnen robes with siluer hemd:
  And on their heads with long locks comely kemd,
  They wore rich Mitres shaped like the Moone,
  To shew that *Isis* doth the Moone portend;
  Like as *Osyris* signifies the Sunne.
For that they both like race in equall iustice runne.

The Championesse them greeting, as she could,   v
  Was thence by them into the Temple led;
  Whose goodly building when she did behould,
  Borne vppon stately pillours, all dispred
  With shining gold, and arched ouer hed,
  She wondred at the workemans passing skill,
  Whose like before she neuer saw nor red;
  And thereuppon long while stood gazing still,
But thought, that she thereon could neuer gaze her fill.

Thence forth vnto the Idoll they her brought,   vi
  The which was framed all of siluer fine,
  So well as could with cunning hand be wrought,
  And clothed all in garments made of line,
  Hemd all about with fringe of siluer twine.
  Vppon her head she wore a Crowne of gold,
  To shew that she had powre in things diuine;
  And at her feete a Crocodile was rold,
That with her wreathed taile her middle did enfold.

One foote was set vppon the Crocodile,   vii
  And on the ground the other fast did stand,
  So meaning to suppresse both forged guile,
  And open force: and in her other hand
  She stretched forth a long white sclender wand.
  Such was the Goddesse; whom when *Britomart*
  Had long beheld, her selfe vppon the land
  She did prostrate, and with right humble hart,
Vnto her selfe her silent prayers did impart.

To which the Idoll as it were inclining,
  Her wand did moue with amiable looke,
  By outward shew her inward sence desining.
  Who well perceiuing, how her wand she shooke,
  It as a token of good fortune tooke.
  By this the day with dampe was ouercast,
  And ioyous light the house of *Ioue* forsooke:
  Which when she saw, her helmet she vnlaste,
And by the altars side her selfe to slumber plaste.

For other beds the Priests there vsed none,
  But on their mother Earths deare lap did lie,
  And bake their sides vppon the cold hard stone,
  T'enure them selues to sufferaunce thereby
  And proud rebellious flesh to mortify.
  For by the vow of their religion
  They tied were to stedfast chastity,
  And continence of life, that all forgon,
They mote the better tend to their deuotion.

Therefore they mote not taste of fleshly food,
  Ne feed on ought, the which doth bloud containe,
  Ne drinke of wine, for wine they say is blood,
  Euen the bloud of Gyants, which were slaine,
  By thundring Ioue in the Phlegrean plaine.
  For which the earth (as they the story tell)
  Wroth with the Gods, which to perpetuall paine
  Had damn'd her sonnes, which gainst them did rebell,
With inward griefe and malice did against them swell.

And of their vitall bloud, the which was shed
  Into her pregnant bosome, forth she brought
  The fruitfull vine, whose liquor blouddy red
  Hauing the mindes of men with fury fraught,
  Mote in them stirre vp old rebellious thought,
  To make new warre against the Gods againe:
  Such is the powre of that same fruit, that nought
  The fell contagion may thereof restraine,
Ne within reasons rule, her madding mood containe.

There did the warlike Maide her selfe repose,   xii
    Vnder the wings of *Isis* all that night,
    And with sweete rest her heauy eyes did close,
    After that long daies toile and weary plight.
    Where whilest her earthly parts with soft delight
    Of sencelesse sleepe did deeply drowned lie,
    There did appeare vnto her heauenly spright
    A wondrous vision, which did close implie
The course of all her fortune and posteritie.

Her seem'd, as she was doing sacrifize   xiii
    To *Isis*, deckt with Mitre on her hed,
    And linnen stole after those Priestes guize,
    All sodainely she saw transfigured
    Her linnen stole to robe of scarlet red,
    And Moone-like Mitre to a Crowne of gold,
    That euen she her selfe much wondered
    At such a chaunge, and ioyed to behold
Her selfe, adorn'd with gems and iewels manifold.

And in the midst of her felicity,   xiv
    An hideous tempest seemed from below,
    To rise through all the Temple sodainely,
    That from the Altar all about did blow
    The holy fire, and all the embers strow
    Vppon the ground, which kindled priuily,
    Into outragious flames vnwares did grow,
    That all the Temple put in ieopardy
Of flaming, and her selfe in great perplexity.

With that the Crocodile, which sleeping lay   xv
    Vnder the Idols feete in fearelesse bowre,
    Seem'd to awake in horrible dismay,
    As being troubled with that stormy stowre;
    And gaping greedy wide, did streight deuoure
    Both flames and tempest: with which growen great,
    And swolne with pride of his owne peerelesse powre,
    He gan to threaten her likewise to eat;
But that the Goddesse with her rod him backe did beat.

Tho turning all his pride to humblesse meeke,   xvi
  Him selfe before her feete he lowly threw,
  And gan for grace and loue of her to seeke:
  Which she accepting, he so neare her drew,
  That of his game she soone enwombed grew,
  And forth did bring a Lion of great might;
  That shortly did all other beasts subdew.
  With that she waked, full of fearefull fright,
And doubtfully dismayd through that so vncouth sight.

So thereuppon long while she musing lay,   xvii
  With thousand thoughts feeding her fantasie,
  Vntill she spide the lampe of lightsome day,
  Vp-lifted in the porch of heauen hie.
  Then vp she rose fraught with melancholy,
  And forth into the lower parts did pas;
  Whereas the Priestes she found full busily
  About their holy things for morrow Mas:
Whom she saluting faire, faire resaluted was.

But by the change of her vnchearefull looke,   xviii
  They might perceiue, she was not well in plight;
  Or that some pensiuenesse to heart she tooke.
  Therefore thus one of them, who seem'd in sight
  To be the greatest, and the grauest wight,
  To her bespake; Sir Knight it seemes to me,
  That thorough euill rest of this last night,
  Or ill apayd, or much dismayd ye be,
That by your change of cheare is easie for to see.

Certes (sayd she) sith ye so well haue spide   xix
  The troublous passion of my pensiue mind,
  I will not seeke the same from you to hide,
  But will my cares vnfolde, in hope to find
  Your aide, to guide me out of errour blind.
  Say on (quoth he) the secret of your hart:
  For by the holy vow, which me doth bind,
  I am adiur'd, best counsell to impart
To all, that shall require my comfort in their smart.

Then gan she to declare the whole discourse   xx
    Of all that vision, which to her appeard,
    As well as to her minde it had recourse.
    All which when he vnto the end had heard,
    Like to a weake faint-hearted man he fared,
    Through great astonishment of that strange sight;
    And with long locks vp-standing, stifly stared
    Like one adawed with some dreadfull spright.
So fild with heauenly fury, thus he her behight.

Magnificke Virgin, that in queint disguise   xxi
    Of British armes doest maske thy royall blood,
    So to pursue a perillous emprize,
    How couldst thou weene, through that disguized hood,
    To hide thy state from being vnderstood?
    Can from th'immortall Gods ought hidden bee?
    They doe thy linage, and thy Lordly brood;
    They doe thy sire, lamenting sore for thee;
They doe thy loue, forlorne in womens thraldome see.

The end whereof, and all the long euent,   xxii
    They doe to thee in this same dreame discouer.
    For that same Crocodile doth represent
    The righteous Knight, that is thy faithfull louer,
    Like to *Osyris* in all iust endeuer.
    For that same Crocodile *Osyris* is,
    That vnder *Isis* feete doth sleepe for euer:
    To shew that clemence oft in things amis,
Restraines those sterne behests, and cruell doomes of his.

That Knight shall all the troublous stormes asswage,   xxiii
    And raging flames, that many foes shall reare,
    To hinder thee from the iust heritage
    Of thy sires Crowne, and from thy countrey deare.
    Then shalt thou take him to thy loued fere,
    And ioyne in equall portion of thy realme:
    And afterwards a sonne to him shalt beare,
    That Lion-like shall shew his powre extreame.
So blesse thee God, and giue thee ioyance of thy dreame.

All which when she vnto the end had heard,   xxiv
  She much was eased in her troublous thought,
  And on those Priests bestowed rich reward:
  And royall gifts of gold and siluer wrought,
  She for a present to their Goddesse brought.
  Then taking leaue of them, she forward went,
  To seeke her loue, where he was to be sought;
  Ne rested till she came without relent
Vnto the land of Amazons, as she was bent.

Whereof when newes to *Radigund* was brought,   xxv
  Not with amaze, as women wonted bee,
  She was confused in her troublous thought,
  But fild with courage and with ioyous glee,
  As glad to heare of armes, the which now she
  Had long surceast, she bad to open bold,
  That she the face of her new foe might see.
  But when they of that yron man had told,
Which late her folke had slaine, she bad them forth to hold.

So there without the gate (as seemed best)   xxvi
  She caused her Pauilion be pight;
  In which stout *Britomart* her selfe did rest,
  Whiles *Talus* watched at the dore all night.
  All night likewise, they of the towne in fright,
  Vppon their wall good watch and ward did keepe.
  The morrow next, so soone as dawning light
  Bad doe away the dampe of drouzie sleepe,
The warlike Amazon out of her bowre did peepe.

And caused streight a Trumpet loud to shrill,   xxvii
  To warne her foe to battell soone be prest:
  Who long before awoke (for she ful ill
  Could sleepe all night, that in vnquiet brest
  Did closely harbour such a iealous guest)
  Was to the battell whilome ready dight.
  Eftsoones that warriouresse with haughty crest
  Did forth issue, all ready for the fight:
On th'other side her foe appeared soone in sight.

But ere they reared hand, the Amazone   xxviii
  Began the streight conditions to propound,
  With which she vsed still to tye her fone;
  To serue her so, as she the rest had bound.
  Which when the other heard, she sternly frownd
  For high disdaine of such indignity,
  And would no lenger treat, but bad them sound.
  For her no other termes should euer tie,
Then what prescribed were by lawes of cheualrie.

The Trumpets sound, and they together run   xxix
  With greedy rage, and with their faulchins smot;
  Ne either sought the others strokes to shun,
  But through great fury both their skill forgot,
  And practicke vse in armes: ne spared not
  Their dainty parts, which nature had created
  So faire and tender, without staine or spot,
  For other vses, then they them translated;
Which they now hackt and hewd, as if such vse they hated,

As when a Tygre and a Lionesse   xxx
  Are met at spoyling of some hungry pray,
  Both challenge it with equall greedinesse:
  But first the Tygre clawes thereon did lay;
  And therefore loth to loose her right away,
  Doth in defence thereof full stoutly stond:
  To which the Lion strongly doth gainesay,
  That she to hunt the beast first tooke in hond;
And therefore ought it haue, where euer she it fond.

Full fiercely layde the Amazon about,   xxxi
  And dealt her blowes vnmercifully sore:
  Which *Britomart* withstood with courage stout,
  And them repaide againe with double more.
  So long they fought, that all the grassie flore
  Was fild with bloud, which from their sides did flow,
  And gushed through their armes, that all in gore
  They trode, and on the ground their liues did strow,
Like fruitles seede, of which vntimely death should grow.

At last proud *Radigund* with fell despight,
  Hauing by chaunce espide aduantage neare,
  Let driue at her with all her dreadfull might,
  And thus vpbrayding said; This token beare
  Vnto the man, whom thou doest loue so deare;
  And tell him for his sake thy life thou gauest.
  Which spitefull words she sore engrieu'd to heare,
  Thus answer'd; Lewdly thou my loue deprauest,
Who shortly must repent that now so vainely brauest.

Nath'lesse that stroke so cruell passage found,
  That glauncing on her shoulder plate, it bit
  Vnto the bone, and made a griesly wound,
  That she her shield through raging smart of it
  Could scarse vphold; yet soone she it requit.
  For hauing force increast through furious paine,
  She her so rudely on the helmet smit,
  That it empierced to the very braine,
And her proud person low prostrated on the plaine.

Where being layd, the wrothfull Britonesse
  Stayd not, till she came to her selfe againe,
  But in reuenge both of her loues distresse,
  And her late vile reproch, though vaunted vaine,
  And also of her wound, which sore did paine,
  She with one stroke both head and helmet cleft.
  Which dreadfull sight, when all her warlike traine
  There present saw, each one of sence bereft,
Fled fast into the towne, and her sole victor left.

But yet so fast they could not home retrate,
  But that swift *Talus* did the formost win;
  And pressing through the preace vnto the gate,
  Pelmell with them attonce did enter in.
  There then a piteous slaughter did begin:
  For all that euer came within his reach,
  He with his yron flale did thresh so thin,
  That he no worke at all left for the leach:
Like to an hideous storme, which nothing may empeach.

And now by this the noble Conqueresse   xxxvi
    Her selfe came in, her glory to partake;
    Where though reuengefull vow she did professe,
    Yet when she saw the heapes, which he did make,
    Of slaughtred carkasses, her heart did quake
    For very ruth, which did it almost riue,
    That she his fury willed him to slake:
    For else he sure had left not one aliue,
But all in his reuenge of spirite would depriue.

Tho when she had his execution stayd,   xxxvii
    She for that yron prison did enquire,
    In which her wretched loue was captiue layd:
    Which breaking open with indignant ire,
    She entred into all the partes entire.
    Where when she saw that lothly vncouth sight,
    Of men disguiz'd in womanishe attire,
    Her heart gan grudge, for very deepe despight
Of so vnmanly maske, in misery misdight.

At last when as to her owne Loue she came,   xxxviii
    Whom like disguize no lesse deformed had,
    At sight thereof abasht with secrete shame,
    She turnd her head aside, as nothing glad,
    To haue beheld a spectacle so bad:
    And then too well beleeu'd, that which tofore
    Iealous suspect as true vntruely drad,
    Which vaine conceipt now nourishing no more,
She sought with ruth to salue his sad misfortunes sore.

Not so great wonder and astonishment,   xxxix
    Did the most chast *Penelope* possesse,
    To see her Lord, that was reported drent,
    And dead long since in dolorous distresse,
    Come home to her in piteous wretchednesse,
    After long trauell of full twenty yeares,
    That she knew not his fauours likelynesse,
    For many scarres and many hoary heares,
But stood long staring on him, mongst vncertaine feares.

Ah my deare Lord, what sight is this (quoth she)
  What May-game hath misfortune made of you?
  Where is that dreadfull manly looke? where be
  Those mighty palmes, the which ye wont t'embrew
  In bloud of Kings, and great hoastes to subdew?
  Could ought on earth so wondrous change haue wrought,
  As to haue robde you of that manly hew?
  Could so great courage stouped haue to ought?
Then farewell fleshly force; I see thy pride is nought.

Thenceforth she streight into a bowre him brought,
  And causd him those vncomely weedes vndight;
  And in their steede for other rayment sought,
  Whereof there was great store, and armors bright,
  Which had bene reft from many a noble Knight;
  Whom that proud Amazon subdewed had,
  Whilest Fortune fauourd her successe in fight,
  In which when as she him anew had clad,
She was reuiu'd, and ioyd much in his semblance glad.

So there a while they afterwards remained,
  Him to refresh, and her late wounds to heale:
  During which space she there as Princess rained,
  And changing all that forme of common weale,
  The liberty of women did repeale,
  Which they had long vsurpt; and them restoring
  To mens subiection, did true Iustice deale:
  That all they as a Goddesse her adoring,
Her wisedome did admire, and hearkned to her loring.

For all those Knights, which long in captiue shade
  Had shrowded bene, she did from thraldome free;
  And magistrates of all that city made,
  And gaue to them great liuing and large fee:
  And that they should for euer faithfull bee,
  Made them sweare fealty to *Artegall*.
  Who when him selfe now well recur'd did see,
  He purposd to proceed, what so be fall,
Vppon his first aduenture, which him forth did call.

Full sad and sorrowfull was *Britomart*   xliv
  For his departure, her new cause of griefe;
  Yet wisely moderated her owne smart,
  Seeing his honor, which she tendred chiefe,
  Consisted much in that aduentures priefe.
  The care whereof, and hope of his successe
  Gaue vnto her great comfort and reliefe,
  That womanish complaints she did represse,
And tempred for the time her present heauinesse.

There she continu'd for a certaine space,   xlv
  Till through his want her woe did more increase:
  Then hoping that the change of aire and place
  Would change her paine, and sorrow somewhat ease,
  She parted thence, her anguish to appease.
  Meane while her noble Lord sir *Artegall*
  Went on his way, ne euer howre did cease,
  Till he redeemed had that Lady thrall:
That for another Canto will more fitly fall.

Cant. VIII.

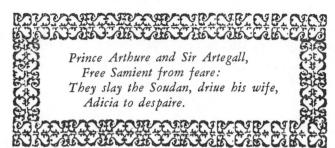

Prince Arthure and Sir Artegall,
Free Samient from feare:
They slay the Soudan, driue his wife,
Adicia to despaire.

NOught vnder heauen so strongly doth allure
  The sence of man, and all his minde possesse,
As beauties louely baite, that doth procure
Great warriours oft their rigour to represse,
And mighty hands forget their manlinesse;
Drawne with the powre of an heart-robbing eye,
And wrapt in fetters of a golden tresse,
That can with melting pleasaunce mollifye
Their hardned hearts, enur'd to bloud and cruelty.

i

So whylome learnd that mighty Iewish swaine,
  Each of whose lockes did match a man in might,
  To lay his spoiles before his lemans traine:
So also did that great Oetean Knight
For his loues sake his Lions skin vndight:
And so did warlike *Antony* neglect
The worlds whole rule for *Cleopatras* sight.
Such wondrous powre hath wemens faire aspect,
To captiue men, and make them all the world reiect.

ii

Yet could it not sterne *Artegall* retaine,
  Nor hold from suite of his auowed quest,
  Which he had vndertane to *Gloriane*;
But left his loue, albe her strong request,
Faire *Britomart* in languor and vnrest,
And rode him selfe vppon his first intent:
Ne day nor night did euer idly rest;
Ne wight but onely *Talus* with him went,
The true guide of his way and vertuous gouernment.

iii

So trauelling, he chaunst far off to heed   iv
    A Damzell, flying on a palfrey fast
    Before two Knights, that after her did speed
    With all their powre, and her full fiercely chast
    In hope to haue her ouerhent at last:
    Yet fled she fast, and both them farre outwent,
    Carried with wings of feare, like fowle aghast,
    With locks all loose, and rayment all to rent;
And euer as she rode, her eye was backeward bent.

Soone after these he saw another Knight,   v
    That after those two former rode apace,
    With speare in rest, and prickt with all his might:
    So ran they all, as they had bene at bace,
    They being chased, that did others chase.
    At length he saw the hindmost ouertake
    One of those two, and force him turne his face;
    How euer loth he were his way to slake,
Yet mote he algates now abide, and answere make.

But th'other still pursu'd the fearefull Mayd;   vi
    Who still from him as fast away did flie,
    Ne once for ought her speedy passage stayd,
    Till that at length she did before her spie
    Sir *Artegall*, to whom she streight did hie
    With gladfull hast, in hope of him to get
    Succour against her greedy enimy:
    Who seeing her approch gan forward set,
To saue her from her feare, and him from force to let.

But he like hound full greedy of his pray,   vii
    Being impatient of impediment,
    Continu'd still his course, and by the way
    Thought with his speare him quight haue ouerwent.
    So both together ylike felly bent,
    Like fiercely met. But *Artegall* was stronger,
    And better skild in Tilt and Turnament,
    And bore him quite out of his saddle, longer
Then two speares length; So mischiefe ouermatcht the wronger.

And in his fall misfortune him mistooke;
  For on his head vnhappily he pight,
  That his owne waight his necke asunder broke,
  And left there dead. Meane while the other Knight
  Defeated had the other faytour quight,
  And all his bowels in his body brast:
  Whom leauing there in that dispiteous plight,
  He ran still on, thinking to follow fast
His other fellow Pagan, which before him past.

In stead of whom finding there ready prest
  Sir *Artegall*, without discretion
  He at him ran, with ready speare in rest:
  Who seeing him come still so fiercely on,
  Against him made againe. So both anon
  Together met, and strongly either strooke
  And broke their speares; yet neither has forgon
  His horses backe, yet to and fro long shooke,
And tottred like two towres, which through a tempest quooke.

But when againe they had recouered sence,
  They drew their swords, in mind to make amends
  For what their speares had fayld of their pretence.
  Which when the Damzell, who those deadly ends
  Of both her foes had seene, and now her frends
  For her beginning a more fearefull fray,
  She to them runnes in hast, and her haire rends,
  Crying to them their cruell hands to stay,
Vntill they both doe heare, what she to them will say.

They stayd their hands, when she thus gan to speake;
  Ah gentle Knights, what meane ye thus vnwise
  Vpon your selues anothers wrong to wreake?
  I am the wrong'd, whom ye did enterprise
  Both to redresse, and both redrest likewise:
  Witnesse the Paynims both, whom ye may see
  There dead on ground. What doe ye then deuise
  Of more reuenge? if more, then I am shee,
Which was the roote of all, end your reuenge on mee.

Whom when they heard so say, they lookt about,   xii
　　To weete if it were true, as she had told;
　　Where when they saw their foes dead out of doubt,
　　Eftsoones they gan their wrothfull hands to hold,
　　And Ventailes reare, each other to behold.
　　Tho when as *Artegall* did *Arthure* vew,
　　So faire a creature, and so wondrous bold,
　　He much admired both his heart and hew,
And touched with intire affection, nigh him drew.

Saying, Sir Knight, of pardon I you pray,   xiii
　　That all vnweeting haue you wrong'd thus sore,
　　Suffring my hand against my heart to stray:
　　Which if ye please forgiue, I will therefore
　　Yeeld for amends my selfe yours euermore,
　　Or what so penaunce shall by you be red.
　　To whom the Prince; Certes me needeth more
　　To craue the same, whom errour so misled,
As that I did mistake the liuing for the ded.

But sith ye please, that both our blames shall die,   xiv
　　Amends may for the trespasse soone be made,
　　Since neither is endamadg'd much thereby.
　　So can they both them selues full eath perswade
　　To faire accordaunce, and both faults to shade,
　　Either embracing other louingly,
　　And swearing faith to either on his blade,
　　Neuer thenceforth to nourish enmity,
But either others cause to maintaine mutually.

Then *Artegall* gan of the Prince enquire,   xv
　　What were those knights, which there on ground were layd,
　　And had receiu'd their follies worthy hire,
　　And for what cause they chased so that Mayd.
　　Certes I wote not well (the Prince then sayd)
　　But by aduenture found them faring so,
　　As by the way vnweetingly I strayd,
　　And lo the Damzell selfe, whence all did grow,
Of whom we may at will the whole occasion know.

Then they that Damzell called to them nie,   xvi
    And asked her, what were those two her fone,
    From whom she earst so fast away did flie;
    And what was she her selfe so woe begone,
    And for what cause pursu'd of them attone.
    To whom she thus; Then wote ye well, that I
    Doe serue a Queene, that not far hence doth wone,
    A Princesse of great powre and maiestie,
Famous through all the world, and honor'd far and nie.

Her name *Mercilla* most men vse to call;   xvii
    That is a mayden Queene of high renowne,
    For her great bounty knowen ouer all,
    And soueraine grace, with which her royall crowne
    She doth support, and strongly beateth downe
    The malice of her foes, which her enuy,
    And at her happinesse do fret and frowne:
    Yet she her selfe the more doth magnify,
And euen to her foes her mercies multiply.

Mongst many which maligne her happy state,   xviii
    There is a mighty man, which wonnes here by
    That with most fell despight and deadly hate,
    Seekes to subuert her Crowne and dignity,
    And all his powre doth thereunto apply:
    And her good Knights, of which so braue a band
    Serues her, as any Princesse vnder sky,
    He either spoiles, if they against him stand,
Or to his part allures, and bribeth vnder hand.

Ne him sufficeth all the wrong and ill,   xix
    Which he vnto her people does each day,
    But that he seekes by traytrous traines to spill
    Her person, and her sacred selfe to slay:
    That O ye heauens defend, and turne away
    From her, vnto the miscreant him selfe,
    That neither hath religion nor fay,
    But makes his God of his vngodly pelfe,
And Idols serues; so let his Idols serue the Elfe.

To all which cruell tyranny they say,   xx
  He is prouokt, and stird vp day and night
  By his bad wife, that hight *Adicia*,
  Who counsels him through confidence of might,
  To breake all bonds of law, and rules of right.
  For she her selfe professeth mortall foe
  To Iustice, and against her still doth fight,
  Working to all, that loue her, deadly woe,
And making all her Knights and people to doe so.

Which my liege Lady seeing, thought it best,   xxi
  With that his wife in friendly wise to deale,
  For stint of strife, and stablishment of rest
  Both to her selfe, and to her common weale,
  And all forepast displeasures to repeale.
  So me in message vnto her she sent,
  To treat with her by way of enterdeale,
  Of finall peace and faire attonement,
Which might concluded be by mutuall consent.

All times haue wont safe passage to afford   xxii
  To messengers, that come for causes iust:
  But this proude Dame disdayning all accord,
  Not onely into bitter termes forth brust,
  Reuiling me, and rayling as she lust,
  But lastly to make proofe of vtmost shame,
  Me like a dog she out of dores did thrust,
  Miscalling me by many a bitter name,
That neuer did her ill, ne once deserued blame.

And lastly, that no shame might wanting be,   xxiii
  When I was gone, soone after me she sent
  These two false Knights, whom there ye lying see,
  To be by them dishonoured and shent:
  But thankt be God, and your good hardiment,
  They haue the price of their owne folly payd.
  So said this Damzell, that hight *Samient*,
  And to those knights, for their so noble ayd,
Her selfe most gratefull shew'd, and heaped thanks repayd.

But they now hauing throughly heard, and seene
  Al those great wrongs, the which that mayd complained
  To haue bene done against her Lady Queene,
  By that proud dame, which her so much disdained,
  Were moued much thereat, and twixt them fained,
  With all their force to worke auengement strong
  Vppon the Souldan selfe, which it mayntained,
  And on his Lady, th'author of that wrong,
And vppon all those Knights, that did to her belong.

But thinking best by counterfet disguise
  To their deseigne to make the easier way,
  They did this complot twixt them selues deuise,
  First that sir *Artegall* should him array,
  Like one of those two Knights, which dead there lay.
  And then that Damzell, the sad *Samient*,
  Should as his purchast prize with him conuay
  Vnto the Souldans court, her to present
Vnto his scornefull Lady, that for her had sent.

So as they had deuiz'd, sir *Artegall*
  Him clad in th'armour of a Pagan knight,
  And taking with him, as his vanquisht thrall,
  That Damzell, led her to the Souldans right.
  Where soone as his proud wife of her had sight,
  Forth of her window as she looking lay,
  She weened streight, it was her Paynim Knight,
  Which brought that Damzell, as his purchast pray;
And sent to him a Page, that mote direct his way.

Who bringing them to their appointed place,
  Offred his seruice to disarme the Knight;
  But he refusing him to let vnlace,
  For doubt to be discouered by his sight,
  Kept himselfe still in his straunge armour dight.
  Soone after whom the Prince arriued there,
  And sending to the Souldan in despight
  A bold defyance, did of him requere
That Damzell, whom he held as wrongfull prisonere.

Wherewith the Souldan all with furie fraught,   xxviii
   Swearing, and banning most blasphemously,
   Commaunded straight his armour to be brought,
   And mounting straight vpon a charret hye,
   With yron wheeles and hookes arm'd dreadfully,
   And drawne of cruell steedes, which he had fed
   With flesh of men, whom through fell tyranny
   He slaughtred had, and ere they were halfe ded,
Their bodies to his beasts for prouender did spred.

So forth he came all in a cote of plate,   xxix
   Burnisht with bloudie rust, whiles on the greene
   The Briton Prince him readie did awayte,
   In glistering armes right goodly well beseene,
   That shone as bright, as doth the heauen sheene;
   And by his stirrup *Talus* did attend,
   Playing his pages part, as he had beene
   Before directed by his Lord; to th'end
He should his flale to finall execution bend.

Thus goe they both together to their geare,   xxx
   With like fierce minds, but meanings different:
   For the proud Souldan with presumpteous cheare,
   And countenance sublime and insolent,
   Sought onely slaughter and auengement:
   But the braue Prince for honour and for right,
   Gainst tortious powre and lawlesse regiment,
   In the behalfe of wronged weake did fight:
More in his causes truth he trusted then in might.

Like to the *Thracian* Tyrant, who they say   xxxi
   Vnto his horses gaue his guests for meat,
   Till he himselfe was made their greedie pray,
   And torne in peeces by *Alcides* great.
   So thought the Souldan in his follies threat,
   Either the Prince in peeces to haue torne
   With his sharpe wheeles, in his first rages heat,
   Or vnder his fierce horses feet haue borne
And trampled downe in dust his thoughts disdained scorne.

But the bold child that perill well espying,
 If he too rashly to his charet drew,
 Gaue way vnto his horses speedie flying,
 And their resistlesse rigour did eschew.
 Yet as he passed by, the Pagan threw
 A shiuering dart with so impetuous force,
 That had he not it shun'd with heedfull vew,
 It had himselfe transfixed, or his horse,
Or made them both one masse withouten more remorse.

Oft drew the Prince vnto his charret nigh,
 In hope some stroke to fasten on him neare;
 But he was mounted in his seat so high,
 And his wingfooted coursers him did beare
 So fast away, that ere his readie speare
 He could aduance, he farre was gone and past.
 Yet still he him did follow euery where,
 And followed was of him likewise full fast;
So long as in his steedes the flaming breath did last.

Againe the Pagan threw another dart,
 Of which he had with him abundant store,
 On euery side of his embatteld cart,
 And of all other weapons lesse or more,
 Which warlike vses had deuiz'd of yore.
 The wicked shaft guyded through th'ayrie wyde,
 By some bad spirit, that it to mischiefe bore,
 Stayd not, till through his curat it did glyde,
And made a griesly wound in his enriuen side.

Much was he grieued with that haplesse throe,
 That opened had the welspring of his blood;
 But much the more that to his hatefull foe
 He mote not come, to wreake his wrathfull mood.
 That made him raue, like to a Lyon wood,
 Which being wounded of the huntsmans hand
 Can not come neare him in the couert wood,
 Where he with boughes hath built his shady stand,
And fenst himselfe about with many a flaming brand.

Still when he sought t'approch vnto him ny,   xxxvi
  His charret wheeles about him whirled round,
  And made him backe againe as fast to fly;
  And eke his steedes like to an hungry hound,
  That hunting after game hath carrion found,
  So cruelly did him pursew and chace,
  That his good steed, all were he much renound
  For noble courage, and for hardie race,
Durst not endure their sight, but fled from place to place.

Thus long they trast, and trauerst to and fro,   xxxvii
  Seeking by euery way to make some breach,
  Yet could the Prince not nigh vnto him goe,
  That one sure stroke he might vnto him reach,
  Whereby his strengthes assay he might him teach.
  At last from his victorious shield he drew
  The vaile, which did his powrefull light empeach;
  And comming full before his horses vew,
As they vpon him prest, it plaine to them did shew.

Like lightening flash, that hath the gazer burned,   xxxviii
  So did the sight thereof their sense dismay,
  That backe againe vpon themselues they turned,
  And with their ryder ranne perforce away:
  Ne could the Souldan them from flying stay,
  With raynes, or wonted rule, as well he knew.
  Nought feared they, what he could do, or say,
  But th'onely feare, that was before their vew;
From which like mazed deare, dismayfully they flew.

Fast did they fly, as them their feete could beare,   xxxix
  High ouer hilles, and lowly ouer dales,
  As they were follow'd of their former feare.
  In vaine the Pagan bannes, and sweares, and rayles,
  And backe with both his hands vnto him hayles
  The resty raynes, regarded now no more:
  He to them calles and speakes, yet nought auayles;
  They heare him not, they haue forgot his lore,
But go, which way they list, their guide they haue forlore.

As when the firie-mouthed steeds, which drew   xl
  The Sunnes bright wayne to *Phaetons* decay,
  Soone as they did the monstrous Scorpion vew,
  With vgly craples crawling in their way,
  The dreadfull sight did them so sore affray,
  That their well knowen courses they forwent,
  And leading th'euer-burning lampe astray,
  This lower world nigh all to ashes brent,
And left their scorched path yet in the firmament.

Such was the furie of these head-strong steeds,   xli
  Soone as the infants sunlike shield they saw,
  That all obedience both to words and deeds
  They quite forgot, and scornd all former law;
  Through woods, and rocks, and mountaines they did draw
  The yron charet, and the wheeles did teare,
  And tost the Paynim, without feare or awe;
  From side to side they tost him here and there,
Crying to them in vaine, that nould his crying heare.

Yet still the Prince pursew'd him close behind,   xlii
  Oft making offer him to smite, but found
  No easie meanes according to his mind.
  At last they haue all ouerthrowne to ground
  Quite topside turuey, and the pagan hound
  Amongst the yron hookes and graples keene,
  Torne all to rags, and rent with many a wound,
  That no whole peece of him was to be seene,
But scattred all about, and strow'd vpon the greene.

Like as the cursed sonne of *Theseus*,   xliii
  That following his chace in dewy morne,
  To fly his stepdames loues outrageous,
  Of his owne steedes was all to peeces torne,
  And his faire limbs left in the woods forlorne;
  That for his sake *Diana* did lament,
  And all the wooddy Nymphes did wayle and mourne.
  So was this Souldan rapt and all to rent,
That of his shape appear'd no litle moniment.

Onely his shield and armour, which there lay,   xliv
　　Though nothing whole, but all to brusd and broken,
　　He vp did take, and with him brought away,
　　That mote remaine for an eternall token
　　To all, mongst whom this storie should be spoken,
　　How worthily, by heauens high decree,
　　Iustice that day of wrong her selfe had wroken,
　　That all men which that spectacle did see,
By like ensample mote for euer warned bee.

So on a tree, before the Tyrants dore,   xlv
　　He caused them be hung in all mens sight,
　　To be a moniment for euermore.
　　Which when his Ladie from the castles hight
　　Beheld, it much appald her troubled spright:
　　Yet not, as women wont in dolefull fit,
　　She was dismayd, or faynted through affright,
　　But gathered vnto her her troubled wit,
And gan eftsoones deuize to be aueng'd for it.

Streight downe she ranne, like an enraged cow,   xlvi
　　That is berobbed of her youngling dere,
　　With knife in hand, and fatally did vow,
　　To wreake her on that mayden messengere,
　　Whom she had causd be kept as prisonere,
　　By *Artegall*, misween'd for her owne Knight,
　　That brought her backe. And comming present there,
　　She at her ran with all her force and might,
All flaming with reuenge and furious despight.

Like raging *Ino*, when with knife in hand   xlvii
　　She threw her husbands murdred infant out,
　　Or fell *Medea*, when on *Colchicke* strand
　　Her brothers bones she scattered all about;
　　Or as that madding mother, mongst the rout
　　Of *Bacchus* Priests her owne deare flesh did teare.
　　Yet neither *Ino*, nor *Medea* stout,
　　Nor all the *Mœnades* so furious were,
As this bold woman, when she saw that Damzell there.

But *Artegall* being thereof aware, xlviii
  Did stay her cruell hand, ere she her raught,
  And as she did her selfe to strike prepare,
  Out of her fist the wicked weapon caught:
  With that like one enfelon'd or distraught,
  She forth did rome, whether her rage her bore,
  With franticke passion, and with furie fraught;
  And breaking forth out at a posterne dore,
Vnto the wyld wood ranne, her dolours to deplore.

As a mad bytch, when as the franticke fit xlix
  Her burning tongue with rage inflamed hath,
  Doth runne at randon, and with furious bit
  Snatching at euery thing, doth wreake her wrath
  On man and beast, that commeth in her path.
  There they doe say, that she transformed was
  Into a Tygre, and that Tygres scath
  In crueltie and outrage she did pas,
To proue her surname true, that she imposed has.

Then *Artegall* himselfe discouering plaine, l
  Did issue forth gainst all that warlike rout
  Of knights and armed men, which did maintaine
  That Ladies part, and to the Souldan lout:
  All which he did assault with courage stout,
  All were they nigh an hundred knights of name,
  And like wyld Goates them chaced all about,
  Flying from place to place with cowheard shame,
So that with finall force them all he ouercame.

Then caused he the gates be opened wyde, li
  And there the Prince, as victour of that day,
  With tryumph entertayn'd and glorifyde,
  Presenting him with all the rich array,
  And roiall pompe, which there long hidden lay,
  Purchast through lawlesse powre and tortious wrong
  Of that proud Souldan, whom he earst did slay.
  So both for rest there hauing stayd not long,
Marcht with that mayd, fit matter for another song.

Cant. IX.

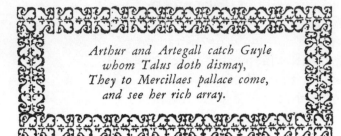

Arthur and Artegall catch Guyle
whom Talus doth dismay,
They to Mercillaes pallace come,
and see her rich array.

WHat Tygre, or what other saluage wight   i
 Is so exceeding furious and fell,
As wrong, when it hath arm'd it selfe with might?
Not fit mongst men, that doe with reason mell,
But mongst wyld beasts and saluage woods to dwell;
Where still the stronger doth the weake deuoure,
And they that most in boldnesse doe excell,
Are dreadded most, and feared for their powre:
Fit for *Adicia*, there to build her wicked bowre.

There let her wonne farre from resort of men,   ii
 Where righteous *Artegall* her late exyled;
There let her euer keepe her damned den,
Where none may be with her lewd parts defyled,
Nor none but beasts may be of her despoyled:
And turne we to the noble Prince, where late
We did him leaue, after that he had foyled
The cruell Souldan, and with dreadfull fate
Had vtterly subuerted his vnrighteous state.

Where hauing with Sir *Artegall* a space   iii
 Well solast in that Souldans late delight,
They both resoluing now to leaue the place,
Both it and all the wealth therein behight
Vnto that Damzell in her Ladies right,
And so would haue departed on their way.
But she them woo'd by all the meanes she might,
And earnestly besought, to wend that day
With her, to see her Ladie thence not farre away.

By whose entreatie both they ouercommen,   iv
 Agree to goe with her, and by the way,
 (As often falles) of sundry things did commen.
 Mongst which that Damzell did to them bewray
 A straunge aduenture, which not farre thence lay;
 To weet a wicked villaine, bold and stout,
 Which wonned in a rocke not farre away,
 That robbed all the countrie there about,
And brought the pillage home, whence none could get it out.

Thereto both his owne wylie wit, (she sayd)   v
 And eke the fastnesse of his dwelling place,
 Both vnassaylable, gaue him great ayde:
 For he so crafty was to forge and face,
 So light of hand, and nymble of his pace,
 So smooth of tongue, and subtile in his tale,
 That could deceiue one looking in his face;
 Therefore by name *Malengin* they him call,
Well knowen by his feates, and famous ouer all.

Through these his slights he many doth confound,   vi
 And eke the rocke, in which he wonts to dwell,
 Is wondrous strong, and hewen farre vnder ground
 A dreadfull depth, how deepe no man can tell;
 But some doe say, it goeth downe to hell.
 And all within, it full of wyndings is,
 And hidden wayes, that scarse an hound by smell
 Can follow out those false footsteps of his,
Ne none can backe returne, that once are gone amis.

Which when those knights had heard, their harts gan earne,   vii
 To vnderstand that villeins dwelling place,
 And greatly it desir'd of her to learne,
 And by which way they towards it should trace.
 Were not (sayd she) that it should let your pace
 Towards my Ladies presence by you ment,
 I would you guyde directly to the place.
 Then let not that (said they) stay your intent;
For neither will one foot, till we that carle haue hent.

So forth they past, till they approched ny   viii
  Vnto the rocke, where was the villains won,
  Which when the Damzell neare at hand did spy,
  She warn'd the knights thereof: who thereupon
  Gan to aduize, what best were to be done.
  So both agreed, to send that mayd afore,
  Where she might sit nigh to the den alone,
  Wayling, and raysing pittifull vprore,
As if she did some great calamitie deplore.

With noyse whereof when as the caytiue carle   ix
  Should issue forth, in hope to find some spoyle,
  They in awayt would closely him ensnarle,
  Ere to his den he backward could recoyle,
  And so would hope him easily to foyle.
  The Damzell straight went, as she was directed,
  Vnto the rocke, and there vpon the soyle
  Hauing her selfe in wretched wize abiected,
Gan weepe and wayle, as if great griefe had her affected.

The cry whereof entring the hollow caue,   x
  Eftsoones brought forth the villaine, as they ment,
  With hope of her some wishfull boot to haue.
  Full dreadfull wight he was, as euer went
  Vpon the earth, with hollow eyes deepe pent,
  And long curld locks, that downe his shoulders shagged,
  And on his backe an vncouth vestiment
  Made of straunge stuffe, but all to worne and ragged,
And vnderneath his breech was all to torne and iagged.

And in his hand an huge long staffe he held,   xi
  Whose top was arm'd with many an yron hooke,
  Fit to catch hold of all that he could weld,
  Or in the compasse of his clouches tooke;
  And euer round about he cast his looke.
  Als at his backe a great wyde net he bore,
  With which he seldome fished at the brooke,
  But vsd to fish for fooles on the dry shore,
Of which he in faire weather wont to take great store.

Him when the damzell saw fast by her side,
  So vgly creature, she was nigh dismayd,
  And now for helpe aloud in earnest cride.
  But when the villaine saw her so affrayd,
  He gan with guilefull words her to perswade,
  To banish feare, and with *Sardonian* smyle
  Laughing on her, his false intent to shade,
  Gan forth to lay his bayte her to beguyle,
That from her self vnwares he might her steale the whyle.

Like as the fouler on his guilefull pype
  Charmes to the birds full many a pleasant lay,
  That they the whiles may take lesse heedie keepe,
  How he his nets doth for their ruine lay:
  So did the villaine to her prate and play,
  And many pleasant trickes before her show,
  To turne her eyes from his intent away:
  For he in slights and iugling feates did flow,
And of legierdemayne the mysteries did know.

To which whilest she lent her intentiue mind,
  He suddenly his net vpon her threw,
  That ouersprad her like a puffe of wind;
  And snatching her soone vp, ere well she knew,
  Ran with her fast away vnto his mew,
  Crying for helpe aloud. But when as ny
  He came vnto his caue, and there did vew
  The armed knights stopping his passage by,
He threw his burden downe, and fast away did fly.

But *Artegall* him after did pursew,
  The whiles the Prince there kept the entrance still:
  Vp to the rocke he ran, and thereon flew
  Like a wyld Gote, leaping from hill to hill,
  And dauncing on the craggy cliffes at will;
  That deadly daunger seem'd in all mens sight,
  To tempt such steps, where footing was so ill:
  Ne ought auayled for the armed knight,
To thinke to follow him, that was so swift and light.

Which when he saw, his yron man he sent,   xvi
  To follow him; for he was swift in chace.
  He him pursewd, where euer that he went,
  Both ouer rockes, and hilles, and euery place,
  Where so he fled, he followd him apace:
  So that he shortly forst him to forsake
  The hight, and downe descend vnto the base.
  There he him courst a fresh, and soone did make
To leaue his proper forme, and other shape to take.

Into a Foxe himselfe he first did tourne;   xvii
  But he him hunted like a Foxe full fast:
  Then to a bush himselfe he did transforme,
  But he the bush did beat, till that at last
  Into a bird it chaung'd, and from him past,
  Flying from tree to tree, from wand to wand:
  But he then stones at it so long did cast,
  That like a stone it fell vpon the land,
But he then tooke it vp, and held fast in his hand.

So he it brought with him vnto the knights,   xviii
  And to his Lord Sir *Artegall* it lent,
  Warning him hold it fast, for feare of slights.
  Who whilest in hand it gryping hard he hent,
  Into a Hedgehogge all vnwares it went,
  And prickt him so, that he away it threw.
  Then gan it runne away incontinent,
  Being returned to his former hew:
But *Talus* soone him ouertooke, and backward drew.

But when as he would to a snake againe   xix
  Haue turn'd himselfe, he with his yron flayle
  Gan driue at him, with so huge might and maine,
  That all his bones, as small as sandy grayle
  He broke, and did his bowels disentrayle;
  Crying in vaine for helpe, when helpe was past.
  So did deceipt the selfe deceiuer fayle,
  There they him left a carrion outcast;
For beasts and foules to feede vpon for their repast.

Thence forth they passed with that gentle Mayd, xx
  To see her Ladie, as they did agree.
  To which when she approched, thus she sayd;
  Loe now, right noble knights, arriu'd ye bee
  Nigh to the place, which ye desir'd to see:
  There shall ye see my souerayne Lady Queene
  Most sacred wight, most debonayre and free,
  That euer yet vpon this earth was seene,
Or that with Diademe hath euer crowned beene.

The gentle knights reioyced much to heare xxi
  The prayses of that Prince so manifold,
  And passing litle further, commen were,
  Where they a stately pallace did behold,
  Of pompous show, much more then she had told;
  With many towres, and tarras mounted hye,
  And all their tops bright glistering with gold,
  That seemed to outshine the dimmed skye,
And with their brightnesse daz'd the straunge beholders eye.

There they alighting, by that Damzell were xxii
  Directed in, and shewed all the sight:
  Whose porch, that most magnificke did appeare,
  Stood open wyde to all men day and night;
  Yet warded well by one of mickle might,
  That sate thereby, with gyantlike resemblance,
  To keepe out guyle, and malice, and despight,
  That vnder shew oftimes of fayned semblance,
Are wont in Princes courts to worke great scath and hindrance.

His name was *Awe*; by whom they passing in xxiii
  Went vp the hall, that was a large wyde roome,
  All full of people making troublous din,
  And wondrous noyse, as if that there were some,
  Which vnto them was dealing righteous doome.
  By whom they passing, through the thickest preasse,
  The marshall of the hall to them did come;
  His name hight *Order*, who commaunding peace,
Them guyded through the throng, that did their clamors ceasse.

They ceast their clamors vpon them to gaze;
  Whom seeing all in armour bright as day,
  Straunge there to see, it did them much amaze,
  And with vnwonted terror halfe affray.
  For neuer saw they there the like array.
  Ne euer was the name of warre there spoken,
  But ioyous peace and quietnesse alway,
  Dealing iust iudgements, that mote not be broken
For any brybes, or threates of any to be wroken.

There as they entred at the Scriene, they saw
  Some one, whose tongue was for his trespasse vyle
  Nayld to a post, adiudged so by law:
  For that therewith he falsely did reuyle,
  And foule blaspheme that Queene for forged guyle,
  Both with bold speaches, which he blazed had,
  And with lewd poems, which he did compyle;
  For the bold title of a Poet bad
He on himselfe had ta'en, and rayling rymes had sprad.

Thus there he stood, whylest high ouer his head,
  There written was the purport of his sin,
  In cyphers strange, that few could rightly read,
  BON FONT: but *bon* that once had written bin,
  Was raced out, and *Mal* was now put in.
  So now *Malfont* was plainely to be red;
  Eyther for th'euill, which he did therein,
  Or that he likened was to a welhed
Of euill words, and wicked sclaunders by him shed.

They passing by, were guyded by degree
  Vnto the presence of that gratious Queene:
  Who sate on high, that she might all men see,
  And might of all men royally be seene,
  Vpon a throne of gold full bright and sheene,
  Adorned all with gemmes of endlesse price,
  As either might for wealth haue gotten bene,
  Or could be fram'd by workmans rare deuice;
And all embost with Lyons and with Flourdelice.

All ouer her a cloth of state was spred,
      Not of rich tissew, nor of cloth of gold,
      Nor of ought else, that may be richest red,
      But like a cloud, as likest may be told,
      That her brode spreading wings did wyde vnfold;
      Whose skirts were bordred with bright sunny beams,
      Glistring like gold, amongst the plights enrold,
      And here and there shooting forth siluer streames,
Mongst which crept litle Angels through the glittering gleames.

Seemed those litle Angels did vphold
      The cloth of state, and on their purpled wings
      Did beare the pendants, through their nimblesse bold:
      Besides a thousand more of such, as sings
      Hymnes to high God, and carols heauenly things,
      Encompassed the throne, on which she sate:
      She Angel-like, the heyre of ancient kings
      And mightie Conquerors, in royall state,
Whylest kings and kesars at her feet did them prostrate.

Thus she did sit in souerayne Maiestie,
      Holding a Scepter in her royall hand,
      The sacred pledge of peace and clemencie,
      With which high God had blest her happie land,
      Maugre so many foes, which did withstand.
      But at her feet her sword was likewise layde,
      Whose long rest rusted the bright steely brand;
      Yet when as foes enforst, or friends sought ayde,
She could it sternely draw, that all the world dismayde.

And round about, before her feet there sate
      A beuie of faire Virgins clad in white,
      That goodly seem'd t'adorne her royall state,
      All louely daughters of high *Ioue*, that hight
      Litæ, by him begot in loues delight,
      Vpon the righteous *Themis*: those they say
      Vpon *Ioues* iudgement seat wayt day and night,
      And when in wrath he threats the worlds decay,
They doe his anger calme, and cruell vengeance stay.

They also doe by his diuine permission   xxxii
 Vpon the thrones of mortall Princes tend,
 And often treat for pardon and remission
 To suppliants, through frayltie which offend.
 Those did vpon *Mercillaes* throne attend:
 Iust *Dice*, wise *Eunomie*, myld *Eirene*,
 And them amongst, her glorie to commend,
 Sate goodly *Temperance* in garments clene,
And sacred *Reuerence*, yborne of heauenly strene.

Thus did she sit in royall rich estate,   xxxiii
 Admyr'd of many, honoured of all,
 Whylest vnderneath her feete, there as she sate,
 An huge great Lyon lay, that mote appall
 An hardie courage, like captiued thrall,
 With a strong yron chaine and coller bound,
 That once he could not moue, nor quich at all;
 Yet did he murmure with rebellions sound,
And softly royne, when saluage choler gan redound.

So sitting high in dreaded souerayntie,   xxxiv
 Those two strange knights were to her presence brought;
 Who bowing low before her Maiestie,
 Did to her myld obeysance, as they ought,
 And meekest boone, that they imagine mought.
 To whom she eke inclyning her withall,
 As a faire stoupe of her high soaring thought,
 A chearefull countenance on them let fall,
Yet tempred with some maiestie imperiall.

As the bright sunne, what time his fierie teme   xxxv
 Towards the westerne brim begins to draw,
 Gins to abate the brightnesse of his beme,
 And feruour of his flames somewhat adaw:
 So did this mightie Ladie, when she saw
 Those two strange knights such homage to her make,
 Bate somewhat of that Maiestie and awe,
 That whylome wont to doe so many quake,
And with more myld aspect those two to entertake.

Now at that instant, as occasion fell,   xxxvi
    When these two stranger knights arriu'd in place,
    She was about affaires of common wele,
    Dealing of Iustice with indifferent grace,
    And hearing pleas of people meane and base.
    Mongst which as then, there was for to be heard
    The tryall of a great and weightie case,
    Which on both sides was then debating hard:
But at the sight of these, those were a while debard.

But after all her princely entertayne,   xxxvii
    To th'hearing of that former cause in hand,
    Her selfe eftsoones she gan conuert againe;
    Which that those knights likewise mote vnderstand,
    And witnesse forth aright in forrain land,
    Taking them vp vnto her stately throne,
    Where they mote heare the matter throughly scand
    On either part, she placed th'one on th'one,
The other on the other side, and neare them none.

Then was there brought, as prisoner to the barre,   xxxviii
    A Ladie of great countenance and place,
    But that she it with foule abuse did marre;
    Yet did appeare rare beautie in her face,
    But blotted with condition vile and base,
    That all her other honour did obscure,
    And titles of nobilitie deface:
    Yet in that wretched semblant, she did sure
The peoples great compassion vnto her allure.

Then vp arose a person of deepe reach,   xxxix
    And rare in-sight, hard matters to reuele;
    That well could charme his tongue, and time his speach
    To all assayes; his name was called *Zele*:
    He gan that Ladie strongly to appele
    Of many haynous crymes, by her enured,
    And with sharpe reasons rang her such a pele,
    That those, whom she to pitie had allured,
He now t'abhorre and loath her person had procured.

First gan he tell, how this that seem'd so faire   xl
  And royally arayd, *Duessa* hight
  That false *Duessa*, which had wrought great care,
  And mickle mischiefe vnto many a knight,
  By her beguyled, and confounded quight:
  But not for those she now in question came,
  Though also those mote question'd be aright,
  But for vyld treasons, and outrageous shame,
Which she against the dred *Mercilla* oft did frame.

For she whylome (as ye mote yet right well   xli
  Remember) had her counsels false conspyred,
  With faithlesse *Blandamour* and *Paridell*,
  (Both two her paramours, both by her hyred,
  And both with hope of shadowes vaine inspyred,)
  And with them practiz'd, how for to depryue
  Mercilla of her crowne, by her aspyred,
  That she might it vnto her selfe deryue,
And tryumph in their blood, whom she to death did dryue.

But through high heauens grace, which fauour not   xlii
  The wicked driftes of trayterous desynes,
  Gainst loiall Princes, all this cursed plot,
  Ere proofe it tooke, discouered was betymes,
  And th'actours won the meede meet for their crymes.
  Such be the meede of all, that by such mene
  Vnto the type of kingdomes title clymes.
  But false *Duessa* now vntitled Queene,
Was brought to her sad doome, as here was to be seene.

Strongly did *Zele* her haynous fact enforce,   xliii
  And many other crimes of foule defame
  Against her brought, to banish all remorse,
  And aggrauate the horror of her blame.
  And with him to make part against her, came
  Many graue persons, that against her pled;
  First was a sage old Syre, that had to name
  The *Kingdomes care*, with a white siluer hed,
That many high regards and reasons gainst her red.

Then gan *Authority* her to appose   xliv
  With peremptorie powre, that made all mute;
  And then the law of *Nations* gainst her rose,
  And reasons brought, that no man could refute;
  Next gan *Religion* gainst her to impute
  High Gods beheast, and powre of holy lawes;
  Then gan the Peoples cry and Commons sute,
  Importune care of their owne publicke cause;
And lastly *Iustice* charged her with breach of lawes.

But then for her, on the contrarie part,   xlv
  Rose many aduocates for her to plead:
  First there came *Pittie*, with full tender hart,
  And with her ioyn'd *Regard* of womanhead;
  And then came *Daunger* threatning hidden dread,
  And high alliance vnto forren powre;
  Then came *Nobilitie* of birth, that bread
  Great ruth through her misfortunes tragicke stowre;
And lastly *Griefe* did plead, and many teares forth powre.

With the neare touch whereof in tender hart   xlvi
  The Briton Prince was sore empassionate,
  And woxe inclined much vnto her part,
  Through the sad terror of so dreadfull fate,
  And wretched ruine of so high estate,
  That for great ruth his courage gan relent.
  Which when as *Zele* perceiued to abate,
  He gan his earnest feruour to augment,
And many fearefull obiects to them to present.

He gan t'efforce the euidence anew,   xlvii
  And new accusements to produce in place:
  He brought forth that old hag of hellish hew,
  The cursed *Ate*, brought her face to face,
  Who priuie was, and partie in the case:
  She, glad of spoyle and ruinous decay,
  Did her appeach, and to her more disgrace,
  The plot of all her practise did display,
And all her traynes, and all her treasons forth did lay.

Then brought he forth, with griesly grim aspect,   xlviii
   Abhorred *Murder*, who with bloudie knyfe
   Yet dropping fresh in hand did her detect,
   And there with guiltie bloudshed charged ryfe:
   Then brought he forth *Sedition*, breeding stryfe
   In troublous wits, and mutinous vprore:
   Then brought he forth *Incontinence* of lyfe,
   Euen foule *Adulterie* her face before,
And lewd *Impietie*, that her accused sore.

All which when as the Prince had heard and seene,   xlix
   His former fancies ruth he gan repent,
   And from her partie eftsoones was drawen cleene.
   But *Artegall* with constant firme intent,
   For zeale of Iustice was against her bent.
   So was she guiltie deemed of them all.
   Then *Zele* began to vrge her punishment,
   And to their Queene for iudgement loudly call,
Vnto *Mercilla* myld for Iustice gainst the thrall.

But she, whose Princely breast was touched nere   l
   With piteous ruth of her so wretched plight,
   Though plaine she saw by all, that she did heare,
   That she of death was guiltie found by right,
   Yet would not let iust vengeance on her light;
   But rather let in stead thereof to fall
   Few perling drops from her faire lampes of light;
   The which she couering with her purple pall
Would haue the passion hid, and vp arose withall.

Cant. X.

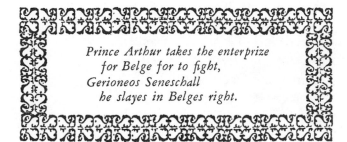

Prince Arthur takes the enterprize
for Belge for to fight,
Gerioneos Seneschall
he slayes in Belges right.

SOme Clarkes doe doubt in their deuicefull art,   i
  Whether this heauenly thing, whereof I treat,
  To weeten *Mercie*, be of Iustice part,
  Or drawne forth from her by diuine extreate.
  This well I wote, that sure she is as great,
  And meriteth to haue as high a place,
  Sith in th'Almighties euerlasting seat
  She first was bred, and borne of heauenly race;
From thence pour'd down on men, by influence of grace.

For if that Vertue be of so great might,   ii
  Which from iust verdict will for nothing start,
  But to preserue inuiolated right,
  Oft spilles the principall, to saue the part;
  So much more then is that of powre and art,
  That seekes to saue the subiect of her skill,
  Yet neuer doth from doome of right depart:
  As it is greater prayse to saue, then spill,
And better to reforme, then to cut off the ill.

Who then can thee, *Mercilla*, throughly prayse,   iii
  That herein doest all earthly Princes pas?
  What heauenly Muse shall thy great honour rayse
  Vp to the skies, whence first deriu'd it was,
  And now on earth it selfe enlarged has,
  From th'vtmost brinke of the *Armericke* shore,
  Vnto the margent of the *Molucas*?
  Those Nations farre thy iustice doe adore:
But thine owne people do thy mercy prayse much more.

Much more it praysed was of those two knights;   iv
  The noble Prince, and righteous *Artegall*,
  When they had seene and heard her doome a rights
  Against *Duessa*, damned by them all;
  But by her tempred without griefe or gall,
  Till strong constraint did her thereto enforce.
  And yet euen then ruing her wilfull fall,
  With more then needfull naturall remorse,
And yeelding the last honour to her wretched corse.

During all which, those knights continu'd there,   v
  Both doing and receiuing curtesies,
  Of that great Ladie, who with goodly chere
  Them entertayn'd, fit for their dignities,
  Approuing dayly to their noble eyes
  Royall examples of her mercies rare,
  And worthie paterns of her clemencies;
  Which till this day mongst many liuing are,
Who them to their posterities doe still declare.

Amongst the rest, which in that space befell,   vi
  There came two Springals of full tender yeares,
  Farre thence from forrein land, where they did dwell,
  To seeke for succour of her and of her Peares,
  With humble prayers and intreatfull teares;
  Sent by their mother, who a widow was,
  Wrapt in great dolours and in deadly feares,
  By a strong Tyrant, who inuaded has
Her land, and slaine her children ruefully alas.

Her name was *Belge*, who in former age   vii
  A Ladie of great worth and wealth had beene,
  And mother of a frutefull heritage,
  Euen seuenteene goodly sonnes; which who had seene
  In their first flowre, before this fatall teene
  Them ouertooke, and their faire blossomes blasted,
  More happie mother would her surely weene,
  Then famous *Niobe*, before she tasted
Latonaes childrens wrath, that all her issue wasted.

But this fell Tyrant, through his tortious powre,   viii
 Had left her now but fiue of all that brood:
 For twelue of them he did by times deuoure,
 And to his Idols sacrifice their blood,
 Whylest he of none was stopped, nor withstood.
 For soothly he was one of matchlesse might,
 Of horrible aspect, and dreadfull mood,
 And had three bodies in one wast empight,
And th'armes and legs of three, to succour him in fight.

And sooth they say, that he was borne and bred   ix
 Of Gyants race, the sonne of *Geryon*,
 He that whylome in Spaine so sore was dred,
 For his huge powre and great oppression,
 Which brought that land to his subiection,
 Through his three bodies powre, in one combynd;
 And eke all strangers in that region
 Arryuing, to his kyne for food assynd;
The fayrest kyne aliue, but of the fiercest kynd.

For they were all, they say, of purple hew,   x
 Kept by a cowheard, hight *Eurytion*,
 A cruell carle, the which all strangers slew,
 Ne day nor night did sleepe, t'attend them on,
 But walkt about them euer and anone,
 With his two headed dogge, that *Orthrus* hight;
 Orthrus begotten by great *Typhaon*,
 And foule *Echidna*, in the house of night;
But *Hercules* them all did ouercome in fight.

His sonne was this, *Geryoneo* hight,   xi
 Who after that his monstrous father fell
 Vnder *Alcides* club, streight tooke his flight
 From that sad land, where he his syre did quell,
 And came to this, where *Belge* then did dwell,
 And flourish in all wealth and happinesse,
 Being then new made widow (as befell)
 After her Noble husbands late decesse;
Which gaue beginning to her woe and wretchednesse.

Then this bold Tyrant, of her widowhed   xii
  Taking aduantage, and her yet fresh woes,
  Himselfe and seruice to her offered,
  Her to defend against all forrein foes,
  That should their powre against her right oppose.
  Whereof she glad, now needing strong defence,
  Him entertayn'd, and did her champion chose:
  Which long he vsd with carefull diligence,
The better to confirme her fearelesse confidence.

By meanes whereof, she did at last commit   xiii
  All to his hands, and gaue him soueraine powre
  To doe, what euer he thought good or fit.
  Which hauing got, he gan forth from that howre
  To stirre vp strife, and many a Tragicke stowre,
  Giuing her dearest children one by one
  Vnto a dreadfull Monster to deuoure,
  And setting vp an Idole of his owne,
The image of his monstrous parent *Geryone*.

So tyrannizing, and oppressing all,   xiv
  The woefull widow had no meanes now left,
  But vnto gratious great *Mercilla* call
  For ayde, against that cruell Tyrants theft,
  Ere all her children he from her had reft.
  Therefore these two, her eldest sonnes she sent,
  To seeke for succour of this Ladies gieft:
  To whom their sute they humbly did present,
In th'hearing of full many Knights and Ladies gent.

Amongst the which then fortuned to bee   xv
  The noble Briton Prince, with his braue Peare;
  Who when he none of all those knights did see
  Hastily bent, that enterprise to heare,
  Nor vndertake the same, for cowheard feare,
  He stepped forth with courage bold and great,
  Admyr'd of all the rest in presence there,
  And humbly gan that mightie Queene entreat,
To graunt him that aduenture for his former feat.

She gladly graunted it: then he straight way
   Himselfe vnto his iourney gan prepare,
   And all his armours readie dight that day,
   That nought the morrow next mote stay his fare.
   The morrow next appear'd, with purple hayre
   Yet dropping fresh out of the *Indian* fount,
   And bringing light into the heauens fayre,
   When he was readie to his steede to mount,
Vnto his way, which now was all his care and count.

Then taking humble leaue of that great Queene,
   Who gaue him roiall giftes and riches rare,
   As tokens of her thankefull mind beseene,
   And leauing *Artegall* to his owne care,
   Vpon his voyage forth he gan to fare,
   With those two gentle youthes, which him did guide,
   And all his way before him still prepare.
   Ne after him did *Artegall* abide,
But on his first aduenture forward forth did ride.

It was not long, till that the Prince arriued
   Within the land, where dwelt that Ladie sad,
   Whereof that Tyrant had her now depriued,
   And into moores and marshes banisht had,
   Out of the pleasant soyle, and citties glad,
   In which she wont to harbour happily:
   But now his cruelty so sore she drad,
   That to those fennes for fastnesse she did fly,
And there her selfe did hyde from his hard tyranny.

There he her found in sorrow and dismay,
   All solitarie without liuing wight;
   For all her other children, through affray,
   Had hid themselues, or taken further flight:
   And eke her selfe through sudden strange affright,
   When one in armes she saw, began to fly;
   But when her owne two sonnes she had in sight,
   She gan take hart, and looke vp ioyfully:
For well she wist this knight came, succour to supply.

And running vnto them with greedy ioyes,   xx
 Fell straight about their neckes, as they did kneele,
 And bursting forth in teares; Ah my sweet boyes,
 (Sayd she) yet now I gin new life to feele,
 And feeble spirits, that gan faint and reele,
 Now rise againe, at this your ioyous sight.
 Alreadie seemes that fortunes headlong wheele
 Begins to turne, and sunne to shine more bright,
Then it was wont, through comfort of this noble knight.

Then turning vnto him; And you Sir knight   xxi
 (Said she) that taken haue this toylesome paine
 For wretched woman, miserable wight,
 May you in heauen immortall guerdon gaine
 For so great trauell, as you doe sustaine:
 For other meede may hope for none of mee,
 To whom nought else, but bare life doth remaine,
 And that so wretched one, as ye do see
Is liker lingring death, then loathed life to bee.

Much was he moued with her piteous plight,   xxii
 And low dismounting from his loftie steede,
 Gan to recomfort her all that he might,
 Seeking to driue away deepe rooted dreede,
 With hope of helpe in that her greatest neede.
 So thence he wished her with him to wend,
 Vnto some place, where they mote rest and feede,
 And she take comfort, which God now did send:
Good hart in euils doth the euils much amend.

Ay me (sayd she) and whether shall I goe?   xxiii
 Are not all places full of forraine powres?
 My pallaces possessed of my foe,
 My cities sackt, and their sky-threating towres
 Raced, and made smooth fields now full of flowres?
 Onely these marishes, and myrie bogs,
 In which the fearefull ewftes do build their bowres,
 Yeeld me an hostry mongst the croking frogs,
And harbour here in safety from those rauenous dogs.

Nathlesse (said he) deare Ladie with me goe,   xxiv
   Some place shall vs receiue, and harbour yield;
   If not, we will it force, maugre your foe,
   And purchase it to vs with speare and shield:
   And if all fayle, yet farewell open field:
   The earth to all her creatures lodging lends.
   With such his chearefull speaches he doth wield
   Her mind so well, that to his will she bends
And bynding vp her locks and weeds, forth with him wends.

They came vnto a Citie farre vp land,   xxv
   The which whylome that Ladies owne had bene;
   But now by force extort out of her hand,
   By her strong foe, who had defaced cleene
   Her stately towres, and buildings sunny sheene;
   Shut vp her hauen, mard her marchants trade,
   Robbed her people, that full rich had beene,
   And in her necke a Castle huge had made,
The which did her commaund, without needing perswade.

That Castle was the strength of all that state,   xxvi
   Vntill that state by strength was pulled downe,
   And that same citie, so now ruinate,
   Had bene the keye of all that kingdomes crowne;
   Both goodly Castle, and both goodly Towne,
   Till that th'offended heauens list to lowre
   Vpon their blisse, and balefull fortune frowne.
   When those gainst states and kingdomes do coniure,
Who then can thinke their hedlong ruine to recure.

But he had brought it now in seruile bond,   xxvii
   And made it beare the yoke of inquisition,
   Stryuing long time in vaine it to withstond;
   Yet glad at last to make most base submission,
   And life enjoy for any composition.
   So now he hath new lawes and orders new
   Imposd on it, with many a hard condition,
   And forced it, the honour that is dew
To God, to doe vnto his Idole most vntrew.

To him he hath, before this Castle greene,   xxviii
  Built a faire Chappell, and an Altar framed
  Of costly Iuory, full rich beseene,
  On which that cursed Idole farre proclamed,
  He hath set vp, and him his God hath named,
  Offring to him in sinfull sacrifice
  The flesh of men, to Gods owne likenesse framed,
  And powring forth their bloud in brutishe wize,
That any yron eyes, to see it would agrize.

And for more horror and more crueltie,   xxix
  Vnder that cursed Idols altar stone,
  An hideous monster doth in darknesse lie,
  Whose dreadfull shape was neuer seene of none
  That liues on earth; but vnto those alone
  The which vnto him sacrificed bee.
  Those he deuoures, they say, both flesh and bone:
  What else they haue, is all the Tyrants fee;
So that no whit of them remayning one may see.

There eke he placed a strong garrisone,   xxx
  And set a Seneschall of dreaded might,
  That by his powre oppressed euery one,
  And vanquished all ventrous knights in fight;
  To whom he wont shew all the shame he might,
  After that them in battell he had wonne.
  To which when now they gan approch in sight,
  The Ladie counseld him the place to shonne,
Whereas so many knights had fouly bene fordonne.

Her fearefull speaches nought he did regard,   xxxi
  But ryding streight vnder the Castle wall,
  Called aloud vnto the watchfull ward,
  Which there did wayte, willing them forth to call
  Into the field their Tyrants Seneschall.
  To whom when tydings thereof came, he streight
  Cals for his armes, and arming him withall,
  Eftsoones forth pricked proudly in his might,
And gan with courage fierce addresse him to the fight.

They both encounter in the middle plaine,
  And their sharpe speares doe both together smite
  Amid their shields, with so huge might and maine,
  That seem'd their soules they wold haue ryuen quight
  Out of their breasts, with furious despight.
  Yet could the Seneschals no entrance find
  Into the Princes shield, where it empight;
  So pure the mettall was, and well refynd,
But shiuered all about, and scattered in the wynd.

Not so the Princes, but with restlesse force,
  Into his shield it readie passage found,
  Both through his haberieon, and eke his corse:
  Which tombling downe vpon the senselesse ground,
  Gaue leaue vnto his ghost from thraldome bound,
  To wander in the griesly shades of night.
  There did the Prince him leaue in deadly swound,
  And thence vnto the castle marched right,
To see if entrance there as yet obtaine he might.

But as he nigher drew, three knights he spyde,
  All arm'd to point, issuing forth a pace,
  Which towards him with all their powre did ryde,
  And meeting him right in the middle race,
  Did all their speares attonce on him enchace.
  As three great Culuerings for battrie bent,
  And leueld all against one certaine place,
  Doe all attonce their thunders rage forth rent,
That makes the wals to stagger with astonishment.

So all attonce they on the Prince did thonder;
  Who from his saddle swarued nought asyde,
  Ne to their force gaue way, that was great wonder,
  But like a bulwarke, firmely did abyde,
  Rebutting him, which in the midst did ryde,
  With so huge rigour, that his mortall speare
  Past through his shield, and pierst through either syde,
  That downe he fell vppon his mother deare,
And powred forth his wretched life in deadly dreare.

Whom when his other fellowes saw, they fled
  As fast as feete could carry them away;
  And after them the Prince as swiftly sped,
  To be aueng'd of their vnknightly play.
  There whilest they entring, th'one did th'other stay,
  The hindmost in the gate he ouerhent,
  And as he pressed in, him there did slay:
  His carkasse tumbling on the threshold, sent
His groning soule vnto her place of punishment.

The other which was entred, laboured fast
  To sperre the gate; but that same lumpe of clay,
  Whose grudging ghost was thereout fled and past,
  Right in the middest of the threshold lay,
  That it the Posterne did from closing stay:
  The whiles the Prince hard preased in betweene,
  And entraunce wonne. Streight th'other fled away,
  And ran into the Hall, where he did weene
Him selfe to saue: but he there slew him at the skreene.

Then all the rest which in that Castle were,
  Seeing that sad ensample them before,
  Durst not abide, but fled away for feare,
  And them conuayd out at a Posterne dore.
  Long sought the Prince, but when he found no more
  T'oppose against his powre, he forth issued
  Vnto that Lady, where he her had lore,
  And her gan cheare, with what she there had vewed,
And what she had not seene, within vnto her shewed.

Who with right humble thankes him goodly greeting,
  For so great prowesse, as he there had proued,
  Much greater then was euer in her weeting,
  With great admiraunce inwardly was moued,
  And honourd him, with all that her behoued.
  Thenceforth into that Castle he her led,
  With her two sonnes, right deare of her beloued,
  Where all that night them selues they cherished,
And from her balefull minde all care he banished.

Cant. XI.

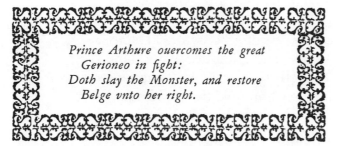

Prince Arthure ouercomes the great
Gerioneo in fight:
Doth slay the Monster, and restore
Belge vnto her right.

I T often fals in course of common life,
  That right long time is ouerborne of wrong,
Through auarice, or powre, or guile, or strife,
That weakens her, and makes her party strong:
But Iustice, though her dome she doe prolong,
Yet at the last she will her owne cause right.
As by sad *Belge* seemes, whose wrongs though long
She suffred, yet at length she did requight,
And sent redresse thereof by this braue Briton Knight.

Whereof when newes was to that Tyrant brought,
  How that the Lady *Belge* now had found
  A Champion, that had with his Champion fought,
  And laid his Seneschall low on the ground,
  And eke him selfe did threaten to confound,
  He gan to burne in rage, and friese in feare,
  Doubting sad end of principle vnsound:
  Yet sith he heard but one, that did appeare,
He did him selfe encourage, and take better cheare.

Nathelesse him selfe he armed all in hast,
  And forth he far'd with all his many bad,
  Ne stayed step, till that he came at last
  Vnto the Castle, which they conquerd had.
  There with huge terrour, to be more ydrad,
  He sternely marcht before the Castle gate,
  And with bold vaunts, and ydle threatning bad
  Deliuer him his owne, ere yet too late,
To which they had no right, nor any wrongfull state.

The Prince staid not his aunswere to deuize,   iv
   But opening streight the Sparre, forth to him came,
   Full nobly mounted in right warlike wize;
   And asked him, if that he were the same,
   Who all that wrong vnto that wofull Dame
   So long had done, and from her natiue land
   Exiled her, that all the world spake shame.
   He boldly aunswerd him, he there did stand
That would his doings iustifie with his owne hand.

With that so furiously at him he flew,   v
   As if he would haue ouerrun him streight,
   And with his huge great yron axe gan hew
   So hideously vppon his armour bright,
   As he to peeces would haue chopt it quight:
   That the bold Prince was forced foote to giue
   To his first rage, and yeeld to his despight;
   The whilest at him so dreadfully he driue,
That seem'd a marble rocke asunder could haue riue.

Thereto a great aduauntage eke he has   vi
   Through his three double hands thrise multiplyde,
   Besides the double strength, which in them was:
   For stil when fit occasion did betyde,
   He could his weapon shift from side to syde,
   From hand to hand, and with such nimblesse sly
   Could wield about, that ere it were espide,
   The wicked stroke did wound his enemy,
Behinde, beside, before, as he it list apply.

Which vncouth vse when as the Prince perceiued,   vii
   He gan to watch the wielding of his hand,
   Least by such slight he were vnwares deceiued;
   And euer ere he saw the stroke to land,
   He would it meete, and warily withstand.
   One time, when he his weapon faynd to shift,
   As he was wont, and chang'd from hand to hand,
   He met him with a counterstroke so swift,
That quite smit off his arme, as he it vp did lift.

Therewith, all fraught with fury and disdaine,
   He brayd aloud for very fell despight,
   And sodainely t'auenge him selfe againe,
   Gan into one assemble all the might
   Of all his hands, and heaued them on hight,
   Thinking to pay him with that one for all:
   But the sad steele seizd not, where it was hight,
   Vppon the childe, but somewhat short did fall,
And lighting on his horses head, him quite did mall.

Downe streight to ground fell his astonisht steed,
   And eke to th'earth his burden with him bare:
   But he him selfe full lightly from him freed,
   And gan him selfe to fight on foote prepare.
   Whereof when as the Gyant was aware,
   He wox right blyth, as he had got thereby,
   And laught so loud, that all his teeth wide bare
   One might haue seene enraung'd disorderly,
Like to a rancke of piles, that pitched are awry.

Eftsoones againe his axe he raught on hie,
   Ere he were throughly buckled to his geare,
   And can let driue at him so dreadfullie,
   That had he chaunced not his shield to reare,
   Ere that huge stroke arriued on him neare,
   He had him surely clouen quite in twaine.
   But th'Adamantine shield, which he did beare,
   So well was tempred, that for all his maine,
It would no passage yeeld vnto his purpose vaine.

Yet was the stroke so forcibly applide,
   That made him stagger with vncertaine sway,
   As if he would haue tottered to one side.
   Wherewith full wroth, he fiercely gan assay,
   That curt'sie with like kindnesse to repay;
   And smote at him with so importune might,
   That two more of his armes did fall away,
   Like fruitlesse braunches, which the hatchets slight
Hath pruned from the natiue tree, and cropped quight.

With that all mad and furious he grew,   xii
  Like a fell mastiffe through enraging heat,
  And curst, and band, and blasphemies forth threw,
  Against his Gods, and fire to them did threat,
  And hell vnto him selfe with horrour great.
  Thenceforth he car'd no more, which way he strooke,
  Nor where it light, but gan to chaufe and sweat,
  And gnasht his teeth, and his head at him shooke,
And sternely him beheld with grim and ghastly looke.

Nought fear'd the childe his lookes, ne yet his threats,   xiii
  But onely wexed now the more aware,
  To saue him selfe from those his furious heats,
  And watch aduauntage, how to worke his care:
  The which good Fortune to him offred faire.
  For as he in his rage him ouerstrooke,
  He ere he could his weapon backe repaire,
  His side all bare and naked ouertooke,
And with his mortal steel quite throgh the body strooke.

Through all three bodies he him strooke attonce;   xiv
  That all the three attonce fell on the plaine:
  Else should he thrise haue needed, for the nonce
  Them to haue stricken, and thrise to haue slaine.
  So now all three one sencelesse lumpe remaine,
  Enwallow'd in his owne blacke bloudy gore,
  And byting th'earth for very deaths disdaine;
  Who with a cloud of night him couering, bore
Downe to the house of dole, his daies there to deplore.

Which when the Lady from the Castle saw,   xv
  Where she with her two sonnes did looking stand,
  She towards him in hast her selfe did draw,
  To greet him the good fortune of his hand:
  And all the people both of towne and land,
  Which there stood gazing from the Citties wall
  Vppon these warriours, greedy t'vnderstand,
  To whether should the victory befall,
Now when they saw it falne, they eke him greeted all.

But *Belge* with her sonnes prostrated low   xvi
     Before his feete, in all that peoples sight,
     Mongst ioyes mixing some tears, mongst wele, some wo,
     Him thus bespake; O most redoubted Knight,
     The which hast me, of all most wretched wight,
     That earst was dead, restor'd to life againe,
     And these weake impes replanted by thy might;
     What guerdon can I giue thee for thy paine,
But euen that which thou sauedst, thine still to remaine?

He tooke her vp forby the lilly hand,   xvii
     And her recomforted the best he might,
     Saying; Deare Lady, deedes ought not be scand
     By th'authors manhood, nor the doers might,
     But by their trueth and by the causes right:
     That same is it, which fought for you this day.
     What other meed then need me to requight,
     But that which yeeldeth vertues meed alway?
That is the vertue selfe, which her reward doth pay.

She humbly thankt him for that wondrous grace,   xviii
     And further sayd; Ah Sir, but mote ye please,
     Sith ye thus farre haue tendred my poore case,
     As from my chiefest foe me to release,
     That your victorious arme will not yet cease,
     Till ye haue rooted all the relickes out
     Of that vilde race, and stablished my peace.
     What is there else (sayd he) left of their rout?
Declare it boldly Dame, and doe not stand in dout.

Then wote you, Sir, that in this Church hereby,   xix
     There stands an Idole of great note and name,
     The which this Gyant reared first on hie,
     And of his owne vaine fancies thought did frame:
     To whom for endlesse horrour of his shame,
     He offred vp for daily sacrifize
     My children and my people, burnt in flame;
     With all the tortures, that he could deuize,
The more t'aggrate his God with such his blouddy guize.

And vnderneath this Idoll there doth lie   xx
   An hideous monster, that doth it defend,
   And feedes on all the carkasses, that die
   In sacrifize vnto that cursed feend:
   Whose vgly shape none euer saw, nor kend,
   That euer scap'd: for of a man they say
   It has the voice, that speaches forth doth send,
   Euen blasphemous words, which she doth bray
Out of her poysnous entrails, fraught with dire decay.

Which when the Prince heard tell, his heart gan earne   xxi
   For great desire, that Monster to assay,
   And prayd the place of her abode to learne.
   Which being shew'd, he gan him selfe streight way
   Thereto addresse, and his bright shield display.
   So to the Church he came, where it was told,
   The Monster vnderneath the Altar lay;
   There he that Idoll saw of massy gold
Most richly made, but there no Monster did behold.

Vpon the Image with his naked blade   xxii
   Three times, as in defiance, there he strooke;
   And the third time out of an hidden shade,
   There forth issewd, from vnder th'Altars smooke,
   A dreadfull feend, with fowle deformed looke,
   That stretcht it selfe, as it had long lyen still;
   And her long taile and fethers strongly shooke,
   That all the Temple did with terrour fill;
Yet him nought terrifide, that feared nothing ill.

An huge great Beast it was, when it in length   xxiii
   Was stretched forth, that nigh fild all the place,
   And seem'd to be of infinite great strength;
   Horrible, hideous, and of hellish race,
   Borne of the brooding of *Echidna* base,
   Or other like infernall furies kinde:
   For of a Mayd she had the outward face,
   To hide the horrour, which did lurke behinde,
The better to beguile, whom she so fond did finde.

Thereto the body of a dog she had,   xxiv
    Full of fell rauin and fierce greedinesse;
    A Lions clawes, with powre and rigour clad,
    To rend and teare, what so she can oppresse;
    A Dragons taile, whose sting without redresse
    Full deadly wounds, where so it is empight;
    And Eagles wings, for scope and speedinesse,
    That nothing may escape her reaching might,
Whereto she euer list to make her hardy flight.

Much like in foulnesse and deformity   xxv
    Vnto that Monster, whom the Theban Knight,
    The father of that fatall progeny,
    Made kill her selfe for very hearts despight,
    That he had red her Riddle, which no wight
    Could euer loose, but suffred deadly doole.
    So also did this Monster vse like slight
    To many a one, which came vnto her schoole,
Whom she did put to death, deceiued like a foole.

She comming forth, when as she first beheld   xxvi
    The armed Prince, with shield so blazing bright,
    Her ready to assaile, was greatly queld,
    And much dismayd with that dismayfull sight,
    That backe she would haue turnd for great affright.
    But he gan her with courage fierce assay,
    That forst her turne againe in her despight,
    To saue her selfe, least that he did her slay:
And sure he had her slaine, had she not turnd her way.

Tho when she saw, that she was forst to fight,   xxvii
    She flew at him, like to an hellish feend,
    And on his shield tooke hold with all her might,
    As if that it she would in peeces rend,
    Or reaue out of the hand, that did it hend.
    Strongly he stroue out of her greedy gripe
    To loose his shield, and long while did contend:
    But when he could not quite it, with one stripe
Her Lions clawes he from her feete away did wipe.

With that aloude she gan to bray and yell,   xxviii
  And fowle blasphemous speaches forth did cast,
  And bitter curses, horrible to tell,
  That euen the Temple, wherein she was plast,
  Did quake to heare, and nigh asunder brast.
  Tho with her huge long taile she at him strooke,
  That made him stagger, and stand halfe agast
  With trembling ioynts, as he for terrour shooke;
Who nought was terrifide, but greater courage tooke.

As when the Mast of some well timbred hulke   xxix
  Is with the blast of some outragious storme
  Blowne downe, it shakes the bottome of the bulke,
  And makes her ribs to cracke, as they were torne,
  Whilest still she stands as stonisht and forlorne:
  So was he stound with stroke of her huge taile.
  But ere that it she backe againe had borne,
  He with his sword it strooke, that without faile
He ioynted it, and mard the swinging of her flaile.

Then gan she cry much louder then afore,   xxx
  That all the people there without it heard,
  And *Belge* selfe was therewith stonied sore,
  As if the onely sound thereof she feard.
  But then the feend her selfe more fiercely reard
  Vppon her wide great wings, and strongly flew
  With all her body at his head and beard,
  That had he not foreseene with heedfull vew,
And throwne his shield atweene, she had him done to rew.

But as she prest on him with heauy sway,   xxxi
  Vnder her wombe his fatall sword he thrust,
  And for her entrailes made an open way,
  To issue forth; the which once being brust,
  Like to a great Mill damb forth fiercely gusht,
  And powred out of her infernall sinke
  Most vgly filth, and poyson therewith rusht,
  That him nigh choked with the deadly stinke:
Such loathly matter were small lust to speake, or thinke.

Then downe to ground fell that deformed Masse,
   Breathing out clouds of sulphure fowle and blacke,
   In which a puddle of contagion was,
   More loathd then *Lerna*, or then *Stygian* lake,
   That any man would nigh awhaped make.
   Whom when he saw on ground, he was full glad,
   And streight went forth his gladnesse to partake
   With *Belge*, who watcht all this while full sad,
Wayting what end would be of that same daunger drad.

Whom when she saw so ioyously come forth,
   She gan reioyce, and shew triumphant chere,
   Lauding and praysing his renowmed worth,
   By all the names that honorable were.
   Then in he brought her, and her shewed there
   The present of his paines, that Monsters spoyle,
   And eke that Idoll deem'd so costly dere;
   Whom he did all to peeces breake and foyle
In filthy durt, and left so in the loathely soyle.

Then all the people, which beheld that day,
   Gan shout aloud, that vnto heauen it rong;
   And all the damzels of that towne in ray,
   Came dauncing forth, and ioyous carrols song:
   So him they led through all their streetes along,
   Crowned with girlonds of immortall baies,
   And all the vulgar did about them throng,
   To see the man, whose euerlasting praise
They all were bound to all posterities to raise.

There he with *Belge* did a while remaine,
   Making great feast and ioyous merriment,
   Vntill he had her settled in her raine,
   With safe assuraunce and establishment.
   Then to his first emprize his mind he lent,
   Full loath to *Belge*, and to all the rest:
   Of whom yet taking leaue, thenceforth he went
   And to his former iourney him addrest,
On which long way he rode, ne euer day did rest.

But turne we now to noble *Artegall*;   xxxvi
  Who hauing left *Mercilla*, streight way went
  On his first quest, the which him forth did call,
  To weet to worke *Irenaes* franchisement,
  And eke *Grantortoes* worthy punishment.
  So forth he fared as his manner was,
  With onely *Talus* wayting diligent,
  Through many perils and much way did pas,
Till nigh vnto the place at length approcht he has.

There as he traueld by the way, he met   xxxvii
  An aged wight, wayfaring all alone,
  Who through his yeares long since aside had set
  The vse of armes, and battell quite forgone:
  To whom as he approcht, he knew anone,
  That it was he which whilome did attend
  On faire *Irene* in her affliction,
  When first to Faery court he saw her wend,
Vnto his soueraine Queene her suite for to commend.

Whom by his name saluting, thus he gan;   xxxviii
  Haile good Sir *Sergis*, truest Knight aliue,
  Well tride in all thy Ladies troubles than,
  When her that Tyrant did of Crowne depriue;
  What new ocasion doth thee hither driue,
  Whiles she alone is left, and thou here found?
  Or is she thrall, or doth she not suruiue?
  To whom he thus; She liueth sure and sound;
But by that Tyrant is in wretched thraldome bound.

For she presuming on th'appointed tyde,   xxxix
  In which ye promist, as ye were a Knight,
  To meete her at the saluage Ilands syde,
  And then and there for triall of her right
  With her vnrighteous enemy to fight,
  Did thither come, where she afrayd of nought,
  By guilefull treason and by subtill slight
  Surprized was, and to *Grantorto* brought,
Who her imprisond hath, and her life often sought.

And now he hath to her prefixt a day,   xl
  By which if that no champion doe appeare,
  Which will her cause in battailous array
  Against him iustifie, and proue her cleare
  Of all those crimes, that he gainst her doth reare,
  She death shall by. Those tidings sad
  Did much abash Sir *Artegall* to heare,
  And grieued sore, that through his fault she had
Fallen into that Tyrants hand and vsage bad.

Then thus replide; Now sure and by my life,   xli
  Too much am I too blame for that faire Maide,
  That haue her drawne to all this troublous strife,
  Through promise to afford her timely aide,
  Which by default I haue not yet defraide.
  But witnesse vnto me, ye heauens, that know
  How cleare I am from blame of this vpbraide:
  For ye into like thraldome me did throw,
And kept from complishing the faith, which I did owe.

But now aread, Sir *Sergis*, how long space,   xlii
  Hath he her lent, a Champion to prouide:
  Ten daies (quoth he) he graunted hath of grace,
  For that he weeneth well, before that tide
  None can haue tidings to assist her side.
  For all the shores, which to the sea accoste,
  He day and night doth ward both far and wide,
  That none can there arriue without an hoste:
So her he deemes already but a damned ghoste.

Now turne againe (Sir *Artegall* then sayd)   xliii
  For if I liue till those ten daies haue end,
  Assure your selfe, Sir Knight, she shall haue ayd,
  Though I this dearest life for her doe spend;
  So backeward he attone with him did wend.
  Tho as they rode together on their way,
  A rout of people they before them kend,
  Flocking together in confusde array,
As if that there were some tumultuous affray.

To which as they approcht, the cause to know,   xliv
  They saw a Knight in daungerous distresse
  Of a rude rout him chasing to and fro,
  That sought with lawlesse powre him to oppresse,
  And bring in bondage of their brutishnesse:
  And farre away, amid their rakehell bands,
  They spide a Lady left all succourlesse,
  Crying, and holding vp her wretched hands
To him for aide, who long in vaine their rage withstands.

Yet still he striues, ne any perill spares,   xlv
  To reskue her from their rude violence,
  And like a Lion wood amongst them fares,
  Dealing his dreadfull blowes with large dispence,
  Gainst which the pallid death findes no defence.
  But all in vaine, their numbers are so great,
  That naught may boot to banishe them from thence:
  For soone as he their outrage backe doth beat,
They turne afresh, and oft renew their former threat.

And now they doe so sharpely him assay,   xlvi
  That they his shield in peeces battred haue,
  And forced him to throw it quite away,
  Fro dangers dread his doubtfull life to saue;
  Albe that it most safety to him gaue,
  And much did magnifie his noble name.
  For from the day that he thus did it leaue,
  Amongst all Knights he blotted was with blame,
And counted but a recreant Knight, with endles shame.

Whom when they thus distressed did behold,   xlvii
  They drew vnto his aide; but that rude rout
  Them also gan assaile with outrage bold,
  And forced them, how euer strong and stout
  They were, as well approu'd in many a doubt,
  Backe to recule; vntill that yron man
  With his huge flaile began to lay about,
  From whose sterne presence they diffused ran,
Like scattred chaffe, the which the wind away doth fan.

So when that Knight from perill cleare was freed,
   He drawing neare, began to greete them faire,
   And yeeld great thankes for their so goodly deed,
   In sauing him from daungerous despaire
   Of those, which sought his life for to empaire.
   Of whom Sir *Artegall* gan then enquire
   The whole occasion of his late misfare,
   And who he was, and what those villaines were,
The which with mortall malice him pursu'd so nere.

To whom he thus; My name is *Burbon* hight,
   Well knowne, and far renowmed heretofore,
   Vntill late mischiefe did vppon me light,
   That all my former praise hath blemisht sore;
   And that faire Lady, which in that vprore
   Ye with those caytiues saw, *Flourdelis* hight,
   Is mine owne loue, though me she haue forlore,
   Whether withheld from me by wrongfull might,
Or with her owne good will, I cannot read aright.

But sure to me her faith she first did plight,
   To be my loue, and take me for her Lord,
   Till that a Tyrant, which *Grandtorto* hight,
   With golden giftes and many a guilefull word
   Entyced her, to him for to accord.
   O who may not with gifts and words be tempted?
   Sith which she hath me euer since abhord,
   And to my foe hath guilefully consented:
Ay me, that euer guyle in wemen was inuented.

And now he hath this troupe of villains sent,
   By open force to fetch her quite away:
   Gainst whom my selfe I long in vaine haue bent,
   To rescue her, and daily meanes assay,
   Yet rescue her thence by no meanes I may:
   For they doe me with multitude oppresse,
   And with vnequall might doe ouerlay,
   That oft I driuen am to great distresse,
And forced to forgoe th'attempt remedilesse.

But why haue ye (said *Artegall*) forborne   lii
  Your owne good shield in daungerous dismay?
  That is the greatest shame and foulest scorne,
  Which vnto any knight behappen may
  To loose the badge, that should his deedes display.
  To whom Sir *Burbon*, blushing halfe for shame,
  That shall I vnto you (quoth he) bewray;
  Least ye therefore mote happily me blame,
And deeme it doen of will, that through inforcement came.

True is, that I at first was dubbed knight   liii
  By a good knight, the knight of the *Redcrosse*;
  Who when he gaue me armes, in field to fight,
  Gaue me a shield, in which he did endosse
  His deare Redeemers badge vpon the bosse:
  The same longwhile I bore, and therewithall
  Fought many battels without wound or losse;
  Therewith *Grandtorto* selfe I did appall,
And made him oftentimes in field before me fall.

But for that many did that shield enuie,   liv
  And cruell enemies increased more;
  To stint all strife and troublous enmitie,
  That bloudie scutchin being battered sore,
  I layd aside, and haue of late forbore,
  Hoping thereby to haue my loue obtayned:
  Yet can I not my loue haue nathemore;
  For she by force is still fro me detayned,
And with corruptfull brybes is to vntruth mis-trayned.

To whom thus *Artegall*; Certes Sir knight,   lv
  Hard is the case, the which ye doe complaine;
  Yet not so hard (for nought so hard may light,
  That it to such a streight mote you constraine)
  As to abandon, that which doth containe
  Your honours stile, that is your warlike shield.
  All perill ought be lesse, and lesse all paine
  Then losse of fame in disauentrous field;
Dye rather, then doe ought, that mote dishonour yield.

Not so; (quoth he) for yet when time doth serue,   lvi
  My former shield I may resume againe:
  To temporize is not from truth to swerue,
  Ne for aduantage terme to entertaine,
  When as necessitie doth it constraine.
  Fie on such forgerie (said *Artegall*)
  Vnder one hood to shadow faces twaine.
  Knights ought be true, and truth is one in all:
Of all things to dissemble fouly may befall.

Yet let me you of courtesie request,   lvii
  (Said *Burbon*) to assist me now at need
  Against these pesants, which haue me opprest,
  And forced me to so infamous deed,
  That yet my loue may from their hands be freed.
  Sir *Artegall*, albe he carst did wyte
  His wauering mind, yet to his aide agreed,
  And buckling him eftsoones vnto the fight,
Did set vpon those troupes with all his powre and might.

Who flocking round about them, as a swarme   lviii
  Of flyes vpon a birchen bough doth cluster,
  Did them assault with terrible allarme,
  And ouer all the fields themselues did muster,
  With bils and glayues making a dreadfull luster;
  That forst at first those knights backe to retyre:
  As when the wrathfull *Boreas* doth bluster,
  Nought may abide the tempest of his yre,
Both man and beast doe fly, and succour doe inquyre.

But when as ouerblowen was that brunt,   lix
  Those knights began a fresh them to assayle,
  And all about the fields like Squirrels hunt;
  But chiefly *Talus* with his yron flayle,
  Gainst which no flight nor rescue mote auayle,
  Made cruell hauocke of the baser crew,
  And chaced them both ouer hill and dale:
  The raskall manie soone they ouerthrew,
But the two knights themselues their captains did subdew.

At last they came whereas that Ladie bode,   lx
  Whom now her keepers had forsaken quight,
  To saue themselues, and scattered were abrode:
  Her halfe dismayd they found in doubtfull plight,
  As neither glad nor sorie for their sight;
  Yet wondrous faire she was, and richly clad
  In roiall robes, and many Iewels dight,
  But that those villens through their vsage bad
Them fouly rent, and shamefully defaced had.

But *Burbon* streight dismounting from his steed,   lxi
  Vnto her ran with greedie great desyre,
  And catching her fast by her ragged weed,
  Would haue embraced her with hart entyre.
  But she backstarting with disdainefull yre,
  Bad him auaunt, ne would vnto his lore
  Allured be, for prayer nor for hyre.
  Whom when those knights so froward and forlore
Beheld, they her rebuked and vpbrayded sore.

Sayd *Artegall*; What foule disgrace is this,   lxii
  To so faire Ladie, as ye seeme in sight,
  To blot your beautie, that vnblemisht is,
  With so foule blame, as breach of faith once plight,
  Or change of loue for any worlds delight?
  Is ought on earth so pretious or deare,
  As prayse and honour? Or is ought so bright
  And beautifull, as glories beames appeare,
Whose goodly light then *Phebus* lampe doth shine more cleare?

Why then will ye, fond Dame, attempted bee   lxiii
  Vnto a strangers loue, so lightly placed,
  For guiftes of gold, or any worldly glee,
  To leaue the loue, that ye before embraced,
  And let your fame with falshood be defaced.
  Fie on the pelfe, for which good name is sold,
  And honour with indignitie debased:
  Dearer is loue then life, and fame then gold;
But dearer then them both, your faith once plighted hold.

Much was the Ladie in her gentle mind
   Abasht at his rebuke, that bit her neare,
   Ne ought to answere thereunto did find;
   But hanging downe her head with heauie cheare,
   Stood long amaz'd, as she amated weare.
   Which *Burbon* seeing, her againe assayd,
   And clasping twixt his armes, her vp did reare
   Vpon his steede, whiles she no whit gainesayd,
So bore her quite away, nor well nor ill apayd.

Nathlesse the yron man did still pursew
   That raskall many with vnpittied spoyle,
   Ne ceassed not, till all their scattred crew
   Into the sea he droue quite from that soyle,
   The which they troubled had with great turmoyle.
   But *Artegall* seeing his cruell deed,
   Commaunded him from slaughter to recoyle,
   And to his voyage gan againe proceed:
For that the terme approching fast, required speed.

Cant. XII.

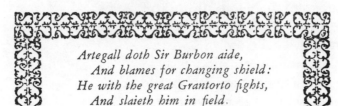

O Sacred hunger of ambitious mindes,　　　　　　　i
　　And impotent desire of men to raine,
Whom neither dread of God, that deuils bindes,
Nor lawes of men, that common weales containe,
Nor bands of nature, that wilde beastes restraine,
Can keepe from outrage, and from doing wrong,
Where they may hope a kingdome to obtaine.
No faith so firme, no trust can be so strong,
No loue so lasting then, that may endure long.

Witnesse may *Burbon* be, whom all the bands,　　ii
　　Which may a Knight assure, had surely bound,
Vntill the loue of Lordship and of lands
Made him become most faithlesse and vnsound:
And witnesse be *Gerioneo* found,
Who for like cause faire *Belge* did oppresse,
And right and wrong most cruelly confound:
And so be now *Grantorto*, who no lesse
Then all the rest burst out to all outragiousnesse.

Gainst whom Sir *Artegall*, long hauing since　　iii
　　Taken in hand th'exploit, being theretoo
Appointed by that mightie Faerie Prince,
Great *Gloriane*, that Tyrant to fordoo,
Through other great aduentures hethertoo
Had it forslackt. But now time drawing ny,
To him assynd, her high beheast to doo,
To the sea shore he gan his way apply,
To weete if shipping readie he mote there descry.

Tho when they came to the sea coast, they found iv
  A ship all readie (as good fortune fell)
  To put to sea, with whom they did compound,
  To passe them ouer, where them list to tell:
  The winde and weather serued them so well,
  That in one day they with the coast did fall;
  Whereas they readie found them to repell,
  Great hostes of men in order martiall,
Which them forbad to land, and footing did forstall.

But nathemore would they from land refraine, v
  But when as nigh vnto the shore they drew,
  That foot of man might sound the bottome plaine,
  Talus into the sea did forth issew,
  Though darts from shore and stones they at him threw;
  And wading through the waues with stedfast sway,
  Maugre the might of all those troupes in vew,
  Did win the shore, whence he them chast away,
And made to fly, like doues, whom the Eagle doth affray.

The whyles Sir *Artegall*, with that old knight vi
  Did forth descend, there being none them neare,
  And forward marched to a towne in sight.
  By this came tydings to the Tyrants eare,
  By those, which earst did fly away for feare
  Of their arriuall: wherewith troubled sore,
  He all his forces streight to him did reare,
  And forth issuing with his scouts afore,
Meant them to haue incountred, ere they left the shore.

But ere he marched farre, he with them met, vii
  And fiercely charged them with all his force;
  But *Talus* sternely did vpon them set,
  And brusht, and battred them without remorse,
  That on the ground he left full many a corse;
  Ne any able was him to withstand,
  But he them ouerthrew both man and horse,
  That they lay scattred ouer all the land,
As thicke as doth the seede after the sowers hand.

Till *Artegall* him seeing so to rage,   viii
  Willd him to stay, and signe of truce did make:
  To which all harkning, did a while asswage
  Their forces furie, and their terror slake;
  Till he an Herauld cald, and to him spake,
  Willing him wend vnto the Tyrant streight,
  And tell him that not for such slaughters sake
  He thether came, but for to trie the right
Of fayre *Irenaes* cause with him in single fight.

And willed him for to reclayme with speed   ix
  His scattred people, ere they all were slaine,
  And time and place conuenient to areed,
  In which they two the combat might darraine.
  Which message when *Grantorto* heard, full fayne
  And glad he was the slaughter so to stay,
  And pointed for the combat twixt them twayne
  The morrow next, ne gaue him longer day.
So sounded the retraite, and drew his folke away.

That night Sir *Artegall* did cause his tent   x
  There to be pitched on the open plaine;
  For he had giuen streight commaundement,
  That none should dare him once to entertaine:
  Which none durst breake, though many would right faine
  For fayre *Irena*, whom they loued deare.
  But yet old *Sergis* did so well him paine,
  That from close friends, that dar'd not to appeare,
He all things did puruay, which for them needfull weare.

The morrow next, that was the dismall day,   xi
  Appointed for *Irenas* death before,
  So soone as it did to the world display
  His chearefull face, and light to men restore,
  The heauy Mayd, to whom none tydings bore
  Of *Artegalls* arryuall, her to free,
  Lookt vp with eyes full sad and hart full sore;
  Weening her lifes last howre then neare to bee,
Sith no redemption nigh she did nor heare nor see.

Then vp she rose, and on her selfe did dight xii
  Most squalid garments, fit for such a day,
  And with dull countenance, and with doleful spright,
  She forth was brought in sorrowfull dismay,
  For to receiue the doome of her decay.
  But comming to the place, and finding there
  Sir *Artegall*, in battailous array
  Wayting his foe, it did her dead hart cheare,
And new life to her lent, in midst of deadly feare.

Like as a tender Rose in open plaine, xiii
  That with vntimely drought nigh withered was,
  And hung the head, soone as few drops of raine
  Thereon distill, and deaw her daintie face,
  Gins to looke vp, and with fresh wonted grace
  Dispreds the glorie of her leaues gay;
  Such was *Irenas* countenance, such her case,
  When *Artegall* she saw in that array,
There wayting for the Tyrant, till it was farre day.

Who came at length, with proud presumpteous gate, xiv
  Into the field, as if he fearelesse were,
  All armed in a cote of yron plate,
  Of great defence to ward the deadly feare,
  And on his head a steele cap he did weare
  Of colour rustie browne, but sure and strong;
  And in his hand an huge Polaxe did beare,
  Whose steale was yron studded, but not long,
With which he wont to fight, to iustifie his wrong.

Of stature huge and hideous he was, xv
  Like to a Giant for his monstrous hight,
  And did in strength most sorts of men surpas,
  Ne euer any found his match in might;
  Thereto he had great skill in single fight:
  His face was vgly, and his countenance sterne,
  That could haue frayd one with the very sight,
  And gaped like a gulfe, when he did gerne,
That whether man or monster one could scarse discerne.

Soone as he did within the listes appeare,   xvi
   With dreadfull looke he *Artegall* beheld,
   As if he would haue daunted him with feare,
   And grinning griesly, did against him weld
   His deadly weapon, which in hand he held.
   But th'Elfin swayne, that oft had seene like sight,
   Was with his ghastly count'nance nothing queld,
   But gan him streight to buckle to the fight,
And cast his shield about, to be in readie plight.

The trompets sound, and they together goe,   xvii
   With dreadfull terror, and with fell intent;
   And their huge strokes full daungerously bestow,
   To doe most dammage, where as most they ment.
   But with such force and furie violent,
   The tyrant thundred his thicke blowes so fast,
   That through the yron walles their way they rent,
   And euen to the vitall parts they past,
Ne ought could them endure, but all they cleft or brast.

Which cruell outrage when as *Artegall*   xviii
   Did well auize, thenceforth with warie heed
   He shund his strokes, where euer they did fall,
   And way did giue vnto their gracelesse speed:
   As when a skilfull Marriner doth reed
   A storme approching, that doth perill threat,
   He will not bide the daunger of such dread,
   But strikes his sayles, and vereth his mainsheat,
And lends vnto it leaue the emptie ayre to beat.

So did the Faerie knight himselfe abeare,   xix
   And stouped oft his head from shame to shield;
   No shame to stoupe, ones head more high to reare,
   And much to gaine, a litle for to yield;
   So stoutest knights doen oftentimes in field.
   But still the tyrant sternely at him layd,
   And did his yron axe so nimbly wield,
   That many wounds into his flesh it made,
And with his burdenous blowes him sore did ouerlade.

Yet when as fit aduantage he did spy,   xx
  The whiles the cursed felon high did reare
  His cruell hand, to smite him mortally,
  Vnder his stroke he to him stepping neare,
  Right in the flanke him strooke with deadly dreare,
  That the gore bloud thence gushing grieuously,
  Did vnderneath him like a pond appeare,
  And all his armour did with purple dye;
Thereat he brayed loud, and yelled dreadfully.

Yet the huge stroke, which he before intended,   xxi
  Kept on his course, as he did it direct,
  And with such monstrous poise adowne descended,
  That seemed nought could him from death protect:
  But he it well did ward with wise respect,
  And twixt him and the blow his shield did cast,
  Which thereon seizing, tooke no great effect,
  But byting deepe therein did sticke so fast,
That by no meanes it backe againe he forth could wrast.

Long while he tug'd and stroue, to get it out,   xxii
  And all his powre applyed thereunto,
  That he therewith the knight drew all about:
  Nathlesse, for all that euer he could doe,
  His axe he could not from his shield vndoe.
  Which *Artegall* perceiuing, strooke no more,
  But loosing soone his shield, did it forgoe,
  And whiles he combred was therewith so sore,
He gan at him let driue more fiercely then afore.

So well he him pursew'd, that at the last,   xxiii
  He stroke him with *Chrysaor* on the hed,
  That with the souse thereof full sore aghast,
  He staggered to and fro in doubtfull sted.
  Againe whiles he him saw so ill bested,
  He did him smite with all his might and maine,
  That falling on his mother earth he fed:
  Whom when he saw prostrated on the plaine,
He lightly reft his head, to ease him of his paine.

Which when the people round about him saw,   xxiv
　　They shouted all for ioy of his successe,
　　Glad to be quit from that proud Tyrants awe,
　　Which with strong powre did them long time oppresse;
　　And running all with greedie ioyfulnesse
　　To faire *Irena*, at her feet did fall,
　　And her adored with due humblenesse,
　　As their true Liege and Princesse naturall;
And eke her champions glorie sounded ouer all.

Who streight her leading with meete maiestie   xxv
　　Vnto the pallace, where their kings did rayne,
　　Did her therein establish peaceablie,
　　And to her kingdomes seat restore agayne;
　　And all such persons, as did late maintayne
　　That Tyrants part, with close or open ayde,
　　He sorely punished with heauie payne;
　　That in short space, whiles there with her he stayd,
Not one was left, that durst her once haue disobayd.

During which time, that he did there remaine,   xxvi
　　His studie was true Iustice how to deale,
　　And day and night employ'd his busie paine
　　How to reforme that ragged common-weale:
　　And that same yron man which could reueale
　　All hidden crimes, through all that realme he sent,
　　To search out those, that vsd to rob and steale,
　　Or did rebell gainst lawfull gouernment;
On whom he did inflict most grieuous punishment.

But ere he could reforme it thoroughly,   xxvii
　　He through occasion called was away,
　　To Faerie Court, that of necessity
　　His course of Iustice he was forst to stay,
　　And *Talus* to reuoke from the right way,
　　In which he was that Realme for to redresse.
　　But enuies cloud still dimmeth vertues ray.
　　So hauing freed *Irena* from distresse,
He tooke his leaue of her, there left in heauinesse.

Tho as he backe returned from that land,
   And there arriu'd againe, whence forth he set,
   He had not passed farre vpon the strand,
   When as two old ill fauour'd Hags he met,
   By the way side being together set,
   Two griesly creatures; and, to that their faces
   Most foule and filthie were, their garments yet
   Being all rag'd and tatter'd, their disgraces
Did much the more augment, and made most vgly cases.

The one of them, that elder did appeare,
   With her dull eyes did seeme to looke askew,
   That her mis-shape much helpt; and her foule heare
   Hung loose and loathsomely: Thereto her hew
   Was wan and leane, that all her teeth arew,
   And all her bones might through her cheekes be red;
   Her lips were like raw lether, pale and blew,
   And as she spake, therewith she slauered;
Yet spake she seldom, but thought more, the lesse she sed.

Her hands were foule and durtie, neuer washt
   In all her life, with long nayles ouer raught,
   Like puttocks clawes: with th'one of which she scracht
   Her cursed head, although it itched naught;
   The other held a snake with venime fraught,
   On which she fed, and gnawed hungrily,
   As if that long she had not eaten ought;
   That round about her iawes one might descry
The bloudie gore and poyson dropping lothsomely.

Her name was *Enuie*, knowen well thereby;
   Whose nature is to grieue, and grudge at all,
   That euer she sees doen prays-worthily,
   Whose sight to her is greatest crosse, may fall,
   And vexeth so, that makes her eat her gall.
   For when she wanteth other thing to eat,
   She feedes on her owne maw vnnaturall,
   And of her owne foule entrayles makes her meat;
Meat fit for such a monsters monsterous dyeat.

And if she hapt of any good to heare,
   That had to any happily betid,
   Then would she inly fret, and grieue, and teare
   Her flesh for felnesse, which she inward hid:
   But if she heard of ill, that any did,
   Or harme, that any had, then would she make
   Great cheare, like one vnto a banquet bid;
   And in anothers losse great pleasure take,
As she had got thereby, and gayned a great stake.

The other nothing better was, then shee;
   Agreeing in bad will and cancred kynd,
   But in bad maner they did disagree:
   For what so *Enuie* good or bad did fynd,
   She did conceale, and murder her owne mynd;
   But this, what euer euill she conceiued,
   Did spred abroad, and throw in th'open wynd.
   Yet this in all her words might be perceiued,
That all she sought, was mens good name to haue bereaued.

For what soeuer good by any sayd,
   Or doen she heard, she would streightwayes inuent,
   How to depraue, or slaunderously vpbrayd,
   Or to misconstrue of a mans intent,
   And turne to ill the thing, that well was ment.
   Therefore she vsed often to resort,
   To common haunts, and companies frequent,
   To hearke what any one did good report,
To blot the same with blame, or wrest in wicked sort.

And if that any ill she heard of any,
   She would it eeke, and make much worse by telling,
   And take great ioy to publish it to many,
   That euery matter worse was for her melling.
   Her name was hight *Detraction*, and her dwelling
   Was neare to *Enuie*, euen her neighbour next;
   A wicked hag, and *Enuy* selfe excelling
   In mischiefe: for her selfe she onely vext;
But this same both her selfe, and others eke perplext.

Her face was vgly, and her mouth distort,　　　xxxvi
　Foming with poyson round about her gils,
　In which her cursed tongue full sharpe and short
　Appear'd like Aspis sting, that closely kils,
　Or cruelly does wound, whom so she wils:
　A distaffe in her other hand she had,
　Vpon the which she litle spinnes, but spils,
　And faynes to weaue false tales and leasings bad,
To throw amongst the good, which others had disprad.

These two now had themselues combynd in one,　　　xxxvii
　And linckt together gainst Sir *Artegall*,
　For whom they wayted as his mortall fone,
　How they might make him into mischiefe fall,
　For freeing from their snares *Irena* thrall,
　Besides vnto themselues they gotten had
　A monster, which the *Blatant beast* men call,
　A dreadfull feend of gods and men ydrad,
Whom they by slights allur'd, and to their purpose lad.

Such were these Hags, and so vnhandsome drest:　　　xxxviii
　Who when they nigh approching, had espyde
　Sir *Artegall* return'd from his late quest,
　They both arose, and at him loudly cryde,
　As it had bene two shepheards curres, had scryde
　A rauenous Wolfe amongst the scattered flockes.
　And *Enuie* first, as she that first him eyde,
　Towardes him runs, and with rude flaring lockes
About her eares, does beat her brest, and forhead knockes.

Then from her mouth the gobbet she does take,　　　xxxix
　The which whyleare she was so greedily
　Deuouring, euen that halfe-gnawen snake,
　And at him throwes it most despightfully.
　The cursed Serpent, though she hungrily
　Earst chawd thereon, yet was not all so dead,
　But that some life remayned secretly,
　And as he past afore withouten dread,
Bit him behind, that long the marke was to be read.

Then th'other comming neare, gan him reuile,   xl
  And fouly rayle, with all she could inuent;
  Saying, that he had with vnmanly guile,
  And foule abusion both his honour blent,
  And that bright sword, the sword of Iustice lent,
  Had stayned with reprochfull crueltie,
  In guiltlesse blood of many an innocent:
  As for *Grandtorto*, him with treacherie
And traynes hauing surpriz'd, he fouly did to die.

Thereto the Blatant beast by them set on   xli
  At him began aloud to barke and bay,
  With bitter rage and fell contention,
  That all the woods and rockes nigh to that way,
  Began to quake and tremble with dismay;
  And all the aire rebellowed againe.
  So dreadfully his hundred tongues did bray,
  And euermore those hags them selues did paine,
To sharpen him, and their owne cursed tongs did straine.

And still among most bitter wordes they spake,   xlii
  Most shamefull, most vnrighteous, most vntrew,
  That they the mildest man aliue would make
  Forget his patience, and yeeld vengeaunce dew
  To her, that so false sclaunders at him threw.
  And more to make them pierce and wound more deepe,
  She with the sting, which in her vile tongue grew,
  Did sharpen them, and in fresh poyson steepe:
Yet he past on, and seem'd of them to take no keepe.

But *Talus* hearing her so lewdly raile,   xliii
  And speake so ill of him, that well deserued,
  Would her haue chastiz'd with his yron flaile,
  If her Sir *Artegall* had not preserued,
  And him forbidden, who his heast obserued.
  So much the more at him still did she scold,
  And stones did cast, yet he for nought would swerue
  From his right course, but still the way did hold
To Faery Court, where what him fell shall else be told.

COMMENTARY

Guide references are to stanza and line.

Notes not otherwise assigned are by the Editor. Editorial comment upon notes is either included in square brackets or designated EDITOR.

In quotations from the *Iliad* and the *Odyssey*, the translations of Lang, Leaf, and Myers, and of Butcher and Lang have been followed. References to Malory in the notes from Miss Walther are to page and line in the reprint of Caxton's edition by H. O. Sommer, 3 vols., London, 1889-1891.

Editions, books, and periodicals frequently cited will be referred to under the following abbreviations:

EDITORS AND COMMENTATORS

HUGHES.   Works of Spenser, ed. John Hughes. 1715.

JORTIN.   Remarks on Spenser's Poems [by John Jortin]. 1734.

WARTON.   Observations on the Fairy Queen of Spenser, by Thomas Warton. 2nd ed., 1762. [1st ed., 1754.]

UPTON.   Spenser's Faerie Queene, ed. John Upton. 1758.

CHURCH.   The Faerie Queene, ed. Ralph Church. 1758.

TODD.   Works of Spenser, ed. H. J. Todd. 1805.

HILLARD.   Poetical Works of Edmund Spenser, ed. G. S. Hillard. 1839.

COLLIER.   Works of Spenser, ed. J. P. Collier. 1862.

WALTHER.   Malory's Einfluss auf Spenser's Faerie Queene, by Marie Walther. *c.* 1895.

SAWTELLE.   Sources of Spenser's Classical Mythology, by A. E. Sawtelle. 1896.

DODGE.   Spenser's Imitations from Ariosto. *PMLA* (1897, 1920).

HEISE.   Die Gleichnisse in Edmund Spenser's Faerie Queene und ihre Vorbilder, by Wilhelm Heise. 1902.

RIEDNER.   Spensers Belesenheit. 1 Theil: Die Bibel und das klassische Altertum, by Wilhelm Riedner. 1908.

BLAKENEY.   The Faery Queene, Book V, ed. E. H. Blakeney. 1914.

GOUGH.   The Faerie Queene, Book V, ed. Alfred B. Gough. 1918.

LOTSPEICH.   Classical Mythology in the Poetry of Edmund Spenser, by Henry G. Lotspeich. 1932.

For references to authors not in this list, consult the Bibliography.

PERIODICALS

Abbreviation	Title
ELH	ELH: A Journal of English Literary History
Engl. St.	Englische Studien
JEGP	Journal of English and Germanic Philology
MLN	Modern Language Notes
MLQ	Modern Language Quarterly
MP	Modern Philology
MLR	Modern Language Review
NQ	Notes and Queries
PMLA	Publications of the Modern Language Association of America
PQ	Philological Quarterly
RES	Review of English Studies
SP	Studies in Philology

Poems

Aen.	Aeneid
F. Q.	Faerie Queene
Ger. Lib.	Gerusalemme Liberata
Il.	Iliad
Inf.	Inferno
Kn. T.	Knightes Tale
Met.	Metamorphoses
Od.	Odyssey
Orl. Fur.	Orlando Furioso
Orl. Inn.	Orlando Innamorato
P. L.	Paradise Lost
P. R.	Paradise Regained
Par.	Paradiso
Purg.	Purgatorio
Rin.	Rinaldo
Sh. Cal.	Shepheardes Calendar
Theb.	Thebais

PROEM

See Appendix to Book II, "Elizabethan Psychology," p. 461.

E. Legouis (*Spenser*, pp. 36-7). It may be said that he merely repeats here very ancient reveries on the age of gold already found in Ovid and many others. That he echoes them is admitted. But he is not a mere echo. He has made those rhetorical disquisitions his own. They are present everywhere in his works. His *Complaints,* especially the *Visions of the World's Vanity,* are full of the same melancholy, of the monotonous description of things falling from a prosperous state into ruin and decay.

It is impossible, then, to call this a poetical fiction used for mere ornament. It is a deep-seated creed, the foundation upon which his poetry was built. His

imagination conspired with his private resentments when conjuring up that beautiful image of times long ago.   In the great controversy between Ancients and
Moderns which was already beginning and was to grow all through the next century, Spenser, without a moment's hesitation, took sides with the Ancients.   He
did not yield to the authority of Jean Bodin, which Harvey invoked against him.
According to Jean Bodin, "it is now that the age of gold flourishes.   Our great-
great-grandfathers had to plod heavily through the ages of iron and bronze, when
all things were rude and imperfect by comparison with the refinement and delicacy
of the present day."   Thus spoke Bodin.   But Spenser would not have it so.
Neither had he any inkling of the ideas already maturing in the mind of young
Bacon which were to culminate in the famous apophthegm: "Antiquitas mundi
juventus sæculi."

GOUGH (pp. [155]-156).   Each book of the *Faerie Queene* opens with
a few introductory stanzas, containing some general reflections, and a dedication or
complimentary allusion to Queen Elizabeth.   In this Proem, which is the longest
and most remarkable of the six, the poet laments the decay of justice.   The moral
degeneration of mankind since the Golden Age had been a commonplace with
the poets since Hesiod.   To a man with the lofty ideals and somewhat melancholy
temperament of Spenser, the condition of affairs when he wrote may well have
appeared to confirm this pessimistic view.   To him, we may well believe, the time
seemed to be out of joint.   With all his Protestantism, there was a strong mediaeval
and conservative current in Spenser's thought.   The religious, political, and social
upheaval of the sixteenth century had weakened respect for the established order.
A succession of terrible wars had shaken the foundations of European society.   The
unparalleled misery of Ireland, chiefly due in Spenser's judgement to the weakness
of government, had deeply impressed his mind.   Feudalism and chivalry were passing away, kings were undermining or sweeping aside constitutional liberties, Jesuits
were plotting to overthrow governments and assassinate rulers, communistic and
anarchistic doctrines were spreading among the masses.   The Counter-Reformation
was gathering force, and the final issue was yet in doubt.

In two parallel passages (2. 7. 16-7 [see UPTON's note, Book II, p. 255] and
4. 8. 29-33) Spenser laments the corruption into which the world has fallen through
lawless lust, which was unknown in "antique age yet in the infancie Of time."
And in the fragmentary seventh book (canto 7) Mutability claims to be sovereign
mistress of the universe, although Nature predicts the end of her reign.   In an
undated letter (perhaps *c.* 1579-1580), Gabriel Harvey rebukes Spenser for complaining of the deterioration of the world.   "You suppose the first age was the
goulde age.   It is nothing soe. . . . You suppose it a foolish madd worlde, wherein
all thinges ar overrulid by fansy" (*G. Harvey's Letter-book*, pp. 82 ff.).   [See
Miss Albright and E. Greenlaw in Appendix to Book VII.]

In the present Proem the poet, crying "All the foundations of the earth are
out of course," fancifully connects the moral disorder of his time with the supposed
progressive derangement of the physical universe.   In this mood he cannot with
Wordsworth look to Duty as the cosmic law and say,

> Thou dost preserve the stars from wrong,
> And the most ancient heavens through thee are fresh and strong.

Elsewhere, it is true, he expressed that idea, e. g. in the present book, 2. 36. 1 ff., 7. 1. 4 ff., but he probably believed that he was living in the midst of violence and treachery to be manifested before the last days (cf. Pr. 4. 9), when the sun shall be darkened (Pr. 7. 9), " and the stars shall fall from heaven, and the powers of the heavens shall be shaken " (Matthew 24. 29).

The quaint and even playful language with which Spenser illustrates the supposed physical deterioration of the universe, especially in the passage describing the displacement of the zodiac (Pr. 10. 6-11. 4) need cast no doubt on the essential gravity of his outlook.

The Proem closes in a less despondent strain. The Almighty, who deals justice to all, has set the Prince as His deputy in His own seat, to dispense righteous dooms at home, and defend the cause of right abroad. The adroit flattery of his " dread Soverayne Goddesse," in which Spenser speaks the usual language of his contemporaries, may grate upon modern ears, but it expresses his proud admiration of the heroic choice which his queen had made in defending a just cause against a tyrannic power, which aimed at the political and spiritual enslavement of Europe.

[On the theory prevailing in Spenser's day, that the world is degenerate, see the following notes, and particularly Richard F. Jones, *Ancients and Moderns, Washington University Studies,* N. S., No. 6, chap. 2, " The Decay of Nature," pp. 23-42; 291-6.]

BLAKENEY. The comparison between Past and Present, to the detriment of the latter, is a hackneyed theme with poet and moralist. Cf. Horace, *Odes* [3.] 6. 46-8 for a classical example (out of many):

Aetas parentum pejor avis tulit
Nos nequiores, mox daturos
Progeniem vitiosiorem.

See Burke's *Thoughts on the Present Discontents* [*Works and Correspondence,* London, 1852, 3. 112], passage beginning: " To complain of the age we live in," etc.

EDITOR. It was a favorite and perhaps natural notion of Spenser's that antique times—of no particular date—were better than ours. See among other passages *Virgils Gnat* 359; *Ruines of Time* 59-61; *Mother Hubberds Tale* 144-151 and note; 1. 12. 14. 8; 2. 7. 16-7 and note in Book II, p. 255; 3. 1. 13 and Appendix in Book III, p. 368; 4. 8. 30-4 and note on 31. 6 in Book IV, p. 211; 6. Pr. 4. 7; 6. 1. 1.

i. H. J. C. GRIERSON (*Cross Currents in English Literature of the XVIIth Century,* pp. 44-6). Spenser's poem, even more than Ariosto's, is lavish of flattery to the Queen and her courtiers; and it reflects vividly the pomp and glitter of courtly life, the pageantry of Court masques and entertainments, the beauty of knightly armour and well-born ladies. But the other side of court life would assert itself too, if more fully in *Mother Hubberds Tale* and *Colin Clouts Come Home Again,* yet in *The Faerie Queene* also; and Spenser will seek escape in dreams of a golden age in the past [st. quoted]. . . . And then he forgets that he is writing of this earlier and greater age, and Sir Calidore is fain to forsake even the ideal court of Gloriana and live the shepherd's simple life [*F. Q.* 6. 9. 19

quoted]. . . . But pastoralism is itself a courtly pose, an aspect of the dream of love. Calidore is only echoing, often translating, the refined and sensuous stanzas of Tasso. Spenser never speaks of the court with Milton's scorn. But the young poet and courtier is also a Puritan whose heart has responded to the appeal of Cartwright, if his first ardour has a little slackened, and he is anxious that his poem should justify itself to those whose supreme interest is a purer religion, a closer walk with God. How is he to reconcile the serious spirit of Protestant Evangelical religion with the vanities of chivalrous romance, the extravagant cult of love, the egoistic conception of personal prowess, the endless absurdities of romantic fiction, a medley of pagan superstitions, Greek gods and goddesses, hermits and monks, the asceticisms and mysteries of mediaeval Catholicism; and running through it all a strain of subtle and elaborate flattery of the Queen and her courtiers? These things and " the Gospel " go not easily together.

7. BLAKENEY. Cf. Shakespeare's *Hamlet* [1. 5. 189]: " The time is out of joint."

ii.   See notes on 4. 8. 31 in Book IV, p. 211.

5-6. UPTON. Cf. Horace, *Odes* 3. 6 and Berni, *Orl. Inn.* 25. 3.

6-7. SAWTELLE (p. 47). Spenser follows *Met.* 1. 399 ff.

LOTSPEICH (p. 53). The way he associates the myth with the stoniness of men since the Golden Age may have been suggested by Natalis Comes 8. 17, who thus interprets the story of the creation of men from stones [ed. Padua, 1637, p. 466]: " At cum rursus rudes homines et religionis cultusque deorum ignari nascerentur, dicti sunt lapides." Cf. also *Georgics* 1. 61-3.

iv ff. EDITOR. Cf. Shakespeare's *Troilus* 1. 3. 93-118.

iv. 6-7. UPTON. This is owing to the precession of the Equinoxes. See Keil, *Astron.*, Lect. 8. *Hudibras* 2. 3. 901-4:

> Some say the Zodiack constellations
> Have long since chang'd their antique stations
> Above a sign, and prove the same
> In Taurus now, once in the Ram.

v. 2. GOUGH. Not the heavenly bodies themselves, but the transparent hollow concentric spheres in which, according to ancient and mediaeval astronomy, they were fixed. The astronomer Ptolemy (see Pr. 7. 6), believing that the earth was the centre of the universe, accounted for the distinct movements of the seven planets (including the sun and moon) by assuming that each of them was fixed in a sphere of its own. Outside of all was an eighth sphere containing the fixed stars, which revolved once in twenty-four hours, carrying the inner spheres with it, each of which however had a slower independent motion of its own. The following lines describe the precession of the equinoxes, i. e. the very slow shifting of the sun's apparent path through the heavens, caused by a progressive alteration of the earth's axis. [See notes to Pr. 7. 6-9 below.]

v. 6–vi. 4. GOUGH. Spenser here mentions the first five signs of the zodiac, viz. Aries, Taurus, Gemini, Cancer and Leo. The twelve signs appear in Babylonia in very remote antiquity with mythological associations. Having been adopted by the Greeks, they were fancifully identified with persons and animals in the Greek mythology by the astronomers of the Alexandrian age, followed by Romans like Manilius and Hyginus. To the examples which Spenser gives here may be added the identification of Virgo, the sixth sign, with Astraea in 1. 11.

6-7. See notes on 3. 11. 30. 5 in Book III, pp. 292-3.

9. SAWTELLE (p. 54). See Hyginus, *Poet. Astron.* 2. "Taurus."

LOTSPEICH (p. 58). For the identification of Europa's bull with Taurus Spenser had the authority of Ovid, *Fasti* 5. 617.

vi. 2. LOTSPEICH (p. 45). Cf. *Ruines of Time* 386-9; *Proth.* 173-4; *F. Q.* 7. 7. 34. The idea . . . that both are "twinnes of Jove," which contradicts the more common myth that Castor was son of Tyndarus, is supported by Natalis Comes 8. 9.

5-9. See the EDITOR's note on sts. 4 ff. above.

9. See note on 9. 47. 6 below.

vii. 5-9. CHURCH. He alludes to the difference of the Zodiac's Obliquity from what it was of old. The curious Reader may consult Mr. Selden's long and learned Note on Drayton's *Polyolbion* [ed. 1613], p. 235 [cf. Hebel's ed. 4. 300-1], which I forbear to transcribe, because such language (as he there observes) is too heavenly for the common Reader.

6. UPTON. Claudius Ptolomaeus, a celebrated astronomer that taught at Alexandria in Ægypt. Spenser alludes to his book called *Almagestum magnum.*

8. G. S. HILLARD (*The Poetical Works of Edmund Spenser* 3. 216-7). This refers to the diminution of the obliquity of the ecliptic, by which the sun recedes from the pole, and approaches the equator. Spenser does not state the amount correctly, however, and it is possible that "thirtie" may be a misprint for "thirteen," which was very nearly the exact amount in his time.

GOUGH. The obliquity of the ecliptic given by Ptolemy after Eratosthenes was 23° 51' 20", and in 1592 it was 23° 29' 56", the difference being nearly 21½ minutes. The sun had really declined less than eleven minutes since Ptolemy's time (A. D. 130), his estimate being 10' 30" too great.

viii-xi. EDITOR (C. G. O.). A. S. COOK ("Notes on Milton's *Ode on the Morning of Christ's Nativity," Transactions of the Connecticut Academy of Arts and Sciences* 15. 314, 327) points out the echo of 8. 1-2; 9. 4-5 in Milton's *Ode* 22-3; 53-4. But this whole passage, 8-11, seems to have been ringing in young Milton's ear that Christmas Day in 1629. Cf. *Ode* 59-60:

> And Kings sate still with awfull eye,
> As if they surely knew their sovran Lord was by.

with stanzas 10. 3; 11.5 (Marlowe's cadence, "Great potentates do kneel with awful fear," mingling with Spenser's) ; and *Ode* 155-6; 163-4:

Yet first to those ychain'd in sleep,
The wakefull trump of doom must thunder through the deep. . . .
When at the worlds last session,
The dreadfull Judge in middle Air shall spread his throne.

with stanza 11. 1-4.

viii.   JORTIN cites Herodotus 2. 142. [*The Faymous Hystory of Herodotus*, translated by B. R. (1584), Tudor Translations, p. 221: "Thus far went the Aegyptians and their priests in describing the continual succession of their kings and governours, alleadging that from the first King unto this priest of Vulcane before mentioned, were 341 generations . . . these strange alterations were marked in the Sunne at four sundry times. Two sundry times it was seene to rise from that place where it is now wont to fall, and in like manner to set in those regions from whence it now ariseth, which also came to passe two several times."]

UPTON cites *Hudibras* 2. 3. 865-8:

The Aegyptians say, the Sun has twice
Shifted his setting and his rise:
Twice has he risen in the West,
As many times set in the East.

GOUGH.   Herodotus, absurdly regarding each reign as equivalent to a generation, reckons the whole time at 11,340 years. His information about Egypt, probably derived from the gossip of dragomans, abounds in misapprehensions. "Perhaps, as Mr. Poole suggests, Herodotus misunderstood the statement that the solar risings of the stars had fallen four times on those days of the vague year on which the settings fell in the time of Sethos" (A. H. Sayce [note on Herodotus 2. 142]). As the Egyptians had no leap-year, the seasons gradually fell later in the calendar, completing the round of the year in the Sothic period of 1,460 years. Thus the summer or the winter solstice would fall four times on New Year's Day in 5,840 years, which would give an average reign of seventeen years.

8.   GOUGH.   With the exception of Mercury, which was not so easily observed owing to its proximity to the sun, Mars, and after it Saturn, have the most eccentric orbits of all the major planets. In Spenser's time it was still believed on *a priori* grounds that the normal form of a planet's orbit was circular. The notable eccentricity of the orbit of Mars therefore seemed to be a proof of derangement until Kepler's great work *De Motibus Stellae Martis* (1609), established the law of eccentric orbits.

With this passage may be compared the words of Mutability in 7. 7. 51-2:

[Mercury] his course doth altar every yeare,
And is of late far out of order gone. . . .

Now *Mars* that valiant man is changed most:
For, he some times so far runs out of square,
That he his way doth seem quite to have lost,
And cleane without his usuall sphere to fare;
That even these Star-gazers stonisht are
At sight thereof, and damne their lying bookes:

> So likewise, grim Sir Saturne oft doth spare
> His sterne aspect, and calme his crabbed lookes:
> So many turning cranks these have, so many crookes.

In a secondary sense Spenser means that wrongful bloodshed and lawlessness (the perversion of Mars and Saturn) have increased.

ix.   JORTIN.   From Ovid, *Met.* 1. 89-102:

> Aurea prima sata est aetas, quae vindice nullo,
> Sponte sua, sine lege, fidem rectumque colebat.
> Poena metusque aberant. . . .
> Non tuba directi, non aeris cornua flexi,
> Non galeae, non ensis, erant. Sine militis usu
> Mollia securae peragebant otia mentes [gentes].
> Ipsa quoque immunis, rastroque intacta, nec ullis
> Saucia vomeribus, per se dabat omnia tellus.

SAWTELLE (p. 106). The reign of Saturn, "the golden age," when peace and plenty abounded, is explained by Ovid, *Fast.* 1. 233 ff., and Macrobius, *Saturnalia* 1. 7 ff.

LOTSPEICH (p. 105) adds Virgil, *Eclogue* 4; Tibullus 1. 3. 35 ff.; Hesiod, *Works and Days* 109-120.

5.   GOUGH.   Cf. Vergil, *Georg.* 2. 538-9:

> Aureus hanc vitam in terris Saturnus agebat.
> Necdum etiam audierant inflari classica. . . .

Ovid [See JORTIN's note above] . . . also Chaucer, "The Former Age" 23: "Ne trompes for the werres folk ne knewe."

7.   GOUGH.   Cf. Hesiod, *Works and Days* 117-8: ["The bounteous earth bare fruit for them of her own will, in plenty and without stint."] Ovid, *Met.* 1. 101-2 [see JORTIN's note above].

x.   2-5.   GRACE W. LANDRUM (*PMLA* 41. 541).   Cf. Matthew 5. 45.

3-4.   EDITOR.   Cf. Shakespeare's *Troilus and Cressida* 1. 3. 93-4:

> And posts, like the commandment of a king
> Sans check, to good and bad.

6.   GRACE W. LANDRUM (*PMLA* 41. 541).   Cf. Jeremiah 23. 5.

xi.   GOUGH.   Some excuse might be found for the extreme flattery of this stanza by a reference to Psalms 82. 1, 6, where rulers are addressed as gods. Spenser here pushes the Tudor doctrine of divine right to its furthest limit. Cf. *F. Q.* 1. Pr. 4. 1-3: "O Goddesse heavenly bright, Mirrour of grace and Majestie divine, Great Lady of the greatest Isle. . . . "

2.   BLAKENEY.   Cf. Proverbs 8. 15: "By me (viz. eternal wisdom of God) kings reign, and princes decree justice."

9.   PAULINE HENLEY (*Spenser in Ireland*, p. 126).   But the hero of Book V gets an Irish name, a sort of symbolically Irish garb, Finn Mac Cumhal's banner

device on his shield, and a magic sword.   Guaire the Hospitable, a famous king of
Connaught in the seventh century, had a son Arthgal, the ancestor of the O'Clerys,
O'Hynes, and Mac Gilla Kellys.   (*Journal R. Society Antiquaries,* vol. 4, 6s. p.
123.)   As the genealogy of Irish chieftains was a matter of deep interest to
Elizabethan statesmen, and also, as the *View* shows, to Spenser, he certainly came
across the name.   But even if he had never heard it, the combination of " Art,"
an Irish name translated by the English Arthur, with " Gall " would have suggested itself to him.   He knew that the Irish called Dermot MacMurrough
" Diarmuid na Gall " (*View,* Globe ed., p. 659), and that the usual term for an
Englishman was " Gall " (a foreigner)—in fact it was a word well-known to all
the English in Ireland. (*View,* Globe ed., p. 628.)

       GOUGH.   The identity of Sir Artegall with Elizabeth's Lord Deputy
in Ireland, Lord Grey de Wilton, is here plainly declared.
       " Artegall ": in *F. Q.* 2. 9. 6, where he is first mentioned, in many places in
F. Q. 3 and occasionally in *F. Q.* 4, he is called Arthegall.   The name is taken from
Geoffrey of Monmouth, who mentions (1) Arthgallo, an early and mythical king
of Britain, who was at first a tyrant, but afterwards " exercised strict justice towards
all men " (*Hist. Brit.* 3. 17), and (2) Arthgal, consul of Cargueit or Carisbrooke,
one of the nobles who were summoned by Arthur to his coronation (*Hist. Brit.* 9.
12).   The former of these two persons, who is the Archigald of *F. Q.* 2. 10. 44
[see notes in Book II, pp. 322-3], is called Arthegal in Hardyng's *Chronicle,* ch. 37.
       Although much is said of Artegall in the earlier books, there is no clear indi-
cation before Book 5 that he represents either the virtue of Justice or Arthur, Lord
Grey de Wilton.   Spenser perhaps chose him to be the hero of the present book
because his name bears some resemblance to that of Arthur Grey.
       Sir Artegall, though he was generally deemed an Elf or Fairy, was a British
prince, son of Gorlois of Cornwall, and had been stolen away into Fairyland in his
infancy (3. 3. 26 ff.).   The maiden Britomart, who had seen his face in Merlin's
magic mirrour, pined for love of him, and was told by Merlin that he was destined
to be her husband, and that many British kings would descend from them (*F. Q.*
3. 2, 3).   Having gone to Fairyland in quest of him, disguised as a knight, she
encountered and unhorsed him at a tournament, without knowing who he was until
she saw his face [4. 6. 26].   When Book 5 opens, Sir Artegall, newly affianced to
Britomart, has left her for three months, " bound upon an hard adventure " (4.
6. 42).

CANTO I

       Arg. 2.   CHURCH.   This Adventure of the Relief of Irena or Irene is plainly
introduc'd as a Compliment to Lord Grey of Wilton, to whom Spenser was Secretary.   That noble Lord was Lord Lieutenant of Ireland.   Irena or Irene is an Anagram
or transposition of the Letters of Ierne, the ancient name of that kingdom.

       GOUGH.   The " distressed Dame " of the " salvage Iland " is called
Irena or Irene (11. 37. 7), by a slight alteration of Ierna (Apuleius, *De Mundo*)
or Ἰέρνη (Strabo), a classical name of Ireland or Erin.   Eirene (εἰρήνη, peace),
who appears in 9. 32. 6, is a different person.
       Irena can hardly be said to represent Ireland as a whole, which regarded Lord

Grey as an oppressor rather than a deliverer, but the small Anglo-Irish minority, chiefly resident in the Pale.

With the name Irena cf. Ireneus, the speaker in *A Veue of the Present State of Ireland*, who expounds Spenser's own opinions on that country.

3. Todd. Perhaps Shan Oneal. [See Appendix, pp. 280, 282, 292, 303.]

i. Editor. The image may in part be a reminiscence, unconscious perhaps, of that in the Gardens of Adonis, 3. 6. 29 ff., especially 39.

ii. 1-5. Upton. Bacchus and Hercules are often joined together: the one as having subdued the tyrants and monsters in the East, the other in the West. Hercules is called in Apuleius [*De Magia* 22] "Lustrator orbis, purgator ferarum." And in Gruter's *Inscriptions*, p. xlix: HERCVLI. PACIFERO. INVICTO. SANCTO. So Bacchus in Sponius, *Miscell. erudit. Antiq.*, p. 43: LIBERO. SERVATORI. SANCTO. SACR.

Sawtelle (p. 36). It was a common tradition that, as Hercules conquered the West, so Bacchus accompanied by numerous raging attendants, swept through the East, especially India, introducing the cultivation of the vine, founding cities, and establishing laws. Apollodorus (3. 5. 2) mentions this, as do Diodorus Siculus (2. 38) and Ovid (*Fast.* 3. 720).

Lotspeich (p. 42). The conception of Bacchus as a champion of justice, like Hercules and Artegal, grows out of the classical tradition of his conquest of the east and his activity as a peacemaker and fosterer of civilization; cf. *Met.* 4. 20 f., 605 f., and Horace, *Epist.* 2. 1. 5-8. Natalis Comes 5. 13 (ed. Lyons, 1602), p. 487, quotes the last passage and adds, "He was exalted as a god because of the many benefits which he brought to men, because of discords and contentions composed by him, because of cities founded and laws given." Spenser may be thinking of him in this capacity also at *Teares of the Muses* 461, where he is mentioned, again with Hercules, as one of those whom the muse, the "nurse of virtue," has glorified.

6-9. Sawtelle (p. 62) cites Apollodorus 2 and Diodorus Siculus 4. [Cf. 2. 1. 5-7 and note.]

Gough. This hero was said to have sailed to the island of Erytheia in the Western Sea, where he slew the monster Geryon and the giant Eurytion (see 10. 9-10) and drove the cattle which they kept. Returning by Spain and Gaul, he founded cities, and became the father of the Celts. He then passed through Italy, where he abolished the human sacrifices of the Sabines, slew the robber Cacus and other lawless men, and established certain religious rites. Horace in the third Ode of his third Book ("Iustum et tenacem propositi virum") mentions Hercules and Bacchus as examples of justice triumphant:

> Hac arte Pollux et vagus Hercules
> Enisus arces attigit igneas . . . .
> Hac te merentem, Bacche pater, tuae
> Vexere tigres indocili iugum
> Collo trahentes.

EDITOR. This stanza reflects the euhemeristic view of myth as actual history, a view especially prevalent in Book V. See LOTSPEICH, p. 216 below.

iii.   A. H. GILBERT (*PMLA* 34. 232) notes this as a transition in the manner of Ariosto.

3-4.   UPTON.   This adventure was hinted at above, 4. 6. 42.

9.   UPTON.   And though Grantorto may signify tyranny and unjustice in general, he may signify sometimes the King of Spain.

A. A. JACK (*A Commentary on the Poetry of Chaucer and Spenser,* p. 222) identifies Grantorto with the Earl of Desmond.

PAULINE HENLEY (*Spenser in Ireland,* pp. 134-5). Spenser does not put any Spanish colouring into the picture of Grantorto, whereas there are many details pointing to an intended Irish figure, and consequently it is likely that the Poet intended to typify the Desmond rebellion rather than the King of Spain. This " strong Tyrant," moreover, does not occur in any of the previous Books of the *Faerie Queene,* and seems to be connected with the period when Grey was Deputy. Spain attacking England through Desmond's rebellion was the special problem that the Deputy was sent to deal with in Ireland. Grantorto is represented as a giant, owing to the formidable strength of the rebellion, and the possibilities that lay behind it. This redoubtable antagonist was accoutred in Irish fashion. [12. 14. 3-8 quoted] . . . in short, a warrior of the period, who fought with an ancient weapon—probably the Catholic religion—but was vanquished by Chrysaor, the Sword of the Lord, with which Artegall strikes off the head of " the cursed felon."

iv.   See note on 9. 34. 5 below.

1.   See notes on Arg. 2 above and " Variant Readings."

2.   Accompanied by old Sir Sergis (11. 37-8).

v-xi.   UPTON. Astraea, the goddess of Justice, lived on this earth during the golden age, but at length offended with our vices she fled to heaven: whilst she was here, she instructed Arthegal, and took him with her " into a solitary cave "—the allegory means, that meditation and philosophy is requisite for a law giver. So Minos was instructed by Jupiter; Numa by the fairy Egeria; Pythagoras, who was a lawgiver, often resorted to a solitary cave at Samos: see Jamblichus [*Life of Pythagoras*], cap. 5—when by proper instruction and meditation Arthegal was fit to wield the sword of justice, this dreaded sword Astraea delivered into his hands: 'tis called Chrysaor; because garnisht all with gold: ($\chi\rho\upsilon\sigma\acute{a}o\rho o\varsigma$ is the epithet of Apollo in Homer, *Il.* 5. 509, from $\chi\rho\upsilon\sigma\grave{o}\varsigma$ " aurum " and $\check{a}o\rho$ " ensis.") 'twas the same sword which Jupiter used in battle against the giants, and taken from his armory, or military store-house, by Astraea. As Justice gives Arthegal a sword; so Judas (2 Macabees 15. 15) sees in a dream or vision the prophet Jeremiah bringing him a sword of gold from God: " kept in store in the eternal house." [Upton merely starts a long list of wise men instructed by wiser women, in which Socrates is conspicuous. It leads in time to the mediaeval vision theme through Boethius, Alanus, etc.

On Chrysaor see also PAULINE HENLEY's note on 9-10 below.]

SAWTELLE (p. 31). We have in Astraea, as here pictured, the ideal of justice dwelling among men in some far-off time before the race fell from its perfect state. Hyginus (*Poet. Astron.* 2. " Virgo "), quoting Aratus [*Phaenom.* 96-137], says that Astraea lived in the golden age of peace and plenty. When, however, justice declined, she could not endure the state of affairs, and so left the earth for the sky.

LOTSPEICH (p. 40). Also Juvenal 6. 19 f. . . . All these classical references are scanty and allusive. The only formal and extended exposition of Astraea as Justice and of her life on earth is by Natalis Comes 2. 2. He says, the Golden Age was the age of perfect justice; laws were impressed in men's hearts, not in books. As human sin increased, Astraea fled the earth, but left behind her a volume of laws. Cf. 7. 7. 37. [Another full account is found in Lactantius, *Divine Institutions* 5. 5-9.]

vi-viii.   See GOUGH's note on stanza 12.

viii. 9–ix. 1. This *concatenatio* or linking of stanza to stanza by verbal echo is common in Spenser. TUCKER BROOKE (*MLN* 37. 223-7) observes that it is the commonest of four linking devices used by Spenser to avoid monotony. (See notes on 5. 4. 18. 9; 5. 10. 32. 2. Cf. below 4. 13-4; 5. 32-3; 9. 23-4; 10. 3-4; 11. 13-4.) " I find forty-eight examples in Books I-III as against twenty-six in Books IV-VI. Book III has many more than any other, namely twenty-two—nearly as many as are found in the whole of the last three books. Book IV has thirteen, as many as are found in either Book I or Book II; Book V has only seven, and Book VI a bare half-dozen. The cantos on Mutability have only one inconspicuous and perhaps unintentional example. It looks as if Spenser made consciously increasing use of the artifice through Book III, and then gradually gave it up as he acquired the uncanny naturalness both of narrative and versification which is so remarkable in the fifth and sixth books." But to accept " R. C.'s " suggestion (Preface to *The Chast and Lost Lovers*, by W. Bosworth, 1651) that Spenser adopted the device from Virgil (cf. *Aen.* 10. 180-1) is to overlook the habitual and traditional use of *concatenatio* by English and Romance poets before Spenser. See Osgood, *The Pearl*, pp. xlv-xlvi and xlv, n. 2, and BROOKE's note on 1. 4. 9. 1 in Book I, p. 215.

viii.   See Appendix, pp. 274, 276-7, 279, 289, 298, 301, 342.

ix-x.   UPTON. 'Tis very common in Romance writers to give their heroes swords, whose force nothing can resist. Hence Amadis de Gaul called himself Knight of the burning sword. We read in Chaucer, that the King of Arabia sent Cambuscan a sword of like sovereign virtue. Compare Ariosto 30. 58 [Ruggiero's sword, " Balisarda "] and 46. 120.

TODD cites *Historia de Carlo Magno* 1. 21. 37: " Fierabras ciño su espada llamada Plorança, y tenia otras dos al arçon de la silla, las quales eran de tal temple que ningun armes porfino que fuesse las mello, ni hizo señal en ellas."

PAULINE HENLEY (*Spenser in Ireland*, p. 127). The magic sword given him by Astraea is called Chrysaor. Though the name is derived from the identical Greek word, it is possible the Poet had in mind a secondary derivation. The word " Christ " united with the Irish word " saor," a workman or artificer, would give a hidden meaning which would delight the colonists, and appeal to

Spenser particularly, for Grey's policy for Ireland, had he been given a free hand, would have been a Mahomedan conquest. His sword would have done the work of Christ, and when he failed to bring Elizabeth round to his views, he wrote dejectedly to Walsingham, " Baal's prophets and councillors shall prevail. I see it is so. I see it is just. I see it past help. I rest despaired." (Froude, vol. 11, chap. 27, p. 242.)

BLAKENEY cites Hesiod, *Theog.* 281 ff.

x.   JORTIN.   So Milton, *P. L.* 6. 320-3:

> but the sword
> Of Michael from the armory of God
> Was giv'n him temper'd so, that neither keen
> Nor solid might resist that edge.

xi.   7.   UPTON.   So he elegantly calls the Zodiack. . . . He had the expression from Manilius [Bentley's ed., 1739] 1. 677: " Sed nitet ingenti stellatus balteus orbe "; 3. [334]: " Atque erit obliquo signorum balteus orbe."

GOUGH.   Cf. Spenser's *Prothalamion* 173 f.: " the twins of Jove . . . Which decke the Bauldricke of the Heavens bright." Quarles imitates this passage in his *Esther* (1621) 128 [Section 13, " Meditatio," lines 30-1]: " Astrea . . . in the shining Baudrike takes her Seat."

8.   CHURCH.   August was first called Sextilis, as being the sixth Month; the year then beginning with March. See note on 7. 7. 37. 6.

9.   See below, EDITOR's note on 2. 30 ff.

xii.   WARTON (1. 97-100).   The character of executing justice, here attributed to Talus, is agreeable to that which he bears in antient story; nor has Spenser greatly varied from antiquity in the [making] of this wonderful man; for he is there said to be formed of brass, and by our author of iron. Plato gives the following account of him, *Minos* [320 C]: [" For Minos used him (Rhadamanthus) as guardian of the law in the city and Talos as the same for the rest of Crete. For Talos thrice a year made a round of the villages, guarding the laws in them, by holding their laws inscribed on brazen tablets, which gave him his name of ' brazen.' "—Translation of W. R. M. Lamb, Loeb Classical Library, *Plato* 8. 417.] As to the circumstances of Talus traversing the isle of Crete, it exactly corresponds with what Spenser says afterwards of his iron man, who did the same in Ierne (5. 12. 26). . . .

Plato has told us, that Talus was denominated " brazen," on account of his carrying the laws about him, written in brazen tables; but Apollonius [cited by JORTIN] informs us, that he was actually made of brass, and invulnerable, *Argon.* 4. [1640-8]: [" He was of the stock of bronze, of the men sprung from ash-trees, the last left among the sons of the gods; and the son of Cronos gave him to Europa to be the warder of Crete and to stride round the island thrice a day with his feet of bronze. Now in all the rest of his body and limbs was he fashioned of bronze and invulnerable . . ."—Translation of R. C. Seaton, Loeb Classical Library.] (Ibycus, quoted by Athenaeus, relates, that Talus was beloved by Rhadamanthus, Lyons, 1657, bk. 13, p. 603.)

Apollonius likewise takes notice of his circuiting Crete three times a year (5. 1646).

Apollodorus will farther illustrate this matter, *Library* 1. 9. 26: [" Some say that he was a man of the Brazen Race, others that he was given to Minos by Hephaestus; he was a brazen man, but some say that he was a bull. He had a single vein extending from his neck to his ankles, and a bronze nail was rammed home at the end of the vein. This Talos kept guard, running round the island thrice every day; wherefore, when he saw the Argo standing inshore, he pelted it as usual with stones."—Translation of J. G. Frazer, Loeb Classical Library.] This marvellous swiftness of Talus is likewise referred to by our author (5. 1. 20):

> His yron page, who him pursewd so light,
> As that it seem'd above the ground he went,
> For he was swift as swallow in her flight.

And is alluded to by Catullus, in his Ode to Camerius, where he tells him that he should not be able to pursue him, *Carm.* 56: "Non Custos si ego fingar ille Cretum." Orpheus, or rather Onomacritus (who lived in the time of the Pisistratic tyranny, about Olymp. 60), calls Talus, in his *Argonautics*, "The brazen triple-giant." The circumstance of the iron flail is added from our author's imagination.

UPTON.   Justice is attended with power sufficient to execute her right-eous doom. The moral is apparent; and the moral should lead us to understand the fable; which yet seems to me to have been misunderstood. Who is ignorant of the history of Talus, mentioned by Plato, Apollonius Rhodius, etc. and by almost all the mythologists? But Spenser's Talus is not the Cretan Talus: though imaged from him. He was a judge; this is an executioner. He was said to have been a brazen man; imaging the laws which were engraven in brazen tables. Ovid, *Met.* 1. 91-2: "Nec verba minacia fixo Aere legebantur." These laws he is said to have carried about with him, when he went his circuit in Crete . . . and partly from his severity, and partly from the tables of brass which he carried about with him, he was called a brazen man. . . . But how properly does Spenser depart from ancient mythology, having a mythology of his own? Spenser's Talus is no judge; there-fore not a brazen man: but he is an executioner, an iron man, imaging his unfeeling and rigid character.

J. G. FRAZER (Loeb ed. of Apollodorus 1. 118-9, n. 1).   As to Talus, see Apollonius Rhodius, *Argon.* 4. 1639-1693; *Orphica, Argonautica*, 1358-1360; Agatharchides, in Photius, *Bibliotheca*, p. 443 b, lines 22-5, ed. Bekker; Lucian, *De saltatione*, 42; Zenobius, *Cent.* 5. 85; Suidas, *s. v.* Σαρδάνιος γέλως; Eusta-thius, on Homer, *Odyssey* 20. 302, p. 1893; Scholiast on Plato, *Republic* 1, p. 337 A. [Frazer cites also *The Dying God*, pp. 74 ff.; A. B. Cook, *Zeus* 1. 718 ff.; A. C. Pearson's ed. of *The Fragments of Sophocles* 1. 110 ff.   See also Frazer's *Pausanias' Description of Greece* 2. 232-4 for further references to Talos.]

GOUGH (p. 165).   The education of Artegall by the goddess Astraea typifies the growth through divine inspiration of the sense of right in the human heart. Astraea's groom, Talus, one of the most vividly conceived characters in the Book, is entrusted to her pupil when she leaves the earth, a symbol of the divinely implanted faculty of executing decrees of the moral judgment, the disciplined energy which translates right belief into action.   In a secondary sense Talus represents the executive force at the bidding of the ruler or magistrate, e. g. the English army in Ireland which carried out the orders of the Lord Deputy, Grey de Wilton.

LOTSPEICH (p. 109). Natalis Comes 2. 2 says that when Astraea departed she left behind her a " testamentum " of laws. The *Minos* passage (320 C) emphasizes Talus' bronze tablet. This tablet, or " testamentum," may have been the connecting link in Spenser's mind, between Astraea and Talus. Considering Spenser's habitual use of " iron " to denote just such qualities as his Talus possesses, it is not surprising to find him changing the tradition in this particular. He may, too, have been aware of the etymology of the Greek name and its connection with τλάω; cf. " Immoveable, resistless, without end." [See note on 4. 6. 17. 1 in Book IV, p. 200 (where " metaphysical " should read " metaphorical ")].

J. W. DRAPER (*PQ* 15. 217). His [Talus's] iron flail . . . Spenser may have borrowed from the Hussite wars in Bohemia in the early fifteenth century. . . . I suggest this origin in spite of Spenser's declaring it a " strange weapon never wont in war " (5. 4. 44). Cf. also the " Protestant flail " used by the London prentices at the time of the Popish Plot. The association of this weapon with Talus is especially apt in his struggles against the Roman Catholic Irish.

[See Appendix, p. 298 below and Appendix to Book I, " On the Propriety of the Allegory," p. 365.]

6. WALTHER (p. 9). Cf. the giants in Malory: Taulus [Taulas], p. 155; Tauleas, p. 369; Taulurd, p. 155.

xiii. 5. GOUGH. When Grey assumed office as Lord Deputy of Ireland, a large part of the country openly repudiated Elizabeth's sovereignty. The crown of Ireland had been accepted by the Pope, Gregory XIII, for his nephew.

xv. 2. UPTON. Translated from Homer, who represents Agamemnon, *Il.* 9. 14: [" weeping like unto a fountain of dark water that from a beetling cliff poureth down its black stream."] And Patroclus, *Il.* 16. 3: [" shed warm tears, even as a fountain of dark water that down a steep cliff pours its cloudy stream."]

7. WARTON (2. 205). That is, " That I might suffer what she did." These words seem an improper imitation of a passage in the new testament, which every serious reader cannot but remember with the greatest reverence. [Warton here probably refers to Matthew 20. 22-3, or to Mark 10. 38-9; see UPTON's note below.]

UPTON. This expression is not only in the scriptures, (Matthew 26. 39, Isaiah 51. 17, Psalm 75. 8) for Plautus uses it, *Casin.* 5. 2. [933]: " Ut senex hoc eodem poculo, quo ego bibi, biberet."

xxiii. 9. GOUGH. " his owne proper good." His own property. Cf. Shakespeare, *Taming of the Shrew* 3. 2. 231-2, where Petruchio says of Katharina:

> I will be master of what is mine own:
> She is my goods, my chattels.

Shane O'Neill, who seized the wife of Calvagh O'Donnell, claimed supremacy over that clan.

xxv. 1-3. WARTON (1. 191). So Chaucer (*Troilus and Cressida* 3. 1048) [cf. Skeat's ed. 1046]: "Where so you list by ordal or by othe." Sacrament is the oath of purgation.

TODD. Concerning the ordeal, or method of purgation by fire or water, see Kilian, in v. "Oor-deel," and particularly Spelman. See also an account of "Of Ordeal in general, and the several sorts of it," in the *Hist. of the Most Remarkable Tryals in Great Britain,* . . . 1715, ch. 1. Spenser adds, "or by blooddy fight," i. e. the trial by combat, the allowed method of settling disputes, if the party to whom the oath was tendered refused to take it (*Hist.,* ch. 3).

R. K. ROOT in a note on *Troilus and Criseyde* 1046-9 (Edition, p. 482) cites, on ordeal and oath, Pollock and Maitland, *History of English Law* 2. 595-9.

xxvi ff. G. L. CRAIK (*Spenser and His Poetry,* 2. 183). It might seem that the most natural and most satisfactory plan would be to appeal to the lady; but she may not perhaps have been so much disinclined as she ought to admit the claim of her bold reaver, with whom she appears both to have gone off somewhat readily and to have been riding along peaceably enough when they were overtaken by Talus; at any rate Artegal takes another method of settling the matter.

xxvi. 1-5. JORTIN. Copied from 1 Kings 3. 16[-27, the "Judgment of Solomon"].

COLLIER notes that Drayton had written in the margin of his *1611* "Sol^n" to indicate the source of the story.

6-9. UPTON. In [Malory] the history of prince Arthur, chap. 118 [Bk. 6, Ch. 17] a knight is doomed to carry the head of a lady, whom he had unjustly slain.

WALTHER (p. 29). Malory 211. 4 [6. 17] sagt Launcelot zu Pedivere, der seine Frau erschlagen hat: "Take this lady and the hede, and bere it upon the, and here shall thou swere upon my swerd to bere it alweyes upon thy back and never to reste tyl thou come to Quene Guenever." (Diese trägt ihm auf, den toten Körper nach Rom zum Papste zu tragen.) Siehe auch Malory 109. 3 [3. 8]: Gawaine muss die von ihm aus Versehen getötete Dame nach Camelot tragen: "The hede of her was hanged aboute his neck and the hole body of hyr lay before hym on his hors mane."

xxviii. 2. GOUGH. In accordance with the rules of courtesy, Sir Artegall addresses his inferior with "thou," his equal in rank, Sir Sanglier, with "you."

xxix. 9. See note on 8. 49. 1-5 below.

CANTO II

i-xxviii. See Appendix, pp. 277-8, 280, 302, 306, 313-4, 345-7.

i. 5-7. See LOTSPEICH's note above on 1. 2. 1-5. Spenser is again thinking of Hercules and Bacchus (see *Ruines of Time* 379-392; *Hymne of Love* 283), to whom he adds Charlemagne (*Teares of the Muses* 462). Lotspeich adds (p. 69):

" On Hercules' final exaltation Boccaccio comments, ' Ideo fictum est quantumque quia pereat corpus viri egregii, fama nomenque eius perpetuae iungitur iuventuti ' (13. 1)."

ii. 9. EDITOR (C. G. O.). " Spousd." Betrothed (cf. 5. 3. 2. 2), as the Red Cross Knight to Una at Book I, canto 12; Phedon to Claribell at 2. 4. 21. See comment on *Proth.*, a poem in celebration of a formal betrothal.

iii. 1-4. UPTON. " Dony " is contracted from Adonio, or Adonis, a knight's name in *Orl. Fur.* 43. [66 ff.]. The construction is, " whom (viz. Dony, her dwarf) she having lost, as ye have heard whyleare," viz. in *F. Q.* 3. 5. 3. " And he (viz. the dwarf) finding in the way Florimel's scattered scarfe, (viz. the scarfe which fell from her as she fled from the Foster in 3. 1. 15 and 3. 4. 45, etc.) did fear a long time the fortune of her life." Spenser gives no hint at all of Florimel's losing her scarfe, as he does of her losing her girdle, which Sir Satyrane found. The omission of these little circumstances makes it often difficult to unravel his meaning.

iv ff. WARTON (1. 212-3). Thus the pagan in Ariosto, [*Orl. Fur.*] 29. 35, keeps a bridge, which no man can pass over unless he fights with him; and which occasions many combats in the water, one of which sort is here described between Sir Arthegall and the Saracen, st. 11.

In *Morte Arthur* [6. 10] we find an account of a knight who kept a bridge, in which a circumstance is mentioned, not in Ariosto, which Spenser seems to have copied from thence, in the passage under consideration. " On the third day he rode over a long bridge; and there start upon him sodainly a passing fowle chorle, and he smote his horse, and asked him, why he rode over that bridge without his licence." So Spenser (st. 11).

HURD (*Letters on Chivalry and Romance*, pp. 226-231). " We hear much of Knights-errant encountering Giants, and quelling Savages, in books of Chivalry."

These Giants were oppressive feudal Lords; and every Lord was to be met with, like the Giant, in his strong hold, or castle. Their dependents of a lower form, who imitated the violence of their superiors, and had not their castles, but their lurking-places, were the Savages of Romance. The greater Lord was called a Giant, for his power; the less, a Savage, for his brutality.

All this is shadowed out in the Gothic tales, and sometimes expressed in plain words. The objects of the Knight's vengeance go indeed by the various names of Giants, Paynims, Saracens, and Savages. But of what family they all are, is clearly seen from the poet's own descriptions [sts. quoted].

Here we have the great oppressive Baron very graphically set forth: and the " Groom of evil guise " is as plainly the Baron's vassal. The Romancers, we see, took no great liberty with these respectable personages, when they called the one a Giant, and the other a Savage. . . .

Now in all these respects Greek antiquity very much resembles the Gothic. For what are Homer's Laestrigons and Cyclops, but bands of lawless savages, with, each of them, a Giant of enormous size at their head? And what are the Grecian Bacchus and Hercules, but Knights-errant, the exact counter-parts of Sir Launcelot and Amadis de Gaule?

For this interpretation we have the authority of our great poet [*F. Q.* 5. 2. 1 quoted].

Even Plutarch's life of Theseus reads, throughout, like a modern Romance: and Sir Arthegal himself is hardly his fellow, for righting wrongs and redressing grievances. So that Euripides might well make him say of himself, " that he had chosen the profession and calling of a Knight-errant ": for this is the sense, and almost the literal construction, of the following verses, *Suppliants* 340: [" I have chosen this custom among the Greeks to be a punisher of evils."] Accordingly, Theseus is a favourite Hero (witness the *Knight's Tale* in Chaucer) even with the Romance-writers.

Nay, could the very castle of a Gothic giant be better described than in the words of Homer, *Od.* 17. [266-8, tr. Pope]:

> High walls and battlements the courts inclose,
> And the strong gates defy a host of foes.

And do not you remember that the Grecian Worthies were, in their day, as famous for encountering Dragons and quelling Monsters of all sorts, as for suppressing Giants?

M. L. Neff (*PQ* 13. 159-167) gathers evidence of widespread abuses of tolls on bridges from the reign of Henry VIII through that of Elizabeth. He summarizes his conclusions thus:

" 1. Spenser, dealing with the virtue of Justice, presents two excesses by the two episodes: Artegall and the toll bridge, and Artegall and the Gyant by the sea. Since the second episode well represents the communistic doctrines against which the poet was allegorically warning the nation, the first episode would be taken as allegorically setting forth the opposite extreme, the danger of private monopolies of public utilities as exemplified in toll bridges.

" 2. History of the sixteenth century reveals that private monopolies in England were numerous and oppressive. Elizabeth, building on the practices of her predecessors, lavished patents of monopoly upon her favorites, many of whom passed their monopolies on to their friends. This practice became so obnoxious that the people finally arose in protest, demanded reform, and secured corrective measures.

" 3. Internal monopolies of England gave excellent opportunity for extortion, bribery, and graft in the control of roads, ferries, dam sites, fishing preserves, and bridges. Laws were made to reform the abuses of justice. The same condition existed in Ireland while Spenser was in an official position, and the Irish people demanded the reform of abuses and the end of extortion under which they suffered. It may have been these politicians of Ireland of whom Spenser wrote that they through ' power ' did unjust acts against the ' feeble ' " [5. 2. 5. 7-8 quoted].

" From the specific monopoly of toll bridges Spenser may have symbolized the general evil of monopolies and patents that choked the commonwealth. The trap door might possibly set forth the methods of bribery and fraud that allowed the unskilled and unwary to be trapped by fierce Pollente. It is worthy of note that Talus, presumably representing the Law, takes no actual part in endeavoring to overcome the taker of toll. Could this not be due to the fact that the patents protected individuals legally in their nefarious business? Talus, the Law, does take an active part, however, against Lady Munera, the keeper of the gold hoard, who endeavors to bribe justice.

" If this view of the episode is correct, it is important to point out that Spenser is bold in his presentation of the monopolistic evil and its necessary reform. He was in advance of the main body of reform legislation, for as late as 1571 a member of the House of Commons had been severely reprimanded by the Council for venturing to complain against licenses and monopolies. Spenser's book, appearing in 1596, presented the need for justice in the economic system, and the reform measures necessary at a time when leaders were strongly remonstrating against patents of privilege. Such a historical view of this canto reveals Spenser's attitude toward social justice when the nobility were thriving on unjust grants from the English sovereign."

LOTSPEICH (pp. 63-4). Pollente may have some affinity with the classical giant Pallans, whom Natalis Comes mentions, 6. 21.

[See Appendix, pp. 302, 313, 345-7.]

vi. 6. UPTON. "A groom of evil guize"; hence called Guizor, one of Dolon's sons, see below, canto 6, stanza 33. Spenser perpetually alludes to the names of the persons whom he introduces.

GOUGH (pp. 175-6). It is needless to identify Pollente with any historical personage. But in his "groome of evill guize," called Guizor in Canto 6, where he is one of three brothers "like treacherous, like full of fraud and guile," there can be little doubt that Henry, the third Duke of Guise, is alluded to [see GOUGH's notes on 6. 32 ff.; 33. 6]. Possibly the words "Whose scalp is bare" and "with scull all raw" (11. 5) refer to the scar on the duke's face, which gave him, like his father, the nickname of "le Balafré." The line, "Which pols and pils the poore in piteous wise," perhaps refers to his ruthless persecution of the Huguenots. But Guizor's resemblance to this prince is not close enough to prevent him from appearing as a low-born "villaine," a touch which simply adds to the baseness of the type depicted.

7. UPTON. The Germans and Franks, with most of the northern nations, thought wearing the hair long a sign of freedom: the contrary bewrayed bondage. This explains Claudian's epithet, de Laud. Stiliconis 1 [. 203]: " Crinigero flaventes vertice reges." And hence will appear the meaning of Ovid, Fasti 1. 645-6:

passos Germania crines
Porrigit auspiciis, dux venerande, tuis.

8. TODD. So, in a letter from Sir Dudley Carleton to Sir Ralph Winwood, dated March 10, 1604: " Pilling and polling is grown out of request, and plaine pillfering come into Fashion," Winwood's Memor. 2. 52. The words " pill " and " poll " appear to have been synonymous. See Barrett's Dict. 1580, in v. " To pill or poll, to take by extortion." In the Statutes and Ordenaunces of War, Emprynted by R. Pynson, 1513, sig. C_{iii}, it is enacted, " that no man be so hardy to go into no chambre or logynge where that any woman lyeth in childbedde her to robbe ne pyll of no goodes. . . ."

EDITOR. According to the NED the literal meaning of the phrase is " to make bare of hair and skin too," but it usually means " to ruin by depredation or extortions; to rifle, strip bare, pillage; . . . rarely to plunder or rob of something." Spenser's use of the phrase is not cited. That Spenser was conscious of the literal meaning seems to be indicated by the reference in line 7 of this stanza and line 5 of stanza 11 to the bare skull of the groome.

vii ff.   C. W. LEMMI (*PQ* 8. 282-3) thinks that Pollente, Lady Munera, and Dolon symbolize three aspects of "corrupting power of money" and that Pollente and Dolon were suggested by the accounts of Plutus in Natalis Comes (2. 10). He cites also Natalis Comes 2. 9 and 7. 1. [See note on 6. 32. 1 below.]

1.   GOUGH.   "Pollente."   Ital. "powerful."   [But also with obvious inclusion of "poll" (6. 8).]

ix-x.   GOUGH.   It was suggested by T. D. Whitaker, in his edition of *Piers Plowman*, that the Lady Meed of that poem (B. Pass. 2-4) was the original of Lady Munera. Skeat (*Piers the Plowman* 2. 31) refers also to "mayden Meed" in Skelton's *Ware the Hauke* 149, and to a passage resembling Langland's description, printed in *Reliquiae Antiquae* 2. 19.

C. R. OWST (*Literature and Pulpit in Medieval England*, p. 97) points out that Spenser's Lady Munera is a survival of the medieval legend of the "Daughter of the Devil." (See Barthelemy Haureau's article in the *Journal des Savants*, vol. for 1884, pp. 225-8.) Mr. Owst notes other literary uses of the legend in Lady Mede of *Piers Plowman* and in Gower's *Mirrour de l'omme*, or *Speculum Meditantis*.

See Appendix to Book I, "On the Propriety of the Allegory," p. 365.

xi-xix.   DODGE (*PMLA* 12. 203) cites the fight between Rodomonte and Brandimarte in *Orl. Fur.* 31. 67 ff.

xii.   EDITOR.   Artegall's fight may be compared with Britomart's on the same bridge, below 6. 36-40. The bridge reappears in Addison's *Vision of Mirzah.*

xiii-xviii.   See Appendix, pp. 275, 313, 314.

xvi. 6-9.   UPTON.   Swimming was always esteemed the necessary qualification of a soldier. Hence Horace by way of reproach says, *Odes* 1. 8: "Cur timet flavum Tiberim tangere?" And by way of praise [3. 7]:

> Nec quisquam citus aeque
> Tusco denatat alveo.

[Swimming is not listed among the courtier's physical accomplishments in *Mother Hubberds Tale* 717-752.]

xviii.   A. H. GILBERT (*PMLA* 34. 231).   Cf. *Orl. Fur.* 46. 140.

5-9.   See 1. 2. 19. 5-9; 2. 8. 45. 6-9; 3. 5. 22. 1-4 and note on 22. 1-2, in Book III, p. 245; 4. 8. 45. 4-9 and note on 45. 6, in Book IV, pp. 212-3; 5. 10. 33. 4-6; 35. 6-9; 5. 11. 14. 6-9; 5. 12. 23. 7-9 and note on 23. 7.

xix.   M. M. GRAY (*RES* 6. 416-8).   In the Fifth Book of the *Faerie Queene*, Sir Artegal, in the moral allegory representing justice, in the political representing Lord Grey, Spenser's chief, has for one of his tasks to undertake adventures which represent the restoration of justice in Ireland. [See Appendix, pp. 325-6.]   Here Spenser's use of Irish material in a very transparent allegory has been easily recognised; but the absolute fidelity to the facts of Irish warfare has not perhaps been sufficiently emphasised, nor has it been noted how the unscrupulous ferocity of both sides in the Irish wars has left its mark on this part of the poem.   Here we have no magnanimous enemies, no "very parfit gentle" knights. Thus in canto 2 Sir Artegal conquers Pollente, a tyrant and robber who preys on all who come in contact with him.   And here is Sir Artegal's triumph, the triumph not of a knight of chivalry, but of a harassed and exasperated enemy [st. quoted].

There is not much allegory or romance in this passage with its curiously definite reference to the River Lee [but see following note]; it is almost what happened to Sir John of Desmond in 1581. The continuator of Holinshed's *Chronicle* (6. 446), Hooker, says, " Sir John's head was sent to Dublin, but his body was hanged up by the heels upon a gibbet and set upon the North Gate of Cork"; " over the River Lee on the North Gate of Cork where it hung for three years," says another account, and the *Dictionary of National Biography* quotes still another which includes the lesson to rebels " hanged up for 3 or 4 years together as a spectacle for all beholders to look on, until at length a great storm of wynd blew it off, but the head was sent to Dublin and then fastened to a pole and set over the city wall." (*DNB.* See also Holinshed, p. 412, *Fate of James FitzMorris*; p. 433, of *James of Desmond*; p. 454, of *Earl of Desmond*.)   And for the fighting in the river a despatch from Byngham to Lord Deputy Perrot in 1586 describes a success against the rebels:

They had no place to fly from us but the river, and as soon as they came hither, our shot beat them from their footing, and the force of the stream carried them to the sea down the river in plumpes. A number of their bodies lie dead upon the rocks in the shallow places of the river and many in the fields. (*Cal. State Papers*, Hamilton, p. 165, 1586. Byngham to Lord Deputy Perrot. See also *Cal. State Papers*, Introd., p. lxvi, " Siege of Carrigafoyle," 1580. Captain Zouche to Walsingham, " The house being entered they yielded and some sought to swim away, but there scaped not one, neither of man, woman or child.")

1.   M. M. GRAY (*RES* 6. 417 n.).   Some commentators gloss this word [" Lee "] here, and in the *Ruines of Time*, simply as river. The *NED* gives no support to this rendering, and an examination of the seven passages [*Proth.* 38, 115; *F. Q.* 4. 11. 29. 7, 44. 3; *Ruines of Time* 135, 603] in which Spenser uses the word shows that he refers certainly in two cases, and possibly in all, either to the English river Lee or the Irish river Lee, the present passage being the only one in which such a definite reference might cause surprise. The actual events which Spenser had in mind seem sufficiently to explain this curious intrusion of reality into the allegory. [See note on *Ruines of Time* 135.]

xxvii.   GOUGH (p. 176).   With the crafty ruffian Pollente is associated his daughter. Lady Munera, the traditional Lady Meed whom Langland had introduced into English literature, represents the allied but subtler and one might say more feminine forms of injustice which consist in taking and giving bribes and favours to pervert the right. Her punishment, which is more severe than that inflicted on any of the other evil women in the poem, reflects the stern temper of the Puritan officers of state, whom Spenser admired. Both Munera and her father stand for forces with which the administration of Grey had to contend in Ireland.

While the rebel leaders planned ambuscades such as that which caused disaster to an English force at Glenmalure in the Wicklow Mountains in the autumn of 1580, at times they endeavoured to seduce English officials from their duty. One of the agents employed for this purpose suffered a fate like that of Lady Munera. Sir William Pelham, lord-justice of Ireland, wrote to the Irish Council on January 26, 1580, that the rebel Earl of Desmond, having failed to lure out the garrison of Adare in Limerick by driving cattle under their walls, " sent a fair young harlot as a present to the constable, by whose means he hoped to get the house; but the constable, learning from whence she came, threw her (as is reported to me), with a stone about her neck, into the river " (R. Bagwell, *Ireland under the Tudors* 3. 36 [cf. *Cal. Carew MSS.*, 1575-1588, pp. 204-5]. Adare is about twenty-three miles from Kilcolman. Cf. also Froude, *Hist. Engl.* [ed. 1870] 10. 611 f.). Perhaps Spenser, who came to Munster in the same year with Grey, heard the story.

[But however specific in allusion or device, Spenser's powerful account of this terrible episode derives its poetic energy from his own passionate sense of justice outraged at all the peculation and venality of his parvenu times. This episode may well be compared with that of Book II, canto 7.—C. G. O.]

5. G. S. HILLARD (*The Poetical Works of Edmund Spenser* 3. 240). Sir James Mackintosh remarks upon this place (see his *Life* 2. 242): " The just execution of a beautiful woman, Munera, by Sir Artegal, was certainly intended to reconcile the mind to the execution (of Queen Mary) at Fotheringay."

6-9. JORTIN. Alluding to Deuteronomy 9. 21: " And I took your sin, the calf which ye had made, and burnt it with fire, and stamped it, and ground it very small, even until it was as small as dust: and I cast the dust thereof into the brook that descended out of the mount." [See also Exodus 32. 20.]

8. WARTON (2. 205). The proverb of getting any thing " by hooke or by crooke " is said to have arisen in the time of Charles I. when there were two learned judges, named Hooke and Crooke; and a difficult cause was to be gotten either by Hooke or by Crooke. But here is a proof that the proverb is much older than that time; and that the form was not then invented as a proverb, but applied as a pun. It occurs in Skelton, [*Col. Cloute* 1240. *NED* lists a much earlier use of the term about 1380 in Wyclif, *Works*, ed. 1880, p. 250; also frequent occurrences throughout the sixteenth century.]

TODD. It appears to have been employed as a proverb by B. Riche, in the second part of his *Simonides*, 1584, sig. N$_{ij}$, which I cite, because it is from a poem in blank verse of nearly 200 lines, and therefore presents a curious specimen of our early unfettered poetry:

Excesse is that whiche onely Athens spoyles,
In that the riche to honours are preferde;
Eche plies it now, by hooke and crooke to gain,
In hope by wealth to clime the steppes of state.

The proverb is also alluded to in Hawes's *Hist. of La Bel Pucell*, ed. 1554, sig. K$_{iii}$. See also Cotgrave's old French Dictionary in v. " Tort." " A tort ou à droict, by hooke or crooke, by right or wrong, by one meanes or another."

BLAKENEY. The phrase derives its origin from the custom of certain manors, where tenants were allowed to take fire-bote " by hook or by crook," that is, so much of the underwood as could be cut by a crook, and as much loose timber as could be pulled from the trees by a hook.

xxix ff.   G. L. CRAIK (*Spenser and His Poetry*, 2. 194-5).   If this had been published in the end of the eighteenth instead of in the end of the sixteenth century—in the year 1796 instead of in the year 1596—the allegory could not have been more perfect, taken as a poetical representation or reflection of recent events, and of a passage in the political and social history of the world generally held to be not more memorable than entirely novel and unexampled.   Here is the Liberty and Equality system of philosophy and government—the portentous birth of the French Revolution—described to the life two hundred years before the French Revolution broke out; described both in its magnificent but hollow show, and its sudden explosion or evaporation.   This is probably one of the instances in which we overrate the advance of modern speculation; the system in question was never indeed before attempted to be carried into practice on so large a scale, or so conspicuous a platform, as in the end of the last century in France; but its spirit, though not perhaps its distinct shape, had appeared before in many popular outbreaks, and as an idea it must long have been familiar to thinking men.   The principles not only of political philosophy but even of what is called political economy, generally assumed to be almost wholly a modern science, were the subject of much more attention, and were much more profoundly investigated, in Spenser's age than is commonly supposed.

Our attention has been directed by a correspondent to a close resemblance between part of Artegal's refutation of the giant's pretensions and the discourse of the angel Uriel in the Fourth Chapter of the Second Book of Esdras in exposure of the ignorance of that prophet.   Our correspondent remarks that the present passage may furnish a notion of what Spenser's lost version of the Book of Ecclesiastes may have been.   [See GOUGH's note on 42. 5. — 43 below.]

GOUGH (p. 177).   Spenser here deals with the question of distributive justice, discussed in the *Nicomachean Ethics* 5. 3 (attributed to Aristotle), where it is laid down that just distribution follows the rule of geometrical proportion, i. e. there must be the same ratio between the merits of the recipients as there is between the values of the things to be distributed.   The relative merit of the recipients will depend upon the political theory adopted, whether democracy, which gives all free men equal shares, oligarchy, which makes wealth the standard, or aristocracy, which is commonly based on the principle of birth, or in its ideal form, upon virtue.   The last, which is Aristotle's theory, is that accepted by Spenser, as by most of the leaders of the Renascence.   The " virtue " of a gentleman entitles him to privileges denied to the " vulgar," the " rascall crew," whom Spenser consistently treats with contempt.   To a mind which was at once conservative (" All change is perillous," 36. 7), aristocratic, and influenced by Calvinistic theology (" What ever thing is done, by him is donne, Ne any may his mighty will withstand," 42. 1-2), society is a divinely established hierarchy (st. 41), comparable with the order of the physical world (st. 36).

This conception was opposed by the gradually rising democratic idea, which in an earlier generation had taken hold of great masses of the servile class in Germany, leading to the Peasants' Rising in 1525 and the commonwealth of visionary Anabaptists at Münster in 1534. In England Robert Kett had established a communistic régime in East Anglia for a brief period in 1549. After his overthrow there was little open advocacy of advanced democratic principles in England, except for a few bold pamphleteers, such as Robert Crowley (d. 1588). The Anabaptist sect, which was associated with levelling tendencies, attracted attention in London in 1575, when two of its members were burnt at Smithfield.

xxx ff.   LOWELL (*Literary Essays* 4. 350).   Despite Spenser's instinctive tendency to idealize, and his habit of distilling out of the actual an ethereal essence in which very little of the possible seems left, yet his mind, as is generally true of great poets, was founded on a solid basis of good-sense. I do not know where to look for a more cogent and at the same time picturesque confutation of Socialism than in the Second Canto of the Fifth Book. If I apprehend rightly his words and images, there is not only subtle but profound thinking here. The French Revolution is prefigured in the well-meaning but too theoretic giant, and Rousseau's fallacies exposed two centuries in advance.

EDITOR (C. G. O.).   These scales of the Giant are in the line of a familiar tradition from Homer (*Il.* 8. 69-72; 22. 209-212) through Virgil (*Aen.* 12. 725-7) to Milton (*P. L.* 4. 990-1015) and Pope (*Rape of the Lock* 5. 71-4). But Spenser modifies the tradition; whereas in Homer and Virgil the losing side fell, in Spenser, Milton, and Pope it flew up. Milton must be thinking of Spenser too in his lines:

> Wherein all things created first he weighd,
> The pendulous round Earth with ballanc't Aire
> In counterpoise.

Cf. 30. 5-31. 4.   The figure is a great favorite with Spenser; see 1. 2. 38. 2; 1. 4. 27. 9; 1. 9. 45. 2; 2. 1. 3. 8; 4. 3. 37. 1; 4. 9. 1. 4; 5. 1. 7. 2; 5. 1. 11. 9.   Possibly the Giant's scales suggested themselves to Spenser as the perverted counterpart of Astraea's.

See Appendix, pp. 275, 294, 304, 336-345.

xxx.   CHURCH.   To this Circumstance Mr. Pope plainly alludes in those fine Lines, *Essay on Man* [1. 113-4, 121-2]:

> Go, wiser thou! and in thy scale of sense
> Weigh thy Opinion against Providence. . . .
> Snatch from his hand the ballance and the rod,
> Re-judge his Justice, be the God of God!

[Any more than to *P. L.* 4. 990 ff.?]

LOWELL (*Literary Essays* 4. 323).   Spenser's giants are those of the later romances, except that grand figure with the balances . . . the most original of all his conceptions, yet no real giant, but a pure eidolon of the mind.

A. A. JACK (*A Commentary on the Poetry of Chaucer and Spenser*, pp. 223-4).   One does not particularly know why it [this stanza] should live forever; it does so, like the ogre with two heads in one's first nursery book. There are inventions of the fancy so striking—The Scarlet Letter, Othello's Sword of Spain—that nothing can erase them from the memory of mankind.

9. WARTON (2. 154). This verse would be improved in its harmony by reading . . . " Yet was admired much of women, fooles, and boyes." But these corrections are made by the critic, upon a supposition that his author must have infallibly written what was best. [See UPTON's note on 3. 1. 14. 9. in Book III, p. 205.]

xxxi-xxxii. GOUGH. It would be as profitless to attempt to explain the exact nature of the giant's operations as it would be to inquire how the scene could be graphically represented. It may, however, be observed that he assumes that the original proportion between the four elements has been disturbed, and he proposes to restore it, after discovering the amount of the excess or deficiency of each.

EDITOR. Cf. Shakespeare's *Troilus and Cressida* 1. 3. 83-125.

xxxii ff. TODD. This fiction is an admirable picture of the absurdity of those levelling principles, which have lately made such a noise in the world. See *The Patriot*, a periodical Paper, published in Ireland in the year 1793, and written (it is supposed) by Baron Smith. See also Mitford's *History of Greece, passim*, and the notes to the second volume in particular. It is well known how the Athenians themselves prepared the way for the iron Man of Macedon by the wild fanaticism of Democracy. It is unnecessary here to enter into the analogical details of Modern Times.—Note supplied by BOYD.

xxxii. Cf. GOUGH's note on 42. 5—43 below.

xxxiii. 3. See UPTON's note on *F. Q.* 1. 1. 23 in Book I, pp. 187-8.

HEISE (p. 117) cites Chaucer's *Persons Tale* 441-2; see also note on 11. 58. 1-2 below.

xxxiv ff. H. S. V. JONES (*Spenser's Defense of Lord Grey*, p. 59) cites Bodin's idea of " harmonic discord."

EDITOR. On Spenser's predilection for the ideas in sts. 34-6 see Book IV, pp. 309-313.

xxxv. 1-4. UPTON. Wisdom 11. 20: " Thou hast ordered all things in measure and number and weight."

GOUGH. Cf. Isaiah 40. 12: " Who hath measured the waters in the hollow of his hand, and meted out heaven with the span, and comprehended the dust of the earth in a measure, and weighed the mountains in scales, and the hills in a balance? " Job 28. 23-5: " God . . . seeth under the whole heaven; to make the weight for the winds; and he weigheth the waters by measure." [See 43. 2 and note below.]

5. GOUGH. The great discovery of Copernicus, which overthrew the geocentric theory of Ptolemy, was published in 1543, fifty years before these lines were written, but only won acceptance very slowly. Bacon rejected it, and Milton, after more than a century, was in doubt [?].

EDITOR. Writers in England, however, supported the new Copernican system before 1596. The first reference in an English book to Copernicus is that in Robert Recorde's *Castle of Knowledge* (1556). John Dee and John Field both approved the new system in written statements at the beginning of Field's *Ephemeris Anni 1557. Currentis Iuxta Copernici et Reinhaldi Canones* (London, 1556), and Thomas Digges printed in 1576 the most important of the English endorsements of Copernicus, *A Perfit Description of the Coelestiall Orbes according to the most aunciente doctrine of the Pythagoreans, latelye reuiued by Copernicus and by Geometricall Demonstrations approued.* This treatise, attached to his father's *Prognostication euerlastinge,* was reprinted at least five times by 1596. See the reprint by Francis R. Johnson and Sanford V. Larkey in the *Huntington Library Bulletin,* no. 5 (April, 1934), pp. 69-117. Spenser would have had no difficulty in obtaining information about Copernicus from the leading mathematicians of his day.

7-9. GOUGH. According to a mediaeval theory the earth is surrounded by successive concentric spheres of water, air and fire. Around these "elemental spheres," and controlling their motions, move the "heavenly spheres" of the planets. See note on Proem 5. 2. Cf. Johannes de Sacro Bosco, *De Sphaera,* a textbook which was still popular in Spenser's time. [See A. H. Gilbert, "Milton's Textbook of Astronomy," *PMLA* 38. 297-307.]

xxxvi. 1-4. GOUGH. Cf. these four lines with the Proem, in which the movements of the heavenly bodies are connected with the idea of justice. The two passages appear to contradict one another with regard to the liability of the universe to change. But while in the Proem it is declared that the heavenly bodies have drifted from their original courses, thereby causing confusion and decay, in the present passage Artegall appears to assert that the elements have not varied in quantity since the creation, which is a different question. Also it must be remembered that in Artegall's time corruption was only beginning (1. 1 ff.).

W. L. RENWICK (*Spenser Selections,* p. 201). Cf. Boethius, *de Consolatione Philosophiae* 1. 5; 4. 6.

2. UPTON. So Manilius 1:

> Sed nihil in tota magis est mirabile mole,
> Quam ratio, et certis quod legibus omnia parent.

And in 4. [14]: " Certa stant omnia lege." [Bentley's ed. (1739) 1. 485-6 reads:

> Nec quicquam in tanta magis est mirabile mole,
> Quam ratio. . . .

A. E. Housman's ed. (1932) 1. 478-9 has the same reading as Bentley.]

7. GOUGH. Cf. Spenser's *Veue of the Present State of Ireland,* p. 649, Globe ed.: " For all Innovation is perilous."

xl. EDITOR (C. G. O.). Commentators have somehow overlooked the familiar Scriptural imagery of fading flower and grass which pervades this stanza; cf. Job 14. 2; Ps. 103. 14-6; Is. 40. 6-8; Jas. 1. 10, 11; 1 Pet. 1. 24; cf. also 3. 6. 37-8.

xli. GOUGH. This stanza, like the two that follow, is partly founded upon several Old Testament texts. See the song of Hannah, 1 Samuel 2, especially 6, 7:

"The Lord killeth, and maketh alive: he bringeth down to the grave, and bringeth up. The Lord maketh poor, and maketh rich: he bringeth low, and lifteth up." . . . Daniel 4. 35: "He doeth according to his will in the army of heaven, and among the inhabitants of the earth: and none can stay his hand, or say unto him, What doest thou?"

5-6. EDITOR (J. G. M.). Cf. Harleian MS 7368, *Sir Thomas More*, scene 6, lines 74-166 (in hand D, frequently identified as Shakespeare's), especially lines 109-125:

> *Moor.* . . . first tis a sinn
> which oft thappostle did forwarne vs of
> vrging obedienc to aucthoryty
> and twere no error yf I told you all
> you wer in armes gainst g[od].
>
> *All.* Marry god forbid that.
>
> *Moo.* Nay certainly you ar
> for to the king god hath his offyc lent
> of dread of iustyce, power and comaund
> hath bid him rule, and willd you to obay
> and to add ampler maiestie to this
> he hath not only lent the king his figure
> his throne and sword, but gyven him is owne name
> calls him a god on earth, what do you then
> rysing gainst him that god himsealf enstalls
> but ryse gainst god, what do you to your sowles
> in doing this o desperat as you are.

See Romans 13. 1-5; 1 Peter 2. 13-4; and Psalms 15. 11 (in the Prayer-Book version and in Parker's revision of the Bishops' Bible): "So shall the king have pleasure in thy beauty, for he is thy Lord God." Cited by R. W. Chambers, *Shakespeare's Hand in The Play of Sir Thomas More*, p. 153, note.

5. GRACE W. LANDRUM (*PMLA* 41. 541). Cf. Proverbs 8. 15-6; ["By me kings reign, and princes decree justice. By me princes rule, and nobles, even all the judges of the earth."]

7. TODD. Compare Psalm 75. [7]: "God is the judge: He putteth down one, and setteth up another." Indeed this and the next stanza are formed entirely from Holy Writ. See 1 Samuel 2. 6-8; Job 36. 7, etc.

EDITOR (C. G. O.). Luke 1. 52.

8. GRACE W. LANDRUM (*PMLA* 41. 541). Cf. Job 1. 21.

9. W. L. RENWICK (*Spenser Selections*, p. 201) cites Job 41. 11; 42. 2.

GRACE W. LANDRUM (*PMLA* 41. 541). Cf. Matthew 20. 15.

xlii. 1. GOUGH. Cf. Psalms 74. 13 (Coverdale [73B in ed. 1535]): "For God is my King of old: the help that is done upon earth he doeth it himself"; and 2 Chronicles 20. 6: "In thine hand is there not power and might, so that none is able to withstand thee?"

xlii. 5—xliii. GOUGH. What follows is apparently suggested by 2 Esdras 4, where the prophet is rebuked by the angel Uriel. Cf. verse 2: "Thinkest thou to comprehend the way of the Most High?" 5: "Weigh me the weight of the fire, or measure me the blast of the wind, or call me again the day that is past." 10-11: "Thine own things, and such as are grown up with thee, canst thou not know; how should thy vessel then be able to comprehend the way of the Highest?"

The parable that follows, verses 13-21, recalls stanza 32. Uriel says that the trees of a wood said, "Come, let us go and make war against the sea, that it may depart away before us, and that we may make [us] more woods. The floods of the sea also . . . said, Come, let us go up and subdue the woods of the plain, that there also we may make [us] another country. The thought of the wood was in vain, for the fire came and consumed it. The thought of the floods of the sea came likewise to nought, for the sand stood up and stopped them." [See CRAIK's note on sts. 29 ff. above.]

xlii. 5-9. GRACE W. LANDRUM (*PMLA* 41. 541). Cf. Romans 11. 33.

xliii.   W. J. COURTHOPE (*A History of English Poetry*, 2. 281). Occasionally he breaks up his stanza in dialogue like the "stichomythia" of the Greek drama [cf. *F. Q.* 1. 2. 43; 1. 7. 41]; not always with a happy effect. But his power of adapting his metre to the purposes of dialectic may be judged from [this] stanza.

2. GOUGH. Cf. Job 28. 25: "to make the weight for the winds."

xliv. 9. UPTON. Very prettily expressed, and literally from Homer [*Il.* 1. 201 *et passim*, *Od.* 1. 122 *et passim*]. *Orl. Inn.* 2. 12. 3:

> Omero, il quale è 'l re degli scrittori,
> Dice, che le parole han tutte l'ale,
> E però quando alcuna uscita è fuori,
> Per trarla indietro il fil tirar non vale.

Horace: "Sed fugit emissum, fugit irrevocabile verbum." [*Epist.* 1. 18. 71 reads "et semel emissum volat inrevocabile verbum." Upton is evidently misquoting from memory.]

xlvii. 5. GOUGH. The thought is obscurely expressed, but perhaps the meaning is that the balances afford a purely objective test of right and wrong. If the giant is angry with the facts, the fault lies with him, not with them. His anger shows that the moral standard in his mind is false.

xlviii-xlix. GOUGH. This stanza and the following allude somewhat obscurely to the Aristotelian theory of virtue as a mean between two extremes, which are contrary vices. See *Nicom. Ethics* 2. 6-9. It follows from this theory that right and wrong (a virtue and a vice) are incommensurable. The same is the case with truth and falsehood. There are no degrees of truth ("truth is one," 48. 6), but there are infinite degrees of falsehood on both sides of truth. The problem is therefore to weigh one falsehood or one wrong against another, e. g. cowardice against foolhardiness. Courage sits "in the middest of the beame alone." [But Aristotle does not use the image of the scales.]

The giant proves himself vicious by disliking the mean. If we think of him as one of the demagogues whom Spenser had in mind, he eschewed liberty, let us say, and set up the two extremes against one another, viz. excessive deference to authority, and licence, exaggerating the viciousness of the former, and extenuating that of the other. He maintains the fallacy that the opposite of a vice must be a virtue.

xlviii. 9. GOUGH. "sate in the middest." This phrase, and "thrust away" in the next line, suggest that right and wrong are conceived as persons. It is in any case difficult to visualize the scene. Spenser has almost forgotten the symbols for the things signified.

xlix. 8—l. EDITOR (C. G. O.). May this picture not owe its vividness to Spenser's recollection of the massacre which possibly he saw at Smerwick, years before, when the bodies of the slaughtered garrison fell or were pushed down the cliffs that supported the fortress to the beach and sea fifty or more feet below?

l. EDITOR. This stanza contains one of Spenser's famous ship similes. Cf. *F. Q.* 1. 6. 1; 2. 1. 2. 9; 2. 2. 24; 6. 4. 1; 6. 12. 1; *Sh. Cal.* Feb. 32; *Teares of the Muses* 139-144; *Amoretti* 34, 56, 59.

li. 6. TODD. From the innovations of modern philosophers, great good and wondrous riches have, in like manner, been expected by the "lawlesse multitude"; but they, who listened with delight to the great-swelling words of these profound reformers, have received no other compensation for their contempt of established usages and the collective wisdom of past times than the privilege (perhaps) of expressing their "certain loss of so great expectation!"

EDITOR. One must realize too that one of the "innovations of modern philosophers" was the modern democratic ideal in government. Spenser may have had in mind particularly the Anabaptist sect, but he was as much concerned as his aristocratic superiors over the general restlessness of the times and growth of democratic ideals. See GOUGH'S note on sts. 29 ff. above and the Appendix, pp. 336-345.

liii. 6. See note on 11. 58. 1-2 below.

liv. DODGE (*PMLA* 12. 203). Cf. *Orl. Fur.* 25. 12.

1-5. HEISE (pp. 111-2) cites *Il.* 17. 755 ff.; 15. 69 ff.; 16. 582 ff.; 17. 46; *Orl. Inn.* 2. 17, 19; *Orl. Fur.* 15. 12; *Met.* 11. 771 ff.; *Inferno* 22. 128. See note on 5. 15 below.

UPTON. Observe here that elegant and Virgilian mixture of tenses. [Cf. Upton's note on 1. 3. 41. 9 in Book I, p. 211.] This simile Dryden has borrowed, and made his own by most excellent versification, *Theod. and Honoria* 315-8:

> So spread upon a lake with upward eye
> A plump of fowl behold their foe on high,
> They close their trembling troop, and all attend
> On whom the sousing eagle will descend.

8. See note on 2. 9. 15. 4 in Book II, p. 285.

CANTO III

i.   1-4.   HEISE (p. 137) cites Tasso's *Rin.* 4. 50.

9.   BLAKENEY.   The last line of this stanza is managed with less than Spenser's accustomed ease and smoothness.

ii ff.   GOUGH (p. 192).   In *F. Q.* 4. 4—5. 27 Spenser has already described a tournament held by Sir Satyrane which resembles the present one in several particulars.   Like Marinell, Cambello is surrounded in the mêlée by a hundred knights, and while he is being led away prisoner is rescued by Triamond, as Marinell by Artegall.   Such impossible feats belong to the romantic tradition.   At both tournaments Braggadochio plays an unknightly part (4. 4. 20), and at both the false Florimell dazzles the beholders by her counterfeit beauty, but is confounded, in the one case by the magic girdle, in the other by the presence of the true Florimell.   In the present case the description is terser, and devoid of the slightly humorous touches which abound in the story in the fourth book.

I. L. SCHULZE (*ELH*, 5. 278-9).   Cf. *F. Q.* 4. 2. 26-7; 4. 4. 5. 6-9.   The occasions of both tournaments are similar to those of jousts in Elizabethan England.   Sir William Segar, an authority on matters of chivalry, writes " Triumphs [in which tilting nearly always played a part] have been commonly used at the Inauguration and Coronation of Emperors, Kings and Princes; at their Marriages, Entry of cities, Enterviews, Progresses and Funerals." (*Honor, Military and Civill*, London, 1602, 3. 138.   Segar, admitted to the College of Arms early in his career, became Garter king-of-arms, January, 1606/7.   The work cited was dedicated to Queen Elizabeth.   See *DNB.*, *sub* Segar.)   Although there is no record of a tournament in Spenser's day for which the prize was a lady's girdle, in the joust celebrating Elizabeth's coronation in January, 1559, the prize was a diamond, " as they jousted for love." (*CSP. Venetian* 7. 18-9.   Albert Way, " Illustrations of Medieval Manners and Costume from Original Documents," *Archaeological Journal*, London, 1847, 4. 231-3, quotes from a 15th century manuscript volume ordinances for a tournament for three prizes of jewels.)   Furthermore, since Florimell's girdle is a symbol of chastity, the first tournament is closely related to the jousts held annually on November 17, to honor Elizabeth's accession to the throne.   As for the second tournament, during Elizabeth's reign tilts were used to celebrate noble, as well as royal, marriages.   When the son of vice-chamberlain Knollys married the daughter of Ambrose Cave, July 16, 1565, jousting followed the wedding supper (*CSP. Spanish* 1. 446, 451-2).   In the same year on November 11, the Earl of Warwick was married to Ann, daughter of the Earl of Bedford, at the royal palace of Westminster.   Tilting formed part of the lavish festivities (John Leland, *Collectanea*, London, 1770, 2. 666 ff.).   The occasions, then, of both tournaments in the poem are exactly paralleled by those of tilts in Spenser's own day.

ii.   1.   See notes on *F. Q.* 3. 8. 30 ff. in Book III, pp. 269-270.

2.   See note on 2. 1. 9 above.

5-9. UPTON. Compare this with the *Orl. Inn.* 2. 20. 60 and *Orl. Fur.*
17. 82. Tilts and tournaments are of the very essence of Romance writings; and
poets who copy from them abound in these kind of descriptions.

GOUGH. Tournaments at wedding festivities were customary in the
age of chivalry (cf. Malory, *Morte Darthur* 7. 35), and were still held in Elizabeth's
reign.

8. TODD (note on *L'Allegro* 121, *Poetical Works of Milton*, 1809, 6. 99)
cites this line beside Milton's "With store of ladies." It would seem as if *L'Al.*
119-124 were not unmindful of this whole description in Spenser. WARTON
(*ibid.*) cites Sidney's *Astrophel and Stella* 106: "But here I doe store of faire
ladies meete." TODD adds Groves's *Songes and Sonnettes*, 1587, and Eluiden's
History of Pesistratus and Catanea.

iii.   WARTON (1. 143-4). After this indirect, but comprehensive manner, Chaucer expresses the pomp of Cambuscan's feast (*Squire's Tale* 83) [cf.
Skeat's ed. 63-72]:

> Of which shall I tell all the array,
> Then would it occupie a sommer's day;
> And eke it needeth not to devise
> At every course the order of service.
> I wol not tellen as now, of her strange sewes,
> Ne of her swans, ne of her heronsewes.
> Eke in that land, as tellen knights old,
> There is some meat that is fully dainty hold,
> That in this lond men retch of it but small:
> There is no man that may reporten all.

Thus also, when lady Custance is married to the Sowdan of Surrie, or Syria
(*The Man of Lawe's Tale* 703-5):

> What shuld I tellen of the rialte
> Of that wedding? or which course goth beforn?
> Who blowith in a trompe, or in a horne?

In these passages it is very evident, that Chaucer intended a burlesque upon the
tedious and elaborate descriptions of such unimportant circumstances, so frequent
in books of chivalry. In the last verse the burlesque is very strong.

It should seem that in some of the old romances, the names of trumpeters in
the lists were sometimes mentioned. Chaucer places in the *House of Fame* 3. 157-9:

> All that usid clarion
> In Casteloigne and Arragon,
> That in their timis famous were.

1-6. WARTON (*History of English Poetry*, 2nd ed., 1. 332-3). They
[heralds] not only committed to writing the process of the list, but it was also
their business, at magnificent feasts, to describe the number and parade of the
dishes, the quality of the guests, the brilliant dresses of the ladies, the courtesy of
the knights, the revels, disguisings, banquets, and every other occurrence most
observable in the course of the solemnity. Spenser alludes expressly to these heraldic
details, where he mentions the splendor of Florimel's wedding.

1-2. Warton (2. 249). At Florimel's wedding. By devisefull sights, Spenser means, sights full of devices, that is, masques, triumphs, and other spectacles, usually exhibited in his time, with great cost and splendor, at the nuptials of noble personages. Hence Milton, in *L'Allegro* [128], selects that species of "masque and antique pageantry," which was celebrated at weddings. On these occasions there was constantly an epithalamium; which is the reason that the author of the *Arte of English Poesie*, separately considers the epithalamium as a species of poetry, and accordingly delivers rules for its composition.

iv. 1-5. I. L. Schulze (*ELH*, 5. 282-4) cites 4. 4. 39 and the close of Bacon's essay no. 37, "Of Masques and Triumphs," to show how common was the fashion of "devices" in Elizabethan tournaments. In 1571 several courtiers appeared as a Red, a White, a Green, and a Black Knight, a Desolate Knight, the Unknown Knight, and even Adam and Eve (*Hist. MSS Com.*, Part 4, *Rutland MSS* 92). He cites also a long account of devices in Nichols's *Progresses* 2. 312-329, and quotes from an account of the Accession Day tournament in 1585, in *Queen Elizabeth and Some Foreigners*, ed. V. von Klarwill, p. 331:

Every knight taking part in the tournament had dressed himself and his attendants in particular colours. . . . Some of the knights had bedizened themselves and their train like savages; some like the natives of Ireland with their hair streaming like a woman's down to their girdles. Some had crescent moons upon their heads; some came into the lists with their horses caparisoned like elephants; some came driving, their carriages drawn by people most oddly attired. Some of the carriages seemed to be drawn along without traction. All these carriages were oddly and peculiarly fitted up, but all the knights had their horses with them, and being ready accoutred for the fight mounted their steeds. Some of them however were dressed like horsemen and bravely decked out.

In 1592 Sir Robert Carey represented the Forsaken Knight (Sir Robert Carey, *Memoirs*, Dublin, 1759, p. 54) ; in 1599 Lord Compton appeared as a fisherman, caparisoned in fish-netting, with six men (*Sidney State Papers*, ed. Arthur Collins, London, 1746, 2. 142). As the author remarks, some of these devices "out-Spenser Spenser completely."

1-2. See Jortin's note on *F. Q.* 2. 2. 39. 3 in Book II, p. 202. Cf. also *F. Q.* 1. 12. 15. 1; 3. 1. 52. 2; 3. 9. 32. 1. Gough notes the use of this Homeric formula (*Il.* 1. 469, etc.) by Tasso, *Ger. Lib.* 11. 17, and by Milton, *P. L.* 5. 451.

iv. 6–vi. 3. I. L. Schulze (*ELH*, 5. 281-2). Cf. *F. Q.* 4. 4. 14. 9. Though Spenser does not deal elaborately with these processions of knights, his courtly reader must have been reminded at once of the glittering parade of Elizabethan knights and their attendants, as, on many occasions, they filed into the field in a grand display of flashing armor, rich plumes, and gaily trapped horses. The entrance of the contestants into the lists at Whitehall, in 1559, is described as follows (Nichols, *Progresses* 1. 80; also *The Diary of Henry Machyn*, ed. J. G. Nichols for the Camden Society, London, 1847-8, pp. 42, 217):

November 5, were great justs at the Queen's Palace; the Lord Robert [Dudley] and the Lord Hunsdon were the challengers, who wore scarfs of white and black; and they had their Heralds and trumpets attending on them: the defendants were the Lord Ambrose Dudley and others; they and their footmen in scarfs of red and yellow sarcenet; and had also their Heralds and Trumpeters.

Much more picturesque, but too long for quotation, is the account of the entrance of The Four Foster Children of Desire in the great tournament for the French ambassadors (Nichols, *Progresses* 2. 312 ff.). A diagram has been preserved showing the actual places of challengers and defendants in a tilt of 1601 (*Salisbury MSS at Hatfield House* 11. 540). Such formal entries were part of the pageantry of every Elizabethan tournament, and Spenser must have had them in mind in the passages I have cited.

iv. 8-9. GOUGH. The custom of maintaining the claim of a lady to superlative virtue or beauty by force of arms against all challengers appears to have originated in the form of ordeal known as trial by battle. According to the childish logic of the Dark Ages the question of fact was thus put to the proof by an appeal to Heaven.

EDITOR. Essex challenged George Villars, Governor of Rouen, to single combat on November 9, 1591, in the following language: " Si vous voulez combattre vous même à cheval ou à pied, je maintendra que le querelle du Roi est plus juste que celle de la Ligue, et que ma Maîtresse est plus belle que la votre." (Quoted by Devereux, *Lives of the Devereux, Earls of Essex* 1. 273, from *Mèm. de Sully* 1. 312.) Cf. Shakespeare's *Troilus and Cressida* 1. 265-283.

I. L. SCHULZE (*ELH*, 5. 280-1). Cf. *F. Q.* 4. 2. 26. 7—27. 4; 4. 4. 5. 7-9; 5. 2. 2. 5-9. Such formal proclamations or challenges were a commonplace of the jousts in Elizabethan England. For three weeks preceding the marriage of the Earl of Warwick to the Lady Ann, referred to above [note on 3. 2 ff.], the following challenge was set at the court gate of Westminster (*Three Fifteenth-Century Chronicles with Historical Memoranda by John Stowe*, ed. James Gairdner for the Camden Society, London, 1880, n. s. 28. 134) :

> Yow that in warlike ways and dedes of arms delight,
> Yow that for countryes cawse or ells for ladyes love dare fyght,
> Know yow foure knyghts ther be that come from foren land,
> Whos hawtye herts and corage great hath movd to take in hand,
> With sword, with speare and shield, on fote, on horse backe, to,
> To try what yow by force of fyght, or otharwyse, can do.
> Prepare yowr selves ther for this challenge to defend,
> That trompe of fame yowr prowes great abrod may sownd and send.
> And he that best can do, ye same shall have the price.
> Ye day, ye place, and forme and fyght, loo here before yowr eys.

The Accession Day tournaments were proclaimed from year to year with regularity. (See " The Originall Occasions of the Yeerely Triumphs in England," quoted by Dyce, ed., *Works of Greene and Peele*, London, 1861, p. 566; also John Nichols, *Progresses of Queen Elizabeth*, London, 1823, 3. 69-70.) When the French commissioners came to England in April, 1581, hoping to conclude negotiations for the marriage of Elizabeth and Alençon, Sidney and his friends planned to entertain them with a tournament representing an attack on the Fortress of Beauty, the Queen herself representing Beauty. The challenge, presented to Elizabeth as she came from church on April 16, the day before the French ambassadors arrived in England, called on her to surrender or to find knights to protect her against Sidney and his companions, who styled themselves The Four Foster Children of Desire (for a complete account of this famous tilt, see Nichols, *Progresses* 2. 312-329). On

November 17, 1592, the Earl of Essex and Sir Henry Lee " issued a challenge to maintain against all comers on the following 26 Feb. ' that ther M. [the Queen] is most worthyest and most fayrest Amadis de Gaule ' " (E. K. Chambers, *The Elizabethan Stage* 3. 268). The foregoing examples clearly show that the proclamations in the poem are reflections of challenges employed regularly in announcing tournaments at the court of Queen Elizabeth.

v.   GOUGH.   The names in this stanza, like many in the *F. Q.*, were probably chosen or invented by Spenser for the sake of the sound rather than for any significance. Names in " Bell- " (fair) are commonly applied to women in the Romances. " Brunell " (little brown man) occurs in its Italian form Brunello as the name of a dwarf in *Orlando Innamorato* and *Orlando Furioso*. Armeddan is a name of Breton type. The Romances occasionally speak of lays as of Briton or Breton origin.

EDITOR (C. G. O.).   Spenser so loved both an etymology and a veiled compliment that one glances twice at his proper names. Orimont, e. g., may be Monmouth.

6. UPTON.   Perhaps Sir Castor; for so he is named in the History of Prince Arthur [12. 4]. These knights were intended perhaps to be shown more fully by our poet in some of his subsequent books.

8. EDITOR (C. G. O.).   " Lansack." A fair Celtic imitation, if not authentic. Cf. Lamerake, Percival's brother, *Morte Darthur* 1. 22; Lamorak de Galis, 7. 13, and *passim*, mentioned at 6. 12. 39. 7.

vi-viii.   So in 4. 4 the tournament was a three-day affair.

vi. 1-2. GOUGH.   Proclamations of great tournaments were sometimes made in many countries, the contests being open to all comers. In the later ages of chivalry, knights would often travel to distant countries in search of the honours they hoped to gain at tournaments. See F. W. Cornish, *Chivalry* (1901), pp. 274-5.

ix.   1. EDITOR (C. G. O.).   A favorite use of a favorite thought. See 1. 1. 44. 7-9; 4. 4. 43. 9, and BLANCHARD's note on 4. 4. 43, Book IV, pp. 191-2.

7. UPTON.   In this tournament though they used cutting swords, yet there was no killing; and the sign of being conquered was being taken captive. So in Chaucer's description of the royal lists and tournament, wherein Palemon and Arcite brought each their hundred knights, the compact was there should be no stabbing, *Knight's Tale* 2553 [cf. Skeat's ed. 2551-2]:

> And he that is at mischief, shall be take,
> And not be slayn, but be brought in to a stake.

And presently after Palemon is taken captive as Marinell [cf. Skeat's ed. 2641-2]:

> And by the force of twenty is he take
> Unyoldin, and ydrawin to the stake.

[Cf. 4. 4. 32. 8-9 and UPTON's note in Book IV, p. 191.]

x-xv.   DODGE (*PMLA* 12. 203).   Cf. *Orl. Fur.* 17. 86-113.

x.   4.   GOUGH.   In *F. Q.* 3. 8, a witch, whose son had wooed Florimell in vain, comforts him by making a counterfeit image of snow and other substances, dresses it in Florimell's garments, and causes an evil spirit to inhabit it. All who are devoid of true insight mistake the false Florimell for the true, "so blind is lust, false colours to descry" (4. 2. 11. 5). Possibly the story was suggested by that version of the tale of Troy followed by Euripides in his *Helena*, according to which it was not the true Helen who was carried off by Paris, and fought for by Greeks and Trojans, but a mere phantom or double of her, made of clouds and sunbeams. [See note on st. 24 below.]

The false Florimell was forcibly taken from the witch's son by Braggadochio, who soon after showed his cowardice by yielding her to Sir Ferraugh (3. 8. 11-19). At Sir Satyrane's tournament she was allowed to return to Braggadochio (4. 5. 25-6).

9.   GOUGH.   Similar incidents are frequent in the Romances.   Cf. Malory, *Morte Darthur* 2. 17; 6. 11; 18. 9. Spenser uses the motive in *F. Q.* 4. 4, where Triamond and Cambello fight in each other's armour.

xiv-xv.   See Appendix, p. 302.

xiv. 8-9. UPTON.   By blazing in heraldry is meant the displaying a coat of arms in its proper colours and metals; and 'tis a fault in blazoning to lay colour upon colour, or metal upon metal. Our poet therefore, if governed by heralds, should have rather written, "Which bore the sunne brode blazed in an azure field." So the arms of Serpentino are blazoned at the tournaments of Charles the Great, *Orl. Inn.* 1. 2. [35]:

> Per insegna portava il Cavaliero
> Nel scudo azzurro una gran stella d'oro.

Whether the poet on purpose falsely blazoned his shield, as he was a false and recreant knight, I leave to the reader's consideration.

xv.   4.   UPTON.   Compare Ariosto 17. 113.

5.   EDITOR.   Cf. Aristotle, *Ethics* 3. 8. 10: "Most foolhardy people are cowards at heart; for although they exhibit a foolhardy spirit where they safely can, they refuse to face real terrors."

xvii ff.   GOUGH (pp. 193-4).   The false Florimell may be compared with the figure made of liquid air by Archimago and inhabited by an evil spirit (1. 1. 45), or again with Duessa, who exhibits a fair form which proves but the mask of foul deformity: false religion which counterfeits the true, personified in Una (*F. Q.* 1). It seems probable that, like Duessa (*F. Q.* 5. 9), the false Florimell is meant to suggest Mary Queen of Scots. "Mary seems at one time the false Florimel, the creature of enchantment, stirring up strife, and fought for by the foolish knights whom she deceives, Blandamour and Paridell (*F. Q.* 4. 4. 5), the counterparts of Norfolk and the intriguers of 1571." [R. W. Church, *Spenser,* p. 128. Cf. GREENLAW in the Appendix, p. 304.]

Be this as it may, the broad spiritual significance of the story is clear. It resembles a Platonic myth. The true Florimell is ideal beauty or goodness, which is not apprehended by the multitude engrossed by base passions. The counterfeit is not to be interpreted as the beauty of the world of sense, which to Plato, and to Spenser after him, leads the soul up to the ideal; but she is yet further removed from reality: she is a mere phantom tenanted by an unclean spirit. Plato teaches in the *Republic* (586) that the multitude who are enslaved by their bodily appetites, and make the satisfaction of them, unreal as they are, the main purpose of their lives, " must fight about these things, as Stesichorus says those at Troy fought about the phantom of Helen, through ignorance of the true one" (cf. note to st. 10. 4 above).

See CHARLES G. SMITH in Appendix 1 of Book IV, pp. 306-7. In his *Spenser's Theory of Friendship*, pp. 55-7, he finds the most apposite expression of the Neo-Platonic doctrine embodied in the two Florimells to be that of Castiglione in *The Courtier*. Among the various passages which he cites from the fourth book of *The Courtier* may be quoted the following:

The beautie that we meane, which is onely it, that appeareth in bodies, and especially in the face of man, and moveth this fervent coveting which we call Love, we will terme it an influence of the heavenly bountifulnesse (Everyman ed., p. 304).

Good and beautifull be after a sorte one selfe thing, especially in the bodies of men: of the beautie whereof the nighest cause (I suppose) is the beautie of the soule: the which as a partner of the right and heavenly beauty, maketh sightly and beautiful what ever she toucheth, (p. 310) . . .

It chanceth also oftentimes, that as to other senses, so the sight is deceived, and judgeth a face beautifull, which in deed is not beautifull. And because in the eyes, and in the whole countenance of some women, a man beholdeth otherwhile a certaine lavish wantonnesse painted with dishonest flickeringes, many whom that manner delighteth, because it promiseth them an easinesse to come by the thing that they covet, call it beautie: but in deede it is a cloked unshamefastnesse unworthie of so honourable and holy name (pp. 311-2).

xvii. 8.   GOUGH.   It is said of the false Florimell in *F. Q.* 3. 8. 5. [4-6]:

> That even Nature selfe envide the same,
> And grudg'd to see the counterfet should shame
> The thing it selfe.

xviii. 1-7.   EDITOR.   See 4. 2. 17. 1-2 and note in Book IV, p. 175.

xix.   UPTON.   This simile is very just.   The mock-Florimell is the mock-sun, or meteor, called by the Greeks παρήλιος.

1-7.   E. KOEPPEL (*Anglia* 11. 358).   Cf. *Rin.* 12. 75:

> Nè stella che risplenda a mezzo giorno . . .
> Nè Ciel ch' appaja di tre Soli adorno. . . .
> Recaro altrui giammi tal maraviglia.

HEISE (p. 137) cites also Dante, *Par.* 1. 61 ff.; *Orl. Fur.* 10. 109; *Rin.* 6. 15.

1.   GOUGH.   The real sun and a mock sun or parhelion.   Generally two mock suns appear, one on each side of the sun.   They are due to the refraction of the sun's light through ice-crystals.

3-4.   EDITOR (C. G. O.).   Within the simile, perhaps by way of strengthening the homologation, Spenser draws upon his own stock phrases of love-poetry:

cf. *Astrophel* 190; *Colin Clouts* 874; *Hymne of Love* 186; *Hymne of Beautie* 241; 2. 3. 23. 1-5; 3. 5. 29. 3; 5. 9. 50. 7.

xx-xxii.   See Appendix, p. 278.

xx.   7.   GOUGH.   This proverbial phrase is derived from Aesop's fable of the jackdaw who adorned himself with peacock's feathers.

xxii. 3.   UPTON.   'Twas a custom for heroes of old to show their wounds. Spenser is all antique. Ovid, *Met.* 13. 262-5:

> Sunt et mihi vulnera cives
> Ipso pulcra loco: nec vanis credite verbis,
> Adspicite en! (vestemque manu diducit) et, haec sunt
> Pectora semper, ait, vestris exercita rebus.

As Arthegall and Ulysses shewed forth their wounds, so does the disappointed Nicomachides in Xenophon's *Memoirs of Socrates* 3. 4.

EDITOR.   See Shakespeare's *Coriolanus* 2. 3. 136-153 for Coriolanus's remarks on this custom of showing one's wounds.

xxiii. 5.   UPTON.   I. e. as if roses were mingled among lilies.   The active passively. . . . Virgil 12. 68-9:

> mixta rubent ubi lilia multa
> Alba rosa: tales virgo dabat ore calores.

Ovid, *Amor.* 2. 5[. 37]: "Quale rosae fulgent inter sua lilia mixtae."
  [Cf. *F. Q.* 2. 3. 22. 5-6, and notes in Book II, p. 214; *Colin Clouts* 336 ff.; *Epithalamion* 226 ff.]

HEISE (pp. 119-120) adds *Orl. Fur.* 7. 11; 10. 96; *Rin.* 1. 55; 4. 45; *Orl. Inn.* 1. 8. 11.

EDITOR (F. M. P.).   This is a veritable commonplace in Elizabethan polite verse. Cf., e. g., Constable, *Diana,* The First Decade 10. 9:

> A field of lilies, roses proper bare.

Lodge, *Phillis* 37. 7 8:

> whereto I medley showers
> Of roses and lilies too, the colours of thy face.

Giles Fletcher, *Licia* 52. 7:

> O rose and lilies in a field most fair.

Sidney, *Astrophel and Stella* 100. 1-2:

> Oh teares, no teares, but shoures from beauties skies,
> Making those Lilies and those Roses growe.

Arcadia 1. 13. 6 (Cambridge ed., p. 90), where Pyrocles is disclosing his love to Philoclea: "Then (I say) indeede me thought the Lillies grew pale for envie, the roses me thought blushed to see sweeter roses in her cheekes."

xxiv.   H. M. BELDEN (*MLN* 44. 526-7).   In support of Gough's suggestion [see note on st. 10, line 4 above] that Spenser's figures of the true and false

Florimell may have owed something to the Stesichorean version of the story of Helen it might be pointed out that Euripides' play gives also a hint for the rather puzzling part played by Proteus in Spenser's poem. Florimell, as Professor Padelford shows, is Spenser's "special embodiment . . . of Beauty," as Amoret is of grace and charm and Belphoebe of chastity. The false Florimell who is created by the witch to solace her loutish son and who thereafter plays so large a part in the story of the third and fourth Books is, of course, false beauty, the beauty of outward show without the inward beauty of the spirit. Helen likewise is the embodiment of the idea of female beauty in Greek legend. According to Euripides, the Helen that made so much trouble for Greece and Troy (compare the quarrels that arise over the false Florimell, F. Q. 4. 2 and 5) was but "a phantom, out of cloudland wrought" by Hera to deceive Paris, and vanishes into thin air (just as the false Florimell does) when the true Helen is restored. Spenser has sharpened his allegory by making his false Florimell out of snow. As Gough points out [see note on 17 ff. above], Spenser might have got the suggestion either from Plato, *Republic* 9. 10, or from Euripides. If, as seems to me probable, Spenser's treatment of Proteus is prompted by the part played by Proteus and his house in the *Helen*, we have additional evidence of the influence of Euripides upon Spenser.

9.   GOUGH.   The famous girdle of Florimell, which confers on its wearer the virtue of chastity, and can only be worn by a chaste woman. Its history is related in F. Q. 4. 5. [3-4; see note in Book IV, p. 193], where Spenser identifies it with the cestus or girdle of Venus (*Iliad* 14. 214), made for that goddess by her husband Vulcan. According to Spenser Florimell dropt it in her flight from the witch's monster, and Satyrane found it and bound the monster with it (F. Q. 3. 7). The latter broke loose and brought it to the witch (F. Q. 3. 8. 2), but we find it again in the possession of Satyrane, who offered it at his tournament as the prize of beauty, where it was awarded to the false Florimell. She was unable to fasten it round her waist, but was nevertheless allowed to keep it (F. Q. 4. 5. 16-20). How she is able to wear it now is not explained, but such inconsistencies are frequent in the F. Q. [Cf. EDITOR's note on 4. 2. 25. 7-9, Book IV, pp. 175-6, and UPTON's note on 5. 2. 3. 1-4.]

xxv.   WARTON (2. 206).   When the false Florimel is placed by the side of the true, the former vanishes into nothing; and as suddenly, says the poet, as all the glorious colours of the rain-bow fade and perish. With regard to the sudden evanescence in each, the comparison is just and elegant: but if we consider, that a rain-bow exists by the presence of the sun, the similitude by no means is made out. However, it is the former of these circumstances alone which the poet insists upon, so that a partial correspondence only is expected.

1.   JORTIN.   Thaumantias Iris, the daughter of Thaumas, not Thaumantes.
    SAWTELLE (p. 114) cites *Met.* 11. 647.
    BLAKENEY.   Iris, the rainbow-goddess. Virgil calls her Thaumantias, *Aeneid* 9. 5 (cf. Cicero, *de Nat. Deor.* 3. 51: "Thaumante dicitur Iris esse nata"). And see Hesiod, *Theog.* 265 ff.
    LOTSPEICH (p. 73).   The form "Thaumantes" may have been caught from the Latin, "Thaumantias" (*Aen.* 9. 5; *Met.* 4. 480), or from Boccaccio 9. 1, "Iris, quam Thaumantis fuisse filiam voluere, id est, admirationis, eo quod sit coloribus et apparitione mirabilis" (cf. 5. 3. 25. 4).

xxvi.   Cf. above 18. 1-7, and note.

xxviii.   A. A. JACK (*A Commentary on the Poetry of Chaucer and Spenser,*
p. 229, n.) notes that Spenser forgets that in Book 4, canto [5, st. 19], the girdle
had fitted Amoret. [See GOUGH'S note on 24. 9 above.]

xxxi.   UPTON.   Guyon tells them the story of the woful couple, viz. Mordant
and Amavia, related in Book 2, canto 1 and their bloody babe, 2. 1. 40, during
which adventure his steed was stolen, 2. 1. 11.

xxxii-xl.   See OSGOOD'S note on 2. 3. 20 ff. in Book II, pp. 210-1.

xxxii.   BLAKENEY.   According to the "law of arms," a challenge refused
was equivalent to a giving up of the contest; but, to make the surer, Artegall asked
whether there were any further "tokens" in the horse.

xxxiii-xxxiv.   UPTON.   Compare this . . . with Ariosto 1. 74, 75.   These kind
of tales told of the great sagacity of horses, and the love which they bear their
masters, have more than poetical warrant for their truth; for historians relate the
same of the horses of Alexander and of Julius Caesar.

      GOUGH cites this story of the horses of Julius Caesar and Alexander
from Montaigne, *Essais* 47 [1. 48 in Florio's translation].

xxxiv.   EDITOR (C. G. O.).   The whole episode accords with that accomplishment of the true courtier which Spenser mentions at *Mother Hubberds Tale* 739
and emphasizes at 2. 4. 1-2; see notes on 2. 4. 1, in Book II, pp. 223-4.

    3.   WARTON (1. 213-6).   Brigliadoro also is the name of Orlando's
horse; from "Briglia d'oro," a golden bridle.
    On the affectation, so common in books of chivalry, of dignifying horses, as
well as knights, with pompous names, the following ridicule in Cervantes is
founded (*Don Quixote* 3. 8).   "And pray, said Sancho, how many persons will
this horse carry?   Two, replied the Afflicted; one upon the saddle, and the other
upon the crupper, and these are commonly the knight and the squire, when there
is no damsel to be stolen. I should be glad to know, Afflicted Madam, what is the
name of that same horse? His name, answered the Afflicted, is not like that of
Bellerophon's horse, which was called Pegasus, nor does it resemble that which
distinguished the horse of Alexander the Great, Bucephalus; nor that of Orlando
Furioso, whose name was Brilliadoro; nor Bayarte, which belonged to Reynaldo de
Montalvan; nor Frontino, that appertained to Rugero; nor Bootes, nor Peritoa, the
horses of the Sun; nor is he called Orelia, like that steed upon which the unfortunate Rodrigo, last king of the Goths, engaged in that battle where he lost his
crown and life. I will lay a wager, cried Sancho, that as he is not distinguished by
any of those famous names of horses, so well known, so neither have they given
him the name of my master's horse Rozinante," etc. After the same manner, they
named their swords. Thus Chrysaor is the name of Arthegal's sword, 5. 1. 9. [7-8];
Caliburn of king Arthur's in *Morte Arthur,* etc. Thus too in Ariosto, we have
Renaldo's Fusberta, Rogero's Balisarda, and Orlando's Durindana. Durinda is the
name of Roland's sword in Turpin's Romance, which Ariosto and Boyardo copy so
faithfully. As a specimen of that historian's style and manner, I shall present the
reader with Roland's soliloquy addressed to this sword, when he was mortally

wounded by a Saracen giant (I. Turpin, *Hist. de Gestis Caroli Mag.* 22). " O ensis pulcherrime, sed semper lucidissime, capulo eburneo candidissime, cruce aurea splendissime, superficie deaurate, pomo beryllino deaurate, magno nomine dei insculpte, acumine legitime, virtute omni praedite, quis amplius virtute tua utetur? Quis," etc. Arthur's sword is called Mordure by Spenser; and his shield, or banner, Pridwen, and his spear Roan, by the romance-writers. Morglay was the sword of sir Bevys of Southampton, and Galantine of sir Gawaine. Tizona was the name they gave the sword of Roderick Diaz de Bivar, the famous Spanish general against the Moors. The French always applied the epithet " joyeuse," jocose, to the sword of their grand hero Charlemagne. This, as one of their own countrymen observes, is a strong characteristic of their natural gaiety; which a phlegmatic Englishman would call ridiculous levity (M. de la Curne de S. Palaye, [*Froissart*] 2. 61 n.) " Ils ont continuellement repandu sur toutes les images de la guerre un air d'enjoue-ment, qui leur est propre: ils n'ont jamais parle que comme d'une fete, d'un jeu, et d'un passe-temps. Jouer leur jeu, ont-ils dit les arbaletriers qui faisoient pleuvoir une grele de traits: Jouer gros jeu, pour donner battaille: Jouer des mains; et une infinité d'autres façons de parler semblables se recontrent souvent dans la lecture de recits militaires de nos ecrivains. Froissart, en rapportant la mort de duc Winceslas, fait ainsi son portrait; En celuy temps (1383) trespassa de ce siecle. . . . le gentil et joly duc Wincelas de Boheme, duc de Luxemburgh et de Brabant, qui en son temps, noble, frisque, sage, amoreux, et armeret avoit este." Some of their late campaigns have begun in the same spirit; which, however, have often ended very seriously: nor have the balls and battles of those lively generals, Soubise and Broglio, been always executed with equal good humour and brilliancy.

See UPTON's note on 3. 1. 1. 9 in Book III, p. 203.

xxxvi. 5-9. EDITOR (C. G. O.). Guyon imparts the lesson of temperance, or continence, in anger, which he learned painfully and at length in Book II, particularly in cantos 4-6.

xxxvii. UPTON. I believe that in describing Braggadochio, Spenser had his eye on the coward Martano, in Ariosto, who runs away at the tournament, 17. 90; he steals the horse and arms of Grison, 17. 110, and is punished, 18. 93.—Cowards in the lists were proclaimed false and perjured, their armour was taken from them, beginning from the heels upwards, and then ignominiously flung piece by piece over the barriours: they were likewise dragged out of the lists, and punished as the judges decreed.

GOUGH (pp. 192-3). The offences of Braggadochio, boaster, coward, liar, and thief, are essentially sins against justice, being due to covetousness, the desire to gain an undue share of honour and property (Aristotle's πλεονεξία). Sir Artegall comes forward as the vindicator of justice against each of the forms of fraud here described, Braggadochio's false claim to the prize, his theft of the horse, and the personation of Florimell. It is noteworthy that his exposure of Bragga-dochio's imposture is the only example of his avenging a wrong done against himself. Contrast his behaviour towards Envy and Detraction in Canto 12 (see . . . note to that canto [below, p. 268]).

See CHURCH's note on 2. 3. 11. 3 in Book II, 210.

5-9. TODD. This was agreeable to the customs of ancient chivalry: the heralds at arms houghed or hamstrung the unfortunate vanquished, whether alive or dead; stript them of their armour; left them naked upon the ground; " scattered their weapons about the lists "; and left their bodies stretched upon the ground until the sovereign's orders were given in what manner they should be disposed of (M. Cousard de Massi, *Hist. of Duelling* 1. 7).

CHILD. These verses describe the process by which a recreant knight was degraded from the rank of Chivalry. Turpin is served in the same way, *F. Q.* 6. 7. 27. 2.

GOUGH. In Hall's *Chronicle*, Henry 8, an. 5 (1548, the first recorded instances of the word) " to bafful " is said to be " a great reproach among the Scottes, and is used when a man is openly periured, and then they make of him an image painted, reuersed, with his heles upward, with his name, wondering, cryenge, and glowing out of (= at) him with hornes, in the most despitefull manner they can." This is evidently a mitigation of the original punishment. Shakespeare uses the word several times in the sense of punishing a recreant knight, e. g. *Twelfth Night* 2. 5. 176; *Richard 2*, 1. 1. 170. Cf. also Beaumont and Fletcher, *King and No King* 3. 2, where a cowardly braggart soldier says, " They hung me up by the heels and beat me with hazel sticks, . . . that the whole kingdom took notice of me for a baffled, whipped fellow."

5. GOUGH cites 1 Chronicles 19. 4.

GRACE W. LANDRUM (*PMLA* 41. 541). Cf. Jeremiah 48. 37.

xxxix. 1. UPTON. This is the punishment inflicted on the Fox in *Mother Hubberd's Tale* [1378-1380]:

> The Fox, first author of that treachery,
> He did uncase, and then abroad let fly.

B. Johnson has this expression in his *Volpone* 5. [609]: " The Fox shall here uncase."

xl. A. H. GILBERT (*PMLA* 34. 232) notes this as a conclusion in the manner of Ariosto.

5. UPTON. This verse is by no means to be altered. Spenser knew his readers would apply it to the ladies, though he places the epithet at such a distance from them. And indeed 'tis his perpetual manner thus to sport with his epithet, and to disjoin it from its proper substantive.

6-7. Cf. *F. Q.* 4. 5. 46. 8-9 and note, Book IV, p. 199.

GOUGH. Cf. *F. Q.* 6. 9. 1, also the closing lines of Book 2 of Vergil's *Georgics:*

> Sed nos immensum spatiis confecimus aequor,
> Et iam tempus equum fumantia solvere colla.

Spenser again expresses weariness in the opening lines of Book 6.

General. Cantos 1-3. UPTON (2. 616). Thus Arthegal finished three adventures. The first is an instance of his sagacity in distributive justice: and imitated from the well known, and first, decision of King Solomon. The second, of his love of publick justice, in punishing a Sarazin, who demanded toll of passengers. The third, of his punishing an impudent accuser, and a pretending amender of God's works: a modern geometrician and conceited metaphysician.

CANTO IV

i-ii.   GOUGH (p. 205).   In the opening stanzas of this canto Spenser emphatically asserts the need for a thorough unflinching prosecution of the duties of government, a thought which runs through the whole Book, and is the leading principle of his *Veue of the Present State of Ireland*, which was written a few years later. Grey's policy of the iron hand had shocked milder men and led to his recall, which to Spenser's mind was a disastrous example of sentimental weakness.

ii-iii.   A. H. GILBERT (*PMLA* 34. 232) notes this as an " Ariosto-like transition from the introductory stanzas of a canto to the narrative."

iv-xx.   See Appendix, pp. 289, 295, 304, 309.

vi. 3-4.   GOUGH.   I. e. their rage was so great that they would allow no settlement of their quarrel but such as the fortune of battle should show to be just.

6.   EDITOR.   This line presents unavoidable metrical difficulties, and may be defective. " Join " is invariably a monosyllable in Spenser, and " cruel " a dissyllable with penultimate stress.

vii. 3.   WALTHER (p. 8).   Cf. Melyas in Malory, p. 628 [13. 12].   Cf. also Myles of the laundes, p. 117 [3. 15], and Mylis, p. 68 [1. 21; ch. 19 in Globe ed.]
          GOUGH.   " Milesio."   This name was probably suggested by an Irish legend concerning the Milesians (sons of Milesius or Milidh), a Scythian race, who were said to have invaded Ireland several centuries before the Christian era. Heber and Heremon, the sons of Milesius, divided the island between them, but the wife of Heber envied the wife of Heremon the possession of a certain valley, and instigated her husband to make war on his brother. A great battle was fought in the plains of Geisol in Leinster, in which Heber was slain, and Heremon became sole monarch. That Spenser knew the legend may be inferred from the fact that in the *Veue of the Present State of Ireland*, Globe ed., p. 627, he discusses and discredits the story of the Milesian invasion and refers to Heberus, after whom the Chroniclers affirm that the land was called Hibernia.

xi.   UPTON.   Compare this stanza with Ariosto, *Orl. Fur.* 6. 5.

2.   UPTON.   This is a scripture phrase, . . . " to taste of death." See Matthew 16. 28; John 8. 52.

xvi. 8.   GOUGH.   Although Spenser usually observes the distinction between " ye " and " you," he occasionally as here and in 17. 5, 6; 18. 5, 6, uses " you " for " ye," possibly for the sake of euphony. Some Elizabethan writers, including Shakespeare, use these pronouns almost indiscriminately, e. g. *Julius Caesar* 3. 1. 159 [157]: " I do beseech ye, if you bear me hard."

xvii. 9.   GOUGH.   This was in accordance with the principles of Roman law; cf. Gaius, *Digest.* 41. 1. 7, " Quod per alluvionem agro nostro flumen adicit iure gentium nobis acquiritur." So also Ulpian, *Digest.* 19. 1. 13.   " Alluvion," or the gradual formation of new land, is a form of accession, i. e. natural growth of property. By Roman law, if a torrent or flood washes away land belonging to one owner and deposits it in a place adjacent to the land of another, the new land becomes the latter's property as soon as any trees which have been deposited with it take root. The English and Scottish laws of alluvion agree substantially with the Roman.

xviii. 2. GOUGH. Brasidas was a Lacedaemonian commander in the Peloponnesian War, but there is no apparent reason for the choice of his name in this connexion. [See note on 20. 2-3 below.]

9. TUCKER BROOKE (*MLN* 37. 224) cites the identity of this line with 17. 9 as one of four devices which Spenser employs to link certain stanzas and overcome monotony. Cf. *F. Q.* 1. 5. 8 and 9; 3. 11. 16. 1 and 17. 9. See also 5. 1. 6-7; 8-9 and note on 8. 9—9. 1.

xix-xx. UPTON. The two brothers submitted their case to Arthegal; who by his doom put an end indeed to their fighting; but had each his right? Amidas and Philtera were displeased no doubt: all the goods in the coffer belonged to her, and were ascertained as her property: but the lands which were by the sea washed away, and thrown on the adjacent island, could not be ascertained. "Alluvius ager—alluviones"—are subjects which the Civilians treat of. See Grotius. Sir Arthegal seems to have made himself a judge of what was proper for each to have; and his intent was to put the two brothers upon an equal footing.

EDITOR. (C. G. O.). This case more than any other in the book seems to involve the issue between law and equity, which Spenser hints at from time to time (cf. 3. 36. 7; notes on 5. 7. 7; 5. 10. 1), and which so much engaged the Elizabethan mind. Mark Edwin Andrews in an unpublished study treats the issue as reflected in *The Merchant of Venice*; he mentions such authorities as Campbell, *Law in Shakespeare*; G. W. Keaton, *Shakespeare and his Legal Problems*; E. J. White, *Commentaries on the Law in Shakespeare*.

xix. GOUGH. According to the old law of wreck ("cicctum" or "iactura maris") whatever is abandoned by its owner and cast ashore by the sea is the property of the sovereign. This principle, derived from the Roman law, prevailed in most countries of Europe. By English law the term "wreck" applied to vessels cast ashore from which neither man, dog, nor cat escaped alive; also to other objects stranded, such as precious stones, whales, and sturgeons ("royal fish"). In many places the right to wreck was among the royalties granted to the lord of the manor. It was not decided till 1771 that the property in wreck on the English coast remained with the owner.

xx. 2-3. EDITOR (C. G. O.). Spenser seems to have invented Philtra as Phil + terra. Perhaps Amidas hints at "fond of possessions ($i\delta\iota a$)" and Bracidas is "Narrowmeans" ($\beta\rho a\chi\acute{v}s + i\delta\iota a$). Hybrids, not to mention vowels and consonants, could not embarrass an etymologizing Elizabethan.

(F. M. P.). May not Spenser have had in mind the root of the verb $\beta\rho\acute{a}\sigma\sigma\omega$— "to throw up," applied to the sea— + $i\delta\iota a$? Cf. *Anthologia Palatina* 6. 222: $\sigma\kappa o\lambda\acute{o}\pi\epsilon\nu\delta\rho a\nu$ . . . $\acute{\epsilon}\beta\rho a\sigma$' $\acute{\epsilon}\pi\grave{\iota}$ . . . $\sigma\kappa o\pi\acute{\epsilon}\lambda o\upsilon s$, and 7. 294, $\tau\grave{o}\nu$ $\pi\rho\acute{\epsilon}\sigma\beta\upsilon\nu$ . . . $\acute{\epsilon}\beta\rho a\sigma\epsilon$ . . . $\epsilon\grave{\iota}s$ $\mathring{\eta}\ddot{\iota}\acute{o}\nu a$.

xxi ff.   DODGE (*PMLA* 12. 203).   Cf. Ariosto's Amazons, *Orl. Fur.* 19. 57 ff.

xxii. 9.   BLAKENEY.   Cf. Judges 9. 54: "Draw thy sword, and slay me, that men say not of me, A woman slew him."

xxiv. 3.   GOUGH.   Artegall will not attack women because the mediaeval code of honour forbade a knight to fight with his inferiors in strength or skill, from the defeat of whom no honour was to be gained. . . . Artegall has no scruple about employing his groom in inflicting ignominious punishment on the women who assail him, Talus not being bound by the laws of chivalry. In *The Wars of Alexander* (EETS 67 [extra series 47]) that king threatens to make war on a queen of the Amazons, who replies that if he were overcome by them it would be great shame to him, and if he overcame them it would bring him no honour. He yields to this reasoning and concludes an alliance with the Amazons, saying that it is more seemly to overcome women with fairness and love than with the sword (lines 3755 ff.).

Circumstances are altered when Artegall hears that Radigund has put many valiant knights to shame. We then find him "swimming in bloody slaughter" of Amazons (st. 41).

xxv. 4.   GOUGH.   The punishment of death by hanging was regarded as a greater disgrace than by decapitation, the former being inflicted on all classes of criminals, and being the usual punishment of such crimes as theft. After the Norman conquest the practice of beheading criminals of high rank was introduced. When, in the reign of Edward II, an Earl of Carlisle was hanged for treason he was first subjected to a long ceremony of degradation, by which he was deprived of his knighthood (see Mills, *Hist. of Chivalry* 1. 2). That hanging was regarded as a peculiarly disgraceful death for a knight may be seen from Guenever's rebuke to a lady who, seeing Sir Lancelot riding in a cart, said she supposed he was going to be hanged. "It was foul mouthed," said the queen, "and evil likened, so for to liken the most noble knight in the world unto such a shameful death" (Malory, *Morte Darthur* 19. 4).

5.   J. W. DRAPER (*MLN* 48. 227) cites "ydrad" as one of "four cases in which Spenser uses the prefix with the imperfect tense. [These] come from verbs that originally contained it throughout their entire conjugation." He adds: "And that should therefore be allowed." "Ydrad" is from O. E. adrædan.

6.   GOUGH cites Psalms 56. 13.

xxvi.   EDITOR.   A fine piece of dramatic irony in anticipation of Artegall's fall in the next canto.

xxviii. 1-2.   GOUGH.   Spenser repeats this thought in 6. 9. 29, and in *Veue of the State of Ireland* [Globe ed., p. 609], lines 35-9.

xxix ff.   WARTON (1. 224).   I shall add, that Spenser, in his Radegond, with her city of females, had an eye upon Ariosto's land of Amazons. It is however to be remembered, that a land of Amazons is a frequent miracle of romance, being taken from the old legends of the Trojan war. Caxton, in his *Destruction of Troy*, gives us a chapter, " How the queene Panthasile cam from Amazonne, with a thousand maydens, to the socoure of Troye. And how she bare her valyantly," etc.

GOUGH. The stories about this mythical race of women warriors, which occur in classical authors from Homer onwards, were repeated and expanded in the mediaeval romances of Troy and Alexander, and in Mandeville's *Travels*. In his account of Radigund Spenser appears to be chiefly indebted to Diodorus Siculus, *Bibl. Hist.* 2. 45; 3. 51 ff. (see notes on 4. 31. 6 and 4. 33. 5), and to the episode of Orontea, the Amazon queen, in Ariosto, *Orl. Fur.* 20 (see note to 4. 30. 1).

EDITOR. Raleigh described a race of Amazons in America. See notes on 4. 11. 21. 8—22. 5 in Book IV, pp. 248-9; and Appendix below, pp. 273, 304.

xxix. 6. GOUGH. "that hold of Maidenhead." Acknowledge allegiance to the Order of Maidenhead. This was founded by Queen Gloriana (see *F. Q.* 2. 2. 42 [and notes in Book II, pp. 202-3]; 2. 9. 6 [and notes in Book II, p. 280; also 1. 7. 46. 4 and PERCIVAL's note in Book I, p. 256; 4. 6. 6. 1 and notes in Book IV, pp. 199-200]); and it was at her annual twelve days' feast that the twelve members of the Order whose adventures were to form the subject of the completed poem, undertook their several quests. (See *Letter to Sir Walter Raleigh*.) The title of the Order is of course a compliment to Elizabeth, the " Virgin Queen."

I. L. SCHULZE (*SP* 30. 155-9) presents evidence to support Upton's identification of the Order of Maidenhead as the Order of the Garter [see notes in Book II, pp. 202-3, 280]. He presents four supporting facts, namely: 1. Arthur was associated with the Garter by Elizabethans. 2. There was an intimate association between the Garter and the legend of Redcrosse through St. George. 3. The Garter was identified with Elizabeth, and the Knights of the Garter were thought of as the Knights of Elizabeth. 4. All the noblemen to whom Spenser addressed dedicatory sonnets, except Walsingham and Raleigh, were Knights of the Garter.

xxx. 1. GOUGH. "her cruel hate." Cf. Ariosto, *Orl. Fur.* 20. 57 ff., where Orontea, the first Queen of the Amazons, is represented as making war on all men to avenge their [the Amazons'] desertion by Phalantus and his companions. The execution of male prisoners is also probably borrowed from the same passage. See 32. 1.

xxxi ff. GOUGH (pp. 207-8). In accordance with his general ethical scheme, the poet makes Radigund a symbol of what in his eyes is a form of injustice, the usurpation of authority by women. Like the giant with the balance, she seeks to overthrow the supposed divine order of society, which binds women " t'obay the heasts of mans well ruling hand " (5. 25. 4). This champion of " the liberty of women " (7. 42. 5), discontented with the condition of " base humilitie " (5. 25. 8) to which the political and theological doctrines of Spenser's age consigned them, this revolutionary who abolishes the privileges of knights, and " doth them compell to worke, to earne their meat " (4. 31. 5), though not lacking in a certain wild grace, as of a tigress, is depicted as treacherous, vindictive, cruel, and subject to fits of uncontrolled rage. Like more modern supporters of the mediaeval view of woman's place in society, Spenser asserts that the rebel woman was led to revolt through unrequited love, which turned to bitter hatred of the whole male sex, expressed in acts of contempt and barbarity. It would be an anachronism to charge the poet with reactionary prejudice in this episode, which reads like a reckless satire on feminist aspirations. He was expressing the general opinion of this time. In spite of the enthusiasm with which Plato's theories were received in the sixteenth century, and although his doctrine of the equality of the sexes, as set forth in the *Republic*, was followed by More in his *Utopia*, and by a few others, little is heard in Elizabeth's reign of such doctrines. Her own position was no precedent for women who desired to govern men without divine sanction. The heavens had lifted her to lawful sovereignty (5. 25. 9). There had been several examples in Spenser's own day of government by women, mostly in his eyes disastrous and destructive of the ideals that he prized. The part that women played in the Counter-reformation is remarkable. Mary Tudor in England (1553-8), Mary of Lorraine (1554-1560) and her daughter Queen Mary (1561-7) in Scotland, Margaret of Parma in the Netherlands (1559-1567), and Catherine de' Medici in France (*c*. 1560-1575) had all laboured strenuously, by legislation, intrigue, persecution, and war, to suppress the reformed faith. The policy of the first two had evoked Knox's *First Blast of the Trumpet against the Monstrous Regiment of Women*, in 1558. Catherine de' Medici, the Queen Dowager, made herself supreme without any constitutional sanction, Mary of Lorraine and Margaret of Parma were appointed Regents; Mary Tudor, according to the theory of some Protestants, was illegitimate, and therefore a usurper, and Mary Stuart forfeited her throne through her connivance at crime. [See GOUGH's note on 5. 11-14 below.]

xxxi.   UPTON.   See an account in Petitus, *de Amazon*. 23 how they misused the men. Consult likewise Apollonius Rhodius [2. 985 ff.] of their cruel nature: and compare Ariosto (who was well acquainted with all ancient literature) of the laws and policy of the Amazons, 19. 57, etc.

4.   GOUGH.   "and cloth in women's weedes." The slavery of male prisoners is a feature common to most later descriptions of the Amazons, but in his description of warriors clothed in women's garments Spenser appears to be thinking of the account of the bondage of Heracles in *Il*. 2. 930 [*sic*], *Od*. 21. 22-[30], where the hero, in order to expiate the murder of his friend Iphitus, sold himself as a slave to Omphale, Queen of Lydia. [William Smith, *Dictionary of Greek and Roman Biography and Mythology* 2. 398, cites *Il*. 2. 730 and *Od*. 21. 22 as sources for the bondage of Heracles. I can find no mention of this story in *Iliad* 2 or elsewhere in that poem; the reference to line 930 is certainly a mistake, for there are not that many lines in the book. Reference should be made to Apollodorus 2. 6. 2-4 and Hyginus, *Fab*. 32, instead of the *Iliad*.] Spenser follows Ovid (*Fast*. 2. [305 ff.] ; *Heroid*. 9. 53), who, as well as other late classical authors, describes him as leading an effeminate life during this period, spinning wool, and wearing the garments of a woman, while Omphale wore his lion skin. Achilles also, in late traditions, was said to have been disguised as a woman by his mother, Thetis, in order to prevent him taking part in the siege of Troy, which she knew would prove fatal to him. She hid him among the maidens of Lycomedes of Scyros, where he was discovered by Odysseus while spinning wool. [See notes on 5. 5. 24 below.]

6.   GOUGH.   Diodorus Siculus (*Bibl. Hist*. 2. 45) says that an Amazon queen, filled with pride at her many victories, constrained the men of her country to spin wool and fulfil all the offices of women, whilst the military and civil functions were reserved for women.

xxxiii. 3.   See note below on 7. 42. 5-9.

5.   GOUGH.   Diodorus Siculus, an author whom Spenser apparently follows in Canto 7, and to whom he refers four times in his *Veue of the State of
Ireland*, recounts the exploits of a Queen of the Amazons in Pontus, who formed
an army of women, enslaved the men of the country (see note to 4. 31. 6), conquered neighbouring nations, and died heroically in battle (*Bibliotheca Historica*
2. 45). He also (*Bibl. Hist.* 3. 53 ff.) describes an earlier race of Amazons in
Libya, whose Queen Myreina founded a city and named it after herself. Cf. 35. 9.

xxxv. 8-9.   UPTON.   The city of the Amazons was named Themiscyra, near
the river Thermodon. Though we are now in Fairy land, yet our poet does not
altogether lose sight of history.

xxxvi. 1.   GOUGH.   The population of the Amazon city does not, as in Greek
legends, consist entirely of women. Cf. however note to 31. 6. We learn from
37. 3-5 that the porter is a man, and another man appears to be mentioned in
5. 34. 3. Aeneas Silvius (Pope Pius II), an author to whom Spenser refers in
another connexion in his *Veue of the State of Ireland*, described the Amazon state
as inhabited by both sexes with the usual relations reversed.
        EDITOR.   Raleigh relates in his *Discoverie of Guiana* a similar account
of the Amazons which he "found" in America. See *Works of Sir Walter Raleigh*,
ed. T. Birch, 2. 170-1. See notes on sts. 29 ff. above.

7.   UPTON cites *Il*. 2. 89.
        HEISE (p. 29) cites other bee images at 1. 1. 41. 5; 2. 9. 51. 4-5; and
(p. 116) other literary originals at *Aen*. 1. 430; *Ars Am*. 1. 95-6; *Fasti* 3. 555-6;
Inf. 16. 1 ff.; *Par*. 31. 1 ff.; Chaucer, *Hous of Fame* 3. 431-2; *Squire's Tale* 196
[204?].

xxxvii. 8.   F. WARRE CORNISH (*Chivalry*, p. 90).   The Barons at Kenilworth
in the "War of the Disinherited" (1266) disdained to wait behind their defences,
and kept the castle gates open in defiance of Prince Edward for ten months,
thinking chivalry more glorious than warfare.

xxxviii. 4, 9.   See WARTON's note on 2. 11. 28. 1-2 in Book II, p. 345.

4.   TODD.   On these passages Milton might have been musing, when he
wrote, *P. L.* 6. 545-6, "no drizzling shower But rattling storm of arrows," etc.
See also *P. R.* 3. 324. Matthew Paris, the historian, uses the same phrase (1242.
587): "Rex Francorum castrum grandine . . . spiculorum." [Quoted inexactly;
see *Chronica Majora* 4. 202, ed. H. R. Luard, London, Longman, 1877.]

xlii. 3.   WARTON (2. 206-7).   Sails are often used by our author for wings;
and after him by Milton [*P. L.* 2. 927]. And by Fletcher (*Purple Island* 12. 59),
"So up he rose, upon his stretched sailes." Again, by our author (1. 11. 10) . . .
Thus Bayardo, in Ariosto, fights with a monstrous bird, whose wings are like two
sails (33. 84): "L'ale havea grandé che parean duo vale." Harington: "Her
wings so huge, they seemed like a saile."

xlviii. 3.   GOUGH.   Spenser abbreviates the name to suit the metre. Cf. Marin
for Marinell in *F. Q.* 4. 12. Arg. A warrior maiden in Tasso's *Gerusalemme Liberata*

(2 ff.) is named Clorinda, which perhaps suggested the name Clarinda for an Amazon.

xlix.   W. J. COURTHOPE (*A History of English Poetry* 2. 281). In [this] . . . stanza there is a fine simplicity which is like Homer.

CANTO V

i.   1-4.   UPTON.   This is translated from Vergil, *Aen.* 11. 182-3.

> [Aurora interea miseris mortalibus almam
>   Extulerat lucem, referens opera atque labores.

The cadence is much the same at *Astrophel* 34; cf. 1. 4. 16. 5].

ii-iii.   UPTON.   As Homer minutely describes his chief heroes, viz. Agamemnon and Achilles, dressing themselves for battle; so Spenser, to raise your ideas of her prowess, minutely arms his Amazonian dame: and I believe he had Q. Calaber 1 [Quintus Smyrnaeus, *Posthomerica*] Παραλειπ· in view, where he describes Penthesilea arming herself for battle.

ii.   1.   GOUGH.   Cf. *F. Q.* 2. 3. 26. 4, where Belphoebe is clad " All in a silken Camus lylly whight "; and see the whole description of her dress (26, 27) which greatly resembles this. [Cf. notes in Book II, pp. 211-2; 216.]

   8.   See WARTON's note on *F. Q.* 3. 9. 20. 4-6 in Book III, pp. 277-8.

iii.   4.   UPTON.   The reader at his leisure may consult Petitus in his treatise of the Amazons; who mentions not a cemitare, but a battle-axe, as their peculiar offensive weapon: but I have seen at Wilton, among my Lord Pembroke's collection, a figure of an Amazonian defending herself with a sword against an horseman.

   5.   UPTON.   One of the labours of Hercules was to get from Hippolyta, queen of the Amazons " her belt of mickell pride."

   6-9.   WARTON (2. 207).   Satan's shield, in Milton, is compared to the moon (*P. L.* 1. 287-291): but to the moon as discerned through a telescope. [See Marjorie Nicolson's article, " Milton and the Telescope," *ELH* 2. 1-32, especially p. 12. However Galileo magnified and glorified Milton's moon, Spenser's image and cadence, as usual, haunted the later poet's ear:

> Hung on his shoulders like the Moon, whose Orb . . .

Cf. 5. 3. 6.   Says UPTON: " Milton had this passage in his mind."]

   UPTON.   Homer, *Il.* 19. 373-4: [" then lastly he took the great and strong shield, and its brightness shone afar off as the moon's."]
   See notes on 2. 3. 1. 9 in Book II, pp. 205-6.

   8.   GOUGH.   Probably after Vergil, *Aen.* 1. 490:

> Ducit Amazonidum lunatis agmina peltis
>   Penthesilea furens,

where Spenser appears to understand " lunatis " as " round and bright like the moon," [cf. 9. 2-3] although an oval shield with a semicircular indentation was among the traditional arms of the Amazons.

iv. 5. GOUGH. The presence of minstrels was customary at tournaments, and Spenser has here introduced them at the single combat. They announced the entry of each knight into the lists, and celebrated any great feat of arms with a flourish.

6. EDITOR. The figure is habitual with Spenser: cf. 1. 5. 16. 9; 4. 3. 49. 9; 5. 11. 34. 2; 7. 6. 52. 7; *Epith.* 141.

v. 6. GOUGH. At the judicial combat, which this somewhat resembles, no spectator was allowed to make any movement or utter any cry that might either encourage or annoy the combatants on pain of losing a limb or even life itself. Cf. Shakespeare, *Richard II* 1. 3. 42: "On paine of death no person be so bold . . . as to touch the lists Except the Marshall."

vii. 6–viii. 4. EDITOR (C. G. O.). The simile—if it be one continuous simile —prolongs itself throughout this passage, though Radigund is at first the malleable metal, then the anvil. HEISE (p. 69) cites the same image at 1. 2. 17. 8; 1. 11. 42. 6-7; 4. 4. 23. 5. See note on 1. 11. 42. 5-8 in Book I, p. 304.

ix. 7. EDITOR (C. G. O.). A repetition of the image in the same connection as at 4. 40. 6-9 above.

xi-xiv. GOUGH (pp. 222-3). Artegall's second error was his conduct at the moment when the queen lay senseless at his feet. He had unlaced her helmet with the intention of striking off her head, an act which, brutal as it seems to the modern mind, the code of chivalry permitted [cf. 1. 3. 37-8; 2. 8. 52; 6. 1. 39]. He ought to have steeled his heart against pity where none was deserved. His treacherous enemy soon showed that she had no such scruples, and meanly took advantage of his misplaced humanity. Here Spenser once more urges the danger of sentimentality in public affairs. It was not only in the Irish policy of Elizabeth's ministers that he saw this danger. There is little doubt that the treatment of Mary, Queen of Scots, was in his mind. Like Radigund, Mary was proud, revengeful, crafty, energetic, and dauntless. On her way to the field of Corrichie she "had uttered her wish to be a man, that she might know all the hardship and all the enjoyment of a soldier's life" (Swinburne, in *Encyclopaedia Britannica*). The almost irresistible charm of her personality had enslaved many brave men. It was even suspected that Lord Grey de Wilton himself, the stern Puritan, had been half won over by her wiles. (His name is in a list of forty noblemen, which Ridolfi showed the Duke of Norfolk in 1571, with the assurance that they "professed to be waiting only for an opportunity to declare in arms against Elizabeth." Froude, *Hist. England*, [ed. 1870], chapter 55.) Prizing power and mastery above all things, she flung them away in the infatuation of passion. When fortune had laid her helpless at the feet of her enemies, and her life, as was believed, was rightly forfeit, she was spared for eighteen years, and was thus enabled to plot for the throne of England, and brought the country into deadly peril. In 1572, after the disclosure of the Ridolfi plot and Norfolk's treason, both Houses demanded Mary's death, and the Bishops waited on Elizabeth with a memorial in which they urged that "to show pity to an enemy, a stranger, a professed member of Anti-Christ, convicted of so many heinous crimes, with the evident peril of so many thousands of bodies and souls of good and faithful subjects, might justly be termed 'crudelis misericordia'" (Froude, *Hist. England*, chapter 57). With this view Spenser would have concurred, though he would have assigned the blame to Elizabeth's ministers rather than to herself.

xi. 8–xii. WARTON (2. 208). This is such a picture as Propertius gives us (3. 10. 13-6):

> Ausa ferox ab equo quondam oppugnare sagittis
> Maeotis Danaum Penthesilea rates;
> Aurea cui postquam nudavit cassida frontem,
> Vicit victorem candida forma virum.

xii-xiv. UPTON. He seems . . . to have in view the story told of Achilles, who having vanquished Penthesilea, when her helmet was loosed, he himself was vanquished with her beautiful face, Propertius, *Eleg.* 3. [10.] 15-6.

There is a similar incident in Tasso's *Ger. Lib.* 3. 21 f., where Tancred, fighting with Chlorinda, strikes off her helmet, and is overcome by her beauty; a passage closely followed by Spenser in *F. Q.* 4. 6.

xii. A. H. GILBERT (*PMLA* 34. 231). Cf. *Orl. Fur.* 32. 79.

[See Appendix, pp. 273-4, 304, 314, 349.]

6-9. See 3. 1. 43; 3. 9. 20; 4. 1. 13; 4. 6. 20-2; and notes on 3. 9. 20. 6-9 in Book III, p. 278.

xiii. 7-9. Cf. 4. 2. 17. 1-2, and note in Book IV, p. 175; 5. 3. 18. 2-7; 5. 3. 26.

xiv-xviii. KATE M. WARREN (p. xx n.). It is just possible that Queen Elizabeth herself, in some of her many moods, may have partly been Spenser's original for Radigund—though, of course, he gives no open clue to this. [See Appendix, pp. 273-4.]

xv. HEISE (pp. 19-25) cites some fifteen similes from falconry in Spenser, and literary analogues for a half dozen. There can be no doubt that Spenser was an enthusiastic hunter with falcon and dog (see note on 3. 11. 35. 7-9, in Book III, p. 286, and on 8. 49. 1-5 below), as well as a fisherman. See note on 2. 54. 1-5 above.

3. GOUGH. Probably one of whose wings; cf. *F. Q.* 5. 7. 7. 4: " her other hand "; *F. Q.* 5. 12. 36. 6: " A distaffe in her other hand she had "; also *F. Q.* 2. 4. 4. 3: " Her other leg was lame "; *F. Q.* 3. 9. 5. 5: " his other blincked eye " (one being blind). According to the *NED.:* " the quots. from Spenser are evidently archaic, and it is possible that in them ' other ' means ' left,' like Germ. ' ander.' " [See UPTON's note on *F. Q.* 2. 4. 4 in Book II, p. 226; cf. 2. 11. 23. 6.]

xvii. 1-3. GOUGH. Spenser repeatedly insists on the voluntary character of Artegall's surrender, by which is apparently meant that he was ready to submit as soon as he found himself attacked while without his sword. Hence Radigund's assault was a mere wanton outrage, quite " bootlesse," for he was already at her mercy.

1. UPTON. Virgil 7. 295, has the like repetition and play on the word, " Num capti potuere capi? "

EDITOR. The Elizabethans were fond of such repetition and play on words. Sister Mary Alphonse McCabe in her unpublished thesis, *Spenser's use of repetition in the " Faerie Queene,"* has listed and classified Spenser's uses of this rhetorical figure. Copies of her thesis are in the libraries of St. Louis University and the Tudor and Stuart Club. See 9. 19. 7 and note below.

9. GOUGH. This sentiment, admirable in other connexions, seems strangely out of place here. The conquest was not gained with Artegall's goodwill, nor was it fair.

xviii. 1-2. GOUGH. It was the custom (still retained in the ceremony of conferring knighthood), when binding a man to feudal service, for his lord to give him a light blow on the shoulder with the flat of the sword. This was called dubbing.

5-9. EDITOR (C. G. O.). This event reflects a shocking poetic injustice on Spenser's part as well as Radigund's. Sir Terpine had been obliged to hear from Artegall a highly patronizing lecture of advice (4. 26), which Artegall in the moment of his trial did not live up to; whereas Sir Terpine when put to the test (4. 32) acquitted himself far more nobly than did Artegall. And now the poor fellow is hanged after all!

xix. 8-9. UPTON. Because by the law of arms (" jure faeciali "[?]) he had forfeited his freedom.

xxi. 3-7. I. L. SCHULZE (SP 30. 154-5) cites the custom of hanging up arms by the Knights of the Garter and by the participants in the Queen's tournament. He quotes Hentzner's description of Windsor Castle (Nichols, *Progresses* 1. 143-4), Lupond von Wedel's description of Whitehall (Victor von Klarwill, *Queen Elizabeth and Some Foreigners*, pp. 320-1), and Gerard Legh's description of a church at the Inner Temple (Nichols, *Progresses of Eliz.* 2. 133). Cf. *F. Q.* 3. 11. 52. 1-5.

8. See 12. 23. 2 and note below.

xxii. 9. GOUGH. Cf. Malory, *Morte Darthur* 6. 11, where Lancelot rescues from a giant threescore ladies, who tell him that most of them have been seven years prisoners, " and worked al manner of sylke workes for our mete, and we are al grete gentylwomen borne."

xxiii-xxv. See Appendix, pp. 304-5.

xxiii. 1-5. C. W. LEMMI (*PQ* 8. 283-4) cites Natalis Comes 7. 1, on the subjection of Hercules to Omphale: " He, after having survived all dangers, after having quelled robbers and rid the earth of monsters, enslaved by his love for Omphale, committed base actions unworthy of his former deeds. Why was this tale sent down to posterity? Because the ancients wished to warn us that a good man must be ever on the watch; for if he turns his eyes from virtue but a moment . . . "

xxiv. 2-9. UPTON. His wife Deianira to cure him of his ignominious love sent him, as she thought a charm, but it happened to be a poisoned shirt, which caused his death. 'Twas not however Iole, but Omphale, a queen of Lydia, with whom he changed his lion's skin and club for the spindle and distaff. Sidney in his *Arcadia* has the same confusion of proper names, viz. Iole for Omphale.

SAWTELLE (pp. 62-3). This picture is based upon classical authority,— probably Ovid, *Her.* 9. [53 ff.],—but Spenser makes a mistake, not in implying the love of Hercules for Iole (see Apollodorus 2. 7. 7; *Met.* 9. 140), but in saying that it was for her sake that he led an effeminate life. Our poet is evidently think-ing of Omphale, queen of Lydia, with whom Hercules at one time passed several years.

W. P. MUSTARD (*MLN* 20. 127). This looks like a bit of "Italianate" mythology. Boccaccio has it in the first book of his *Fiammetta*, in his *Amoroso Visione* 26, and in his *Filocopo* 5. 7. Probably it came to Spenser through Tasso, *Ger. Lib.* 16. 3:

> Mirasi qui fra le mëonie ancelle
> favoleggiar con la conocchia Alcide.
> Se l'inferno espugnò, resse le stelle,
> or torce il fuso; Amor se 'l guarda, e ride.
> Mirasi Iole con la destra imbelle
> per ischerno trattar l'armi omicide.

3-4. LOTSPEICH (pp. 72-3). But Boccaccio [*De Genealogia Deorum*] 13. 1 makes the same confusion and his version of the story is the closest parallel to Spenser: "Eurito occiso, Iolem obtinuit [Hercules]. Huius enim amore ardens ea iubente leonis spolium et clavam deposuit, sertis et unguentis et purpura annulisque usus est, et quod turpius, inter pedissequas amatae iuvenis sedens, penso suscepto venit."

3. CHURCH. Mr. Jortin supposes that Spenser makes the second syllable in Iōla long. The old English Poets (he says) regard not Quantity. With respect to our Poet, I incline to think that in the present Instance, and in the above mention'd (4. 10. 27. 4) he himself would have pronounc'd, and intended that we should pronounce, according to the true Quantity.

xxv. H. S. V. JONES (*Spenser's Defense of Lord Grey*, p. 60). Compare with these quotations [this stanza and 7. 42] the following from the *Republic* (ed. Paris, 1577):

Il n'y a jamais eu loy ny coustume, qui ayt exempté la femme de l'obeissance, et non seulement de l'obeissance, ains aussi de la reverence qu'elle doit au mari (p. 19); il n'y a rien plus grand en ce monde, comme dit Euripide, ny plus neces-saire pour la conservation des Republiques, que l'obeissance de la femme au mari (p. 19); la loy de Dieu et la langue saincte, qui a nommé toutes choses selon sa vraye nature et proprieté appelle le mari Bahal, c'est à dire, le seigneur et maistre, pour monster qu'à luy appartient de commander. Aussi les loix de tous les peuples, doivent passer les femmes en sagesse et vertu, ont ordonné, que l'honneur et splendeur de la femme, dependroit du mari (p. 20); celles, qui prennent si grand plaisir à commander aux maris effeminez, resemblent à ceux, qui ayment mieux guider les aveugles, que de suivre les sages et clairvoyans (p. 20).

[See Appendix, pp. 278-9, 297.]

9. JORTIN. The last line was inserted on account of Queen Elizabeth.

CHURCH. This Line, as Mr. Jortin observes, was probably inserted on account of Queen Elizabeth: and, if I mistake not, there is a twofold propriety in the Epithet lawfull; as it ascertains, in that case, the right of the woman over the man; and in Queen Elizabeth's case, in particular, asserts the Legality of her Title to the Crown, which in the preceding Reign had been call'd in question.

[See Gough's note on 4. 31 ff. above.]

xxvii. 2. EDITOR. Same image at 3. 10. 18. 1; 5. 6. 19. 2.

xxxi ff. UPTON. Clarinda, like Anna in Virgil, is the confident of this love-sick queen. Whilst her mistress is in earnest, she is jesting, and ringing the changes on the word " dread," like a professed punster; I suppose with intention to make her mistress smile, and to change her melancholy mood. I know not whether 'tis worth mentioning that Sir Lancelot in the History of Prince Arthur, is taken captive by four queens, and led thence into a strong castle, and released from thence by a damsel who falls in love with him, [6. 3-4; 19. 7-8]. These kind of adventures are common in Romance writers. [See WALTHER's note on 36 ff. below.]

xxxi. 1-4. GOUGH. This stanza affords a good example of the alliterative inter-lacing of words and phrases of which there are many examples in the F. Q. Similar play upon words is a frequent characteristic of Elizabethan English; cf. Shake-speare, Love's Labor's Lost 5. 2. 21 ff. For the address " deare dread," cf. F. Q. 1 Proem 4: " O dearest dred " (Queen Elizabeth); 1. 6. 2. 3: " Una his deare dreed "; 3. 2. 30. 6 (Britomart); 4. 8. 17. 1 (Belphoebe). Dread = object of reverence.

xxxiv. 3. See GOUGH's note on 4. 36. 1.

xxxv. 2, 4, 5, 7. GOUGH. " indevour . . . labour . . . favour . . . behaviour." These words have all different rime-endings, a case which it would be difficult to parallel in the F. Q. The careless rimes in Book 5 are perhaps a sign that Spenser's interest in his work was flagging.

xxxvi ff. WALTHER (p. 30). Malory 186. 36 ff. [6. 3]. Launcelot ist von vier Königinnen gefangen genommen. Er soll sich eine davon als Paramour wählen oder sterben. Die Damoysel der Fay Morgan verhilft ihm zur Flicht (187).
Ferner: Malory 785. 20 [19. 8]. Meliagraunce hat Launcelot verräterisch in einer Falle gefangen. Die Damoysel, die ihm Essen bringt, sagt: . . . " but woldest thow but kysse me ones I shold delyver the and thyne armour and the best hors that is within sir Mellyagraunce's stable."

xxxvi-xlii. See Appendix, p. 297.

xxxvi. 2. TODD. See the note on F. Q. 2. 9. 8. 1 [in Book II, p. 281.] . . . But I find it also in Chaucer, where Troilus thus complains, Troilus and Cressida 1. 837: " For well finde I, that Fortune is my fo."
See UPTON's note on 2. 9. 8. 1 in Book II, p. 281.

xxxix. 3. GRACE W. LANDRUM (PMLA 41. 541). Cf. Hosea 2. 15: [" a door of hope." It may be observed from quotations in the Concordance that, while Spenser more often makes figurative use of doors than windows, the door asso-ciates itself in his mind with death and fate, the window with light and hope.]

xl. 5-6. GOUGH. Cf. Tasso, Ger. Lib. 6. 73, where Erminia, debating with herself whether she shall go to the Christian camp and seek Tancred whom she loves, soliloquizes:

Nata non sei tu già d'orsa vorace
Nè d'aspro e freddo scoglio, o giovinetta.

So Vergil, Aen. 4. 366-7, where Dido addresses the fugitive Aeneas:

Duris genuit te cautibus horrens
Caucasus, Hyrcanaeque admorunt ubera tigres.

xlii. 6-9.   Heise (p. 143) cites Chaucer's *Troilus* 5. 774 and Hawes' *Pastime of Pleasure* (ed. for Percy Society, 1846), p. 84.

Editor (C. G. O.).   The *Concordance* shows that this figure of the bait is one of Spenser's most characteristic images. It occurs no less than 26 times. He was evidently a devoted angler. See notes on 4. 8. 32. 4; 4. 11. 33; 4. 11. 47. 7-9, in Book IV, pp. 211-2, 257, 273.

xlvi. 5.   A Spenserian formula; see 3. 1. 9. 5; 3. 5. 45-7; 3. 8. 42. 3; 5. 11. 55. 9.

xlix. 1-4.   Jortin.   He that compares this with *Aen.* 4. 424 ff. will be inclin'd to think that Spenser had Virgil's Dido in view: " I, soror, atque hostem supplex adfare superbum," etc. That gifts can pacifie even the Gods, was a proverb amongst the Heathen. Euripides, *Medea* 964: [" 'Tis written, gifts persuade the gods in heaven." Tr. Gilbert Murray.]

3-4.   Blakeney.   Contrast the words of Plato in *Alcibiades* 2. 149 E: " The Gods, methinks, are not like base usurers to be won over by gifts." Perhaps Spenser was thinking of an old Greek proverb (quoted by Plato in the *Republic* 390 E: " gifts persuade even Gods and venerable kings " [cf. Jowett's note in his translation, 2. 213: " Quoted by Suidas as attributed to Hesiod."]), or Ovid, *Art. Amat.* 3. 653:

Munera (crede mihi) capiunt hominesque deosque;
Placatur donis Jupiter ipse datis.

liii. 1-4.   Gough.   Cf. Bartholomew Anglicus, *De Proprietatibus Rerum* (in R. Steele, *Mediaeval Lore,* ed. 1893, p. 46): " A nurse . . . cheweth meat in her mouth, and maketh it ready to the toothless child, that it may the easilier swallow that meat." [Cf. *Batman Vppon Bartholome*, ed. 1582, fol. 74r. See note on 6. 14 below.]

7-8.   E. B. Fowler (*Spenser and the System of Courtly Love*, pp. 28-31) remarks the inflammatory function of love in the courtly convention. He cites Ovid, *Amores* 1. 1; Jaufre Rudel, in Raynouard, *Poésies des Troubadours*, Paris, 1818, vol. 3, p. 99; *Romance of the Rose* 2467-2471; M. E. *Court of Love* 883-5; Petrarch 55, " Quel foco."

lvi. 1-3.   See Fowler's note on 6. 17-8 below.

lvii.   A. H. Gilbert (*PMLA* 34. 232) notes this as a conclusion in the manner of Ariosto.

CANTO VI

i.   See Appendix, p. 298.

7.   Upton cites 1 Corinthians 10. 12.

ii.   4.   See notes on 5. 42. 6-9 above.

5. See FOWLER's note on 6. 17-8 below.

iii ff.   DODGE (*PMLA* 12. 177). Britomart waiting impatiently for the return of Arthegall, seeing the time appointed for his return slip by, tormented by fears and jealousies, is the exact counterpart of the lovesick Bradamante waiting for the return of Ruggiero (*Orl. Fur.* 30. 84 ff.; 32. 10 ff.). Talus, who brings back news of Arthegall's defeat by Radegund and his captivity, thereby rousing Britomart's jealousy, corresponds to the "cavalier guascone" who brings to Bradamante the report that Ruggiero is betrothed to the warrior maiden, Marfisa. The conduct of Britomart when she receives the news is exactly like that of Bradamante: she first indulges in resentful despair, then sets out to go to her lover.

GOUGH (p. 233).   The selfish distress of the two enamoured Amazons, described in Canto 5, serves as a foil to the much tried devotion of Artegall's true lover. Nowhere in this book, and seldom in the poem, is a state of the soul portrayed with so intimate and delicate strokes as here, where Artegall's apparent breach of faith with his betrothed rouses a tumult of emotions in her breast. It is worthy of remark that Book 5 was probably written during Spenser's courtship of Elizabeth Boyle. . . . If his sonnets are in the main a record of that courtship, as seems probable, and not mere literary exercises, it may be inferred that for a time Elizabeth Boyle was estranged from Spenser, owing to "false forged lies," which, he says, "in my true love did stirre up coles of yre" (Sonnet 86). The thought of the beloved a prey to doubt, jealousy, and wrath may well have occupied his mind while he was writing these cantos.

[See Appendix, pp. 283-4, 348.]

iii-iv.   E. B. FOWLER (*Spenser and the System of Courtly Love*, pp. 15-7). In an enumeration of the evils which afflict lovers Spenser stresses the idea of fear (*Hymne in Honour of Love* 259-262):

> The gnawing envie, the hart-fretting feare,
> The vaine surmizes, the distrustfull showes,
> The false reports that flying tales doe beare,
> The doubts, the daungers, the delayes, the woes.

The God of Love inspires terror in the beholder. In the Masque of Cupid he brandishes his darts and claps his wings (*F. Q.* 3. 12. 23), "That all his many it affraide did make.". . .

The lover's fear and his jealousy are scarcely separable. So much is implied in Spenser's use of the term "jealous fear." Jealousy is recommended by mediaeval writers on courtly love as a sure means of increasing the lover's affection. (This idea is probably derived from Ovid. See *Ars amatoria* 2. 445-6, and cf. Andreas Capellanus, *De Amore*, ed. by Trojel, p. 311, and Froissart, *Le Paradys d'Amour* 661-7.) Spenser, however, holds quite the opposite view. He denounces the passion as destructive of all love (*F. Q.* 3. 11. 1):

> O hateful hellish snake! what Furie furst
> Brought thee from balefull house of Proserpine,
> Where in her bosome she thee long had nurst,
> And fostred up with bitter milke of tine,
> Fowle Gealosy! that turnest love divine

> To joylesse dread, and mak'st the loving hart
> With hatefull thoughts to languish and to pine,
> And feed it selfe with selfe-consuming smart?
> Of all the passions in the mind thou vilest art.

In the *Hymne in Honour of Love* he again attacks it as an enemy of love (266-272):

> Yet is there one more cursed then they all,
> That cancker worme, that monster Gelosie,
> Which eates the hart, and feedes upon the gall,
> Turning all loves delight to miserie,
> Through feare of losing his felicitie.
> Ah, gods! that ever ye that monster placed
> In gentle love, that all his joyes defaced.

One of Spenser's most repulsive creations is Malbecco, an embodiment of marital jealousy (*F. Q.* 3. 9. 3 ff.). Sir Guyon rescues from Furor a young squire who had been driven by jealousy to slay his lady and poison his friend (*F. Q.* 2. 4. 3 ff.). Love of Amyas makes Paeana jealous of Aemylia and Placidas (*F. Q.* 4. 9. 9). The shepherd Coridon resents Sir Calidore's attentions to Pastorella (*F. Q.* 6. 9. 39),

> and even for gealousie
> Was readie oft his owne hart to devoure,
> Impatient of any paramoure.

Yet some of Spenser's noblest lovers suffer the pangs of jealousy. The Redcross Knight "burnt with gealous fire" when he saw the counterfeit Una in the embrace of a supposed lover (*F. Q.* 1. 2. 5). Sir Scudamour is stirred to action against Britomart and Amoret by the false accusations of Ate (*F. Q.* 4. 5. 31),

> The which like thornes did pricke his gealous hart,
> And through his soule like poysned arrow persed.

Even Britomart is thrown into a jealous fit by the news that Artegall is held captive in the castle of the Amazon Radigund (*F. Q.* 5. 6. 11 ff.).

iii. 6-7. UPTON. Arthegal promised Britomart to return after the expiration of three months. See 4. 6. 43.

v. 6-9. GOUGH. It is difficult to understand what reckoning Spenser intended. The emendations suggested are impossible and uncalled for. Mr. J. C. Smith suggests a possible interpretation which requires no alteration of the words, viz. that she reckoned the time in months and days rather than weeks and hours, i. e. three months, to sound less than twelve weeks, &c. This makes tolerable sense, though it is not very forcible or convincing. The whole passage is a characteristic, if somewhat puerile example of a " concetto " in the artificial Italian manner. [Cf. " Critical Notes on the Text."]

EDITOR (F. M. P.). It is strange that this passage should have raised any question in the minds of editors, or that Smith should have felt any uncertainty about his own suggested, though partial, interpretation. When Britomart reviews the " passed time " she thinks of days and months, rather than hours and weeks, as Smith says " to make the time look shorter." When she thinks of the unexpired separation, however, she can no longer play tricks with her mind, for her emotions get the best of her; consequently, in anticipation each hour seems a month, and each month a year. Cf. Juliet's " 'tis twenty years till then [tomorrow]," *Romeo and Juliet* 2. 2. 171.

vi. 7-8. EDITOR (C. G. O.). Cf. 11-12. Just why she suspected his weakness, unless from her suspicion of every man's susceptibilities, is not clear. Una, with plenty of reason, did not distrust her man. Britomart is again sternly suspicious of Artegall's candor at 16. 6-9.

EDITOR (F. M. P.). But is not Britomart's apprehension, her "iealous feare, Lest some new loue had him from her possest," singularly true to life, at least as an Elizabethan conceived it? The more intense the love, the more haunting such fears. Since her judgment is overpowered by her emotions, at one moment Britomart blames herself; the next moment, Artegall. Una is of a very different temperament. In any case, Britomart's perturbation adds dramatic interest to the story.

vii. J. W. MACKAIL (*The Springs of Helicon*, pp. 114-5). Spenser's Chaucerianism was no mere muddle of antiquarian pedantry; it was a real love and admiration, a poetical sympathy that makes him write now and then, for a few lines together, with the freshness and charm of Chaucer. If I may venture to put it so, he sometimes drops into poetry. When he has almost wearied us with Britomartis, he suddenly writes of her thus [st. quoted]. . . . It is like cool water. The same clear simplicity comes with the same lovely effect in many single lines. [Cf. notes on *F. Q.* 5. 5. 39. 3; 5. 7. 40. 2; 6. 4. 17. 3; 6. 10. 34. 1-2.]

4-5. UPTON. Ireland lies west of England. 'Tis from these little circumstances, well attended to, that we may get acquainted with the historical allusions of our poet.

4. DODGE (*PMLA* 12. 203). Cf. the " alta torre " in *Orl. Fur.* 32. 14. 5.

viii. DODGE (*PMLA* 12. 203). Cf. the " cavalier guascone " in *Orl. Fur.* 32. 28.

ix. 5. GOUGH. The statement in this clause can hardly be reconciled with the words immediately preceding. In any case Talus is not a mere automaton, but is endowed with a rudimentary or subhuman personality, and is even capable, as here, of a certain delicacy of feeling.

xi. 4. See UPTON'S note on 2. 2. 2, Book II, pp. 195-6.

xii. DOROTHY BUCHANAN (see note on 25 below) cites this stanza as an example of the objective method of the complaint in Spenser. " Obviously this is a paraphrase of a complaint rather than the real lyric. Furthermore it is singularly barren of all the familiar themes." Besides the examples cited in Book IV, p. 277, Miss Buchanan lists the following " complaints " in *F. Q.*: 1. 1. 51-2; 1. 2. 22-6; 1. 3. 7; 1. 7. 22-3; 3. 4. 8-10; 36-9; 3. 5. 45-7; 3. 11. 9-11; 6. 8. 19-22.

xiv. A. A. JACK (*A Commentary on the Poetry of Chaucer and Spenser*, p. 347). The picture is as inappropriate as it is lively and more cannot be said. [A like image is found at 1. 10. 35. 9; 5. 5. 53. 2; 6. 2. 11. 9; 6. 12. 21. 1.]

xvii-xviii.   E. B. FOWLER (*Spenser and the System of Courtly Love*, pp. 50-5) notes that " a second general law demands of the courtly lover absolute loyalty both to the beloved and to the God of Love." He cites *Court of Love* 316-9:

> The thrid statut was clerely write also
> Withouten chaunge to live and dye the same,
> Non other love to take, for wele ne wo,
> For brind delyt, for ernest nor for game.

xix. 6.   See below note on 32 ff.

xxii. 1.   UPTON.   Matthew 24. 33: " [know] that is it neere, even at the doors."

xxiv. 5-9.   E. B. FOWLER (*Spenser and the System of Courtly Love*, p. 33). The vicissitudes of the lover's fortunes keep him in a state of nervous restlessness— or *malaise*—accompanied with loss of sleep. Thus in the *Romance of the Rose* the lover complains (2631-2):

> A man to lyen hath gret disese
> Which may not slepe ne reste in ese.

(Ovid, *Ars. am.* 1. 735: " Attenuent juvenum vigilatae corpora noctes." See also *Amores* 1. 2. 1-4 . . . , Bernard de Ventadorn, in Raynouard, *Poésies des Troubadours*, Paris, 1818, vol. 3, p. 66.)

xxv.   See note on 4. 12. 25, in Book IV, p. 277; note on st. 12 above. Miss Dorothy Buchanan in an unpublished paper on " The Love Complaint in *The Faerie Queene*," which constitutes part of her larger study of the tradition of the " complaint," describes Spenser's practice thus: " Words that have medieval connotations are used, such as the power of the eyes, the dart of Cupid and other mythological references in the manner of the Court of Love. Climax and dénouement are emphasized by question and answer, so common a device that it is almost a trademark of the 'plaint [quotes stanza]. The rhetorical style of this stanza, a characteristic of the euphuistic prose of the period, is another common mark of the love complaint. Notice for example the artful repetition of words: betray, watch, sleepe, wake, and the intellectual contrast of ideas."

xxvi. 8.   Cf. 1. 29. 9 above and note on 8. 49. 1-5 below.

xxvii ff.   See LEMMI's note on 2. 7 ff. above; and Appendix, pp. 314, 316.

xxvii-xxx.   EDITOR (C. G. O.).   One of the most vivid and memorable scenes in the whole poem. According to one opinion it may have prompted in Milton's *Lycidas* the obscure and much dissertated " two-handed engine at the door." See *RES* 1. 339-341.

xxvii. 2.   W. RIEDNER (*Spensers Belesenheit*, p. 19).   Cf. Mark 14. 30; Luke 22. 34. [Complete references would include Matt. 26. 34, 69-75; Mark 14. 68-72; Luke 22. 60-1; John 13. 38; 18. 27. But only in Mark 14. 68, 72 was the cock's crow a warning.]

6-9.   UPTON (2. 672).   These kind of adventures are frequent in romances: in like manner the knight of the sun by a trap-door, that sunk under him, as he was in a certain castle, found himself in a deep dungeon. See *Don Quixote* 3. 1.

GOUGH. There is a similar instance of treachery to a guest in Malory's *Morte Darthur* 19. 7. Sir Launcelot, who has been hospitably received by Sir Mellygraunce at his castle, treads on a trap-door, and falls down into a prison, where he is kept until released by a damsel.

xxviii. 9. See notes on 2. 3. 1. 9 in Book II, pp. 205-6.

xxix. 4. " raskall rout." See note on 2. 9. 15. 4, Book II, p. 285; also on 11. 44-47; 11. 59. 6-8, below.

xxxii ff. GOUGH (pp. 234-6). At the meeting with Dolon it seems that we again enter the world of allegory. Britomart, the royal British virgin, the future slayer of Radigund, is one of the types of Elizabeth, and in the two treacherous attempts to murder her we cannot fail to recognize allusions to some of the plots to assassinate the Queen. In the watchfulness of Britomart and Talus, by which her life is saved, Spenser refers to the activity of Elizabeth's spies, who repeatedly frustrated the designs of the plotters.

It has already . . . been shown that Guizor, the " groome of evill guize " (5. 2. 6. 6), is probably Henry, the third Duke of Guise. His two brothers, the Duke of Mayenne and the Cardinal of Lorraine, were, like himself, bitter and unscrupulous enemies of Elizabeth. A complete and consistent allegory is not to be looked for. It is Spenser's habit to give a hint of a political meaning, and then deliberately to confuse the trail. The slaughter of Guizor can hardly have a historical reference. Nor can Dolon be the great Guise, the father of the three brothers, for he had nothing to do with plots against Elizabeth, and was murdered in 1563. Though it is difficult to identify Dolon, " the crafty," the particularity of the description of him in stanzas 19 and 32 appears to point to some real person.

Perhaps Philip of Spain is intended, a prince whose character corresponds well with that of Dolon. He only once appeared in the field of battle, at the assault on St. Quentin in 1557, when he was thirty years of age (cf. 5. 6. 32. 3), and he preferred " slie shiftes and wiles " to open war. He had treacherously brought to shame many " noble Knights, which were adventurous," such as Counts Egmont and Hoorn (1568). Like Elizabeth, he was anxious to avoid a conflict between Spain and England as long as possible, and in 1573 he made overtures to the Queen which resulted in a treaty. Elizabeth deserted the insurgent Netherlanders, and even held out hopes of her conversion to the Roman Church. The apparent friendship between the two Powers, which lasted several years, may be suggested by Dolon's hospitality to Britomart. Philip was insincere throughout. He had approved the Ridolfi plot to murder Elizabeth in 1571, and his aim now was merely to frustrate an Anglo-French alliance, and to keep his hands free for a time to deal with the Netherlands. Through his ambassador Mendoza, whom Elizabeth expelled in 1583, he supported the Jesuit mission in 1580, which worked for the overthrow of Elizabeth. He was a party to Throckmorton's plot for her assassination in 1583, and probably to several other schemes of the kind. At this time Philip was " well shot in yeares " (5. 6. 19. 6), having been born in 1527.

The three brothers of the house of Guise, who were much younger men than Philip, and were closely bound to him by party interests, might be figuratively described as his sons. They were as ready as he to intrigue against Elizabeth. The two armed knights, apparently the surviving sons of Dolon, who tried to force their way into Britomart's chamber, followed by "a raskall rout," with the intention of murdering her, may represent the Duke of Guise and his brother the Duke of Mayenne, who planned an invasion of England in 1583. Guise was to land with an army in the North, and Mayenne in Sussex, while Philip's fleet was to hold the Channel. The failure of the assassin whom the brothers had hired to kill the Queen, and the subsequent detection of Throckmorton's plot, were among the causes of the abandonment of the scheme.

EDITOR (C. G. O.). It is the not uncommon practice of the satirist to base his satirical portrait upon his knowledge of one or more actual human instances, and then to generalize it through the energy of his very hatred of the defect or offence which they illustrate. Examples abound in Dryden and Pope. Surely Spenser hated nothing more than the treachery all about him, and his feeling in the matter asserts itself again and again throughout his poet's life, and with especial force in this portrait of Dolon. Regard for such evolution of an allegorical portrait or character is always salutary in discussing the historical allegory.

xxxii.   LOTSPEICH (p. 55). Spenser translates (*Virgils Gnat* 536) the very brief allusion at *Culex* 328 in a way that indicates his acquaintance with the story. Cf. *Il.* 10. 314 ff.; *Met.* 13. 241-6 [also 98, 244].

EDITOR (C. G. O.). The whole tale of Dolus is told by Boccaccio in *De Genealogia Deorum* 1. 20, where Spenser doubtless read it. This stanza suggests a reminiscence of Boccaccio's words explaining the pagans' moral interpretation of Dolus's parentage (by Erebus out of Night): "Arbitror eos pro Herebo intimum cordis humani recessum intellexisse. Ubi enim cogitationum omnium sedes est, et ideo si aeger animus virtute neglecta, ut ad optatum deveniat, si desint vires, illico dirigit ad artes ingenium. Et quoniam facilius dolo capiuntur amantes, eo cogitationibus pessimis fabricato, et quos capit et seipsum letifero alligat laqueo, et sic ex nocte id est mentis caecitate, per quam ea via, qua minime decet, in desiderium suum tendit, et aegri pectoris ignominiosa concupiscentia ferventis dolus creatur, et nascitur, et ut plurimum non ante visus in lucem, quam is in praecipitium venerit in quem struitur."

1.   UPTON. Dolon is mentioned by Homer, *Il.* 10. [314-478]. Hector sent him as a scout by night into the Grecian camp. He had his name from δόλος, to which Spenser alludes, "He was nothing valorous, but with slie shiftes, etc." And Ovid likewise alludes to this Etymology, in a passage which is misunderstood, *Epist.* 1. [39-42]:

> Rettulit et ferro Rhesumque Dolonaque caesos,
>   Utque sit hic somno proditus, ille dolo.
> Ausus es, o nimium nimiumque oblite tuorum
>   Thracia nocturno tangere castra pede.

WALTHER (p. 8) cites Dolon [Dalan] in Malory, p. 454 [10. 25].

C. W. LEMMI (*PQ* 8. 283). [See note on 2. 7 ff. above.] There is no parallel to this statement in the *Mythologiae* [cf. Natalis Comes], but I think it supports my thesis that Boccaccio (*Gen. Deor.* 8. [5]) says as follows: "His [Pluto's] chariot is nothing but the manoeuvres of those who want to get rich; it

runs on three wheels to indicate the labor, risk, and uncertainty of such a quest."
So also it is said that three are the horses, of which the first is called Metheus
[Ametheus], or blind determination; the second Abaster, or anxiety; the third
Nuvius [Novius], or fear. [The Latin for this last sentence reads: " Sic et equi
trahentes tres esse dicuntur. Quorum primus Ametheus dicitur, qui interpretatur
obscurus, ut per eum intelligatur insana deliberatio acquirendi quod minime oppor-
tunum est, qua trahitur seu impellitur cupidus. Secundus Abaster dictus est, qui
idem quod niger sonat, ut appareat discurrentis moeror, et tristitia circa incum-
bentia fere semper pericula et pavores. Tertius Novius nuncupatur, quem intel-
lexere sonare repentem, ut per eum advertamus, quoniam ob timorem periculorum
ardor ferventissimus acquirendi tepescat aliquando.]

xxxiii. 6. GOUGH. "Guizor." The "groome of evill guize" (2. 6. 7);
but Spenser has evidently forgotten that he described him there as a thrall "whose
scalp is bare, that bondage doth bewray," and here makes him the son of a knight.

xxxvi-xxxix. DODGE (*PMLA* 12. 203). Britomart passing the bridge despite
Dolon's sons is like Bradamante: she alone passes it without being forced into the
water, *Orl. Fur.* 35. 38 ff.

  EDITOR (C. G. O.). No pitfalls await Britomart as they did Artegall.

xxxvi. 8. BLAKENEY. The bridge was narrow ("streight"), like the famous
bridge Al-Sirat in Mohammedan legend; it was narrower than the sword edge,
and cast across the abyss of hell. Over this ordeal bridge all must pass to resur-
rection; but the wicked will fall over into the gulf.

  EDITOR. "Pollente," at 5. 2. 7. 1 a trisyllable, is here a disyllable.

xl. 4.7. GOUGH. "Engine." Here used for the lightning, possibly by association of ideas with a battering ram or a missile, in which senses "engin" was
used. . . . The description is not true to nature, for lightning cannot uproot a tree,
though it may shatter the trunk.

CANTO VII

  FRIEDRICH ZANDER (*Stephen Hawes' Passetyme of Pleasure ver-
glichen mit Edmund Spenser's Faerie Queene unter Berücksichtigung der alle-
gorischen Dichtung in England,* p. 50) points out that both Graunde Amour (who
visits the temple of Pallas, *Passetyme of Pleasure* 4963 ff.) and Britomart seek the
help of a deity before completing their quests and have a vision of the coming
ordeal.

  E. B. FOWLER (*Spenser and the Courts of Love,* pp. 4, 13) uses this
episode as an example of the court of love "setting in a temple or castle." He
adds: "This episode could be omitted without prejudice to the general argument,
but it is included for the sake of completeness because structurally it conforms to the
type, because the figure of Isis has certain close affinities with that of Venus in
Spenser's Temple of Venus, and because the whole situation, with Britomart
worshipping in the temple before going forth to combat for her lover, provokes

comparison with similar situations in court of love literature. Cf., for example, the scene in Chaucer's *Knightes Tale* 1351-1412, where Palamon prays in the Temple of Venus before the combat with Arcite for the love of Emelye." [See below notes on 7. 8. 9.]

H. S. V. JONES (*Spenser's Defense of Lord Grey*, p. 53 n.). Although it is Artegall who personifies Justice, his close association with Britomart suggests the classical personification of Justice as a beautiful virgin. This symbolism de l'Hôpital dwells upon in the *Traité* (1. 68-9), opposing to his portrait of Justice another one of Injustice. The two allegorical figures correspond interestingly with the contrasted portraits of Radigund and Britomart in the *Faerie Queene*.

i-xxiv.   See JONES's note on 9. 38 ff. below.

i.   GOUGH. Cf. the whole of this stanza with Proem, st. 10. Plato (*Republic* 4. 443) identifies justice in the deeper sense of the word with virtue itself, i. e. it is the inward harmonizing and unifying principle which regulates all the desires and actions of the good man.
[See Appendix, pp. 281, 284-5, 287 ff., 295-6.]

3.   UPTON. "Suum cuique tribuens." Cicero, *de Off*. 1. 5; *De Fin. Bonor. et Malor.* 5. 23; *De Nat. Deor.* 3. 15.

6.   GRACE W. LANDRUM (*PMLA* 41. 541). Cf. 2 Chronicles 9. 8.

9.   UPTON. Complimenting Q. Elizabeth.

BLAKENEY cites Proverbs 8. 15: "By me kings reign, and princes decree justice." [See GOUGH's note on Pr. 11 above.]

ii ff.   JORTIN cites the following in Plutarch's *Isis and Osiris* [13]: [*The Complete Works of Plutarch*, The Kelmscott Society, *Essays and Miscellanies* 1. 376, where Osiris is called "A great king, beneficent"; p. 377: "That when Osiris reigned over the Egyptians he made them reform their destitute and bestial mode of living, showing them the art of cultivation, and giving them laws, and teaching them how to worship the gods."]

SAWTELLE (p. 69). This entire passage, which describes the attributes and worship of the Egyptian divinities, Isis and Osiris, is based upon Plutarch's *Isis and Osiris*. Spenser, however, does not feel himself at all bound by the original, but follows it at times afar off. Thus he says the priests wore their hair long, while Plutarch says their heads were shaved. The interpretation of the crocodile, also, which he gives in Stanza 22, is not authorized by the original. The other points which Spenser cites,—the justice of Osiris when king of Egypt; the equity attributed to Isis; the linen garb of the priests; the crescent miters; the interpretation of Osiris as the sun, and Isis as the moon; the continence of the priests; their abstinence from fleshly food; the reason why they did not drink wine,—all these are consistent with the account given by Plutarch.

E. GREENLAW (*SP* 20. 239-240). The true explanation seems to me to be that Spenser has transferred, consciously or unconsciously, to the priests of Isis some of the characteristics of the galli. In the standard descriptions of these priests we are told that they were dressed in flowing robes, like women, and wore long hair fragrant with ointment. (Cf. the account taken from Apollonius Rhodius, *Argon.* 1. 1092-1150.) This observation leads to several other points of interest. While Spenser is undoubtedly indebted to Plutarch, he omits several striking details which he appears to use elsewhere. Thus, he follows Plutarch in tracing the descent of Osiris from ancient kings; in explaining Osiris as significant of the sun and Isis of the moon; and in the details describing the priests—their linen robes, their avoidance of flesh or wine (the detail about wine being thought to be the blood of the Titans is common to both), and their ascetic habits. But in Plutarch the crocodile is not Osiris but Typhon. There is no mention of the justice-equity interpretation of Osiris-Isis; he gives a different philosophical explanation, made up of elements used by Spenser elsewhere, not here. Spenser's representation of Isis with one foot on the crocodile is not a happy one if, as he says, the crocodile is her lover Osiris; that is, it is not a happy one for the lover, or for romantic views of the marital relation. Plutarch is more satisfying. To him Typhon, the crocodile, is the passionate, irrational and brutal part of the soul. Isis therefore represents the reason subduing this irrational principle. The symbolism would fit Spenser's treatment of the legend of Guyon. Again, Plutarch speaks of the "intelligible part" (form) plus matter as joining to bring the cosmos into being; material that suggests some of the details in Spenser's account of the Garden of Adonis [3. 6] and is no doubt related to it. Plutarch also discourses on the triangle and the mystical significance of numbers, following Plato's *Republic*, of course, but also reminding one of a portion of Spenser's allegory of the body [2. 9]. Finally, Plutarch speaks of Isis as the mother of the world, both male and female principles being present in her, sending forth the generative principle into the air. This detail reminds us of Spenser's comment on Nature as both male and female, not found in Alanus; it also introduces the title "mother of the world" which is applicable to *Mater Deum* as well as to the goddess Natura; and it suggests the Garden of Adonis. For these reasons it appears to me that in order to make the temple scene fit the necessary allegory of his legend of justice, Spenser modifies Plutarch greatly; but it also appears that he read it attentively, for the contrast between the rational and irrational principles in the soul, the form-matter theory of the cosmos, and the conception of a goddess who is mother of the world, are important philosophical elements found in other parts of the *Faerie Queene. Isis and Osiris* must have fascinated him, also, for its catholicity. Plutarch was really writing on comparative religion. He makes the point that the names given to the gods by various peoples indicate not different deities but the same supernatural principles operating under different titles. Thus the whole treatise dwells on allegory, and would therefore appeal with special meaning to allegory's chief poet.

LOTSPEICH (pp. 73-4). [This comment, though suggesting no new sources, is printed as a convenient summary of details noted by others.] Spenser's use of Isis and Osiris is based on Plutarch, *De Iside,* and Diodorus 1. 11 f. . . . , with perhaps some additional suggestions from Natalis Comes 5. 13. He uses his sources with freedom and independence. The conception of Osiris as a just king (st. 2) who, because of his reputation, afterwards became a god of justice, is found in Plutarch 13, Diodorus 1. 17, and Natalis Comes. Isis as "that part of justice which is equity" is probably founded on Plutarch 3 and Diodorus 1. 14, where she is said to have "caused men to practice justice among themselves." The identification of Osiris with the sun and of Isis with the moon is in Diodorus 1. 11 and Plutarch 52. For the description of the character and habits of Isis' priests, Spenser is indebted mainly to Plutarch 2-6, who tells of their austere and continent rule, their linen robes, their abstinence from flesh and wine. Spenser contradicts Plutarch in giving them long hair; he may be remembering Natalis Comes's remark (noted by LEMMI, *P. Q.* 8. 274) that, in commemoration of his triumphs, Osiris commanded that men's hair should be worn long. Spenser may also owe something to Natalis Comes's description of the "galli" (9. 5), the priests of Rhea, with whom Isis was identified. The " galli " were vowed to chastity and were clothed in the habit of women. The crocodile (st. 7) may represent a memory of what Plutarch has to say about Typhon, the enemy of Isis and Osiris, and a symbol of the powers of disorder and confusion. Plutarch says (ch. 50) that Typhon once assumed the form of a crocodile. Plutarch may also have given a suggestion for Britomart's dream (st. 12 ff.). In ch. 81 he says that sleeping in a temple, near burning incense, is a stimulus to the " imaginative and prophetic part of dreams."

EDITOR (C. G. O.). As between Plutarch and Diodorus, both of whom Spenser evidently consulted, no one has observed that the strongly euhemeristic opinion in 7. 2. 5-9 favors Diodorus, whose account of Isis and Osiris is entirely euhemeristic, whereas Plutarch explicitly disapproves of that interpretation.

Strangely enough every commentator has overlooked the obvious traces in this passage of Spenser's reading in the *Metamorphoses* of Apuleius. The experience of Britomart in " Isis Church "—the vigil, the dream, the investure for the sacrifice, the encounter with the high priest at dawn—is all clearly based upon that of Lucius the Ass in *Met.* 11. 4-8, where Isis restores him to human form and he becomes a priest of Isis and then of Osiris. Spenser has simplified and altered certain details and omitted many from Apuleius's elaborate account. Lucius has several dream-visions of Isis (cf. " visions," 7. Arg. 2). They always occur at night. In the first on the shore at Cenchris the goddess promised Lucius release from his asinine form through her chief priest, and Britomart seeks the help of the high priest appointed to that service, " to guide me out of errour blind." Lucius after his restoration to human form hired a house within " the cloisture of the temple," and had a dream of the high priest which puzzled him; so at dawn he went in to pray, and found the priest as he " prepared and set the divine thinges on every Aultour, and pulled out of the fountaine the holy vessell with solempne supplication. Then they began to singe the mattens of the mornyng, . . . " (Cf. 17.) Like Britomart Lucius was invested in a robe of fine linen for his participation in the sacrifice (13). Spenser may have read Apuleius in Adlington's translation, 1566, who speaks not only of " mattins " (cf. " morrow Mas ", 17. 8), but of Isis " Church " in Rome. See *Hymne of Love* 287; 3. 6. 50 and notes in Book III, p. 261; this passage, 7. 1 ff., seems to resolve the uncertainty there expressed by Lotspeich whether Spenser read Apuleius. See notes on 8. 9. 12 ff. below.

ii. BLAKENEY. The prominent part which Justice plays in Plato's system is well known. In the *Republic*, Justice is equated with Virtue in general. Solon had already spoken of Justice as the daughter of Zeus (following the lead of Hesiod, *Works and Days* 256) [cf. Pr. 11. 4]. For the Altar of Justice cf. Aeschylus, *Agam.* [392-5]: " There is no defence in riches for a man who hath spurned the Altar of Justice"; *ib.*, *Eumen.* 538: "At all times I bid thee reverence the Altar of Justice." And read Swinburne's fine poem "The Altar of Righteousness."

iii. 1. GOUGH. According to Diodorus, *Bibl. Hist.* 1. 14, after the death of Osiris his wife Isis devoted herself to the exact administration of justice among her people, in which, as well as in mercy, she excelled all other rulers.

5. A. H. GILBERT (*PMLA* 34. 232) notes this as an "Ariosto-like transition from the introductory stanzas of a canto to the narrative."

iv. 1-5. JORTIN. The Priests of Isis wore ἐσθῆτα λινέην μούνην, "vestem tantummodo lineam," Herodotus 2. 37, and are called "Linigeri" by many writers. Their heads were close shaved, though Spenser gives them long locks.

UPTON. Spenser never thinks himself tyed down to exactness in minute descriptions: he has an allegory and a mythology of his own, and takes from others just as suits his scheme. 'Tis very well known that the Ægyptian priests wore linnen robes, and were bald, quite contrary to what Spenser says, Juvenal 6. 533: "Qui grege linigero circumdatus, et grege calvo." But Spenser does not carry you to Ægypt; you stand upon allegorical and Fairy ground. He will dress therefore the priests of Justice, like the priests of Him, the assessors of whose throne Justice and Judgment are, Psalms 89. 14; 97. 2. In the prophet Ezekiel though 'tis said [44. 17], "the priests shall be clothed with linnen garments": yet 'tis ordered [44. 20], "they shall not shave their heads [nor suffer their locks to grow long]." The original command seems to intend that a distinction should be kept up between the Jewish and Ægyptian priests even in their dress. See Leviticus 21. 5.
[See notes on sts. ii ff. above.]

5. C. W. LEMMI (*PQ* 8. 274-5) cites Natalis Comes, *Mythologiae* 5. 13: "Thus Osiris, having started on his way, resolved not to cut his hair till he returned to his native land; wherefore the custom afterwards obtained that travelers should let their hair grow until they returned home."

7-8. JORTIN. So Plutarch, *De Isid.* [52].

BLAKENEY. Such was the usual interpretation among old writers (and still is, even among modern scholars of good repute). Frazer, however, has shown, in *The Golden Bough* (third edition, "Adonis, Attis, Osiris," vol. 2, chaps. 7, 8), that there is good reason for holding that both these divinities were rather vegetation than solar powers. Isis was similar, in a number of points, to the Greek Demeter (the Earth Mother), goddess of corn and fruits of the earth.

GOUGH. Diodorus 1. 11, identifies Osiris and Isis with the sun and moon.

v. F. HARD (*Sewanee Review* 42. 301). Two smaller buildings which reflect [Spenser's] architectural interest are the Temple of Venus and Isis Church. [See HARD's note on 9. 21 ff.]

EDITOR (C. G. O.). Though it has not been noticed, one can hardly doubt that this stanza entered into Milton's elaborate description of Pandemonium, *P. L.* 1. 710 ff.—the temple, the pillars, the gold, the arched roof (though in a building of Egyptian or Greek style), the wonder of those who entered at both the workman and his skill; and Milton includes Egyptian temples in his magnificent compound simile (717-722). There is a Miltonic cadence about lines 4-6.

3-6. See FOWLER'S notes on *F. Q.* 4. 10. 37. 4-5, 6-8, in Book IV, pp. 228-9.

6. F. HARD (*Sewanee Review* 42. 304-5). He [Spenser] thinks the architect is to be praised, as witness his frequent comments on workmanly skill [quotes 1. 4. 5. 2; 2. 9. 21. 8 (add 23. 3); 2. 9. 46. 9]. Incidentally, Spenser's appreciation of fine workmanship in the several arts is characteristic. Repeatedly he mentions the "workeman's passing skill," the "cunning craftsman's hand," etc. Compare 2. 9. 47; 3. 12. 20. 3; 4. 4. 15. 8; 4. 10. 29. 8-9; 5. 9. 27. 8.

vii. 3-4. GOUGH. The crocodile was said to lure its victims by feigned weeping. Note the inconsistency between this interpretation and that in stanza 22, where the crocodile symbolizes "the righteous knight" and "faithfull lover" Artegall, and the just Osiris. This is a proof, if any is needed, that Spenser's allegory is not rigidly systematic, but adapts itself spontaneously to the mood of the moment.

EDITOR (C. G. O.). In relation to stanzas 15 and 22 I see no inconsistency in this stanza. The theme throughout is the issue between clemency or equity and the literal application of the law, which Spenser often saw perverted to serve "forged guile and open force." It was an issue which much preoccupied the Elizabethan mind as appears in the trial in *Merchant of Venice*. See above 5. 7. 3. 4-5; 5. 4. 19-20 and note; 10. 1 and notes.

viii. 4-5. UPTON. Virgil, *Aen.* 12. 260: "Accepit omen"; 'tis frequently mentioned that the idols, by some sign or other, gave tokens of their favouring or disfavouring the request of their votaries. [EDITOR. *Aen.* 12. 260 reads: "Accipio agnoscoque deos; me, me duce ferrum." The index in the Lemaire edition of Virgil and Wetmore's *Index Vergilianus* show that the phrase, "Accepit omen," does not occur in Virgil. Cf. Cicero, *De Divinatione* 1. 46. 103.]

9. JORTIN. Britomartis sleeps in the temple of Isis, and has visions of what should befal her. It was not unusual for those who consulted the Gods, to sleep in their temples, where, as we are informed, they used to have their fortunes told them.

Virgil, *Aen.* 7. 86-91:

> Huc dona sacerdos
> Cum tulit, et caesarum ovium sub nocte silenti
> Pellibus incubuit stratis, somnosque petivit,
> Multa modis simulacra videt volitantia miris:
> Et varias audit voces, fruiturque deorum
> Conloquio, atque imis Acheronta adfatur Avernis.

Servius: "Incubare proprie dicuntur hi, qui dormiunt ad accipienda responsa: unde est: Ille incubat Jovi, . . . id est, dormit in Capitolio, ut responsa possit accipere."

GOUGH. This kind of divination, which was called "incubatio," was as a rule only practised in the temples of under-world divinities or departed heroes, but Diodorus (1. 25) says that according to the Egyptians Isis appears to those who seek her help in this manner, and reveals methods of healing.

ix. 1-3. JORTIN. So the Selli in Homer, *Il.* 16. 233-5: [" And around thee dwell the Selloi, thy prophets, with unwashen feet, and couching on the ground."]

GOUGH. Sleeping on the bare ground was a custom with several priesthoods, . . . and is still practised by the Parsi priests. Plutarch, although he does not mention the custom in the case of the priests of Isis, speaks of their " austere and hard services in the temples " (*De Iside* 2).

7. GOUGH. This was strictly enjoined on the priests of Isis (Plutarch, *De Iside* 2).

x. 1-2. GOUGH. Cf. Plutarch, *De Iside* 5: " they abstain from mutton and swine's flesh." [Also from certain fish and onions, 7-8.]

2. GOUGH. Cf. Genesis 9. 4: " But flesh with the life thereof, which is the blood thereof, shall ye not eat."

x. 3–xi. 6. JORTIN cites Plutarch, *Isis and Osiris* [6].

[William W. Goodwin, *Plutarch's Morals* 4. 69: " They have likewise many purgations, wherein they prohibit the use of wine, in which they study philosophy, and pass their time in learning and teaching things divine. . . . And they began first to drink it in the reign of Psammetichus; but before that time they were not used to drink wine at all, no, nor to pour it forth in sacrifice as a thing they thought any way grateful to the Gods, but as the blood of those who in ancient times waged war against the Gods, from whom, falling down from heaven and mixing with the earth, they conceived vines to have first sprung; which is the reason, (say they) that drunkenness renders men besides themselves and mad; they being, as it were, gorged with the blood of their ancestors."]

EDITOR. See notes on 1. 7. 9, in Book I, p. 249, especially LEMMI'S quotation from Natalis Comes 6. 21, which seems to be an expansion of remarks by Boccaccio in his *De Genealogia* 4. 68. Either passage may have lurked in Spenser's mind.

UPTON. The following Epigram is worth reading, viz. Caelii Calcagnini Ferrariensis, " de vini origine." [Cf. *Opera Aliquot* (1544), ed. by Antonius Musa Brasavolus.]

Terrigeniae victi; victor Saturnius; actis
Undique Phlegraeis molibus horror erat.
Maesta parens Tellus in vites ossa redegit
Caesorum, et vinum est qui modo sanguis erat.
Ah ne quis mala vina bibat! de sanguine nata
Qui biberit, caedes exitiumque bibet.

x. 5. SAWTELLE (p. 74). The adjective " Phlegrean," . . . is explained in the light of Apollodorus 1. 6. 1; Claudian, *Gigantomachia* 4; Diodorus Siculus 4. 21. 5; 5. 71. 4: it was in Phlegra in Italy, the home of the Giants, that the contest took place.

GOUGH. Among other giants, Porphyrion was struck down by Zeus with a thunderbolt. Cf. Horace, *Odes* 3. 4. 73-6:

Iniecta monstris Terra dolet suis
maeretque partus fulmine luridum
missos ad Orcum, nec peredit
impositam celer ignis Aetnam.

"the Phlegrean plaine." Cf. Spenser, *Virgils Gnat* 39-40: "that dreadfull stound, When Giants bloud did staine Phlegraean ground"; after *Culex* 27: "Phlegra Giganteo sparsa est quo sanguine tellus."

See notes on *F. Q.* 2. 10. 3. 4 in Book II, p. 304; also *Ruines of Rome* 12. 1-8; 6. 7. 41. 6-7.

9. GOUGH. "swell." Alluding to the rising of volcanic cones, as in the Phlegrean Fields near Naples, where in 1538 a new hill (Monte Nuovo) rose in a few days to a height of 400 feet.

xi. 3. GOUGH. Volcanic soil is peculiarly fitted for the cultivation of the vine.

xii ff. UPTON. Our poet certainly had in view the story told by Jeffry of Monmouth [1. 11], that Brutus had a vision in the temple of Diana, and that the goddess foretold his success; her oracle is well known, "Brute sub occasu solis," etc. "Sic de prole tua reges nascentur." Jeffry of Monmouth says, Brutus laid himself down "upon a harts skin, which he had spread before the altar": this was according to ancient superstition; see the commentators on Virgil 7. 88: "Pellibus incubuit stratis." In like manner Britomart has a vision figuring the future glory of Britain. St. 13, "The scarlet robe and crown of gold," are the dress of the British Kings and Queens; st. 14, "The tempest and outrageous flames" image her own troubles; which are put an end to by the Crocodile, st. 15, imaging Arthegal. The crocodile is the guardian Genius of the place; and among the Ægyptians, according to their sacred emblems, represented Providence.

xii. 2. UPTON. "Under the wings of Isis," i. e. under the protection of Isis. 'Tis a Hebrew phrase; and frequently used by the Psalmist [e. g. 57. 1].

CHURCH cites Psalms 17. 8.

BLAKENEY. The votaries of Isis (as of Aesculapius) spent the night in the temple in the hope of a personal communication from the goddess. See the description of this ἐγκοίμησις in Aristophanes, *Plutus* 654 ff.

xiv. EDITOR. Cf. 3. 12. 1-2; 27; WARTON's note on 3. 12. 1. 5-6, Book III, p. 301; GREENLAW's remarks, Book III, pp. 359-364.

xvi. 5-6. UPTON. Meaning a British king; see st. 23. This is no new invention of our poet; for the mother of Alexander the Great, and of Augustus Caesar, were both enwombed of a dragon; so likewise the mother of Scipio: see Milton, *P. L.* 9. 509. [See 3. 3. 29-30; HARPER's note, Book III, p. 229; also 23. 7-8 below.]

xxi. 8. UPTON. Viz. King Ryence; see *F. Q.* 3. 2. 18-22 [and notes in Book II, pp. 216-7].

9. UPTON. Cf. *F. Q.* 5. 5. 20.

xxii. 2. BLAKENEY. One is reminded of Homer's words, *Iliad* 1. 63: "Dreams come from Zeus." So in the Old Testament, God is often represented as "coming" or speaking in a dream (Genesis 20. 6; 41. 15 ff.). Cf. Herodotus 2. 141.

xxiii. 7-8. UPTON. Cf. *F. Q.* 3. 3. 29-30 [and notes in Book III, pp. 229-230; also 16. 6 above].

xxv ff. See Appendix, p. 316.

xxvi ff. DODGE (*PMLA* 12. 177). The combat of Britomart with Radegund might be likened to the combat of Bradamante with Marfisa (*Orl. Fur.* 36). As Bradamante discovers her jealousies to have been causeless, so Britomart.

SUSANNAH J. MCMURPHY (*Spenser's Use of Ariosto for Allegory,* p. 36). Bradamante's corresponding victory over Marfisa . . . Formari and Toscanella interpret as the victory of virtue over pride.

GOUGH (pp. 246-7). The theme here chosen, however, a duel between two jealous women, requires the utmost delicacy of treatment, if it is to escape being either repulsive or ludicrous. Ariosto failed, or rather perhaps did not try to avoid this danger, for he deliberately introduced a ridiculous element into the story; the fight becoming at last a vulgar scuffle carried on with the aid of fists and feet. But in Spenser's narrative the high spirit and pride of the two women maintain the action at the heroic level. Britomart's motive is not so much the wresting of a lover from a rival as the execution of vengeance for a wrong, and a wrong done not only to her knight, but to knighthood itself. Her victory is the vindication of social justice against a revolutionary polity (cf. stanza 42).

We have already seen that Radigund is probably Mary Queen of Scots, and that Britomart is Elizabeth. The two historic queens, the champions of rival ideals of religious and civil government, waged, though mainly with the weapons of diplomacy and intrigue, a long and bitter fight, in which their lives were at stake. The "vile reproch" (34. 4) which Radigund cast at Britomart, if it was an accusation of wantonness, which is not quite clear, resembled a charge which the partisans of Mary were never weary of laying against her rival. Again, Radigund lies senseless on the plain before the fatal blow is aimed at her head (5. 5. 11. 4), which seems to suggest Mary's helplessness in the hands of Elizabeth. The ruthless slaughter of the Amazons which Britomart mercifully stops may represent the punishment of those who conspired on Mary's behalf, especially the cruel reprisals after the Rising of the North in 1569-1570, when six or seven hundred of the common people were hanged. Lastly, the execution of Mary effected the liberation of many brave Englishmen from spiritual thraldom, so that when the Armada came in the following year the nation rallied as one man round the queen.

2. GOUGH. "She." It is not clear to whom this refers. From the context apparently Radigund is meant, in which case we must understand that she set up her pavilion for Britomart's use as an act of courtesy. The clause "as seemed best" suits this interpretation best, for Britomart had no choice.

xxvi. 4. As in 5. 6. 26. 5-9.

xxviii. 5-9. UPTON. Perhaps he had Homer in view, *Il.* 22. 261, where Hector, propounding terms to Achilles, he scorn'd to treat with him.

xxx.   HEISE (p. 106) cites *Knight's Tale* 1768 ff.

xxxii. 4-7. GOUGH. Radigund apparently wishes Britomart to believe that Artegall is dead. For a warrior to accompany a mortal blow with a message to be delivered to a person already dead, is a frequent incident in epic, e. g. in *Aeneid* 9. 742, Turnus before slaying Pandarus says, " Hic etiam inventum Priamo narrabis Achillem." Cf. also *Aen.* 11. 689.

EDITOR. See Redcrosse's message to Sansfoy, 1. 5. 13; also Romeo's statement to Tybalt, *Romeo and Juliet* 3. 1. 130-4.

5. TODD. Radigund, we are to suppose, discovered in the heat of the conflict that her antagonist was a woman; for the poet has not elsewhere told us how the Amazon queen knew this circumstance.

8-9. GOUGH. This speech of Britomart's is not very clear. " My love " is probably not " my beloved," but " the love I bear to Artegall," which is " depraved " or misrepresented by Radigund's ironical taunt.

EDITOR. Britomart gives no indication here or elsewhere of believing Radigund's hint that Artegall is dead. The phrase " my loue deprauest " refers to her suspicion that Artegall has been seduced by the Amazon. This suspicion is not dispelled until she discovers " her loue " in " womanishe attire " (st. 37-8). " My loue," then, refers to Artegall. Cf. 34. 3; 37. 3; 38. 1.

xxxiii. 2. GOUGH. " shoulder plate." This piece of armour, also called the pauldron, came into use about 1400, and gradually increased in size. In the Elizabethan age it was very large, and like many other pieces, was chiefly used in tournaments and for display. Spenser's knights are for the most part equipped after the fashion of the age of expiring chivalry.

xxxvii-xli. See Appendix, pp. 274, 279.

xxxviii ff. GOUGH. Cf. the similar scene in 1. 8. 42 ff., where Una finds the Red Cross Knight in prison. In each case shame prevents the knight from answering the lady's enquiries. [And there, as here, the lady blames " misfortune " for his humiliation.]

xxxviii. 4. BLAKENEY. Britomart has been the fierce fighter till recently; but at the sight of her lover spinning and in woman's garb, her instinctive womanhood at once asserts itself: " abasht she turned her head aside." This is a delicate touch, worthy of the tender-hearted poet.

xxxix. UPTON. When Penelope goes to meet Ulysses, she uses great caution, and does not receive him with transport, not well knowing the features of his face, Homer, *Od.* [Pope's tr.] 23. 96-100:

> That she knew not his favours likelynesse,
> But stood long staring on him through uncertain fears.

Amaz'd she sate, and impotent to speak:
Oer all the man her eyes she rolls in vain,
Now hopes, now fears, now knows, then doubts again.

[Cf. lines 85-110 in the original.]

xl.   2.   J. W. MACKAIL (*The Springs of Helicon*, p. 115).   [So] the Amazon [Britomart] asks Artegall when she finds him in prison, touched by surprise to forget all her rhetoric. [Cf. MACKAIL's note on 6. 7 above.]

GOUGH.   An allusion to the custom of a man disguised in woman's clothes taking the place of the May Queen. He was supposed to represent Maid Marian, and was accompanied by Robin Hood as May Lord and his merry men. Strutt considers this addition to the May games to date from the sixteenth century or a little earlier (*Sports and Pastimes* 4. 3. 16).

xlii.   See JONES's note on 5. 25 above.

3.   GOUGH.   If Radigund was debarred by her sex from the right of governing, it may be asked by what right Britomart reigned and legislated. Spenser perhaps shows that he felt this difficulty by making her transfer the sovereignty to Artegall.

5-9.   UPTON.   Compare above, 5. 25:

But vertuous women wisely understand
That they were born to base humilitie.

'Tis well and artfully added, with a view to his royal mistress, "Unlesse the heavens them lift to lawful soveraintie." *Samson Agonistes* 1053-1060:

Therefore God's universal law
Gave to the man despotic power
Over the female, in due aw;
Not from that right to part an hour,
Smile she or lour:
So shall he least confusion draw
On his whole life, not swayd
By female usurpation, or dismayd.

The allegory in the historical view seems to allude to the Salic law in France, which excludes women from the throne: This methinks is plain from the French name, Radigund; the name of a French Queen. The moral allusion is, that women should not be trusted with government; much less be Queens: but to say this directly was too dangerous; the poet therefore endeavours to hide his general meaning by particular exception.

xlv.   A. H. GILBERT (*PMLA* 34. 232) notes this as a conclusion in the manner of Ariosto.

CANTO VIII

i.   See Appendix.

3.   See notes on 5. 42. 6-9 above.

5-7.   See WARTON's note on 2. 12. 67. 2-5 in Book II, p. 384.

BLAKENEY. One is reminded of Pope's lines, *Rape of the Lock*
2. [28]:

> Fair tresses man's imperial race ensnare,
> And beauty draws us with a single hair.

The curious student should not fail to read Burton's *Anatomy of Melancholy* 3. 2. 2. 2 [" Other Causes of Love-Melancholy, Sight, Beauty from the Face, Eyes, other parts, and how it pierceth." Burton quotes this stanza].

6. TODD. From this passage Butler probably adopted part of his description of Love, *Hudibras* 2. 1. 417-9:

> Love is a burglarer, a felon,
> That at the windore-eye does steal in
> To rob the heart. . . .

ii. 1-3. UPTON. See Judges 16. 17, 19.

4-9. GOUGH. Spenser here appears to follow Tasso, *Ger. Lib.* 16. 3 ff., where on the gates of Armida's palace are sculptured two scenes which represent the triumph of Love, viz. Hercules with the distaff in the company of Iole, who bears his club and lion's hide, and Antony and Cleopatra at the battle of Actium. [See 5. 24 and notes.]

4. UPTON. Hercules burnt himself on mount Oeta, and after this fiery consecration was made a god: therefore he calls him Oetean. Seneca has a tragedy named *Hercules Oetæus*. [See 5. 24. 3-4 and notes above.]

iv. 6-9. EDITOR (C. G. O.). Compare the fleeing Florimell, 3. 4. 46-51, especially 49. 4-9; 50. 6-9; also 1. 9. 21.

8. BLAKENEY. "all to-rent," altogether rent (torn to pieces). The best-known example of this combination, all + to, occurs in the Authorised Version of Judges 9. 53: "and all to brake his skull." Wright, *Bible Word Book*, gives a crowd of examples. "All to" is supposed by many to be an intensive form of "to." See Abbott, *Shakespearian Grammar* § 28 . . .; but in the *NED*, s. v. "All," c. 14, it is observed that the "to" originally belonged to the verb (= asunder; Ger. "zer-," Lat. "dis-"). Another instance occurs below, st. 44; again in 9. 10 [see notes below].

v. 4-5. UPTON. Bace, or Prison-bace, is a country sport where the chasers are chased, as explained in the second line. See notes on *F. Q.* 3. 11. 5. 5 [in Book III, p. 288; also *Sh. Cal.* Oct. 5 and notes].

GOUGH. Cf. *Shep. Cal.* Oct. 4-5:

> Whilome thou wont the shepheards laddes to leade,
> In rymes, in ridles, and in bydding base.

vii. 1. See below notes on 36. 4-5; 49. 1-5.

ix. 9. EDITOR (C. G. O.). See *Sh. Cal.*, Feb. 6; *Ruines of Time* 517; *F. Q.* 1. 2. 20. 2; 1. 8. 23 and note, Book I, p. 259; 2. 8. 35. 7 and note, Book II, p. 277. HEISE (p. 147) cites Pulci, *Morgante Maggiore* 24. 123. Spenser had an eye for towers and masonry, especially when they were "ruinous and old."

xiv. 7. WARTON (2. 84). Mr. Upton observes, that we have here an instance of Spenser's learning, and that he makes his knights swear by their swords, agreeably to such a custom practiced among the Goths and Hunns, and related by Jornandes, and Ammianus Marcellinus. But I am inclined to believe, that our author drew this circumstance from books that he was probably much better acquainted with, old romances. (Mr. Upton, *Letter to G. West*, pp. 17, 19, while he is professedly speaking of Spenser's imitations from the romance writers, by specifying only such romance writers as Heliodorus and Sydney, did not appear, at that time, to have had any notion of the species of romances in which Spenser was principally conversant, and which he chiefly copied: I mean the romances of the dark ages, founded on Saracen superstitions, and filled with giants, dwarfs, damsels, and enchanters.) In *Morte Arthur* we have frequent instances of knights swearing in this manner. The same ceremony occurs again (6. 1. 43), "He made him sweare, By his own sword." See also 6. 7. 13.

In another place (6. 3. 18), one of the knights swears by his knighthood; an oath which we likewise frequently meet with in romance.

TODD. This ancient custom of swearing upon the sword, or upon the cross which the old swords had upon the hilt, has been satisfactorily shewn in the extracts from our elder writers by Dr. Farmer, in his *Essay on the Learning of Shakspeare* [ed. 1821, p. 61]. See also the other commentators on Hamlet's desiring Horatio and Marcellus to swear upon his sword [*Hamlet* 1. 5. 145 ff.].

GOUGH cites Spenser's *Veue of the State of Ireland*, Globe ed., p. 634.

xvii ff. See Appendix, pp. 272, 291, 316.

xix-xx. See Appendix, p. 305.

xix. 2-3. GOUGH. Roman Catholic conspiracies to assassinate Elizabeth were generally attributed to the instigation of Mary Stuart and Philip of Spain. The plot of 1571 against her life originated with the Spanish. There were so many plots that in 1584 the Protestants formed a Bond of Association for the protection of the Queen's life (Froude, *Hist. of England* [ed. 1870], ch. 67).

5-6. JORTIN. Virgil, *Aen.* 2. 190: "Quod Di prius omen in ipsum Convertant."

UPTON. This manner of averting curses from ourselves to our enemies is used almost by all nations. So in Psalm 140. 9: "Let the mischief of their own lips fall upon the head of [cover] them."

8. GOUGH. Spenser refers to the enormous riches which the King of Spain derived from the plunder of the Indies.

EDITOR. The description of Marinell's "Rich strond" (3. 4. 23) may have been intended originally to apply to Philip of Spain in the same way as this passage does.

xx-xxiii. GOUGH (p. 258). The Souldan's wife Adicia represents the injustice to which the King of Spain was "wedded," and probably, in particular, the iniquitous government that he maintained. Mercilla's honest endeavour to establish peaceful relations with her, instead of waging the implacable war that justice demanded, will then symbolize Elizabeth's prolonged efforts to avoid a breach with

Spain. Elizabeth hated bloodshed, and had no love of military glory; but her desire to keep the peace, a desire which for many years was fully reciprocated by Philip, was mainly due to prudent statesmanship, and to the knowledge that war would put everything to the hazard. The actual relations between the two governments were far from corresponding with the symbolic narrative, in which courtly bias is evident. There was extreme provocation on both sides. If Philip secretly supported schemes for the overthrow of Protestantism and of Elizabeth's government, the latter encouraged the unofficial war which Drake and other sea-rovers waged against Spain, and she gave open, though reluctant, support to the revolted Netherlands. Both sovereigns strove long to restrain the ardent desire of their subjects to determine the religious quarrel by force of arms. In 1587 Elizabeth sent commissioners to the Prince of Parma in the Netherlands to re-open negotiations with Spain. Parma, who foresaw the danger of a conflict, sincerely promoted the plan, but his master Philip, who had at last decided on invasion, took good care that the negotiations should come to nothing, and continued his warlike preparations. The mission of Samient to Adicia and her violent expulsion may have a vague reference to these events.

xx. 3. G. S. HILLARD (*The Poetical Works of Edmund Spenser* 3. 344). Adicia may represent the Catholic religion, of which the king of Spain was so bigoted an adherent.

GOUGH. Adicia: Greek ἀδικία, injustice.

xxi. 8. GOUGH. "attonement." Here four syllables.

xxii. 1-2. UPTON. In the allegorical interpretation meaning Embassadors. "Sanctum populis per saecula nomen." And particularly hinting at Philip K. of Spain (the Souldan) who detained the deputies of the States of Holland, being sent to complain unto him, and to beg a redress of their grievances. This action was violating the sacred privilege of Embassadors.

7. See note on 49. 1-5 below.

xxiv. 7. H. H. BLANCHARD (*SP* 22. 220). Solimano (*Ger. Lib.* 9. 2), il Soldano (9. 22), in Tasso is King of the Turks, a mighty pagan conqueror.

xxviii. 2-9. See UPTON'S note on sts. 30-45 below; cf. 2. 8. 37; 5. 8. 39. 4 below.

4-6. JORTIN. See an account of these chariots, "currus falcati," in Q. Curtius 4. 9. Alexander bid his soldiers avoid them, "laxatis ordinibus" (4. 13).

A. S. COOK ("Notes on Milton's *Ode on the Morning of Christ's Nativity*" in *Transactions of the Connecticut Academy* 15 (1909). 328, note on line 56, cites this passage and adds: "Silius Italicus (17. 417-8) assigns the scythe-bearing chariot to the barbarians of the North. . . . In 2 Maccabees 13. 2 we have a mention of 'three hundred chariots armed with hooks.'" [See note on 41. 6 below.]

xxx-xlv. UPTON. The Briton Prince, having conquered the proud Souldan, hung his armour on a tree as a perpetual monument [st. 45]. So acted Aeneas having slain the tyrant Mezentius, Virgil, *Aen.* 11. 5. And as Virgil often alludes to the customs and history of his own country, so does our poet; led thereto by the very nature of his poem. Almost all nations dedicated their spoils taken in war to their deities. We read in Scripture of such kind of trophies of victory. The Philistines hung up the arms of Saul in the temple of their god Ashtaroth, 1 Samuel 31. 10. And it appears that David hung up the sword of Goliah in the temple of Jerusalem, 1 Samuel 21. 9. These acknowledgments to the Lord of Hosts, the giver of all victory, seem as reasonable as religious. And so Queen Elizabeth after that most signal victory obtained over the Spanish Armada, " went to Paul's church, (where the banners taken from the enemy were hung up to be seen) gave most hearty thanks to God, and heard a sermon, wherein the glory was given to God alone " (Cambden [ed. 1630, Bk. 3, p. 144]). For to this historical fact Spenser (as I believe) here alludes: and I believe likewise, that in this whole episode he keeps his eye (as far forth as his fairy tale will permit) on this remarkable victory over this falsly called Invincible Armada. Let us go back a little. The Soldan is the King of Spain: his swearing and banning, st. 28: " Swearing and banning most blasphemously." This may be supposed to hint at those many pious cursings and papistical excommunications so liberally thundered out against the Queen and her faithful subjects. Next the Soldan is described, " And mounting straight upon a charret hye." Cambden more than once mentions the great hight of the Spanish ships, built with lofty turrets upon their decks like castles. He says, " With yron wheeles and hookes armed dreadfully." The Prince of Parma likewise in the Netherlands built ships—" and prepared piles sharpened at the neather end, armed with yron and hooked on the sides " (Cambden, [ed. 1630, Bk. 3, p. 130]). Let it be added moreover that 'twas reported that this Armada carried various instruments of torture; and thus literally " was armed dreadfully with yron wheeles and hookes."

> And drawne of cruell steedes which he had fed
> With flesh of men.

What were the captains and soldiers of this Armada, but persecutors, or those who acted under the commands of persecutors, inquisitors, devourers of men? " And by his stirrup Talus did attend." Justice prepares now for execution. And here we are led to consider the various preparations made in England for its just defence: By land, the Earl of Leicester and Lord Hunsdon, etc. By sea, Lord Howard of Effingham, Vice Admiral Drake, etc. Submitting always to God's providence, and trusting in the truth of their cause. " More in his causes truth he trusted then in might." The fight of the two fleets is imaged in sts. 31, 32, etc. The Armada was high-built, and of great bulk; the Spanish captains thought they could by their bulkiness over-set the English fleet [31. 7-9 quoted]. But the English ships " could turn about with incredible celerity and nimbleness, which way soever they pleased, to charge, wind, and tack about again " (Cambden, p. [138]). See too p. [139]: " Neither did the Lord Admiral think good to adventure grappling with the Spanish ships: for the enemy had a strong army in his fleet, but he had none: their ships were far more for number, of bigger burthen, stronger and higher built; so as their men fighting from those lofty hatches, must inevitably destroy those who should charge them from beneath." 'Tis easy to apply this history to the fable. There were four engagements between the two fleets. I know not but it may seem too particular to suppose the first imaged in sts. 30, 31; the second in sts. 32, 33; the third in sts. 34, 35; and the last and final overthrow in sts. 37, 38. Where the Prince draws aside the veil, that covered his bright shield, and flashed lightning and terrour and confusion in the face of the tyrant, and his terrified horses. Now this may allude not only to the burning of the Spanish fleet, but to the easiness of the victory over this Invincible Armada: and to this allude likewise the medals, which were coined in memory of this success, with a fleet flying with full sails, with this inscription, " Venit, vidit, fugit," i. e. (applied to the Soldan, or the Armada) it came to attack the Briton prince: it saw, the brightness of the uncovered shield: it fled, in confusion and terrour. Cf. notes on 42. 9 below.

xxxi. 1-4. LOTSPEICH (p. 54). Spenser may be following *Met.* 9. 194-6, but is closer to Boccaccio 13. 1: "Diomedes, king of Thrace, whose custom it was to kill his guests and feed them to his animals, Hercules conquered and killed and to the same animals gave him to be devoured."

EDITOR. Warner tells the story of Hercules' slaying of Diomedes in *Albions England* (1586), book 1, chap. 12, pp. 50-1.

xxxv. 5-9. JORTIN cites Homer, *Il.* 11. [547-553].

UPTON. The prince wounded by the souldan in his armed chariot is compared to an enraged lion wounded by a hunter, who defends himself with trees and with burning brands. 'Tis observed by Aristotle and Pliny (great observers of nature) that lions are frightened with fire: and this circumstance poets frequently mention. Claud. *in Ruf.* 2. 252-4:

> vacuo qualis discedit hiatu
> Impatiens remeare leo; quem plurima cuspis,
> Et pastorales pepulerunt igne catervae.

Compare Homer, *Il.* 11. 547 [-555] with Barnes' notes. And likewise *Il.* 17. 657 [-664].

HEISE (pp. 106-7) adds *Aen.* 9. 792-6.

xxxvi. 4-5. HEISE (p. 97) cites *Rin.* 3. 4; *Orl. Fur.* 29. 61; *Orl. Inn.* 3. 44; *Morgante Maggiore* 11. 116; also *Met.* 1. 533 ff.; *Il.* 10. 360 ff.; 15. 579 ff. See note on 49. 1-5 below.

xxxvii. A. H. GILBERT (*PMLA* 34. 231). Cf. *Orl. Fur.* 10. 107-110; 22. 85-7.

xxxvii. 6–xxxviii. 3. WARTON (2. 208). The Aegis is represented with the same effect on horses, in the spirited poem of Valerius Flaccus, [*Argonautica*] 6. 396:

> Aegida tum primum virgo, spiramque Medusae
> Tercentum saevis squalentem sustulit hydris;
> Quam soli vidistis Equi; pavor occupat ingens,
> Excussis in terga viris.

xxxvii. 6-7. UPTON. This is the first time that P. Arthur voluntarily makes use of the power of his inchanted shield. [See 1. 7. 33-6 and notes in Book I, pp. 253-4.]

xxxix ff. C. W. LEMMI (*PQ* 8. 284).   This episode is based chiefly on the myth of Phaeton, to which Spenser refers. The chariot with its scythed wheels, racing here and there, is the chariot of Phoebus; the blinding terrible shield is the thunderbolt of Jove.

This episode is usually understood to allude to the arrogant failure of the Armada.

Natalis Comes 6. 1 [cited by JORTIN below]: " As regards ethical significance, it was intended by this fable [Phaeton] to humble the arrogance of some who believed themselves equal to anything and, because of their nobility, thought themselves ignorant of nothing. Arrogance more than anything else brings down great calamities upon men."

Natalis Comes 6. 10, " De Phaethonte": " The wise thus admonished us that honors desired by the inexperienced in the management of affairs are sometimes disastrous to those who desire them and to those who grant them; for ambition and undeserved honors have been ruinous to many."

xl.   JORTIN. If the reader examines these lines, he will find in them a figure call'd [anacoluthon], a figure which Spenser deals very much in, a want of construction. He imitates Ovid here, but varies a little from him: for Ovid tells us, that the Scorpion frightned Phaethon, *Met.* 2. 198-201:

> Hunc puer ut nigri madidum sudore veneni
> Vulnera curvata minitantem cuspide vidit,
> Mentis inops, gelida formidine lora remisit.

" Scorched path." Natalis Comes 6. 1: " Finxerunt eum [Phaethontem] in ea parte praecipue signiferi delirasse, quae est ultima Librae in Scorpionem, ubi via dicitur usta: quae gradus decem utrinque continet."

CHURCH.   Our Poet, 'tis true, is not always exact; but I think we may now venture to say that much of this supposed want of Construction is owing to the almost numberless Blunders and false pointings which run through all the former editions.

SAWTELLE (p. 99) cites Ovid, *Met.* 1. 748 ff.

LOTSPEICH (p. 99).   See *Teares of the Muses* 7-12; *Virgils Gnat* 197-200; *F. Q.* 1. 4. 9; 3. 11. 38.

1. UPTON. Ovid, *Met.* 2. 119: " ignem vomentes . . . Quadrupedes "; 85: " Quos [ignes] ore et naribus efflant."

LOTSPEICH (p. 99) cites *Met.* 2. 153-5.

3-9. LOTSPEICH (p. 99) cites *Met.* 2. 195-200.

9. UPTON. Alluding to the poetical account of the galaxy or milky way; which see in Chaucer, in the *House of Fame* 2. 428 ff. And in Manilius 1. 727:

> An melius manet illa fides per saecula prisca,
> Illac solis equos diversis cursibus isse,
> Atque aliam trivisse viam; longumque per aevum
> Exustas sedes, incoctaque sidera flammis
> Caeruleam verso speciem mutasse colore;
> Infusumque loco cinerem, mundumque sepultum.
> Fama etiam antiquis ad nos descendit ab annis,

Phaethontem patrio curru per signa volantem.
(Dum nova miratur propius spectacula mundi,
Et puer in caelo ludit, curruque superbus
Luxuriat, magno [nitido] cupit et majora parente)
Monstratas liquisse vias. . . .

GOUGH cites also Gower, *Conf. Amant.* [Pauli's ed.] 2. 34. [Cf. G. C. Macaulay's ed. 4. 979-1034; especially 1020-1.]

xli. 6. UPTON. These kind of chariots, here alluded to, armed with hookes and keene graples, were called by the Latins, " Falcati currus," and by the Greeks δρεπανηφόροι. Xenophon describes them, both in his *Cyropaedia* [6. 1. 30, 50] and in his *Anabasis* [1. 7. 10; 1. 8. 10]. They seem to be much older than the times of Cyrus; and perhaps are called in Scripture " chariots of iron." [See notes on 28. 4-6 above.]

xlii. 4-5. UPTON. The passage before us seems translated from Homer, *Il.* 5. [585-6: " and he fell gasping from the well-wrought chariot headlong in the dust on crown and shoulders."]

8. UPTON. From Ovid, *Met.* [15.] 528-9, speaking of Hippolitus:

Nullasque in corpore partes
Noscere quas posses. Unumque erat omnia vulnus.

9. G. L. CRAIK (*Spenser and his Poetry* 2. 233-4). The conquest of the Soldan has therefore been achieved only by a supernatural means. Have we not here a covert acknowledgment that the defeat of the Armada was in truth the work rather of the tempest than of any human exertion,—as it was expressed on the medal struck at the time, with the inscription, " Flavit Jehovah et dissipati sunt," Jehovah blew and they were scattered? Cf. end of note on 30-45 above.

xliii. 1-7. WARTON (2. 209). Hippolitus was not torn in pieces by his own horses, but by a monster sent from Neptune, as Euripides relates, *Hipp. Cor.* 1220, and from other authors. In this account of the death of Hippolitus, he greatly varies from himself, 1. 5. 37 ff. [Warton misunderstands 1. 5. 37. 3-8; see LOTSPEICH'S note below.]

UPTON. I. e. Hippolitus the son of Theseus whom his father cursed. Ovid, *Met.* 15. 504:

Immeritumque pater projecit ad urbe;
Hostilique caput prece detestatur euntis.

See *F. Q.* 1. 5. 37.

EDITOR. Modern texts give the first line: " Meritumque nihil pater eicit urbe."

LOTSPEICH (pp. 69-70). Spenser's telling of the Hippolytus myth does not agree with any one classical version. . . . He seems to be following Boccaccio's chapter on Hippolytus (10. 50), which may be summarized as follows. Hippolytus gave his whole life to hunting and " with a constant heart spurned all women. He was loved by his stepmother, Phaedra, who, when she found that he would not requite her desire, accused him before Theseus." Theseus, " overcome by rage, prayed for his son's death." As a result, Hippolytus, fleeing in his chariot, encountered some sea-monsters ("phocae"), who so frightened his horses that they escaped control, overturned the car, and dragged Hippolytus, who was tangled in the reins, over cliffs and rough places, so that "pro mortuo a circumvicinis collectus sit." He was restored to life by Aesculapius. Boccaccio here supplies all the material of Spenser's version, in Spenser's order, [see 1. 5. 37-9] except two details: that Phaedra killed herself with a knife, and that Theseus, with Diana's help, gathered up Hippolytus' remains. Both of these points seem to be peculiar to Spenser, but for the latter he may have received a suggestion from *Aen.* 7. 765-9.

1-4. W. RIEDNER (*Spensers Belesenheit*, p. 111) cites *Met.* 15. 497-9, 524-9. See notes on 1. 5. 37-9 in Book I, pp. 235-7.

xlv. 1-3. See UPTON's note on sts. 30-45 above.

1. GOUGH. The practice of hanging up the armour of a conquered enemy on a tree as a trophy was common with the Greeks and Romans; cf. *Iliad* 10. 458 ff.

EDITOR. See also 4. 1. 21-4, and notes, Book IV, p. 168, on st. 21-3. In his *Spenser's Theory of Friendship*, p. 18, n. 7, C. G. SMITH points out a similar hanging of trophies in Sackville's *Induction* together with other indications that Spenser had Sackville in mind. Cf. also *Virgils Gnat* 126-8.

xlvi. 1-2. HEISE (p. 98) cites Ovid, *Fasti* 4. 459-462; *Met.* 2. 623 ff.; 13. 870 ff.; *Theb.* 6. 186.

xlvii. 1-2. JORTIN. See Natalis Comes 8. 4.

C. W. LEMMI (*PQ* 8. 284) notes that the story of Ino in Natalis Comes 8. 4 is explained as symbolical of "the insane pride and ambition of ancient princes 'whose temples and priests and ceremonies were as those of the immortal gods.'"

WARTON (1. 101). Ovid reports, *Met.* 4. 528, that Ino threw herself, together with her son Melicerta, from the summit of a rock into the sea. Others relate that she murdered Melicerta, and afterwards leaped into the sea. It is difficult to fix upon Spenser's precise meaning in these verses.
[See notes on 4. 11. 13. 6 in Book IV, pp. 243-4.]

3-6. See notes on 2. 12. 43-5 in Book II, pp. 372-3; see also *Virgils Gnat* 397-400.

5-6. JORTIN. By the "madding Mother" he means, I suppose, Agave, who tore her son Pentheus to pieces.

WARTON (1. 101). Her son Pentheus being of a very temperate disposition, and consequently averse to the rites of Bacchus, she, together with the rest of the Maenades, tore him in pieces, in the midst of the Bacchanalia.

SAWTELLE (p. 36) cites Ovid, *Met.* 3. 601 ff.

LOTSPEICH (p. 35). At *Virgils Gnat* 170-6 Spenser is translating freely from *Culex* 110-114, which gives all the material and is unique in speaking of the vengeance of King Nictileus (Bacchus). There is enough in the *V. G.* passage to explain the allusion [here], although Spenser may well have known other treatments of the story of Pentheus and Agave and the Maenads, especially *Fasti*

4. 457-9; *Met.* 3. 701 ff. He remembers the Maenads chiefly for their mad fury: according to Boccaccio 5. 25, they were called Bacchae " ob fuorem potius quam ob virtutem."

8. SAWTELLE (p. 80) cites Euripides, *Bacchanals, passim*, on the fury of the Maenades.

xlix. 1-5. HEISE (pp. 7-9) cites 28 dog similes in *F. Q.*, of which there is none at all in Book I and an increasing number in the later books (4 in this canto— st. 7, 22, 36, 49). One who is at all acquainted with Ireland cannot resist the guess that his Irish life made Spenser more familiar with dogs, especially hunting and sporting dogs. For 13 of these similes Heise (pp. 95-7) finds literary precedent in ancient and Italian poets (cf. notes in Book III, pp. 207, 277, 287; Book IV, pp. 212, 215); but Spenser invariably treats them with a first-hand energy, and the one before us has every mark of direct observation. See also 2. Pr. 4. 5 and UPTON's note, Book II, p. 186; 5. 9. 6. 7-8; 11. 12. 2; 12. 38. 5-6, below.

9. UPTON. Viz. Ἀδικία. See canto 9, stanza 1. In this transformation he seems to have in view that of Hecuba [to a bitch]. See Ovid, *Met.* 13; *Fab.* 2 [404-7; 565-571]; Eurip., *Hecuba* 1265, ed. Barnes. Plautus, *Menaech.* [713-8]. [The tiger interests Spenser; cf. Maleger's tiger, 2. 11. 20 ff.; also 5. 7. 30. 1-4 and *Concordance*, s. v.]

l. 7-8. H. H. BLANCHARD (*PMLA* 40. 847-8). There are two similar similes in Boiardo descriptive of similar situations. I have been unable to find this simile elsewhere. *Orl. Inn.* 1. 4. 44:

> Ranaldo è con lor sempre mescolato,
> Ed a destra e sinistra il brando mena;
> Chi mezzo 'l capo, chi ha un braccio tagliato,
> Le teste in gli elmi cadon a l'arena.
> Come un branco di capre disturbato,
> Cotal Ranaldo avanti sè li mena.

Orl. Inn. 2. 17. 11:

> Ora la gente a lui fugge davante,
> Nè si ritrova alcun, che si conforte
> Di star con seco volentieri a faccia,
> Ma come capre avanti ognun si caccia.

[Cf. 9. 15. 4; 6. 3. 49. 3.]

li. A. H. GILBERT (*PMLA* 34. 232) notes this as a conclusion in the manner of Ariosto.

CANTO IX

J. W. MACKAIL (*The Springs of Helicon*, p. 110) thinks that in this and the following cantos " the poetry is at its lowest temperature; they are not so much poetry as versified politics."

i. A. H. GILBERT (*PMLA* 34. 232) notes this as a transition in the manner of Ariosto.

2. EDITOR (F. M. P.). An expression which Spenser frequently employs. Cf. 1. 2. 15. 4, 8. 39. 6, 11. 24. 2; 2. 8. 31. 1; 3. 1. 6. 2. So Sir David Lyndsay, *The Dreme* 166: "In flame of fyre, rych furious and fell."

ii. 1-5. So Duessa, 1. 8. 50. See UPTON's note in Book I, p. 263.

iv-xix. See Appendix, pp. 275, 279, 281, 303, 305, 316-7.

v-xix. GOUGH (pp. 271-2). The character of Malengin and his methods of attack resemble those of the Irish kerns and galloglasses, as they appeared to their English enemies. Spenser had much experience of the guerilla warfare with which Lord Grey's term of office was filled, and took the usual contemporary English view of the depravity of the insurgents, and the necessity for extreme severity. The outlawed Irish chiefs, such as the Earl of Desmond, were followed by their armed retainers, who acknowledged no allegiance except to the heads of their own septs. The English armies, encumbered with baggage and artillery, despaired of hunting down their nimble and wily enemies, who moved swiftly from one fastness to another, amid almost impenetrable mountains, forests, and bogs, seldom making a stand, but perpetually harassing the marching columns at fords and passes (cf. stanzas 5, 15). They often, like Malengin, sheltered in caves, and lived upon the cattle which they drove from the pastures. The appearance of these unhappy outcasts, with their sunken eyes, flowing locks, and outlandish ragged garments is vividly described in stanza 10. Not less aptly portrayed is Malengin's character: his wily wit, his smooth tongue, and subtle talk "that could deceive one looking in his face," his "pleasant trickes," his mental and bodily alacrity and elusiveness. Spenser, as we know from his *Veue*, was a close, though unsympathetic, observer of the Irish character. [See also 2. 9. 13-16 and WINSTANLEY's notes in Book II, pp. 284-5.]

There is an unconscious irony in the selection of the most atrocious chapter in English history as an example of the virtue of justice. Yet the elder Essex, who with the express approbation of Elizabeth massacred 600 women and children in the caves of Rathlin, and Grey, who would have depopulated Munster in the name of the gospel, had not humaner counsels led to his recall when the work was half done, were pious and upright men, who honestly did what they conceived to be their painful duty. The legal fiction that Ireland was the property of the English sovereign by right of conquest, incomplete though that conquest was, justified in their eyes the arbitrary and violent supercession of Irish law, land tenure, and religion by those of England. The faithfulness of the peasantry to their chiefs, who had, in many cases, illegally, been set aside and outlawed, was held to justify a policy of systematic extermination by the sword, the gallows, and famine.

Spenser, it is true, like Elizabeth and Burghley, disapproved of extermination, but complained of the vacillation and half-measures which prolonged the agony of the country. Unflinching military terrorism, would, he believed, stamp out rebellion. Level-headed statesmen like Burghley might say with justice that "the Flemings had not such cause to rebel by the oppression of the Spaniards, as is reported the Irish people" (Froude, *Hist. Engl.* [ed. 1870], ch. 62), but to the poet's impetuous idealism this was dangerous and cruel sentimentality. Admiration for the stern and fanatical Lord Grey had warped his judgement.

v. 2. GOUGH. Spenser in the *Veue of the Present State of Ireland* describes the Irish outlaw as " being for his many crimes and villanyes bannished from the townes and howses of honest men, and wandring in waste places," where " he still flyeth from his foe and lurketh in the thicke woodes and straite passages " (Globe ed., p. 631). [Cf. above 9. 2. 1-5 and note.]

v. 8–vi. UPTON. " Malum ingenium: mala mens, malus animus." " Malengin: dolus malus: c'est l'action d'une personne ingenieuse à mal faire," Le Duchet. His den seems imaged from the den of Cacus in Virgil 8. 190 and Ovid, *Fasti* 1. 555-6:

> Proque domo longis spelunca recessibus ingens
> Abdita; vix ipsis invenienda feris.

vi. 5. GOUGH. A cave as one of the entrances to hell is found elsewhere in literature. Cf. e. g. Vergil, *Georg.* 4. 467-[9]: " Taenarias etiam fauces, alta ostia Ditis . . . Ingressus, manesque adiit "; also *Aen.* 6. 237 ff.

EDITOR (C. G. O.). This habitat is not unlike that of Demogorgon in Boccaccio's *De Genealogia Deorum* 1. 1. Lines 3-5 find an echo in *Comus* 517:

> And rifted Rocks whose entrance leads to Hell,

where Milton is referring to the allegorical value of Greek myth.

7-8. See note on 8. 49. 1-5 above.

viii-xix. See Appendix, pp. 275, 279, 281, 303, 305, 316-7.

viii-ix. See GOUGH'S note on 2. 27. above for the plan of sending a woman as a decoy.

x. MARION GRUBB (*MLN* 50. 168-9) thinks that the following passage in *Arden of Feversham* (2. 1; ed. Brooke, in *Shakespeare Apocrypha*, pp. 11, 12) is taken from this stanza:

> *Brad.* . . . so vile a rogue as he
> Lyves not againe upon the earth . . .
> *A leane faced writhen knaue,*
> Hauke nosde and verye *hollow eied,* . . .
> *Long haire downe his shoulders curled*; . . .
>
> *Will.* What apparell had he?
>
> *Brad.* A watchett sattin doublet *all to torne,* . . .
> A paire of velvet threadbare hose, seame rent,
> A worsted *stocking rent aboue the shoe,*
> A liuery cloake, but all the lace was of.

EDITOR. The parallels, noted by the usual italicizing, are all commonplace. Hollow eyes, long hair, and ragged clothes were usually associated with villains. The expression " all to torne," which seemed to attract Miss Grubb is itself a commonplace, as can be seen by a glance at the *NED* under " all." (See BLAKENEY'S note on 8. 4. 8 above.) Miss Grubb's suggestion that this " parallel " points to the passing around of the MS of Book V as early as 1592 (the date of *Arden*) is without any support.

5-9. Gough. Spenser describes the Irish as "wearing Mantells and long glibbes, which is a thick curled bush of heare, hanging downe over theyr eyes and monstrously disguising them" (*Veue*, Globe ed., p. 630).

xi. 6-8. Warton (1. 217). This net seems to be borrowed from the like expedient used by the giant Caligorante [*Orl. Fur.*] 15. 44. 1-2:

Piacer fra tanta crudelta si prende
D'una Rete. . . .

Harrington:

And in this crueltie he has great sport
To use the service of a certaine net.

[See notes on 13. 1-7; 14. 2-3, below.]

Gough. According to Italian commentators Caligorante represents a famous theological sophist of Ariosto's day. . . . The gruesome horror of Ariosto's description is replaced in Spenser by light humour.

xii. 6-7. Upton. There are herbs, 'tis said, in Sardinia, that distort the mouths of those who eat them with something between grinning and laughing: see Virgil, *Ecl.* 7. 41. Hence when a person feigns a laugh, or laughs with his lips only, as Homer expresses it, he is said to laugh a Sardonian laugh. Homer, *Il.* 15. 101-2: ["And she laughed with her lips, but her forehead above her dark brows was not gladdened."] Compare *Od.* 20. 302. Plato [*Republic* 337 A] and Cicero [*Letters* 7. 25. 1, no. 668.] likewise use this proverb. And Ariosto alludes to it, 13. 35: "Sorrise amaramente."

Church. Of this Adage Erasmus has collected many different Interpretations. Here it means a forced smile. In the Island Sardinia there grows an Herb called Sardoa, like smallage, which is fatal to those that eat it; and affects them in such a manner that they die with a smile upon their faces.

Editor. The expression "laugh on" seems to be a favorite with Spenser. At 1. 9. 12. 9 the "Faults Escaped" corrected "laugh at" to "laugh on"; see "Variant Readings" in Book I. He uses the expression also in 3. 6. 2. 7 and 3. 12. 15. 3.

xiii. 1-7. Heise (pp. 144-5) cites *Orl. Fur.* 9. 67; *Orl. Inn.* 1. 14. 29; see also 3. 1. 54. 8-9, and Heise's note, Book III, p. 212; *Sh. Cal.* Mar. 106-111.

1-2. Jortin. So in *Colin Clout's come home again* [1-5]:

The Shepherd's boy . . .
Sat, as his custom was, upon a day,
Charming his oaten pipe unto his peers.

Upton. He has the same allusion, 3. 1. 54. 8. . . . And the same expression in [*Sh. Cal.* Oct. 118]: "Here we our slender pipes may safely charme," i. e. says the old Glossary [to *Sh. Cal.*], "temper and order: for charmes were wont to be made by verses." He had Virgil's expression in view, *Ecl.* 10. 51 and *Aen.* 1. 1, "Carmen modulatus." [Upton refers to the apocryphal beginning of the *Aeneid*:

Ille ego, qui quondam gracili modulatus avena
Carmen . . .

See notes on 1. Pr. 1, Book I, p. 173; also note on *Sh. Cal.*, Oct. 118].

8-9.   EDITOR.   So the Ape as a courtier, *Mother Hubberds Tale* 700-1. This line, by mentioning fashionable court pastimes, may glance at particular " Malengins " in Court.

xiv. 2-3.   UPTON.   Spenser might have in view the Retiarius, who fought with a net to intangle his adversary: or rather the giant Zambardo, in *Orl. Inn.* 5. [See WARTON's note on 11. 6-8 above.]

xv.   4.   Cf. 8. 50. 7-8 and note; 6. 3. 49. 3.

8-9.   GOUGH.   An allusion to the difficulties experienced by English commanders in waging a guerilla war with the Irish. Grey's successor, Sir John Perrot, said that " the work of trotting the mountains " was not suited to English soldiers (R. Bagwell, *Ireland under the Tudors* 2. 207).

xvii-xix.   GOUGH.   In the account of the transformations of Malengin Spenser probably follows the myth of Proteus (*Od.* 4. 399 ff., Vergil, *Georgics* 4. 440 ff.), which he describes at length in *F. Q.* 3. 8. 39-41. Similar incidents are common in folk-tales, e. g. in the ballad of Tam Lin.

EDITOR.   LOTSPEICH adds *Met.* 8. 731-7. Homer mentions the tree and the snake, Ovid a stone; the rest of the transformations seem to be Spenser's ingenious own. See Stith Thompson's *Motif-Index of Folk-Literature* 2. 29-60 for stories of transformations.

EVELYN M. ALBRIGHT (*PMLA* 41. 497-516) elaborates Reyher's (*Les Masques Anglais*, p. 148 n.) suggestion that this episode in the then unpublished second part of the *Faerie Queene* was used as a source for Davison's Proteus Masque, performed in the Christmas Revels at Gray's Inn and at court in the winter of 1594-5. From this, Miss Albright goes on to suggest a friendship between Davison and Spenser and that in return for Spenser's permission to use his unpublished *Faerie Queene* Davison allowed him to use certain official maps and documents in the preparation of his *Veue of Ireland* (1596).

xix.   7.   EDITOR (C. G. O.).   The same rhetorical device, with the same word, occurs at 2. 5. 34. 8:

So, them deceiues, deceiu'd in his deceipt.

See John Hoskins, *Directions for Speech and Style*, ed. Hoyt H. Hudson, p. 17: " Polyptoton, or Traductio, is a repetition of words of the same lineage, that differ only in termination." The figure was much affected by Sidney, as Hoskins's illustrations show.

EDITOR (R. H.).   Sister Mary Alphonse McCabe in her unpublished thesis lists more than a hundred illustrations of this figure in the *Faerie Queene*. See note on 5. 17. 1 above.

xx ff.   B. E. C. DAVIS (*Edmund Spenser, A Critical Study*, p. 248).   The doctrine of " Divine Right " glanced at in the Mercilla episode was defended at some length by John Leslie in his *Treatise Touching the Right of Mary Queen of*

Scotland (1584) and by Thomas Bedingfield in his preface to the *Florentine History of Machiavelli* (1595).

[See Appendix, pp. 319-320.]

xxi ff.   HARD (*Sewanee Review* 42. 299-300; 304).   The most conspicuous evidence of Spenser's interest in architecture is to be found, of course, in the temples, castles, and palaces described in the poems; and the most important of these are to be found in the *Faerie Queene:* the House of Pride, the House of Temperance, Busyrane's Palace, Castle Joyeous, and the palace of Mercilla.   It is true that these buildings are in some respects highly fantastic,—that they contain features, for the expression of allegory and symbolism, which actual buildings may not possess; yet it is a mistake to regard them as mere castles in the air.   Careful and deliberate description, with some attention to architectural detail, gives them form and substance, and makes them rise before the mind's eye as real structures. This is not to say that Spenser sets forth a meticulous report of architectural design; but it is worth observing that Spenser's structures impress us as being far more substantial and orderly than those found in the conventional examples of " literary " architecture. . . .

Spenser's buildings have porches sustained by stately columns; or secure gateways attended by porters or wardens; the entrance may have a screen; the roof is traced with foliated designs, or it is gilded; the walls are hung with tapestry, or carved with curious emblems; the pinnacled turrets or the terraces are reached by substantial stairways.   Altogether, the buildings are convincing.   [See HARD's note on 7. 5; also on 4. 10. 6. 8-9, Book IV, p. 219.]

xxi. 4-6.   See FOWLER's notes on *F. Q.* 4. 10. 37. 4-5, 6-8, in Book IV, pp. 228-9.

6.   TODD.   Such is Milton's address to Sabrina in *Comus* [934-5]:

May thy lofty head be crown'd
With many a tower and terrace round.

And thus of the imperial palace in Rome, *P. R.* 4. 54, is adorned with " Turrets and terraces."   On both which passages Mr. Warton has remarked, that Milton was impressed with this idea from his vicinity to Windsor Castle.   But I think it more probable that Spenser, in the stanza before us, suggested the idea to Milton; for Milton's " imperial palace " strongly resembles also in other respects the old " stately pallace " of Mercilla [*P. R.* 4. 51-4]:

high
The structure, skill of noblest architects,
With gilded battlements conspicuous far,
Turrets, and terraces, and glittering spires.

EDITOR.   Spenser frequently refers to the towers in describing a city; see Osgood's *Concordance*.   He was probably influenced not only by the classical idea but also by the habit of Saxton of representing on his maps important cities by clusters of towers.   See OSGOOD's note on 4. 11. 28. 6-9 in Book IV, p. 253.

xxii-xxvii.   EDITOR.   Spenser is here describing an entrance to Elizabeth's (Mercilla's) Court, most likely Hampton Court.   E. K. Chambers (*Shakespeare's England* 1. 90-1) gives the following convenient description:

The arrangement of the principal rooms of a Tudor palace can perhaps be best studied in the plan of Hampton Court. Upon the dais at the back of the great Hall is the entrance to a Guard or Watching Chamber. Out of this opens the Presence Chamber, and out of this again the Privy Chamber, which gives access to the private apartments of the sovereign. From the opposite end of the Guard Chamber runs a gallery, which passes round two sides of a court and leads to the royal Closet, over-looking and forming part of the Chapel. Into this gallery also opens the Council Chamber. The presence chamber and the privy chamber were the essential elements of the scheme, and these had to be contrived, however humbly the court was lodged. The crowd of courtiers filled the presence chamber, and waited until it was the pleasure of the sovereign to appear in public.

He quotes an account of such an audience from P. Hentzner's *Travels in England* (cf. Rye, *England as seen by Foreigners*, 1865, pp. [103]-4). Another description, more to our purpose, is that of Il Schifanoya (*Cal. State Papers*, Venetian, 1558-1580, 7. 91):

On the morrow, Wednesday the 24th, after dinner, accompanied *ut supra*, they went to the Court at Whitehall Palace, where the Queen now resides, and having entered the great hall on the ground floor, hung with very choice tapestries, with the canopy, throne, and royal cushions, they were received by the Earl of Arundel, the Lord Steward, with all the rest of the Lords of the Privy Council, and mounting the stairs they went to kiss [hands] and do reverence to the Queen, who received them very joyfully and graciously, going to meet them as far as the guard chamber at the head of the stairs (*doppo le scale*); and being conducted to the presence chamber, they presented their credentials, and explained their embassy, everybody standing.

Artegall and Arthur pass from the porch into the Great Hall, where they find the usual throng of courtiers and seekers after favors. They are conducted through this crowd to the rear of the room, where, at the entrance to the Guard Chamber, as they pass a "Scriene," they see Bon Font nailed by his tongue to a post. From thence, they were "guyded by degree" into the Presence Chamber. The screen here is at the entrance to the Guard Chamber at the rear of the Hall and not at the entrance to the Hall, as in 10. 37. 9. Spenser distinguishes the set-up in a royal palace from that in a castle, or private house. See notes on 25. 1 and 10. 37. 9 below.

xxii. 5-9. See FOWLER'S note on 2. 9. 25 in Book II, p. 291.

6. GOUGH. In the galleries at Hampton Court is a portrait of Queen Elizabeth's porter, a giant said to have been eight feet six inches in height.

xxiii. 7-9. WARTON (2. 210-11). Here Spenser paints from the manners of his own age; in which the custom of celebrating a

Feast,
Serv'd up in hall with sewrs and seneshalls,

was not entirely dropt. (Stow, *Survey*, ed. 1599, p. 315, speaking of a magnificent feast in Ely-house, at which were present king Henry VIII and queen Catharine, says, that "Edward Nevil was Seneshall or Steward.") One of the officers at these solemnities was styled the marshal of the hall: an office for which Chaucer tells us, his host at the tabard was properly qualified (*Prologue* 753 [Skeat's ed. 751-2]):

A semely man our hoste was withal
To ben a Marshall in a lordis hall.

As the guests at these pompous and public festivals were very numerous, and of various conditions; I suppose the business of this office, was to place every person according to his rank, and to preserve peace and order.

8.   TODD.   In Hawes's *Hist. of Graunde Amoure*, Reason is the officer thus named in the Tower of Doctrine, sig. B$_{iiij}$, ed. 1554 [ll. 477, 483]:

The Marshall yclipped was dame Reason . . .
And the hye Stewarde (i. e. Seneshall,) Liberalitye.

In Massinger's *New way to pay old debts*, the Steward's name, I may add, is Order.

xxv-xxvi.   A. B. GOUGH (*MLR* 12. 140-5) thinks that the allusion here may be to Ulpian Fulwell, in whose *Ars Adulandi* (1576) he finds many puns on the name, e. g., " Ful well I do finde, that Fortune is blinde." His enemies may have, in his own punning vein, called him " Foul Well," which is like Spenser's " Malfont." In the *Ars Adulandi* are several passages which suggest that Fulwell had been considered " a very saucy and presumpteous foole " at court. In Dialogue 4 (p. 17) is an attack on Leicester as " Lady Fortune's minion." Mr. Gough thinks that the bitter satire in *Ars Adulandi* was remembered by Spenser, and that he meant in " Malfont " a reference to Fulwell.

EDITOR.   Mr. Gough may, of course, be right in his suggestion, but the evidence he gives does not seem sufficient to prove his case; Fulwell's remarks in *Ars Adulandi* were made at " Fortune's court " and may very well refer only to the affairs of Ulpian Fulwell with fickle Dame Fortune without any recognizable satire on Elizabeth's court. If Malfont is to be identified with any particular person, he should be someone who deserted Elizabeth for Mary Stuart. Malfont is probably a reference to all Elizabeth's subjects who attacked her in " rayling rymes." Cf. Appendix, p. 321.

xxv. 1.   WARTON (2. 209).   " Screene" occurs again, 5. 10. 37. [9]. The screen, or entrance into the hall, was as familiar a term in Spenser's age, as the ceremonies, mentioned in the next note, to have been performed within it, were frequent: This is still to be seen before the halls of antient houses. Stow uses it as a well-known word, " A maypole, to stand in the hall, before the scrine, decked with holme and ivie, at the feast of christmas." It is yet remembered in our universities.

EDITOR.   It is clear that this screen was not at the entrance to the hall, for the great throng would not have had room to mill about. See the Editor's note on sts. 22-7 above. Cf. also 23. 2.

UPTON.   Meaning Westminster hall.   The Chancellor, and judges have scrines, lattices, " Cancelli," around their seats: the Chancellor has his name particularly from hence.

5.   GOUGH.   " blaspheme." The use of this word indicates the sacred character of the Queen's office, on which the panegyrists of Elizabeth laid great stress. Cf. 1 Kings 21. 10: " Thou didst blaspheme God and the king."

xxvii ff.   E. B. FOWLER (*Spenser and the Courts of Love*, p. 70).   Aside from the self-evident political allegory we note in the description of this exalted personage certain court of love features. The sovereign seated on her jewelled throne in regal splendor is a court of love inheritance from the classical tradition. . . .

Compare Ovid's description of Apollo throned in his palace (*Met.* 2. 23-4):

> Purpurea velatus veste sedebat
> In solio Phoebus, claris lucente smaragdis.

See also the throne of Lady Loyaltè in the *Assembly of Ladies* 475-490 (text in Skeat's *Chaucerian Pieces*, pp. 380 ff.):

> And there I saw, withouten any fayl,
> A chayrë set, with ful riche aparayl.

> And fyve stages it was set fro the ground,
> Of cassidony ful curiously wrought;
> With four pomelles of golde, and very round,
> Set with saphyrs, as good as coud be thought;
> That, wot ye what, if it were thorugh sought,
> As I suppose, fro this countrey til Inde,
> Another such it were right fer to finde! . . .
> Above ther was a riche cloth of estate,
> Wrought with the nedle ful straungëly,
> Her word thereon; and thus it said trewly,
> " A endurer," to tel you in wordës few,
> With grete letters, the better I hem knew.

A similar impression of magnificence is conveyed by the description of Queen Eleutherillida and her throne in *The Strife of Love in a Dream*, Lang's ed., p. 117:

In the middle prospect, opposite against our going in upon a degreed regall throne, set full of glystering stones in a marvelous order, farre more excellent then the seat in the temple of Hercules at Tyre, of the stone Eusebes. The Queene with an imperiall Maiestie sitting uppon it, goddesse like, and of a woonderfull magnanimitie in countenance: gorgiously apparrelled in clothe of goulde, with a sumptuous and curious attyre, upon hir head of a purple couler, with an edging of Orient Pearle, shadowing over hir large forhead, aunciently and princelike, euer pressing hir plemmirrulate trammels of hayre, as blacke as iet descending downe hir snowie temples. . . .

Spenser secures the same effect in the representation of Mercilla, not by an elaborate description of the queen herself—a hazardous undertaking—but by enlarging upon the cloudlike appearance of the cloth of state spread above her [st. 28 quoted].

      EDITOR.   The description, however, was obviously intended to apply to Elizabeth's court, the lavish display and richness of which is described by Harrison in his *Description of England* (ed. Furnivall, for the New Shakespeare Society, pp. 270-7).

See Appendix, pp. 272-3, 299, 317, 321-4.

xxvii. 8.   See HARD's note on 7. 5. 6 above.

    9. UPTON.   This is pointing out the allegory very particular.

      GOUGH.   The charges on the royal arms of England and France, borne by Elizabeth, and all other English sovereigns from Edward III to George III.

The French arms were quartered with the English as "arms of pretension" in 1340, to indicate Edward III's claim to the French crown, and were abandoned with the empty title in 1802, at the Peace of Amiens.

xxviii. 4. HEISE (p. 133) cites *Met.* 3. 183-5; *Aen.* 8. 622-3; but the application of the simile is, in both, quite different.

xxviii. 9–xxix. See *Epithalamion* 229-233 and Van Winkle's notes.

xxix. 2. UPTON. "And on their purpled wings." Perhaps he gave it "purple wings." Ovid, *Rem. Am.* 701: "Nec nos purpureas pueri resecabimus alas." Horace, *Odes* 4. 1. 10: ["purpureis . . . aloribus."] Consult Bentley on Horace, *Odes* 3. 3. 12: "purpure[o] ore." See note on *F. Q.* 2. 3. 1. 1 [in Book II, p. 205].

4-5. GRACE W. LANDRUM (*PMLA* 41. 541). Cf. Isaiah 6. 3. [Also Rev. 7. 11-2; 15. 3-4.]

9. WARTON (2. 212-3). Spenser frequently uses the expression "kings and kesars," 3. 11. 29. 9; 4. 7. 1. 4; 6. 3. 5. 7; 6. 12. 28. 7 [also 2. 7. 5. 9]. It is a very antient form of speaking, and is found, among other poets, in the *Visions of Pierce Plowman:*

Death came driving after, and all to dust pashed
Kynges and Kaysers, knights and popes.

(It was not unfamiliar in Ben. Jonson's time; thus, in his *Tale of a Tub* 2. 2:

Tu. I charge you in the queen's name keep the peace.
Hil. Tell me o' no queene or kersar.

It occurs likewise in Harrington's *Ariosto,* 44. 47:

For myters, states, nor crownes may not exclude
Popes, mightie kyngs, nor keysars from the same.)

xxx. 7. GOUGH. An allusion to the prolonged peace which Elizabeth contrived to maintain for her English subjects, after the suppression of the Rising of the North in 1569. [See Appendix, pp. 303, 307, 309.]

xxxi-xxxii. JORTIN. Homer, *Il.* 9. 498 ff.: ["Moreover prayers of penitence are daughters of great Zeus, halting and wrinkled and of eyes askance, that have their task withal to go in steps of sin. . . . Now whoso reverenceth Zeus' daughters when they draw near him they greatly bless and hear his petitions. . . ."] So, according to Homer, the Litae are not very handsome. Homer does not give us their names, or number. Dice, Eunomie, and Eirene, according to Hesiod, are the Horae, daughters of Jupiter and Themis. *Theog.* 901-2: ["Next he wedded bright Themis, who bare Hours (Horai), even Good Government (Eunomia), and Justice (Dike), and blooming Peace (Eirene)."] "Sacred Reverence" seems to be taken from Ovid, *Fast.* 5. [19-25]:

Saepe aliquis solio, quod tu, Saturne, tenebas,
     Ausus de media plebe sedere Deus. . . .
Donec, Honor, placidoque decens Reverentia vultu
     Corpora legitimis imposuere toris.
Hinc sata Majestas. . . .

SAWTELLE (pp. 79-80). This name is a personification of the Greek word for "prayers" (λιταί), as in *Iliad* 9. 502 ff.—a passage which is the source of the general conception here expressed. With Homer, as with Spenser, they are daughters of Jove, who attend their father as mediators between him and man; and they bend the wills of mortals also. But while Homer describes them as "halting and wrinkled and of eyes askance, that have their task withal to go in the steps of Sin," Spenser says they are fair virgins and lovely daughters. . . .

The fusion of the Litae with the Hours is arbitrary on the part of our poet: it may have been suggested, however, by the ethical conception of the Hours, which is evident in Hesiod, *Theog.* 901 ff., and Pindar, *Olymp.* 13. It is clear, from the names themselves, that the Hours of Hesiod are something more than those of Homer, who represents them as divinities of the seasons only: with Hesiod there is an ethical conception, and they administer justice, good laws, and peace to men, as their names indicate. This idea held its own as time went on, as will be seen from the passage by Pindar, referred to above [lines 6-9]: "For therein dwell Order, and her sisters, sure foundation of states, Justice and like-minded Peace, dispensers of wealth to men, wise Themis' golden daughters."

This conception, however, is so different from that of Homer concerning the Litae that, as said above, it could not have done more than suggest to Spenser the fusion of the two.

LOTSPEICH (pp. 78-9). For this confusion of Litae and Hours, Natalis Comes is partly responsible. At 2. 1 Natalis Comes mentions the Litae in close connection with Themis and discusses their activities in regard to the prayers of kings in terms which parallel st. 32. 1-4. At 4. 16 he attaches similar meaning to the Hours, quotes *Theog.* 901-3, and shows that their names mean justice, law, and peace, which well suits Spenser's purpose in his passage on the Litae.

xxxii. 6-9. E. B. FOWLER (*Spenser and the Courts of Love*, p. 79). Although these characters are of classical origin, the facts that three are specially chosen and named by Spenser and that they are beautiful young virgins in close attendance upon Queen Mercilla make the situation strikingly analogous to the court of Venus with the three Graces in attendance upon the goddess. (In the *De Nuptiis* of Claudianus Venus is seated in her chair of state (100-101):

> Dextra laevaque sorores
> Stabant Idaliae.

In the *De Venus la Deesse d'Amor* 122 the goddess is attended by "trois puceles.")

xxxiii. 4. GOUGH. Emblem of the power of England. It was adopted as a device by Henry I, to whom Geoffrey of Monmouth alluded as "the Lion of justice" in the prophecy of Merlin. The first king of England to display the lion on his shield was Richard I.

In *Mother Hubberd's Tale* 624-6 the Mule, who has come from Court, relates that the Lion lives there,

> Enchaste with chaine and circulet of gold:
> So wilde a beast so tame ytaught to bee,
> And buxome to his bandes, is joy to see.

Here the lion appears to denote the Earl of Leicester, who bore a lion on his coat-of-arms, though he can hardly be alluded to in the present passage.

CANTO IX 243

xxxiv. 5. CHURCH. It seems to have been a Compliment (in times of Knight-errantry) paid by strangers, when introduced at the Courts of Princes, humbly to desire that they might have the atchievement of any adventure which, during their stay, should happen. See Letter to Sir W. Raleigh: "In the beginning of the feast," etc. See too 5. 10. 15. 9. [Also Book I, pp. 391-5; 399-401.]

xxxvi ff. E. B. FOWLER (*Spenser and the Courts of Love*, pp. 107-8). Certain features of this allegorical trial are paralleled in Rolland's *Court of Venus* (c. 1560, ed. Rev. W. Gregor for Scottish Text Society, Edinburgh and London, 1884). Though differing in detail the two scenes are alike in their adherence to elaborate legal form. In an argument between Hope and Despair over the relative merits and demerits of love, Hope is worsted. Venus comes to the aid of her knight and orders Despair before her court to answer a charge of blasphemy against love. The goddess sends Nemesis, her sheriff, to summon the culprit. As an interested party to the proceedings Venus declines to act as judge and appoints Lady Rhamnusia in her stead. Venus assumes the rôle of prosecutor. After a long search for counsel Despair finally secures the services of Vesta. The clerk is Fremmitnes and the "sergiands" are Rigour, Impacience, Evill Will, and Unkindness. The "assyis," or jury, consists of twenty-five famous women of mythology including Dione the mother of Venus. As spectators are gathered the celebrated women of history and mythology. In the capacity of attorney for Despair Vesta vainly challenges a number of the jury—notably Dione—as incompetent. The indictment as read charges Despair with having slain Hope and slandered Venus. Vesta answers the first charge by pointing to the knight, who stands there alive, and the second, by attempting to prove that love is the root of all mischance. After long arguments by Vesta and Venus the case goes to the jury. This body commends both Venus and Vesta and tempers the verdict of guilty with recommendation to the mercy of the court. Venus is finally appeased and court adjourns for a feast and tournament.

We note that both in Spenser and Rolland a woman acts as judge, and in both a throne is endangered; for, as Nemesis says in Rolland's poem (890), "this caus concernis the croun." The functions of Order and Nemesis as officers of the court are similar. (Cf. also the serjeants Rigour, Impacience, Evil Will, and Unkindness.) Attention may be called to certain differences in procedure. In Rolland, Venus quits the chair of state to conduct the prosecution in person; whereas, in Spenser Zele acts for the queen. In Rolland we have trial by jury, but in Spenser the decision rests with Mercilla. But since in the *Court of Venus* the defendant is turned over to the goddess for punishment, it is fair to say that in both cases the fate of the prisoner is left in the hands of the injured sovereign. In both, also, there are advocates for the defendant, the rôle of Pittie and the rest corresponding to that of Vesta. The spectators in Rolland are chiefly women; whereas, in Spenser the distinguished guests are men. Accordingly, in the latter court we find Arthur himself, but in the former "Guanour" his queen. The two trials are alike in the indefiniteness of the ending. The postponement of sentence in the case of Duessa is also noticeably similar to the stay of judgment in *Le Parlement d'Amour*.

xxxvi. 4. UPTON. I. e. indifferently, as we use it in our Common Prayer, "administering justice indifferently."

xxxvii. 8. CHURCH. The Poet, if I mistake not, by seating Prince Arthur and Arthegall in this manner, would insinuate that Queen Elizabeth, in the unfortunate

Case of the Queen of Scots, was supported in her determination by Justice and Glory, or The good of her Kingdom. See st. 43, line 8.

xxxviii ff. H. S. V. JONES (*Spenser's Defense of Lord Grey*, p. 56). There can be no mistake about the general significance of the Isis Church and Mercilla episodes. Grey is vowed heart and soul to the service of the Queen, who is at once merciful and militant. It is not simply that he owes allegiance to her, but that he loves those twin ideals of justice and mercy which, as the poet would have it, are the essence of her character and the inspiration of her life. In the person of Mercilla the merciful disposition of the Queen is further celebrated; and there is significance in representing Leicester and Grey as taking with them on their respective missions to the Netherlands and Ireland the lesson to be drawn from the trial of Mary Queen of Scots. That process has shown that the forces that make for order, justice, and peace (Eunomie, Dike, Eirene)—in a word those that informed the nationalistic and eirenic policy of "les politiques"—were arrayed against the Catholic menace in the person of the Scottish queen; and Arthur and Artegall address themselves to their respective tasks with the example of the stern but sorrowful justice of Mercilla fresh in their minds. In Ireland, Spenser implies, Grey followed the example that the Queen had set in the execution of Mary and that was recommended to Leicester for his campaign in the Netherlands. Moreover, the association of the Scottish queen (the kinswoman of the Guises) with Grey and Leicester in this episode stresses the international significance of Grey's mission to Ireland.

xxxviii. EDITOR. It was this episode, without doubt, at which James took offence. The following extract of the letter of Robert Bowes to Lord Burghley, Nov. 12, 1596, from the *State Papers relating to Scotland in the Public Record Office in London,* is printed in Carpenter's *Reference Guide,* pp. 41-2:

The K[ing] hath conceaued great offence against Edward Spencer publishing in prynte in the second book ["Book" deleted in MS] p[ar]t of the Fairy Queene and ix*th* chapter some dishonor*a*ble effects (as the k. demeth thereof) against himself and his mother deceased. He alledged that this booke was passed w*i*th previledge of her mats Commission[er]s for the veiwe and allowance of all wrytinges to be receaued into Printe. But therin I haue (I think) satisfyed him that it is not given out wth such p[ri]viledge: yet he still desyreth that Edward Spencer for his faulte, may be dewly tryed & punished.

See Appendix, pp. 317, 319-324.

2. UPTON. Mary Q. of Scots: whom in st. 42 he calls "untitled queen."

3-9. Cf. *Hymne of Beautie* 148-161.

9. GOUGH. This must allude rather to the years of Mary's captivity in England than to the actual time of her trial, when Parliament presented a petition to Elizabeth requesting that she might be put to death, and the country was flooded with pamphlets making the same demand.

xxxix. 7. EDITOR (C. G. O.). Milton liked the image, the more perhaps for the Spenserian precedent. Cf. *P. L.* 2. 656; *Samson Agonistes* 235, 906.

xl.	See Appendix, pp. 299, 319-324.

6. GOUGH. The commission by which Mary was tried was not empowered to deal with anything that had occurred before 1585, and therefore not with her complicity in the plot for the murder of her husband, Lord Darnley, 1567, or in the Rising of the North, 1569, conspiracies which had caused the death or ruin of many prominent men whom Mary had "beguiled." Mary was charged only with having "conspired the destruction of the Queen of England and the subversion of religion."

xli. 3. UPTON. The Earls of Northumberland and Westmorland.

E. G. HARMAN (*Edmund Spenser*, pp. 92 ff.) identifies these with Henry Percy, eighth Earl of Northumberland and Philip Howard, thirteenth Earl of Arundel. They were the most prominent men alleged to be implicated in Throckmorton's plot for the murder of Elizabeth and the release of Mary in 1583. They were both committed to the Tower. GOUGH accepts this identification.

xlii. 3. GOUGH. This may be taken to refer generally to all the conspiracies formed against Elizabeth in favour of Mary Queen of Scots, including the Ridolfi plot, 1571, the Throckmorton plot, 1583, and the Babington plot, 1585. These plots were detected by the Government spies, and such of the ringleaders as could be arrested were executed.

8. GOUGH. After her surrender to the Scottish Lords at Carberry Hill in 1567, Mary abdicated the crown. She was also Queen Dowager of France.

xliii-xlv. EDITOR (F. M. P.). In connection with these stanzas it is interesting to read an anonymous little volume that appeared in 1587, entitled *A Defence of the honorable sentence and execution of the Queene of Scots*, attributed by Herbert (*Typographical Antiquities* 2. 1226, first ed.), without authority, to Maurice Kyffin, author of *The Blessedness of Brytaine*, 1587. (See J. P. Collier, *Bibliographical and Critical Account* 3. 252-4.) In the sixth chapter, "containing an aunswere to certaine objections latelie made by certaine fauorites of the Queene of Scottes," many precedents and laws are cited to show that England had technical sovereignty over Mary; that England acted in accordance with the civil law, the law of nature, the divine law, and the law of nations; that Mary's nobility of birth did not protect her from the consequences of her treasonable acts; and that her execution was in accordance with the dictates of both justice and mercy. Spenser's summary of these arguments corresponds closely to this tract. Less apposite is Richard Crompton's *A short declaration of the ende of traytors*, etc., another justification of the execution of Mary, for the line of reasoning does not parallel Spenser's. For a review of all the controversial literature relative to Mary Stuart's claim to the English throne, see Kerby Neill, "*The Faerie Queene* and Mary Stuart" in the Appendix, pp. 319-324.

xliii. 1. Cf. the Franklin, Zeal, 1. 10. 6.

7-8. UPTON. The Lord Treasurer Burleigh.

xliv. 2. GOUGH. Mary was only brought to trial by "peremptory power" of an Act passed in 1584, embodying the aims of the "Bond of Association," and providing penalties for any act or counsel to the harm of the Queen's person. This statute, it was maintained with doubtful legality, removed the obstacle to a trial presented by Mary's prerogative as a foreign prince.

7.   GOUGH.   The House of Commons twice petitioned Elizabeth that the Queen of Scots might be put to death. When a joint address to this effect from both Houses was received with a request to find some other way, Lords and Commons voted unanimously that there was no other way. Public opinion, which in the end overcame Elizabeth's doubts and scruples, was mainly swayed by the dread of civil war and the suppression of religious liberty, and was particularly excited by the revelation of Babington's plot for the assassination of Elizabeth.

xlv. 2.   GOUGH.   Chiefly chivalrous considerations which would weigh especially with the poet. Some of them were mentioned by Elizabeth in her reply to a petition for Mary's execution. "I protest there is nothing hath more grieved me, than that one not differing from me in sex, of like rank and degree, of the same stock and most nearly allied unto me in blood, hath fallen into so great a crime" (Lloyd, *State Trials*, p. 34).

5-6.   GOUGH.   The execution of Mary was at once a challenge to Scotland, France, and Spain, though it was well known that only the last of these powers would make more than a formal protest. James VI was powerless to avenge his mother, and Henry III of France, whose brother Francis II had been Mary's first husband, was endeavouring to check the aggressively Papal policy of her kinsmen the Guises, and he had no desire to see Spanish influence supreme in the British Isles. But the death of Mary precipitated the conflict with Philip II of Spain, whom the Roman Catholics regarded as her heir to the crown of England. It was to enforce this claim that he sent the Armada in the following year.

EDITOR.   See *King James's Secret: Negotiations between Elizabeth and James VI relating to the Execution of Mary Queen of Scots, from the Warrender Papers* (London, 1927), by Robert S. Rait and Annie I. Cameron, for evidence that James connived at his mother's death in order to assure himself of the succession to the English throne.

5.   See notes on 3. 12. 11 in Book III, p. 302; and on 4. 10. 16. 5—19 in Book IV, p. 221.

6.   UPTON.   Viz. to France and Scotland.

xlvi.   See Appendix, pp. 306-7, 317, 322.

2-3.   UPTON.   The Earl of Leicester (often imaged in P. Arthur) was thought inclined to the party of the Q. of Scots.

xlvii. 6.   Same cadence at *Ruines of Time* 422; 3. 7. 41. 9; cf. above Pr. 6. 9.

xlviii.   See Appendix, pp. 319-324.

2.   UPTON.   Viz. of her husband, the Earl of Darnley.

l. 6-8.   B. E. C. DAVIS (*Edmund Spenser, A Critical Study*, p. 150). The length of Spenser's stanza and the eclectic nature of his vocabulary increases this tendency to diffuseness, the common characteristic of the school to which he belonged.

l. 6—li.   TODD.   If the poet had lived to read and examine the notices which, in later times, have been produced to shew the unfair treatment which Mary experienced; he might have been led perhaps to vindicate her character. His gentle spirit, however, I conceive, even while apologising for Elizabeth, undoubtedly felt the force of what Brantome has asserted, that " No one ever beheld the person of Mary without admiration and love, or will read her history without sorrow." [See 38. 9.]

COLLIER. Pity and justice seem, throughout the trial, to maintain a contest in the mind of Spenser, and even his Mercilla, at the conclusion, would fain have concealed the grief by which she was overcome.

CANTO X

DODGE (*PMLA* 12. 203). Cf. *Orl. Fur.* 9. 17 ff. Arthur's exploit in behalf of Belge is very much like Orlando's exploit in behalf of Olimpia. Note that Olimpia's dominions are in the Low Countries. It seems probable that Spenser, determining to allegorize the English wars in the Low Countries under Leicester, remembered this story of the *Furioso* and adopted certain of its features.

GOUGH. Comparing Spenser's allegory with the reality, we find that Belge's miseries and the atrocities perpetrated by her oppressor are imaginatively, but in a broad sense truthfully, rendered. The horrors of the Inquisition and of Alva's infamous " Council of Blood," the ruin of some of the fairest cities, and the suppression of liberty everywhere except among the moors and marshes of the sea-board, are features on which the poet rightly dwells. But the part played by England is entirely misrepresented. As an idealized version of history a great part of Cantos 10 and 11 would be ridiculous. [See Appendix, pp. 299, 306-8, 316-8.]

i.   BLAKENEY. For the sentiment expressed in this stanza cf. Shakespeare, *Merchant of Venice* 4. 1 [196-7]:

And earthly power doth then show likest God's,
When Mercy seasons Justice.

[Cf. 5. 7. 7 and note.]

3-4. UPTON. By divine extraction: as derived from justice originally, and a part of her. Milton very scriptural says, *P. L.* 10. 59: " Mercy collegue with Justice."

7-8. Perhaps an allusion to the mercy seat in recollection of such passages as Ex. 25. 21-2; 30. 6; 33. 8-19; Lev. 16. 2; Num. 7. 89; Is. 16. 5.

ii.   BLAKENEY. The thought embodied in this rather difficult stanza is this: Justice, by strict adherence to legal formulas, will sacrifice the good of the individual, or society, in order to maintain its rules unimpaired; hence the phrase, " summum jus, summa injuria." Mercy, on the other hand, without questioning the rules of justice, is prepared to make the necessary exceptions.

3. UPTON. He seems to have Ovid in view, [*Met.* 1. 190-1]:

Sed immedicabile vulnus
Ense recidendum, ne pars sincera trahatur.

To preserve right inviolated, often takes away the chief, or principal, corrupted part, to save the other part which is not corrupted.

iii. 6-7.　JORTIN.　Armoric I suppose.

UPTON.　Even from Bretagne in France, called formerly Aremorica or Armorica (which Spenser spells Armericke, or his printer, I cannot determine whether) unto the Molucca islands in the East Indian Seas. Chaucer, ed. Urry, p. 108 [*Franklin's Tale* 729]: "In Armorike that clepid is Britaine."

CHURCH cites "Armorick" in *F. Q.* 2. 10. 64. 5.

TODD.　Armorick, however, in the passage to which Mr. Church refers, is a substantive, as it also is in Chaucer; and is moreover accented on the first syllable; whereas Armericke is accented on the second, and is an adjective. May we not then be permitted to suppose an errour of the press, and that Armericke might have been intended for Americke? This reading presents a just compliment both to the Queen, and to the poet's friend Sir Walter Raleigh; (who had named, in honour of Elizabeth, the first country which the English planted in America, Virginia;) while the opposition to the Moluccas is thus more strongly marked, and renders the meaning the same as if the poet had written "From the Western to the Eastern shores the Queen's honour is enlarged." [Cf. allusion in 2. Pr. 2-3.]

GOUGH.　Probably Todd's emendation "Americke" is correct. . . . Otherwise Armericke stands for Armoricke, i. e. Armorican, Breton. If so, there is a reference to Elizabeth's operations in Brittany in aid of Henry IV in his struggle against the Catholic League, which held that Duchy. There was much anxiety in England owing to the seizure by a Spanish force of the Breton port of Blavet (near the present L'Orient), nominally to support the League, but really to secure the Duchy for Philip's daughter, the Infanta Isabel. Sir John Norris was sent to Brittany in April, 1591, with 3000 men. In 1593 Spain sent large reinforcements to Brittany, and occupied Brest. Elizabeth replied by sending more English troops, and in 1594 Brest was recovered from the Spaniards with the aid of an English fleet under Frobisher.

Book 5 was probably written in 1592-3, and revised not later than 1595. These events in Brittany were therefore current topics when Spenser wrote. On the other hand, the words "th'utmost brinke" and "Nations farre" are more appropriate to America than Brittany.

EDITOR (J. G. M.).　But cf. the spelling of the title licensed to Thomas Woodcocke (*SR* 2. 411) on 21 May 1582: *Diuers voiages touchinge the discoue[r]y of Armerica.*

7.　GOUGH.　The Moluccas or Spice Islands, and archipelago between Celebes and New Guinea. They attracted much attention at this time on account of the lucrative spice trade, which was in the hands of Spain. In 1579 Francis Drake, in the course of his famous voyage round the globe, stayed a month at Ternate, where he was warmly welcomed by the Sultan of that island, the most powerful prince in the Moluccas. The Portuguese had established themselves in Ternate, but in 1580, on the union with Spain, their colonial policy was directed by that power. In 1588 Thomas Cavendish, an English navigator, sighted one of the Moluccas. Sir James Lancaster sailed in 1591 on the first English voyage specially directed to the East Indies. Spenser may have this expedition in view, although Lancaster, who returned in 1594, went no further than the Malay Peninsula.

8. GOUGH. The cruelties practised by the Spaniards on the natives of their colonies were often made a pretext for the piratical actions of the English seamen, who professed to avenge their wrongs.

EDITOR. Reference may be to the expedition of Drake in 1579 and his report of the acceptance of Elizabeth as ruler by the Sultan of Ternate.

iv. 6. GOUGH. Elizabeth was anxious that it should appear that her hand had been forced, and indeed it is probable that her disinclination to sign the death-warrant was not altogether feigned. Her personal feelings were overborne by the strongly urged advice of her ministers, and her own sense of political necessity.

vi. 2. GOUGH. The springals can hardly, as Upton suggests [see Appendix, p. 301], be the Marquess of Havré and Adolf Meetkercke, who came to England in 1577 as envoys from the States, to ask for help against Spain. They obtained from the queen a promise of money and troops. More probably the incident refers quite generally to the repeated appeals from the Netherlands. In this case the springals are probably the provinces of Holland and Zeeland, which took the lead in the national struggle. As the springals are Belge's eldest sons [so stated at 14. 6; here they are " of full tender yeares," though they have fifteen younger brothers who had passed " their first flowre "!], and her seventeen sons are the provinces [cf. Upton on 10. 7. 4], this interpretation is more consistent than the other with the general sense.

4. UPTON. 'Tis thus to be scanned, " To seek | for succour | of her | and of | her peares." But the Folio of 1609: " To seek for succour of her and her peares." [See Variants.]

8. UPTON. Philip king of Spain. [In his note on st. 25 below, Upton seems to imply that Geryoneo is the Duke of Alva. Is he not Philip, or the Spanish power generally, and the " Seneshall " in 30. 2 a representation of Alva?]

vii. 4. UPTON. The seventeen provinces of the Netherlands.

8-9. LOTSPEICH (p. 91). Spenser seems here to adapt *Met.* 6. 152-5. [See note on *F. Q.* 4. 7. 30. 5-9 in Book IV, pp. 207-8.]

viii. 2. UPTON. The cruelties which were exercised in the Netherlands by the Duke of Alva, and the schemes which were pursued by the subsequent Regents, to introduce the Roman religion, and to make the King of Spain absolute, stirr'd up the Prince of Orange to unite as many of the provinces, as he possibly could, in one confederacy. These provinces were five, which " Belge complains were the only five left of all her numerous brood," viz. Holland, Friesland, Zealand, Guelderland, and Utrecht.

8. UPTON. Aeschylus, *Agamemnon* [870, " three-bodied Geryon."] Hesiod, *Theog.* 287: [" three-headed Geryoneus."] Lucretius [5. 28]: Quidve tripectora tergemini vis Geryonai."

ix-x.   UPTON.   This monster makes a very picturesque figure in a romance or fairy tale. If the reader wants to know particularly concerning the mythology here alluded to, let him consult Servius and the commentators on Virgil 7. 662 and Hesiod, *Theog.* 287, etc.; Silius Italicus 13. 845; Apollodorus, Schol. Apoll. Rhod. *Argon.* 2. 1215; Hyginus, *Fab.* 151; Natalis Comes 7. 1.

LOTSPEICH (p. 63).   In his use of Geryon here to cloak historical allegory, Spenser may have been helped by Servius, *ad Aen.* 7. 662, where Geryon's triple form is said to signify the three islands over which he ruled (in Spenser, the three parts of the Spanish dominions). For a good share of the descriptive material in this passage, he is indebted to Natalis Comes 7. 1: "Dicitur Geryon . . . triplex corpus habuisse, canemque duorum capitum, . . . ex Typhone et Echidna genitum. . . . Habuit vero suae crudelitatis ministrum impigrum atque diligentem Eurytionem." Geryoneo, an example of Spenser's habit of independently multiplying mythical figures, shares the characteristics of his father.

C. G. OSGOOD (*Classical Mythology in Milton's English Poems*, p. 37) notes Milton's reference to Spenser when he calls Spaniards "Geryons sons." Cf. *P. L.* 11. 410-11.

> Guiana, whose great Citie Geryons Sons
> Call El Dorado.

x. 1-2. UPTON.   Apollodorus [2. 5. 10]: φοινικὰς βοῦς; Natalis Comes [7. 1]: "Jussit [Herculem] Eurystheus, ut puniceos Geryonis, Hispaniae regis, boves, qui hospites vorarent, ad se adduceret."

6-8. JORTIN.   Hesiod, *Theog.* 306-9: ["With her (Echidna) they say Typhaon met in loving union, a dread and blustering wind with a bright-eyed maid. And she conceived and bare stout-hearted children. First Orthos she bare to be the dog Geryoneus."] See also Silius Italicus 13. 845.

7-8. WARTON (1. 102).   I wonder that Spenser should in this place have omitted the mention of a seven-headed dragon, who, together with Orthrus, was stationed to guard these oxen, and was likewise the offspring of Typhaon and Echidna [mentioned by Natalis Comes, Spenser's obvious authority]. A dragon was too tempting a circumstance to be omitted.

xi. 5-9. UPTON.   The allegory is very elegant and learned, considered either in a general and poetical sense, or in the historical view of the state of Belge; when the Spaniards had subverted the liberties of the States, after the assassination of the Prince of Orange. The description of Belge as a Widow, is scriptural likewise: this superadds to its dignity. Lamentations 1. 1: "How doth the city sit solitary, that was full of people! how is she become as a widow!" "To widow" is used in the Greek language for "to make desolate". . . . And in this sense Virgil most elegantly uses it, 8. 571.

8. GOUGH.   The allegory in this canto is, like most of Spenser's allegories, so vague and loose that it is difficult to determine the allusion. It is commonly supposed that the husband is William the Silent, Prince of Orange and Stadtholder of Holland, who was assassinated in 1584. But in this case, line 9 and the two following stanzas are entirely opposed to the facts. It is better, following Craik, to identify the husband with Charles the Bold, Duke of Burgundy, who was

slain at the battle of Nancy in 1477. The house of Burgundy, which had ruled in the Netherlands for nearly a century, although not popular, was preferred to the house of Habsburg. This family inherited the Netherlands through the marriage of Charles's daughter and heiress Mary to Maximilian, Archduke of Austria, immediately after her father's death. Their grandson was the Emperor Charles V.

If this interpretation be followed, the tyrant Geryoneo must be taken to represent not only Philip II but the dynasty to which he belonged, and the beginning of Belge's " woe and wretchednesse " will date from the acquisition of the Netherlands by the house of Habsburg.

xiii. 2. GOUGH. This of course is not to be taken literally, as the king of Spain was the lawful sovereign of the Netherlands, which had no choice in the matter. Charles V governed the country for many years with studied moderation, and redressed many grievances. In 1549 he presented to the States of the Netherlands his son Philip, who swore to maintain their rights, in return for the oath of allegiance which they gave him.

5-9. GOUGH. Charles V, who had been gradually increasing the severity of his enactments against heresy, issued in 1550 a " placard " or edict, which ordained the burning of men, and the burying alive of women convicted of heresy. It was enforced with extreme rigour, and was one of the chief causes of the subsequent revolt.

7. UPTON. Meaning the papisticall religion inforced by persecution; particularly the inquisition, which the Duke of Alva set up in the Netherlands.

8-9. LOTSPEICH (p. 63). Spenser may have received a suggestion from Boccaccio 1. 21, where, referring to Dante, he describes an image of Fraud, with the face of a man and the body of a serpent, ending in a scorpion's tail, the name of which was Geryon.

xiv. 6. See note on 6. 2 above.

xv-xvi. See note on 9. 34. 5 above.

xvi. 5. See UPTON's note on *F. Q.* 2. 3. 1. 1 in Book II, p. 205; also on 9. 29. 2 above. Cf. " Aurora with her rosie heare," *Virgils Gnat* 68, from Virgil's " crinibus . . . roseis . . . Aurora," *Culex* 44.

xvii. 2. GOUGH. In reality Leicester had to borrow money on the security of his lands before he started to take up his post in the Low Countries, and complained that no pay was forthcoming for his men, who were in danger of starving. In seven months half of them were dead. Froude, *Hist. Eng.* [ed. 1870], ch. 68.

xx. 3-9. GOUGH. Although he afterwards became very unpopular, Leicester at his arrival in Holland was greeted with the utmost joy. The States of Holland writing to Elizabeth said " they looked upon him as sent from Heaven for their deliverance." See *Cambridge Modern History* 3. 619. Among those who actually met him on his arrival were the widow of the Prince of Orange and his son Maurice, then eighteen years old (*Leycester Correspondence.* Camden Soc. [O. S. 27,] p. xi). [See Appendix, p. 319.]

7-8.   LOTSPEICH (p. 60).   Cf. *Daphnaida* 498.   The wheel and the blindness are common in the tradition of Fortuna which originates in the classics; see H. R. Patch, *The Goddess Fortuna in Medieval Literature*, pp. 11-2, 38, 44, 150. Natalis Comes 4. 9 also calls Fortuna blind and, on the subject of her wheel, quotes Tibullus 1. 5. 70.

xxii-xxiv.   See Appendix, p. 274.

xxii. 4.   GOUGH.   " deepe rooted dreede."   These expressions may refer to the suspicion with which many of the Dutch regarded the arrival of Leicester and his English forces.   It was due to Elizabeth's hostility to religious freedom, her unwillingness to break with Spain, her demand that three sea-ports should be handed over to her (which it was feared she would restore to Spain), and other discouraging indications of half-heartedness or treachery.

9.   BLAKENEY.   Cf. Shakespeare, *Measure for Measure* 3. [1. 2-3]:

> The miserable have no other medicine,
> But only hope.

Good advice is given by Cicero, *Tusc. Disp.* 2. 23. 55: " Hoc quidem in dolore maxime est providendum, ne quid abjecte, ne quid timide, ne quid ignave, ne quid serviliter muliebriterve faciamus."   And in Plautus, *Rudens* 402 [2. 3. 71], we read: " Ergo animus aequos optumumst aerumnae condimentum."

xxiii. 3-5.   GOUGH.   In 1572 Alva gave orders that every Flemish town which refused to admit a Spanish garrison should be sacked " and all its inhabitants put to death.   At Mechlin, Zutphen, and Naarden these orders were almost literally carried out " (Creighton, *Age of Elizabeth*, ch. 5).   At Zutphen and Naarden scarcely a house was left standing.   Haarlem was sacked in 1573, and in 1576 a mutinous Spanish army sacked Antwerp, burning the splendid City Hall and a great part of the city, and massacring thousands of the inhabitants.

4.   " sky-threating."   Spenser seems always to have liked this image.   See *Concordance*, s. v. *threat*.   The whole passage 4-9 reflects an actuality which Spenser in Ireland had not far to seek.

xxiv. 6.   Cf. Matthew 8. 20.

xxv.   UPTON.   This city I suppose to be Antwerp; and the castle, the citadel, which was built by the Duke of Alva, to keep the people in awe.   In this citadel the Duke caused to be erected his statue, representing him trampling upon the conquering [*sic*] states of the Netherlands.   [See note on 6. 8 above.]

3.   GOUGH.   It was especially to save Antwerp, which was being besieged by the Spaniards under the Prince of Parma, that the States appealed to Elizabeth in 1585.   She haggled long over the terms, and two days after an agreement was signed the city fell.   Leicester and his troops landed at Flushing.

6.   GOUGH.   This probably refers to the long siege of Antwerp in 1585. Parma threw a bridge across the Scheldt below the city, by which means supplies were cut off.

8. "in her necke." In the "neck" of her territory, i. e. on the Scheldt, which was the main thoroughfare for overseas traffic.

xxvii. 1. GOUGH. Soon after his accession Philip II took strong measures to strengthen his hold upon the Netherlands. A Spanish army was maintained. Many of the privileges and liberties of the provinces and communes were curtailed or abrogated. A new diocesan organization was imposed. The Council of State was practically superseded by the *Consulta,* a body of three ministers whose powers were almost absolute. From 1567 to 1573 the Duke of Alva was Governor-General, and set up an arbitrary tribunal, the Council of Troubles, or "Council of Blood" as it was popularly called, which attempted to stamp out heresy and sedition by establishing a reign of terror.

2. GOUGH. "inquisition." Primarily, apart from the allegorical significance, this must mean vexatious inquiry, espionage. But in stanzas 25-7 Spenser nearly forgets the mythical Geryoneo and Belge, and tells almost literally the story of Spanish oppression in the Netherlands.

Charles V had established the Papal Inquisition in the Netherlands. Its activities were greatly increased under Philip II, and thousands of persons were tortured and burnt to death. See Motley, *Rise of the Dutch Republic,* Part 2, ch. 3. On Feb. 16, 1568, the Inquisition condemned all the inhabitants of the Netherlands to death, with the exception of a few persons specially named. This sentence rendered further legal forms unnecessary.

4. GOUGH. This probably refers to such politic compromises as the Union of Brussels, 1577, which was signed by William of Orange and nearly all the States. The signatories pledged themselves to maintain the Roman Catholic religion and the authority of King Philip, but at the same time to expel the Spanish army from the country.

xxviii-xxix. See 1. 8. 36 and note in Book I, p. 261.

xxviii. 2. GOUGH. The chapel is probably intended to symbolize the worship of the Roman Catholic Church forced upon the Netherlands by the Spaniards, but it may be noted that Alva built a church in the middle of the citadel of Antwerp. (See Motley, *Dutch Republic,* Part 3, ch. 1.)

4. GOUCH. "Idole." The Host, which in Roman Catholic churches is kept in the pyx above the altar.

6. GOUGH. The public burning to death of persons convicted by the Holy Office of heresy, which being regarded as a solemn act of faith ("auto de fe"), and accompanied by much religious ceremonial, might without great impropriety be described as a form of human sacrifice.

7. GRACE W. LANDRUM (*PMLA* 41. 541). Cf. Genesis 1. 26.

9. TODD. "yron eyes." This is a bold expression, and seems to have suggested to Milton *Il Penseroso* 107, "Pluto's iron tears." I meet with a similar phrase, which, in my opinion, very happily describes a pompous griping lawyer in *The Ant and the Nightingale,* Lond., 1604. This lawyer is introduced addressing himself to tenants waiting upon their new landlord, his client: "With an iron

looke, and shrill voice, he began to speake to the richest of our number, ever and anon yerking out the word ' Fines,' which serued instead of a full point to euery sentence! "

[See notes on 4. 6. 17. 1, in Book IV, p. 200 (where " metaphysical " should read " metaphorical ").]

xxix. 1-5. WARTON (2. 220-1). We are apt to conceive something very wonderful of those mysterious things which are thus said to be unknown to us, and to be out of the reach and compass of man's knowledge and apprehension. Thus a cave is said to be (5. 9. 6. [4]) :

A dreadfull depth, how deepe no man can tell.

If the poet had limited the depth of this cave to a very great, but to a certain number of fathoms, the fancy could still have supposed and added more; but, as no determinate measure is assigned, our imagination is left at liberty to exert its utmost arbitrary stretch, to add fathom to fathom, and depth to depth, till it is lost in its own attempt to grasp the idea of that which is unbounded or infinite. " Omne ignotum pro magnifico est," says Tacitus, somewhere [*Annales* 30. 13]; a writer of the strongest imagination.

3. GOUGH. The Inquisition. The following lines allude to the profound secrecy with which its operations were conducted. [On this monster see notes on 11. 23-5, below.]

6. TODD. " him." Spenser has made the Monster a female in the next canto, sts. 21, 22, etc.

xxx. 2. UPTON. Meaning the Regent of the Netherlands, set up by Philip, King of Spain. The cruellest of all was the Duke of Alva. [See note on 6. 8 above.]

xxxii. 2. Here the new b rime is the old c rime of the preceding stanza. TUCKER BROOKE (*MLN* 37. 224) points this out as one of four linking devices used by Spenser to overcome monotony. Other examples are 2. 1. 20-1; 4. 10. 42-3. For other devices see above 1. 8. 9—9. 1 and note; 4. 18. 9 and note.

6-8. See 1. 7. 33-6; 8. 19 and notes in Book I, pp. 250-4; 259; also 8. 37 above and notes on 37-8; cf. 2. 11. 41. 8; 5. 11. 10. 7-9; 26. 2.

xxxiii. 1-6. See above 5. 2. 18. 5—9 and note.

xxxiv. 6-9. See 1. 7. 13 and note, in Book I, p. 249.

xxxv. 8-9. BLAKENEY. The final lines of this stanza are highly reminiscent of Homer's *Iliad*, 5. 56-8; 14. [516-9], and elsewhere.

[See above 5. 2. 18. 5—9 and note.]

xxxvii. EDITOR (C. G. O.). There is no more realistic episode in the whole poem.

9. EDITOR. This is a different setting from that in 25. 1, which is a royal palace. This is a private house, having a screen at the entrance to the Hall, rather than at the rear (entrance to the Guard Chamber). Professor F. A. Comstock of

Princeton University visualizes this scene thus: "Arthur chased the two knights into the rear of the castle and across the courtyard to the door (postern) at the opposite end of the screen from the main entrance. He slew them at the screen in the front of the Hall." According to the *NED* "Postern" may mean any entrance other than the main one. See notes on 9. 25. 1; 22-7 above.

CANTO XI

i-xxxv.   See Appendix, pp. 310, 318-9.

i. 1-6. BLAKENEY.   Horace's well-known lines ([*Odes*] 3. 2. 31-2) fitly illustrate the theme of the opening part of this stanza:

> Raro antecedentem scelestum
> Deseruit pede Poena claudo.

The thought was a commonplace with the Greeks: take, for example, Aeschylus (in one of the fragments): "Vengeance surely follows in the wake of him who transgresses Justice." [Fragment 9 (22).]

ii.   6. EDITOR (C. G. O.).   A hackneyed *contentio* of the sonneteers from Petrarch down. Cf. *Am.* 32; 55.

v.   9. See 2. 9. 24. 3 and notes in Book II, pp. 290-1; also 6. 8. 16. 3; 7. 6. 41. 1, which suggest that Spenser may have had in the back of his mind the impregnable cliffs of Galtymore.

vi.   C. W. LEMMI (*PQ* 8. 285).   Natalis Comes 7. 1: "Others have believed that by the fable of Geryon, who had had many legs, hands, and eyes, governed by one will, was symbolized concord among citizens, which makes them invincible when all those who are just men act in concert, as Plutarch says in his *Politics*."

2. Cf. 14. 1.   That is, six, not nine.   This "triplicity" he seems to have inherited from his father (10. 9. 6), though Spenser has not said so.

9. UPTON.   Berni, *Orl. Inn.* 2. 20. 20: "Innanzi, in mezzo, in ogni parte."

viii. 8. COLLIER.   It was not unusual, in romances, to apply the word "child" to Squires and others who had not yet been received into the order of knighthood: it was also given to knights, as here, and elsewhere [4. 8. 44. 8; 6. 8. 15. 7] to Prince Arthur. [Cf. "Chyld Tristram," 6. 2. 36. 3.]

ix. 7. UPTON.   The poet mixes the ludicrous with the dreadful. So Milton of Death, 2. 846: "Grin'd horrible a gastly smile."

x. 7-8. See above 10. 32. 6-8 and note.

xii. 2. See notes on 8. 36. 4-5; 49. 1-5 above.

3. See above 5. 8. 28. 2-9 and note.

xiv. 1. See note on 6. 2 above.

5-9. See above 5. 2. 18. 5-9 and note.

xvi.   UPTON. Belge offers herself and all her castles to the Briton Prince: see below the handsome answer which the Prince makes. Does not this plainly allude to the States' offer, and to the Queen's refusal of the sovereignty of the Netherlands?

9. UPTON. "But ev'n that which thou sá-vedst, thine still to remain." So the verse is to be read in scansion.

GOUGH. "thine still to remaine." Viz. that it (the land which thou savedst) shall ever remain thine. Belge offers to make Prince Arthur her over-lord, or feudal superior.

On Leicester's arrival in the Netherlands " there was an eager desire to confer sovereign powers on him; and he was nothing loth. Without consulting Elizabeth he allowed himself, February 4, 1586, in the presence of the States General and of Maurice of Nassau, to be solemnly invested with almost absolute authority, under the title of Governor-General " (*Camb. Mod. Hist.* 3. 619).

xvii. 2. EDITOR. Almost the same line, *Colin Clouts* 232.

9. GOUGH. The proverbial saying " Virtue is her own reward " occurs in Silius Italicus, *Punica* 13. 663: " Ipsa quidem virtus sibimet pulcherrima merces."

EDITOR. Very common in classical literature. Cf. Clement of Alexandria, *Stromata* 4. 7. 56; Cicero, *Fin.* 2. 72; Plautus, *Amphitruo* 2. 2. 17 (cf. Prologue 78) ; Claudian, *De Consul. Maltii Theod.* 5. 1; Seneca, *Epist.* 81 and *De Vita Beata* 9. 4. See also 2. 3. 10. 8-9; 3. 1. 13; 3. 10. 31. 7; 3. 12. 39. 5-6.

xix. 5-7. T. WARTON (*Poems upon Several Occasions . . . By John Milton,* 2nd ed., pp. 279-280, note on *Hymn on the Morning of Christ's Nativity* 205-210). A book, popular in Milton's time, thus describes the dreadful sacrifices of the worship of the idol Moloch (Sandys's *Travels,* p. 186, ed. 1615). " Wherein (the valley of Tophet) the Hebrews sacrificed their children to Moloch; an idol of brass, having the head of a calf, the rest of a kingly figure with arms extended to receive the miserable sacrifice, seared to death with his burning embracements. For the idol was hollow within, and filled with fire. And lest their lamentable shrieks should sad the hearts of their parents, the priests of Moloch did deaf their ears with the continual clangs of trumpets and timbrels." This imagery, but with less effect, was afterwards transferred into the *Paradise Lost* 1. 392-6. . . . These dreadful circumstances, of themselves sufficiently striking to the imagination, are here only related: in our *Ode,* they are endued with life and action, they are put in motion before our eyes, and made subservient to a new purpose of the poet by the superinduction of a poetical fiction, to which they give occasion. " The sullen spirit is fled of a sudden, and has left his black burning image in darkness and solitude. The priests, dancing in horrid gesticulations about the blue furnace from which this idol was fed with fire, in vain attempt to call back their griesly king with the din of cymbals, with which they once used to overwhelm the shrieks of the sacrificed infants." A new use is made of the cymbals of the disappointed priests.

He does not say, "Moloch's idol was removed, to which infants were sacrificed; while their cries were suppressed by the sound of cymbals." In Burnet's treatise *De Statu Mortuorum et Resurgentium*, there is a fine picture of the rites of Moloch.

Grace W. Landrum (*PMLA* 41. 541). Cf. 2 Kings 23. 10. [See also Jeremiah 32. 35; Psalms 106. 37-8; and Leviticus 18. 21.]

xxi. 6-9. See note on 10. 29. 6.

xxi. 5. Upton. He displays the brightness of Truth against superstitious illusions. See note on 1. 8. 19. [3, in Book I, p. 268; note on 5. 10. 32. 6-8 above].

xxii. 1-2. Upton. See this custom explained in a note on *F. Q.* 4. 10. 9. [4, in Book IV, p. 220].

Gough. Striking with sword or spear upon an opponent's shield was a recognized method of challening him. Thus, in Malory, *Morte Darthur* 1. 22, Sir Griflet challenges a knight who has hung his shield upon a tree, by striking it "that the shield fell down on the ground. With that the knight came out of the pavilion and said, Fair Knight, why smote ye down my shield? For I will just with you, said Griflet."

xxiii-xxv. Upton. Compare Berni, *Orl. Inn.* 1. 5. 75. Compare likewise the description of Errour in the note on *F. Q.* 1. 1. 13. [6-7, in Book I, pp. 182-3].

Lotspeich (p. 63). Probably suggested by Natalis Comes [7.] 1 [ed. Padua, 1637, p. 362], who says that Geryon also had a dragon, born of Typhaon and Echidna.

Lotspeich (p. 108). Spenser has taken over Natalis Comes's description of the Sphinx (9. 18) and applied it to his own monster [ed. Padua, 1637, p. 525]: "Caput et manus puellae, corpus canis, vocem hominis, caudam draconis, leonis ungues, alas avis, . . . cum alas haberet aquilae, citissimeque ad illos convolaret. . . ." The kinship is inward as well. The monster represents the Inquisition; a wrong answer to the Sphinx's riddle means death.

Gough. The Sphinx of Greek mythology, which, according to Apollodorus (3. 5. 8), was, like Spenser's monster, a daughter of Typhaon and Echidna. Unlike the Egyptian Sphinx, she is represented as a winged lioness, with the head and breasts of a woman. She settled on a rock at Thebes in Boeotia, and slew all those who could not solve her riddle, viz. "A being with four feet has two feet and three feet, and only one voice; but its feet vary, and when it has most it is weakest." Oedipus, "the Theban Knight," son of a king of Thebes, told the Sphinx that the answer was "a man," whereupon she cast herself from the rock and perished.

xxiii. Cf. *F. Q.* 6. 6. 9-12 and notes in Book VI.

7. Todd notes this feature in Hawes's *Graunde Amour*.

xxv. 3. Upton. He calls the progeny of Oedipus fatal, as if Providence had marked them out for extraordinary punishments on account of his incestuous marriage.

Gough. A curse had been pronounced against the house of Laius, the father of Oedipus, in consequence of which the sons of the latter, Eteocles and

Polynices, quarrelled and slew each other, and their sister Antigone was immured for honouring the body of Polynices with funeral rites, contrary to the decree of the new king, Creon.

xxvi. 2.   See note on 10. 32. 6-8 above.

xxix. 1-5.   EDITOR.   HEISE (pp. 76-9) cites more than a dozen similes in Spenser of ships in peril or distress. Of these he finds possible literary sources for but four: 1. 6. 1 (see note in Book I, p. 239) ; 2. 2. 24; 2. 7. 1; 3. 4. 53; cf. 5. 2. 50; 5. 12. 18. 5-9 and notes.

xxxi. 5.   Same figure in the same situation at 1. 11. 22. 6.   In fact this fight should be compared with that of Red Cross with the dragon in 1. 11, from which Spenser here repeats a number of details, even to the rejoicing procession of maidens (34; cf. 1. 12. 6).

9.   UPTON.   The image is odious (as he intends it) rather than terrible. Compare 1. 1. 20.

xxxii. 1-5.   See Appendix, p. 285.

4.   LOTSPEICH (p. 108).   The epithet "loathed" preserves the Greek meaning of the name; cf. Natalis Comes 3. 2 [ed. Padua, 1637, p. 100], "Styx odium est" and its waters are "odiosae." Styx as the place where waiting souls pass over into Hades figures several times. [See notes on 2. 5. 22. 7 in Book II, p. 237.]

xxxiii. 7-9.   UPTON.   Meaning the popish religion was destroyed, and the protestant established.

xxxiv.   See UPTON's note on *F. Q.* 1. 12. 9 in Book I, p. 306.

4.   TODD.   The poet seems to have had in mind 1 Samuel 18. 6.

xxxv.   UPTON.   Namely, his seeking Gloriana. . . . 1. 9. 15.

8.   Almost the same as *Muiopotmos* 146.

xxxvi.   A. H. GILBERT (*PMLA* 34. 232) notes this as a transition in the manner of Ariosto.

1.   UPTON.   So the Italian romance poets, "Ma torniamo," etc.

xxxvii ff.   GOUGH (pp. 302-3).   Sir Sergis evidently represents some retired statesman, experienced in Irish affairs, whom Lord Grey de Wilton consulted when he took up the office of Lord Deputy in 1580. He is probably Sir Henry Sidney, the father of Sir Philip. The greater part of his career was spent in Ireland, of which he was thrice Lord Deputy (1565-7, 1568-71, 1575-8). He was the ablest administrator of Ireland in the reign of Elizabeth, and the frequent harshness of his policy did not detract from Spenser's admiration of him. (Spenser had perhaps been with him in Ireland in 1577.) On Lord Grey's appointment as Lord Deputy in 1580, Sir Henry Sidney visited him at Wilton, and gave him valuable advice.

Although his age was only fifty-one at this date, he was prematurely aged, and died worn out by his arduous labours in 1586. On his recall from Ireland in 1578 he had resumed the more peaceful and less onerous duties of Lord President of the Welsh Marches (cf. 37. 3-4). [See Appendix, pp. 324-330.]

xxxvii. GOUGH. See canto 1, stanza 4 above. Sir Sergis is not mentioned there.

xxxix. 3. GOUGH. "The salvage Iland" is Ireland, a country not inaptly so called in Spenser's time. Cf. his dedication of the *Faerie Queene* to the Earl of Ormonde [in Book III, p. 193]:

> Receiue most noble Lord a simple taste
> Of the wilde fruit, which saluage soyl hath bred,
> Which being through long wars left almost waste,
> With brutish barbarisme is ouerspredd.

xl. 1. GOUGH. The fixing of a day by which a champion must appear to defend a lady's innocence, failing which she will be condemned to death, arises from the mediaeval custom of trial by combat (see note to 5. 1. 25. 1-3). It is a frequent incident in the Romances. Cf. Malory, *Morte Darthur* 18. 4, where Guenever is accused of poisoning a knight, and given fifteen days in which to find a champion to defend her. Lancelot arrives at the last moment, just as Arthur [*sic*] does in this case.

xli. UPTON. This Apostrophe of Arthegal to vindicate his honour from neglecting the adventure, which he had taken in hand, to relieve Irena, is very like that most elegant apostrophe, which Aeneas makes, when he relates to Dido the siege and destruction of Troy. Arthegal stands much more cleare; his thraldome is mentioned above, 5. 5. 17. But how supinely did the wise and brave Aeneas behave in suffering the Greeks to impose on the Trojan credulity? and yet see how he apostrophizes [*Aen.* 2. 431]: "Iliaci cineres." [See Upton's note on 1. 7. 49. 7 in Book I, p. 256.]

6-9. GOUGH. The flat contradiction between this avowal and lines 1-5 can only be explained by supposing that Artegall suddenly realizes the fact that the cause of Irena's new trouble was his servitude to Radigund to which his honour had bound him. We know from the *Veue of the State of Ireland* that Spenser attributed much of the misery of that country to the vacillating, dilatory, and ineffective policy of the English Government. He could not of course lay the blame on the Queen, who was really responsible. He had no desire to reflect on Grey, whose measures he thoroughly approved.

xliii-xlv. GOUGH (pp. 303-5). The episode of Burbon, which concludes this canto, thereby making it the longest in the book, is perhaps an afterthought. The argument to Canto 12 shows that Spenser intended at first to insert it at the beginning of that canto [see CHURCH's note on 12. Arg. 1-2]. The episode refers to the latest historical event definitely alluded to in Book 5, viz. the recantation of Protestantism by Henry IV of France in July, 1593.

This action finds a suitable place in the book as an example of a form of injustice not elsewhere dealt with—the desertion of the religious faith that one has pledged one's self to maintain. The conversion of King Henry to Catholicism (which was obviously due to self-interest rather than conviction) was no merely personal matter, it was an act of faithlessness towards the Reformed Church of France of which he was the protector.

Henry of Bourbon, king of Navarre, who had been brought up as a Calvinist, was the leader of the Huguenots in the French wars of religion. On the assassination of Henry III in 1589 he was recognized as king of France by the moderate Catholics as well as the Protestants, but was resisted by the League, which dominated North-eastern France with the aid of Philip II of Spain. For a time Henry IV had a much smaller force at his disposal than his enemies (cf. 45. 6). In October 1589, Elizabeth sent him 4,000 men under Lord Willoughby, and 7,000 in 1591, including a contingent under the Earl of Essex to aid him in the siege of Rouen. In 1593 she concluded an informal treaty with him.

In the Burbon episode Artegall does not represent Lord Grey, who had no part in the French wars. If Spenser refers to any English leader, it is probably Essex, whom he had addressed in 1590 in one of the dedicatory sonnets published with Books 1-3 of the *Faerie Queene*, promising to commemorate his " heroicke parts " in a later instalment of the poem. He has greatly exaggerated the part played by the small English auxiliary force in securing the victory of Henry IV. That king, who was also aided by German and Dutch Protestants, fought with varying success, winning the victories of Arques (1589) and Ivry (1590) (cf. 53. 7), but failing to take Rouen and Paris.

The Catholic League was greatly weakened by its inability to produce a claimant with a good title to the throne, while the attempts of its leaders to dismember France, and the danger of Spanish predominance alienated all good Frenchmen. The cry of the exhausted country for peace became more and more insistent, and Henry's religion appeared to be the only obstacle to a general pacification. There was little personal conviction in his faith; he is reported to have observed cynically, " Paris vaut bien une messe." Accordingly he consented to " receive instruction," and after a decent interval was admitted into the Church of Rome in July, 1593. Earnest Protestants like Spenser were naturally shocked, and Elizabeth sent him a grave remonstrance.

His conversion had not at once the full effect that he perhaps expected (cf. 54. 6). It was too obviously a political move to disarm suspicion. Paris opened her gates to the king in March 1594, but the country was not entirely pacified till 1595, when a formidable insurrection in the West was suppressed.

Not only has Spenser made Henry IV owe too much to the English army (Talus), a fault which, as in the case of Belge, may be due to his anticipating events, but he has misrepresented the king's character. Henry was no craven (stanza 46), but one of the bravest, as well as one of the wisest, though not the most high-minded of French kings.

[See Appendix, pp. 282, 299, 330.]

xliv-xlvii.   EDITOR.   The "rude rout" here in action, and again in 51, 57-9, is unmistakably such as Spenser saw in Ireland, the same in conception as that in 2. 9. 11-5; see note in Book II, pp. 281-2; also 2. 11. 5-7, 17-9, and notes on 59. 6-8 below.

xliv. 2-3.   UPTON.   Henry of Navarre.   " The rude rout," his rebellious subjects.   " The Lady," France, or the Genius of France, hight Flourdelis (st. 49).

xlv. 3. UPTON. Alluding to the courage and activity which Henry show'd in his various battles against his subjects.

xlvi. 3. UPTON. I. e. to renounce his protestant faith. In allusion to Ephesians 6. 16: "Above all, taking the shield of faith." [See 1. 1. 1 and note on 1-2, in Book I, p. 176; and below 54. 4.]

CHURCH. To part with the shield was ever esteem'd dishonourable. See below sts. 52 and 55. David laments that circumstance as being an aggravation of Saul's misfortunes. 2 Samuel 1. 21: "For there the shield of the mighty is vilely cast away, the shield of Saul."

xlvii. UPTON. Alluding to the assistance given to Henry IV by Q. Elizabeth.

9. TODD. "Like scattred chaffe." This is a frequent simile in Holy Writ. See Job 21. 18; Psalm 1. 4 etc.

EDITOR. Of a half dozen passages Spenser is here nearest to Is. 41. 15-6 (Geneva version): "Thou shalt thresh the mountaines, and bring them to powder, and shalt make the hilles as chaffe. Thou shalt fanne them, and the wind shall scatter them." Cf. Psalms 35. 1-5, which is nearer the situation, but not the phrase.

l. 3. UPTON. The K. of Spain. [See notes on 1. 3. 9 above.]

lii-lvi. See DODGE's note on 12. 22. 7 below.

liii. UPTON. 'Tis rightly done of our poet to put us in mind now and then of his heroes; for they are all to be brought together in the last book, when they make their appearance, with P. Arthur, before the Fairy Queen. [See Upton's note on *F. Q.* 3. 3. 62. 9 in Book III, p. 237.]

2. GOUGH. The Knight of Holiness, the hero of the first book of the *Faerie Queene.* He symbolizes the ideal Christian of the reformed faith, and his conferring knighthood upon Burbon alludes to the fact that Henry IV was baptized and brought up as a Protestant.

liv. 4. See note on 46. 3 above; cf. 1. 1. 1. 3-4.

lv. 9. BLAKENEY. There is a striking parallel in the *de bello Gildonico* of Claudian (451), which has hitherto escaped the notice of commentators: "Nonne mori satius vitae quam ferre pudorem?" Cf. Shakespeare, *1 Henry VI,* 4. 5. [32-3]:

> Here on my knee I beg mortality,
> Rather than life preserved with infamy.

EDITOR. See note on 5. 46. 5 above.

lvi. See Appendix, p. 330.

lviii. 1-2. HEISE (p. 116) cites like similes at 1. 1. 38. 2; 5. 2. 33. 3 (see note); 5. 2. 53. 6; 6. 8. 40. 2; 6. 11. 48. 1-4, as "diejenigen, in welchen von einem Fliegenschwarm die Rede ist und teils die grosse Menge oder die Ohnmacht des Verglichenen angedeutet werden soll; vgl. vor allem *Il.* 2. 469-471; 16. 641-3; 17. 570-2; *Orl. Inn.* 2. 30. 8; 3. 8. 14; *Orl. Fur.* 10. 105."

7-9. HEISE (pp. 125-6) cites *Morgante Maggiore* 27. 236; *Rin.* 6. 52; 10. 48; *Aen.* 12. 365-7; *Theb.* 6. 107-8.

LOTSPEICH (p. 43). Cf. *Ruines of Rome* 16, 26; *Sh. Cal.* Feb. 226; *F. Q.* 1. 2. 33. 7. The epithets and general characteristics which Spenser gives to Boreas ("bitter bleake," "bitter," "blustering," "wrathful") are in agreement with classical usage; cf. *Met.* 6. 685-6; *Aen.* 3. 687. Spenser is closer to Vergil than to Ovid. Ovid anthropomorphizes Boreas completely and tells of his love affair, playing with his character as a wind. Vergil and Spenser see him rather as a natural force, vaguely personified.

lix. 6-8. BLAKENEY. Spenser had as poor an opinion of the rank and file as Homer himself, who, in the *Iliad*, represents them mainly as a mob, without much discipline and without much fighting spirit. Verily " one man of you (the Heroes) shall chase a thousand." Spenser was aristocratic in his sympathies to the backbone.

EDITOR. Spenser uses the word "raskall" only to describe a mob or rout; see *Mother Hubberds Tale* 1193; *F. Q.* 1. 7. 35. 5; 1. 12. 9. 1; 2. 9. 15. 4 (and TODD's note in Book II, p. 285); 2. 11. 19. 2; 3. 11. 46. 3; 5. 2. 52. 5; 5. 2. 54. 8; 5. 6. 29. 4; 5. 11. 65. 2; *Axiochus,* ed. Padelford, p. 52. His attitude toward a mob can hardly be used to indicate his lack of sympathy for the poor and lowly.

lxiii 8-9. See FOWLER's note on 6. 17-8 above.

CANTO XII

See Appendix, pp. 324 ff.

Arg. 1-2. CHURCH. These lines should have been part of the Argument of the preceding Canto; to this they have no relation. [See GOUGH's note on 11. 43-5 above and Appendix, p. 331.]

i. EDITOR (C. G. O.). Such apostrophe, not uncommon in Spenser's predecessors, is found at 3. 1. 13 (see note in Book III, p. 204), where it is a concluding or intervening choric comment, as often in Chaucer.

1-2. UPTON. Spenser is classical in his expressions; and to understand him you must often translate him. " Sacred hunger "; Virgil 3. [57]: " Sacra fames." " Impotent desire of men to raigne: Impotens regnandi cupido ": i. e. ungovernable, violent.

BLAKENEY. Ambition may indeed, as Quintilian [1. 2. 22] reminds us, often become the cause of virtue; it no doubt is (as Milton says [*Lycidas* 71]) " the last infirmity of noble mind "; yet it is none the less true that in itself it is a vice. As Shakespeare has said [*Henry VIII,* 3. 2. 440-1]:

> Cromwell, I charge thee, fling away ambition;
> By that sin fell the angels.

For the sentiment embodied [condemned?] in this stanza cf. Milton, *P. L.* 1. 262: " To reign is worth ambition, though in hell."

3. GOUGH. Cf. James 2. 19: " the devils also believe and tremble."

4-6.   UPTON.   Perhaps he had in view, what Cicero [*De Officiis* 3. 21] tells us was Caesar's favourite sentiment from a speech in Euripides, [*Phoenissae* 527-8]:

> Nam si violandum est jus, regnandi gratia
> Violandum est; aliis rebus pietatem colas.

7-9.   UPTON.   Reflections of this kind are very frequent: so in 2. 10. 35. . . . Chaucer, *Knighte's Tale* 1623-6:

> O Cupido, out of all charitee!
> O reign, that wouldst have no felaw with thee!
> Full sothe is said, that Love ne Lordship
> Will not his thankes have any felawship.

So the Italian Proverb, " Amor et seignoria non vogliano compagnia." And Ovid, [*Ars Amat.* 3. 564], " Non bene cum sociis regna Venusque manent."

ii.   3.   GOUGH.   There is no hint in Canto 11 of this motive, which refers rather to Henry IV than to Burbon.

8-9.   See Appendix, p. 318.

v.   9.   See 3. 4. 49. 4-9, and notes in Book III, p. 243; cf. 6. 8. 49. 9.

vii.   9.   HEISE (p. 143) cites TODD's note on 11. 47. 9 above.

viii-ix.   EDITOR.   The settlement of causes between armies by single combat was, of course, common in the Middle Ages and in the Romances. In Spenser's own time, however, the Earl of Essex continued this chivalric tradition. In the expedition with Drake and Norris to Portugal in 1589 he thrust his pike into the gate of the tower of Lisbon " demanding alowd, if any Spaniard mewed therein, durst aduenture forth in fauour of his Mistress to break a staffe with him " (Speed's *Chronicle*, ed. 1632, p. 1190). Again at the siege of Rouen, Nov. 9, 1591, he challenged the Governor, Villars, in this manner: " Si voux voulez combattre vous même à cheval ou à pied, je mainteindra que le querelle du Roi est plus juste que celle de la ligue, et que ma Maîtresse est plus belle que la votre." (Quoted by Devereux, *Lives of the Devereux, Earls of Essex* 1. 273, from *Mem. de Sully* 1. 312.)

If Spenser had Essex in mind here, as he certainly had in the *View*, as the one person who could settle the Irish problem (see Appendix, p. 324), he must have thought of his chivalric method of settling disputes. The temptation is strong to suppose that Essex had this passage in mind when in 1599 he attempted to settle the Irish affair by challenging Tyrone to single combat. He is reported to have sent the following message by Tyrone's agent, Henry O Hagan, who came to ask for a parley:

If thy master have any confidence either in the justness of his cause, or in the goodness and number of his men, or in his own virtue, of all which he vainly glorieth, he will meet me in the field so far advanced before the head of his kerne as myself shall be separated from the front of my troops, where we will parley in that fashion which best becomes soldiers. (Quoted by Bagwell, *Ireland under the Tudors* 3. 340, from Dymnok's *Treatise* and a Journal in *Carew MS*, no. 135.)

The whole thing is too fanciful and neat for serious consideration but furnishes good matter for a certain type of speculation.

viii.   H. S. V. JONES (*Spenser's Defense of Lord Grey*, pp. 56-7). That Grey like the Queen was merciful as well as just Spenser declares in his poetry as he had done in his prose. More than once Artegall recalls Talus from the stern execution of justice. (The rôle of Talus in the administration of justice corresponds to that of force as described in the following passage from de l'Hôpital, *Traité* 1. 88-9. . . .) For example, when the iron man sets upon the wild rout in Irena's kingdom [st. quoted].

x.   4. GOUGH. Cf. Froude, *Hist. Eng.* [ed. 1870], ch. 62: "Those who were now in office, Grey, Malby, and Bingham . . . regarded the Irish nation as divided into two classes, the kernes, or armed followers of the chiefs, and the churles, who were the tillers of the ground. The kernes were marked for death whenever they were found. The churles they wished to befriend, but the churles who accepted their friendship were killed by the kernes, as traitors to their country."

xiii.   DODGE (*PMLA* 12. 203). Cf. *Orl. Fur.* 32. 108. This comparison is one of the commonest in Italian literature: see Dante, *Inf.* 2. 127-9; Boccaccio, *Teseide* 9. 28; Fr. Bello, *Mambriano* 8.—(st. quoted by Panizzi, *Orl. Inn.*, vol. 1, p. 318) ; *Ger. Lib.* 18. 16; 20. 129. It is evident that Spenser is following Ariosto's version.

K. WAIBEL (*Engl. St.* 58. 360) cites *Purple Island* 11. 38.

D. BUSH (*Mythology and the Renaissance Tradition in English Poetry*, pp. 92-3). This is quite lovely, but overloaded, and it does not approach "the portion of weeds and outworn faces," nor can it be set beside Virgil on the death of Euryalus. Thus Spenser's similes, whether or not they involve mythology, have a diffuse richness and lack of salience. They are—and this is true of most of his incidental allusions to myth—patches stuck on rather than a growth from within. To say that is of course only to say that Spenser was a poet of the Renaissance.

xiv. 3, 7.   CHILD. The Irish foot-soldier was armed " in a long shirt of mayle downe to the calfe of his leg, with a long broad axe in his hand" (*View of the State of Ireland*, [Todd's ed.], p. 392).

[See PAULINE HENLEY's note on 1. 3. 9 above.]

xviii. 5-9.   UPTON. Compare this simile with the following, Rowe's *Lucan* 6. 494-8 [cf. *Pharsalia* 6. 286-7; 7. 125-7]:

> So when the seamen from afar descry
> The clouds grow black upon the low'ring sky,
> Hear the winds roar and mark the seas run high,
> They furl the flutt'ring sheet with timely care,
> And wisely for the coming storm prepare.

[See above 11. 29. 1-5 and note.]

xxii. 7.   R. E. N. DODGE (" Cambridge Spenser "). That Arthegall, so soon after condemning Burbon sternly for abandoning his shield (11. 52-6), should abandon his own, is one of the grosser inconsistencies of the poem, due to the allegory. Burbon's shield has a meaning, Arthegail's not.

xxiii. 2.   CHURCH. Chrysaor, the sword of Arthegall, was broke by Radigund. See 5. 5. 21. [8]. These slips of the Memory are very excusable in a Poem of such uncommon Length and Beauty. [Cf. meaning of Chrysaor—Law and Order, as implied in 5. 1. 9 (see notes on 9-10), which, though violated in one case may triumph in another.]

7. UPTON. The construction is, that falling he fed on (he bit) his mother earth, Virgil 11. 418: "Procubuit moriens et humum [simul] ore momordit." [See above 2. 18. 5-9 and note.]

xxiv. HENLEY (p. 135). True to the policy of the English in asserting that they were saving the Irish from the cruel exactions of the Anglo-Irish lords, Spenser would represent the people as rejoicing in the overthrow of the Earl of Desmond.

xxv-xxviii. [C. L. FALKINER] (*Edinburgh Review* 201. 184). Spenser has been reproached in relation to Irish politics with an arrogant contempt for Ireland, and Mr. Lee censures his *View of the State of Ireland* as "a mere echo of the hopeless and helpless prejudices which infected the English governing class." But whatever may be said of the narrowness of Elizabethan views of the Irish question, this picture of the difficulties of an Irish Viceroy is intensely modern. So little difference have three centuries wrought in Ireland, so perennial are the problems that at recurring periods compel the attention of English statesmen, that they might with equal applicability have been written by some uncompromising Unionist of the present day in reference to Mr. Arthur Balfour's Chief Secretaryship and his administration of the Crimes Act!

CHILD. The severity of Lord Grey during his administration as Deputy of Ireland (represented here by the destructive activity of the truculent Talus) exposed him to very serious accusations on his return to England. See Spenser's statement of the case [see UPTON's note on st. 28 below], pp. 432, 433, of his *View of The State of Ireland* (Todd's ed.), and also p. 419, where he recommends the most violent measures.

EDITOR. Reproach of Spenser for his attitude toward Ireland and the Irish is usually based on the assumption that he advocated in his *View* the extermination of the whole Irish nation. Spenser advocates no such thing; his critics do not read far enough. He says in the character of Irenaeus (Globe ed., p. 650):

. . . for by the swoorde which I named, I doe not meane the cutting of of all that nation with the swoorde, which farre be it from me that I should ever thinke soe desperatly, or wish soe uncharitably, but by the swoorde I meane the royall power of the Prince, which ought to stretche it self foorthe in the chiefest strength to the redressing and cutting of of those evills, which I before blamed, and not of the people which are evill. For evill people by good ordinaunces and government may be made goode; but the evill that is of itself evill will never become good.

xxv. 9. GOUGH. Before Grey's departure from Ireland most of the insurgent leaders had perished by war, by execution or by assassination. In particular the powerful house of the Fitz Geralds of Desmond was almost exterminated.

xxviii ff. See Appendix, pp. 281, 292, 307, 318-9.

xxviii-xlii. See Appendix to Book II, "Elizabethan Psychology," p. 461.

xxviii. UPTON. Spenser's *View of Ireland* [cf. Globe ed., pp. 655-6]: I remember that in the late government of the good Lord Grey, when, after long travail, and many perillous assays, he had brought all things almost to that pass that it was even made ready for reformation, and might have been brought to what her majesty would; like complaint was made against him, that he was a bloody man, and regarded not the life of her subjects. . . . Whom, who that well knew, knew to be most gentle, affable, loving, and temperate. . . . Therefore most untruly and maliciously do these evil tongues backbite and slander the sacred ashes of that most just and honourable personage, whose least virtue, and of many that abounded in his heroic spirit, they were never able to aspire unto.

xxviii. 4–xxxvi. UPTON. These griesly creatures were Envy and Detraction. Compare Envy feminine, with Envy masculine, 1. 4. 30-2. See too Ovid, *Met.* 2. [760-832], where Minerva pays a visit to this imp of hell.

xxix-xxxii. See notes on 1. 4. 30-2 in Book I, pp. 221-2.

EDITOR (C. G. O.). In his note on 1. 4. 30-2 just cited, JORTIN quotes much of the passage in *Met.* 2. 760-782. But strangely enough he leaves out three lines which evidently furnished Spenser with two or three conspicuous details:

> Pallor in ore sedet, macies in corpore toto.
> Nusquam recta acies, livent robigine dentes,
> Pectora felle virent, lingua est suffusa veneno.

As the whole passage in Ovid is quoted by Boccaccio in his chapter on Invidia, *Gen. Deorum* 1. 18, it seems likely that Spenser after his habit consulted it there.

xxx. 6. TODD. The very circumstance of Envy devouring a snake, is also described in Alciat's *Emblems* [no. 141, ed. 1583]. And, in the French edition of the *Emblems* printed at Lyons in 1549, the following remarkable lines are subjoined to the Emblem, p. 93:

> Envie.
> Vne femme est chair de serpent mangeant,
> A qui les yeulx font mal, son coeur rongeant
> Fort palle, et maigre, et d'espineuse poincte
> Tient vng baston. Tell est enuie pincte.

Having mentioned these Emblems in regard to Envy, I take this opportunity of observing that, in the same collection, Gluttony is represented exactly as Spenser has painted the monster, namely, " with an upblown belly and a crane-like neck," *F. Q.* 1. 4. 21. See the *Embl.,* ed. cited, p. 112 [no. 165, ed. 1583]:

> Gourmandie.
> A col de Grue, et grand ventre de Tor
> Vng homme tient. . . .

[See MCMANAWAY's note on 2. 4. 4 in Book II, pp. 226-7.]

xxxi. 6—xxxii. K. WAIBEL (*Engl. St.* 58. 341-2) cites *Purple Island* 7. 66.

xxxi. 7-8. EDITOR (C. G. O.). Expands Ovid's " carpitque et carpitur una Suppliciumque suum est " (781-2), reiterating his iteration. 32 dilates: " videt ingratos intabescitque videndo Successus hominum " (780-1). See notes on 5. 17. 1 and 9. 19. 7 above; also on *Virgils Gnat* 377—384.

xxxii. 8. BLAKENEY. The state of mind which, pining at another's well-being, rejoices at their mishaps, is described by Aristotle, *Ethics* 2. 7. 15 [18]: "A man is called righteously indignant when he feels pain at the sight of undeserved prosperity; but your envious man goes beyond him, and is pained by the sight of anyone in prosperity; while the malevolent man is so far from being pained that he actually exults in the sight of prosperous iniquity" (F. H. Peters' translation). This malignity is called in the Greek ἐπιχαιρεκακία. See Plutarch's *Moralia*, "On Envie and Hatred" (in my edition of Philemon Holland's translation of 1603, [pp. 233-6; *Plutarch's Morals*, ed. Goodwin, 2. 95-9]).

xxxvi. 2-5. TODD. Compare Psalm 140. 3: "They have sharpened their tongues like a serpent: adder's poison is under their lips." [Cf. also Ovid as quoted in note on 29-32 above.]

xxxvi. 6. See UPTON's and McMANAWAY's notes on *F. Q.* 2. 4. 4 in Book II, pp. 226-7; also 2. 11. 23. 6; 3. 9. 5. 5; 5. 5. 15. 3 and note above.

xxxvii. 5. GOUGH. This is the only indication that Irena had fallen into the power of Grantorto through the agency of Envy and Detraction. The vituperation of Elizabeth and her ministers by the Roman Catholic party fostered Irish disaffection.

7. UPTON. Spenser generally gives you some hint, and a short transitory kind of view, of what he intends afterwards to display more fully. The Blatant beast, here just mentioned, he tells you is under the direction of Envy and Detraction: we shall read more of him in the next book. His name is derived from "Blaterare," to babble idly and impertinently, like defamatory and detracting tongues: or the Italian "blatterare." See note on 6. 12. 39.

xxxviii. 5-6. See notes on 8. 36. 4-5; 49. 1-5 above.

xxxix. WARTON (1. 70-1). It may be objected, that Spenser drew the thought of Envy throwing her Snake at Arthegall, from Alecto's attack upon Amata (*Aen.* 7. 346-7):

Huic Dea caeruleis unum de crinibus anguem
Conjicit, inque sinus [sinum] praecordia ad intima condit [subdit].

But Spenser's application of this thought is surely a stronger effort of invention than the thought itself. The rancour, both of Envy and of her Snake, could not have been expressed by more significant strokes. Although the snake was her constant food, yet she was tempted to part with her only sustenance, while she could render it an instrument of injuring another; and although the snake, by being thus constantly fed upon, was nearly dead, some life, as he finely says, remaining secretly, yet its natural malignity enabled it to bite with violence.

UPTON. This half-gnawen snake she throws at Arthegal, which secretly bit him: intimating that he felt the effects of his envyers and calumniators. The conduct of other poets is different: those bit by the serpent of Envy are poisoned with the malignity, and become the envyers, not the envyed.

xl. 5. See 5. 1. 9 above.

8-9. UPTON. When Lord Grey was deputy of Ireland, he put to the sword the Spaniards, who surrendered to his mercy. His enemies said 'twas done with treachery and unjustly. This is the historical allusion: and 'tis mentioned by Spenser in his *View of Ireland* [Globe ed., pp. 655-6].

xli. 4-6. See note on *Epithalamion* 18.

7. See WARTON's note on *F. Q.* 6. 12. 27 ff.

xlii. 9. GOUGH. Evidently Grey's behaviour towards his detractors reminded Spenser of David's, when on his flight from Jerusalem. Shimei cursed him, cast stones at him (cf. 12. 43. 7), and called him " a bloody man," because he had shed the blood of the house of Saul (cf. *Veue of* . . . *Ireland*, Globe ed., p. 655, . . . where it is twice said that Grey was called " a bloody man "). Like Talus, Abishai was rebuked by his master for desiring to avenge the insult. See 2 Samuel 16. 5-13.

xliii. A. H. GILBERT (*PMLA* 34. 232) notes this as a conclusion in the manner of Ariosto.

APPENDIX I

THE VIRTUE OF JUSTICE AND THE PLAN OF BOOK V

JOHN UPTON (*Spenser's Faerie Queene* 2. 632-3). Let us, as usual, take a review of this Fifth Book, which treats, in the form of an allegory, of the most comprehensive of all human virtues.

Herodotus informs us, that the Persian kings celebrated with the highest magnificence their birth-day; when they granted to every one his boon. Nor with less magnificence the Fairy Queen kept her annual feast, on twelve several days, and granted to every just petitioner the requested boon.

In one of those days a disconsolate queen, named Irena, attended by Sir Sergis, made her entry according to the custom established; and complaining that an oppressive tyrant kept by violence her crown from her, prayed that some knight might be assigned to perform that adventure; her boon was granted, and Sir Arthegal was the knight assigned.

This hero we have been long acquainted with; and have seen him in Fairy land, seeking adventures, and perfecting himself in many a chivalrous emprise. But we must suppose that he was not to proceed on his grand quest, till joined by his faithful Talus; a man of iron mold, without any degree of passion or affection, but the properest person imaginable to put in act the righteous decrees of Arthegal, or in one word, to be an executioner. Thus is justice (imaged in Arthegal) armed with power (imaged in Talus:) and thus accoutred, he relieves the oppressed, distributes right, and redresses injured kingdoms and nations.

Though Arthegal appears in a fuller view in this book, than hitherto, yet our chief hero, who is to be perfected in justice, that he might in the end obtain true glory, is not forgotten. If Homer dwells on the exploits of Diomed, or shows you at large Agamemnon, or describes the success of Hector; yet ever and anon you are put in mind of Achilles; and you plainly perceive the fatal effects of that pernicious wrath, which brought so many woes on Greece. Hence the unity of the poem is preserved. Why will you not consider Spenser's poem in the same view, only built on a more extensive plan?

The Briton prince becomes acquainted with Arthegal by a rencounter, which often happens among knight-errants: as soon as they are reconciled (for the real great and good never disagree) they go in quest of adventures; and afterwards visit Mercilla at her royal palace. And here the Briton prince undertakes the relief of Belge from an oppressive tyrant: Mean time Arthegal goes to reinstate Irena in her pristine dignity.

KATE M. WARREN (Introduction to her edition of Book V, pp. vii-xxxi). The fifth book of the *Faerie Queene,* containing the Legend of Justice, is in both form and matter the simplest of all the six books of the poem. The main narrative is clearly outlined, the digressions are few, and throughout the movement of the story we are never allowed to forget the end in view—the rescue, by the Knight of Justice, of the Lady Irena from Grantorto, her oppressor. The allegorical matter,

269

too, is, on the whole, quite easy to follow. It is chiefly historical, and the historical meaning, in its main outline, stands clearly forth. Much of the narrative in this book will bear nothing beyond an interpretation by history; it is impossible to find in it any moral or spiritual meaning. . . . In the greater part of the poem there is no double allegory, and where any other meaning does appear it is often of the simplest, as in the story of the vanishing of the false Florimell when brought before the true lady of that name.

In its simplicity of form the fifth book is a return to the manner of Books I and II. It is even simpler than these, while the contrast between this Legend and the crowded narrative of Books III and IV is very great. In its simplicity of allegory, however, it is unlike any of the other books.

Again, the same mark of simplicity, in some cases almost of bareness, may be found in many of the descriptive passages. There is an absence of colour and ornament, fewer similes are used, and less variety of detail. Compare the account of the arrival of the two Knights at the court of Mercilla with that of the Red Cross Knight and Duessa at the court of Lucifera—a not unfair comparison, because, if we may judge from some of the expressions used in each narrative, Spenser seems to have had in his mind the earlier description as he was writing the later one. The first is richer in detail than the second, yet there was equal opportunity for detail.

Or compare, again, the picture of the Temple of Isis (7.) with the description of the House of Busyrane (3. 11) or of the Temple of Venus (4. 10). It is remarkable that in this fifth book we find really no long episode of pictorial description done with that delight in the mere " word painting " such as we have at least once, and sometimes more than once, in every one of the other books. . . .

Throughout the book there is a less hopeful air than in the other Legends, and after almost every strife in which Justice is the conqueror, we feel that the triumph is but fleeting, and before long Injustice will become bold again.

A careful reader of this poem will also discover another special mark upon it— a kind of studied conscientiousness in the treatment of a certain portion of his subject which we are not accustomed to in Spenser—a conscientiousness which gives us the idea that other motives than the keen pleasure of the artist at times impelled him in his work. There seems almost a business-like air about the plan of the poem. It follows the stereotyped arrangement which he had originally planned as the frame-work of every book of the *Faerie Queene*.

In due order, at the beginning of canto 1, the Faerie Queene commits the succour of the lady in distress to the representative knight of the Legend; there is the usual attendant upon this knight; there is the usual appearance of Prince Arthur and his usual action—though Artegall is less in need of him than the other knights, save Britomart, have been. All is done decently and in order in this book. The poet never once sails away upon any meandering digression which may take him out of sight of the main adventure to be accomplished; the digressions he admits are always, at the least, indirectly concerned with Artegall himself. It will be noticed, however, that where Spenser appears to enjoy his own work the most is in those very parts of the book the least directly connected with the main quest of the Knight of Justice—in those incidents which, carried on from previous books, he now concludes, such as the story of Florimell, of Trompart and Braggadocchio, of Britomart.

Throughout this book, too, the quality of the verse maintains an even level. It has few stanzas in it that will compare with the most magnificent of his metrical work in the well-known " show " passages in the other books; but, on the other hand, there are, even in the least imaginative parts of the poem, very few lines that are defective in melody, and the general level of the verse is very high. It is the work of a great metrist who is making his music carefully, but is not often ravished away into that mood where no other expression but the highest music is possible to him. If we had nothing else left us of Spenser's metrical work but the Legend of Justice, we should admire and wonder, and enjoy it as the verse of a master; but having so much more from the same hand with which to compare it, we say, it is very fine, but not the finest of which this poet is capable. And what we say here of the metre is to a certain extent true of the greater part of the work in the whole of the fifth book. It is noble work, but not the noblest. Spenser's imagination here was working less frequently at white heat than in the other books, though he still creates for us things of very great interest and beauty. To these we shall presently refer.

We see, then, that the fifth book has marks upon it which give it a character distinct from the other books of the *Faerie Queene,* and it is not difficult to find a reason for this. The Legend of Justice was written with a more definite purpose than any of the other Legends, and this purpose imposed limitations upon the poet. It fettered his thought, his feeling, and his imagination. It was written to stand not only as a picture of the virtue of Justice in its place among the other virtues of which the *Faerie Queene* had to tell, but chiefly as a defence before the world of the character and conduct of a personal friend and hero of the poet.

And here we must for a moment turn aside from the poem to speak of history.

One of the leading qualities of Spenser's nature was a capacity for strong, faithful and admiring friendship. Gabriel Harvey, Sir Philip Sidney, Sir Walter Raleigh, all shared in this warm-hearted loyalty, and Arthur, Lord Grey de Wilton, was another, for whom the poet conceived such a strong attachment that he became his champion before the world. . . .

In this fact, that the Legend of Justice is an apology and vindication for Lord Grey's rule in Ireland, we find the chief explanation of the character of the poem as we have described it above. And to follow out this explanation is our next point.

The book calls itself the Legend of Justice, but it is not the presentation of the universal principle of Justice, but of Justice (?) as displayed in the British Islands in the 16th century. It treats it, too, much more as a political than a private virtue. Artegall, the Knight of Justice, does not often stand for a power of the soul, or a human being fighting for justice in a tangled world of injustice, but most frequently for Lord Grey de Wilton dealing out a more than doubtful sort of justice amidst the bewilderment of Irish difficulties. Here at once, then, begins the poet's limitation; he links the illimitable principle of justice far too closely to a special time, place, and personality. And having thus localized Artegall, he does the same by Prince Arthur, the companion of the Knight of Justice.

In all the incidents in which the Briton Prince appears he stands as the scarcely veiled historical figure of Leicester, or of some other representative English leader in war. Having begun by making his Legend an allegory of contemporary history in Ireland, his political mood continued more or less throughout, even when he was not writing with Ireland in his mind. Having therefore so far localized the virtue of Justice, the range of his imagination was at once limited, and the matter upon which he wished it to work was not of the kind which could most move a poet of Spenser's nature. . . .

Nor was he much more fortunate in the chief quality that his hero attached to Justice under the pressure of Irish affairs. Relentlessness was not the temper which could most appeal to a man like Spenser, who felt so keenly graciousness in character and person. And we may be sure that other qualities drew forth his affection to Lord Grey than those which appeared in that nobleman's Irish policy. Indeed in this Legend of Justice, he shows his dissatisfaction with the cruelty of that policy. He makes Artegall (Lord Grey) a striking and noble figure, but all the most unpleasant results and the useless slaughters which follow from his judgments or action are taken in hand by Talus, the Iron Man. This would seem to say that Spenser felt the cruelties involved in Grey's government of Ireland to be incompatible with the ideal of a Knight of Justice. Several times in the poem he makes Artegall forbid the slaughter which Talus is carrying out with such a grim pleasure, though it is plain from history that Lord Grey made no attempt to stop the massacres in Ireland. Talus, as the groom of Artegall, is usually supposed to stand for the executive power which carries out the decrees of justice, and as such he has some rightful place in the story; but that an Iron Man, incapable of human feeling, should be the sole attendant upon Justice is a woeful limitation to impose upon our conception of the virtue which Aristotle thought the most perfect of all. And this brings me to another point. Spenser having limited himself to a picture of Justice as he saw it during a short period of his own century, and in a few places, had then of necessity to limit his conception of the virtue itself. He treats it very largely in its political, not its private aspect, and his mind, as he writes, is full of its sterner attributes. Where are Mercy, Succour, Pity, and the rest which true Justice in a world like ours must take into companionship? To Spenser, Justice was not much more than an Avenger. And, for the time at least, he was blind to the fact that it has as much to do with exalting and blessing the good as with the overthrow and punishment of evil. Could he but have imagined Justice in a woman's form, with her train of attendants both awful and gracious, moving through the world, giving forth reward as well as punishment, and where she punished, punishing in a remedial way, what noble and lovely things might not the creator of Fidelia and Speranza have made for us in his Legend of Justice! He does, indeed, once present Justice in the person of a woman, Queen Mercilla, but it is a meagre conception, and is not born of sympathetic imagination. Mercilla, on her canopied throne, with the lion at her feet, is a stately figure, but the description both of the Queen and her attendants (9. 27-35) is given mostly in general terms, and, as we have before noticed, there is in it scarcely any of the rich and symbolic detail which Spenser always used when his imagination was on fire. We do not vividly realize the scene unless we read into it from our knowledge of history what Spenser plainly means,—the court of Elizabeth and the trial of the Queen of Scots, who is most unfairly represented as Duessa.   And this very insistence upon the historical meaning of the picture makes it impossible for us to view it as a true presentation of the universal principle of Justice. Spenser himself cannot have felt it so.

At times, too, Spenser's imagination turned sullen in her fetters, and refused to work, so that a dulness creeps over the narrative, as when he writes of Sanglier and the headless lady, or of Amidas and Bracidas; or he loses inventiveness, and reproduces old stories afresh; or is driven to a repetition which weakens the force of a narrative, such as the petition of Belge to Prince Arthur to undertake another battle for her, immediately after he has slain her worst enemy. . . .

We turn, then, to those parts of the fifth book where criticism becomes admiration.   There is the whole of the third canto, with its joyful opening, and the lingering charm of the old court-poetry at its close.   In that canto we find the Marriage Tournament and the dramatic meeting of the two Florimells; the half-humorous picture of the end of Braggadocchio and his man, and the quaint, almost tender, little episode of Guyon and his horse.   There is the story of Radigund the Amazon, with its touches of humanity and grace; there is Guile; there is Britomart, a world of delightfulness in herself.   There is also, from first to last, a certain interest about the character of Artegall.   Students of the poem will be struck by the fact that all these portions of it which are more truly Spenserian in feeling and treatment than any others, are, as far as we know, built up very little, if at all, upon actual history, but upon Spenser's own imagination working upon his personal experience of life, and, in some cases, his memory of the *Orlando Furioso*.   But of all the shorter stories in this book, among these none is perhaps more striking than the meeting of the two Florimells.   It is told with great beauty, and it is a piece of the best kind of allegory, where the meaning is as clear as it is deep. . . .

The Story of Radigund the Amazon has the double charm of vivid narrative and true human feeling.   Radigund herself was, in the first place, suggested by Ariosto's Amazon, but the manner of presenting her is Spenser's.   She is a mixture of the wild Amazon and a more natural womanhood.   We see her several times in a fury of rage, and she has a savage glee at the thought of battle, which Britomart, warrior as she is, never shows; war is a delight to her for its own sake. Yet she looks after the sick and wounded carefully when the fight is over, and she can fall in love.   She is, too, a great princess, and knows the dignified way of doing things, as when she sends her ambassador to challenge Artegall to battle (4. 49-51).   She clothes herself magnificently for the same contest (Spenser devotes eighteen delightful lines to her attire), and she is so beautiful of countenance that Artegall, when about to kill her, beholding her face—"a miracle of Nature's goodly grace"—throws down his sword in anger with himself "that had this visage mard."   But his impulsive generosity cost him dear, for she has none of that virtue herself, as the Knight might have known if he had paid attention to her "spightful speaches" in the course of the fight.   She takes immediate advantage of his weaponless condition, and, springing on him, easily beats him down.   The stanzas which describe the end of this contest are of great vigour, and the shrewish and unrelenting viciousness of the Amazon is skilfully shown. So incisively is this episode sketched that one feels as if the poet had some especially vindictive woman in his mind. Her treatment of him afterwards is characteristic of a selfish and cruel female type. . .

But if Spenser makes a woman mar the career of the Knight of Justice, he also makes a woman restore him to honour. Britomart now comes into the story again, and this scene, the last in which we are to meet her, is consistent with the character the poet has given her since she first appeared in the Legend of Chastity. He devotes nearly the whole of two cantos (6 and 7) to her doings. She is the same impulsive, warm-hearted, daring, inventive creature that we have known before, though she is perhaps a little more wayward. . . .

Artegall is the only other person in the book who has any distinction of character. Prince Arthur enters the story as nothing more than a valiant and courteous knight, and the scene where he comforts the troubled Belge with cheerful speeches is a repetition, in a shorter form and less well done, of his comforting of Una in Book I. But Artegall has a certain individuality. He is made from the first superior in strength of character and prowess to either the Knight of Holiness or of Temperance. He is never foolhardy, as they were inclined to be, but is secure enough in his own courage, as Prince Arthur is, to avoid danger when to encounter it would lead to no special end. Only once is he overcome, and that is through his too great susceptibility to woman's beauty, which is one of the few touches that make him human: his silence, when Britomart releases him from the bondage of the Amazon, is another.

His upbringing has been of the noblest, and he is more on an equality with Prince Arthur (as perhaps Spenser meant his name to signify) than any other Knight we meet. Arthur does not intervene to succour him as he does some of the other knights, but fights side by side with him as a " peer." It is the goddess Astræa herself who has endowed him with his mighty sword and his " groom." His leading quality, as might be expected, since Spenser was drawing Lord Grey in Ireland, is a stern firm-mindedness. Whatever he enters upon he carries through without turning aside or wavering. His attendant Talus is wholly a subordinate, and never acts the part of mentor to him, as did Una and the Palmer to their respective knights. When he is delayed in the accomplishment of his quest, the delay is not in his own will (11. 41). Even Britomart cannot detain him, though his attachment to her is steady in its faithfulness. When he has once given his word, even though foolishly, as in the case of his promise to abide by the conditions of Radigund if she overcome him, he holds to it, " falsely true." It would have been greater honour here to break loose from her captivity and continue his quest. He is an " antique Roman," and it is as such that he stands out from among the other knights of the poem. But it is always necessary, when speaking of Spenser's delineation of character, to guard against misunderstanding. There are critics of Spenser who see in all his men and women only types of human beings, having no special marks of individual character upon them. There is, of course, some truth in this view, but it does not seem the whole truth. Many of the persons in the *Faerie Queene* are types and nothing more, and it would be absurd to claim for Spenser the high dramatic power of creating character which belongs to Shakspere. Spenser's mode, also, of presenting his subject matter was not the dramatic, but the romantic mode, in which incident and sentiment count for more than individual character. Yet it seems possible to discern, in several places in the *Faerie Queene,* the delineation of a character as distinct from the delineation of a type, especially in some of the women,—certainly in the case of Britomart.   Spenser's men are always less distinctive than his women; but Artegall, Calidore, Malbecco, Timias have about them individual touches.   But what there is of character drawing in the *Faerie Queene* is rendered less vivid than it would be on account of the dream-like atmosphere and the lulling verse in which it is presented.   It is only perhaps when the scattered sayings and doings of a personage are drawn together and viewed as a whole, somewhat apart from the mazy windings of the verse in which they are involved, that it is possible to realize how far Spenser could draw a life-like character.   Within certain limits, then, it seems reasonable to say that Spenser could pourtray characters as well as types.

There are many other things in the poem that might be dwelt upon, but there is only room to notice a few more.   There is the vigorous account of the fight in the river between Artegall and the pagan Pollente (2. 13-18), and the description of the flight and capture of Guile, is one of the best of Spenser's grotesque pieces of work, which in some places will recall to the student of Spenser parts of the description of Despair, Mammon and Maleger.   There is also the story of the Giant, in which the material and the abstract are curiously mixed.   What conception does it give us to hear of the clumsy giant—a fairly real personage—weighing in a real pair of scales such immaterial things as "winged words," "the true and the false," "the right and so much wrong"—what are the colour, size and shape of these things?   Had the poet's imagination been fully at work on this passage, he would have given some more definite form to these abstractions to make the picture real.   The somewhat prosy speech of the giant, too, does not rouse in us enough indignation to make us sympathize with the swift punishment visited upon him—a speech which, however, some commentators have seized upon as the text for a sermon against the principles underlying the French Revolution.   But the end of the story is vividly done, even though we do not feel the "justice" in the action of Talus when he quietly interrupts the wearisome old giant to shoulder him over the cliff.   He was hardly used—and it would have been better to let him go on talking and blundering with his scales.   But the simile of the ship here is very spirited, and the vigour and fine adaptability of the verse to argument cannot fail to impress the reader.   This story, however, plainly shows that Spenser was not beyond his age in the way he viewed the "democratic movement."   There is here the unsympathetic, aristocratic air which the Elizabethan gentleman too often adopted towards the people, and from which Shakspere himself was not free.   What contempt there is in the line about the giant's influence— He "was admired much of fooles, women and boys"; and in Artegall's attitude towards these followers—"Loth he was his noble hands t'embrew, In the base blood of such a rascall crew."

The giant, it is true, was a foolish demagogue, but the principles which he ignorantly preached were not so foolish as himself; and Artegall's own answer to them is flimsy enough.

It is impossible in a brief introduction to say the half that there is to say about a poem like this.   I have been unable to touch upon many important points which the student of Spenser needs to keep before him when reading any portion of the *Faerie Queene.* . . . But I would especially remind him that he will not find the main interest of the poem in its narrative—scarcely an incident of which but was taken by Spenser from the classics or from English or Italian writers—nor in the allegory, but in the simple humanity, the high idealism, and the exquisite art of the poem.

We have seen, then, something of the peculiar interest of the Legend of Justice; but there is still another point about it that no lover of Spenser can overlook, and which, though I have already touched it, needs a little more notice. There is in this book a revelation of the poet's attempt to work out in a special instance in his own personal life the ideal of true manhood about which he wrote so much. In its defense of Lord Grey, the Legend of Justice is another evidence of Spenser's quality of loyal-heartedness, as well as of his scorn of all time-serving. The open defence of his friend was not a politic thing; judged by the world's standard, it was an imprudent and foolish act. Lord Grey, it was well known, was no favourite with the Queen at any time, and he had failed in Ireland. Spenser knew that his forthcoming books of the *Faerie Queene* would be read and criticised at Court—for he was not now the "new poet" Immerito. Yet he devotes—and makes what he means absolutely clear—the larger portion of this poem to that unpopular nobleman, who was his friend: it was a knightly deed. Further, it has been laid to Spenser's charge—by Professor Courthope and by Dean Church—that he grossly flattered Queen Elizabeth in the *Faerie Queene*. The witness of this fifth book should help to free him from that accusation. We have seen that he chooses for his hero a man disliked by Elizabeth, and boldly commends him to her notice. But more than this. He introduces in canto 9 a direct description of Elizabeth and her Court, making it quite unmistakable to whom he refers. Here was the finest opportunity for flattery. But what do we find? In the description of Elizabeth not a word of praise to which any real exception can be taken (unless the epithet "angel-like" may offend some). As a great Queen and a stately figure in the history of the time, she deserved, even in her old age, all that he says of her here, and the incident of her reluctance and tears at the condemnation of Mary Queen of Scots is said to be historical. In the introductory stanzas he commends her, but chiefly for her justice—"the instrument whereof loe here thy Artegall." If this was flattery, it was dashed with an audacity which risked something for its speaking.

If, then, on the whole Spenser has lavished less of colour and richness of design upon this fifth book than upon the others, he has told in it perhaps more of his own outward personal history, and this gives it a unique place in the *Faerie Queene*.

FREDERICK M. PADELFORD ("Talus: The Law," pp. 97-104, abridged). In his *English Writers,* Morley identifies Talus, the attendant or squire of Artegall, the hero of the Legend of Justice in the *Faerie Queene*, with "the abstract principle of Justice—swift to overtake offenders, strong to punish, untouched by passion or pity, irresistible." Now if Talus is justice in the abstract, Artegall must be justice in the concrete. In that case, however, Artegall ought to be the squire of Talus, and not Talus the squire of Artegall. As a matter of fact, the real office of Talus is explicitly stated when the character is first introduced. While Astraea was upon earth, Talus was her attendant (1. 12),

> But when she parted hence, she left her groome
> An yron man, which did on her attend
> Alwayes, to execute her stedfast doome,
> And willed him with *Artegall* to wend,
> And doe what euer thing he did intend.
> His name was *Talus,* made of yron mould,
> Immoueable, resistlesse, without end.
> Who in his hand an yron flale did hould,
> With which he thresht out falshood, and did truth vnfould.

That which executes the judgments of justice, threshes out falsehood and unfolds truth, is not the "abstract principle of Justice," but the law and its ministers. I take the character of Talus, then, to represent the law and the agents who enforce it. The epithets "immoueable" and "resistlesse" well express the rigor of the law, and the "yron flale," the pitiless methods by which the iron law wrenches the truth from those suspected of guilt or punishes those proved guilty. In a verse which lends further support to this interpretation, Talus is called, "The true guide of his [Artegall's] way and vertuous government," for the law is the foundation of government, and the guide of the courts in the application of justice.

This interpretation of the character of Talus will be borne out, I think, by a review of the episodes in which the character figures. The first canto shows justice dealing with a domestic problem. As Artegall and Talus are proceeding on their journey to assist Irena, they come upon a youth lamenting beside the headless body of a lady. It develops that a certain knight, Sir Sanglier, had been riding in attendance upon this lady, but that when he saw the beautiful companion of the squire who is now lamenting, he took possession of this lady and renounced his former love. Imploring death rather than desertion, she met death at his hands. Talus is sent in pursuit of Sanglier, and identifies him by circumstantial evidence:

> Whom at first he ghessed by his looke,
> And by the other markes, which of his shield he tooke.

After sentence is passed upon the disdainful miscreant—to bear the murdered lady's head upon his breast, it is Talus who executes sentence.

In the second canto, justice deals with extortion, in the persons of Pollente and Munera, the sarazin and his daughter who exact toll from all who pass their castle, and with communism, in the person of the blustering giant who pretends to be the champion of the common herd, the victims of his demagogism. When Talus storms the castle, Munera tries to appease him with fair words (23),

> But when as yet she saw him to proceede,
> Vnmou'd with praiers, or with piteous thought,
> She ment him to corrupt with goodly meede;
> And causde great sackes with endlesse riches fraught,
> Vnto the battilment to be vpbrought,
> And powred forth ouer the Castle wall,
> That she might win some time, though dearly bought
> Whilest he to gathering of the gold did fall.
> But he was nothing mou'd, nor tempted therewithall.

In other words, finding that the law is unmoved by entreaty, the extortioner tries to corrupt it with bribes.

Entered within the castle, it is Talus who at last finds Munera, suggesting the power of the law in tracing crime. Though Artegall rues the unhappy plight of Munera,

> Yet for no pity would he change the course
> Of Justice, which in Talus hand did lye,

for justice must allow the law to punish such an enemy of society.

In the second episode of the canto Talus shoulders the loud-mouthed giant off the land, just as the law forced the Anabaptists to leave England in 1568. The assault which the noisy rabble then makes upon Talus corresponds to the protest that was made against this legislation by those who sympathized with the sect, and just as the " lawlesse multitude " hid in holes and bushes when Talus retaliated, so these Anabaptist sympathizers were silenced by the law. (See Strype, *Life and Acts of Archbishop Grindal,* p. 181.)

In the third canto, justice deals with defrauders, personated by the false Florimel, Braggadochio, and Trompart. Talus shows how the law treats such imposters by breaking the sword of Braggadochio, depriving him of his shield, and scourging him and his accomplice out of court.

In the opening episode of canto 4, the settlement of the dispute between Bracidas and Amidas, justice is concerned with property rights. In this unique episode, Talus, " that great yron groome," is in attendance upon Artegall as " his gard and government," a most significant expression, as defining his office.

The concluding episode of this canto introduces the question of woman's place in government. A crowd of women, followers of Radigund, who prides herself on reducing all knights to servitude, " like tyrants mercilesse " are leading forth an unfortunate captive, Sir Turpine, to execution. When Artegall inquires as to the offence, the women swarm about him, thinking to lay hands on him as well (24):

> But he was soone aware of their ill minde,
> And drawing backe deceiued their intent.
> Yet though him selfe did shame on womankinde
> His mighty hand to shend, he *Talus* sent
> To wrecke on them their follies hardyment;
> Who with few sowces of his yron flale,
> Dispersed all their troupe incontinent,
> And sent them home to tell a piteous tale,
> Of their vaine prowesse, turned to their proper bale.

Although I am satisfied that there is a rather specific historical allegory lurking in this episode, in its universal import it concerns the old question of woman's political and legal rights, which had been freshly brought to the fore by Knox's *Monstrous Regiment of Women* and the lively and persistent discussion which it aroused. Knox makes elaborate citations from the laws and quotes abundantly the opinions of Aristotle and the church fathers upon this question. [Arber ed., pp. 12-4 quoted.]

Spenser compresses the same conclusions into the following stanza, taking pains—as also in the character of Britomart (Elizabeth)—to make due allowance for the exceptional woman whom the heavens have lifted "to lawful soueraintie." In his harsh dispersal of the troops of women who attend Radigund, Talus obviously figures as the law.

The fifth canto is peculiarly significant. Artegall, having made the foolish compact with Radigund that whichever was worsted in combat should become subject to the other, is paying the price of his folly by abject servitude. Now, although Talus is the squire of Artegall, expressly assigned the office by Astraea, he refrains from any effort to rescue his lord because he holds an agreement to be sacred. Thus scrupulously does the poet imply that it is the duty of the law to recognize the inviolability of a contract, even though the contract itself be a vicious one.

In the sixth canto, Talus exemplifies—as elsewhere—the watchfulness of the law by his nocturnal vigilance in the castle of Dolon, where he guards the person of Britomart, who, now become the exemplar of justice, is hastening to the relief of Artegall. With his flail he scatters the "raskall rout" who seek to capture Britomart, for the law is the defender and the preserver of justice.

In the seventh canto, while Britomart is engaged in overcoming Radigund, Talus enters the castle of the Amazon and slays her women, until Britomart in pity stays his hand. The law itself knows no pity.

With the eighth canto, Spenser turns his attention to the display of justice in national and international situations. In these episodes Talus would seem to represent military force, that force which is the instrument of national or international justice. The defeat of the Spanish Armada is commonly thought to be represented in the struggle of Prince Arthur and the Soldan. Prince Arthur—the Grace of God—wins this signal victory for England. He is attended by Talus (29. 6-9):

> And by his stirrup *Talus* did attend,
> Playing his pages part, as he had beene
> Before directed by his Lord; to th' end
> He should his flale to finall execution bend.

If my general thesis be correct, this is a figurative way of saying that in this struggle English arms were the strong ally of the Divine Purpose.

In the ninth canto, as Artegall and Prince Arthur journey to the court of Mercilla (Elizabeth), they learn of Guyle, who lives in a nearby cave. They agree to exterminate the monster, and it is Talus who, after the monster has assumed, in his cunning, a variety of shapes, finally captures and kills him. As the remainder of this canto and the opening stanzas of the next are given over to the vindication of England's policy in executing Mary Queen of Scots, it seems not unlikely that the character of Guyle is intended to represent Mary's crafty allies in England, especially the unfortunate Duke of Norfolk, who, after many sinuous turnings and twistings, was finally brought to execution in 1572.

The major portion of the tenth canto and the first half of the eleventh are concerned with England's succor of the Low Countries. Talus does not accompany Prince Arthur on this expedition, but attends his own knight, Artegall, who in the meantime has returned to his original quest of relieving Irena.

As they proceed, Artegall, after much indecision, is induced to lend his aid to

Bourbon. Literally, this of course means that Spenser entertained some doubt as to whether or not justice was on the side of Henry IV. In the struggle which ensues, Talus chases the base rabble over hill and dale (65),

> Ne ceassed not, till all their scattred crew
> Into the sea he droue quite from that soyle,
> The which they troubled had with great turmoyle.

Such were the stern methods of military suppression by which Henry established his beneficent reign.

In canto 12 Artegall finally achieves his quest, the relief of Irena. Artegall represents justice as personified in Lord Grey, and Talus represents the harsh laws that were made for the subjugation of the Irish and the harsh military methods by which Lord Grey sought to enforce these laws [st. 26 quoted].

The last mention of Talus is in the concluding stanza of the book, where he is barely restrained from attacking Envy, who has sought to poison the good name of Artegall upon his return to Faerie Land, a manifest reference to the abuse which Grey received upon his return to England:

> But *Talus* hearing her so lewdly raile,
> And speake so ill of him, that well deserued,
> Would her haue chastiz'd with his yron flaile,
> If her Sir *Artegall* had not preserued,
> And him forbidden, who his heast obserued.

This means, I take it, that mere detraction does not properly come within the scope of the law. The public servant, or that justice which he embodies, must expect to be misunderstood, and defamation is not to be remedied by a harsh resort to law, however strong the inclination to attempt it.

Such, in brief, is the interesting part that Talus plays in this legend of justice. There can be little doubt, I think, that Spenser intends the character to stand for the law.

E. DE SELINCOURT (Introduction to one-vol. Oxford ed., pp. xlviii-xlix). The peculiar nature of the theme seemed to demand a special treatment; and the allegory, which is to present the character necessary to him who would be his sovereign's "instrument," and to expound Spenser's whole theory of government, finds its substance not in legend or romance, but in those three great events which led up to the final clash with the power of Spain—the suppression of rebellion in Ireland, encouraged and supported by Philip, the execution of Mary Queen of Scots, and the war in the Netherlands. The first of these, of which Spenser had himself personal experience, bulks the largest; and the several adventures which befall Sir Artegall are vivid illustrations of points which he has emphasized in his prose indictment of the present state of Ireland. Before the Knight of Justice can subdue Grandtorto, the great enemy who keeps Irena in subjection, he meets with lawless outrage and deceit in Sir Sanglier, with the venality of Pollente and Munera, by whom justice is bought and sold, with the misunderstandings of a mob ever ready to stir up civil faction at the specious bidding of the Giant of demagogy, with the insolence of Braggadocchio, who takes to himself credit for the deeds done by the knight that he defames. Hardest of all he must subdue

Malengiǹ, type of that guile which will cross his path at every turn, and is capable of assuming any form if only it can elude his vigilance. And if for a moment he give way to womanish pity, however noble may seem to be its promptings, his work will be undone, and he will himself be enslaved to the Radegund whom he should destroy. True Justice " had need have mightie hands " (5. 4. 1. 5-8) :

> For vaine it is to deeme of things aright,
> And makes wrong doers iustice to deride,
> Vnlesse it be perform'd with dreadlesse might.

Sir Artegall must have at his right hand Talus (5. 1. 12. 6-7),

> made of yron mould,
> Immoueable, resistlesse, without end.

Even after rebellion has been crushed and Grandtorto is destroyed, his task is not complete. There is still need of a wise but relentless government; and in the recall of Sir Artegall to the Faerie Court, leaving Irena " in heavinesse," and himself pursued by the revilings of the witches Envy and Detraction and by the barkings of the Blatant Beast, Spenser views with passionate regret the fate meted out to his chosen knight of Justice. (A masterly exposition of Book V, to which I am much indebted, will be found in E. A. Greenlaw's " Spenser and British Imperialism," *MP*, January 1912.) [See below.]

WILLIAM FENN DEMOSS (*The Influence of Aristotle's "Politics" and "Ethics" on Spenser*, pp. 40-2). In discussing his fifth virtue, Justice, Spenser expresses the mean in almost the exact words of Aristotle. Aristotle tells us that particular Justice has to do with the goods of fortune (*N. Eth.* 5. 2). He defines Justice as follows: " Just conduct is a mean between committing and suffering injustice; for to commit injustice is to have too much, and to suffer it is to have too little " (*N. Eth.* 5. 9). In the proem to Book V Spenser in describing the Golden Age, when all men were just, says: " And all men sought their owne, and none no more "

Again, in Book V proper, Spenser's treatment of Justice as a mean is unmistakable. In canto 2 we have the Gyant with his " huge great paire of ballance." Complaining that this world's goods are unjustly, because unequally, distributed, the Gyant proposes to weigh everything and make a just distribution. He has asserted that he " could justly weigh the wrong and right," and Artegall (Justice) is testing him. Artegall finally tells him [2. 48-49. 5 quoted]. At this point Talus, Artegall's iron squire (the iron hand of Justice) hurls the Gyant into the sea and drowns him. This mean which the Gyant " misleekes," and which Justice demands, is not simply a mean, but Aristotle's mean of Justice; for it is the mean in regard to the distribution of the goods of fortune. Moreover, the episode is Aristotelian in every particular. Aristotle teaches that equality as applied to Justice must be proportionate, not absolute. Justice, he holds, demands that the goods of fortune be distributed proportionately to the varying degrees of virtue in the citizens. (*N. Eth.* 5. Aristotle makes the same point in his discussion of Friendship. See *N. Eth.* 8. 9.) He even protests particularly against an equalization of property and reiterates this protest (see, for example, *Politics* 8. 9).

Spenser's characters in this Book represent not only the mean but also the two Aristotelian extremes in regard to Justice: that of accepting less than rightfully belongs to one, and that of taking more. The first is represented by the Squire who is wronged by Sir Sanglier. Sanglier will not "rest contented with his right" (5. 1. 17), but, "the fairere love to gaine," takes the Squire's Ladie and slays his own. The Squire complains to Artegall. Brought before Artegall for judgment, Sanglier defies his accuser, and testifies falsely that (5. 1. 23, 24)—

> neither he did shed that Ladies bloud
> Nor tooke away his love, but *his owne proper good.*

Then

> Well did the Squire perceive himself too weake,
> To aunswere his defiaunce in the field,
> And rather chose his challenge off to breake,
> Then to approve his right with speare and shield.
> And rather guilty chose him selfe to yield.

Only by imitating Solomon is Artegall able to discover to whom the live Ladie belongs and who is the murderer. The other extreme is represented by Sanglier, the robber Pollente, his daughter Munera, the Gyant with the huge "ballance," and so on. Like Aristotle, Spenser puts the emphasis on the extreme of taking too much. The opposite of general Justice is represented by such characters as Grantorto (Great Wrong). The mean is seen in Artegall, Arthur, Britomart, and Mercilla (Equity).

The various phases of Justice discussed by Aristotle are clearly presented by Spenser, such as distributive justice, corrective justice, retaliation, equity, and so on. Spenser also plainly makes Reason the determiner of the mean in respect to Justice. See, for example, his literal exposition of Justice in 5. 9. 1 ff.

ALFRED B. GOUGH (*Spenser's Faerie Queene Book V,* pp. xli-xlvii). The Fifth Book of the *Faerie Queene* is so distinct from the rest in tone and temper that it seems to mark a definite phase in the poet's development. It may of course contain some passages of an earlier date than the rest, though the first canto is the only one without feminine rimes, the presence of which distinguishes Books IV-VI from I-III. Broadly speaking, it is probable that IV-VI were written between Spenser's return to Kilcolman from England early in 1591 and a date shortly before his marriage in June, 1594 (see Sonnet 80). As Book V presupposes events narrated in IV, viz. the betrothal of Artegall and Britomart (4. 6), and that of Marinell and Florimell (4. 12), it was probably written mainly in 1592-3. The story of Belge, difficult as it is to interpret, is more intelligible if we assume that it was written before Spenser heard of the complete reduction of the southern provinces by Spain in 1592. The latest event clearly referred to is the abjuration of Protestantism by Henry IV of France in July, 1593. (This episode is perhaps one of the last additions to the Book; see note to 12, Arg.)

What was Spenser's mood when he was writing Book V? The high hopes with which he had set out for England with Raleigh in 1589 had been only partially satisfied. The publication of the first instalment had brought him the Queen's favour, abundant fame, and a pension of £50 a year (February, 1591), worth perhaps £400 at the present day. But his hope of being called away from his Irish exile to some political office in England remained unfulfilled, and it became clear that Burghley's hostility was a bar to preferment.   His personal disappointment mingled with his indignation at the treatment accorded to his patron and hero, Lord Grey, the faithful servant of the Crown, whose offence had been, as it appeared to Spenser, his stern devotion to duty, who had been recalled and disgraced because Burghley had listened to the voices of envy and detraction.   In *The Ruines of Time* (440 ff.), in 1590, Spenser had lamented:

> learning lies unregarded,
> And men of armes doo wander unrewarded . . .
> For he [Burghley] that now welds all things at his will,
> Scorns th' one and th' other in his deeper skill.

In a famous passage in *Mother Hubberds Tale* (895 ff.), added in or about 1591, Spenser vividly describes his painful experiences as a suitor at court:

> Full little knowest thou that hast not tride,
> What hell it is, in suing long to bide, &c.

And in *Colin Clouts Come Home Again* (690 ff., 727 f.), in 1591, he spoke of the court

> Where each one seeks with malice and with strife,
> To thrust downe other into foule disgrace,
> Himselfe to raise: and he doth soonest rise
> That best can handle his deceitfull wit,
> In subtil shifts . . .
> Whiles single Truth and simple honestie
> Do wander up and downe despys'd of all.

In the letter, written December 27, 1591, in which Spenser dedicates this poem to Raleigh, he complains of "the malice of evill mouthes" (again mentioned, with a pointed reference to Burghley, in the last stanza of Book VI).

In his fortieth year Spenser settled down once more, after his visit to the brilliant but corrupt society of London, to his great task in his lonely post at Kilcolman, realizing not only the vanity of his longing for a public career, but also the baseness and injustice that prevailed in public life, but not yet fully reconciled to the loss of his hopes.   Book IV, perhaps the weakest and most inconsequent of the six, maintains, in spite of some noble passages, a less exalted level than those that preceded it.   Book V however reflects the poet's dejection far more evidently, from the Proem, which laments the universal and progressive decay of justice, to the final scene where the hero is assailed by Envy, Detraction, and the Blatant Beast.   The poet's habitual joyous lingering over scenes of beauty and splendour is almost entirely absent; there are a severe brevity and austerity in the descriptions not found elsewhere, and not entirely due to the subject.   The obvious flagging of inspiration has been well attributed to the obtrusion of the moral motive. Spenser's mind was full of the sense of injustice.   He wrote from a sense of duty; he felt called to vindicate his hero.   His best poetry was only produced when his heart overflowed with a serene delight in the beauty of the world.

A new emotional disturbance which probably occurred while Spenser was writing this Book still further depressed his genius.   It was, as it seems, late in

1592 that he fell in love with Elizabeth Boyle, and if we are justified in treating the *Amoretti* as broadly autobiographical, all through the following year he was a prey to the torments and fears of the unsuccessful lover, feelings exceptionally acute in a sensitive nature like his. (He calls his lady a " cruell warriour," proud and defiant, who keeps him " in cruell bands," while he spends his days " in pining languor," and she daily augments his miseries—Sonnets 5, 11, 12, 36; cf. 20, 52, 57. Conventional as this language is, it may be pertinently compared with the account of Artegall's imprisonment by Radigund in 5, written about the same time. Note also the masterly characterization of Britomart.) In this year (1593) he also suffered from a long illness, which he distinguishes from his " harts wound " (Sonnet 50), and he was sued by Lord Roche for unlawfully appropriating some land of his (possibly the " false forged lyes " of Sonnet 86). In October Lord Grey de Wilton died, without having been received back into favour.

The subdued temper continued while Spenser was writing the earlier part of Book VI, which describes the pursuit of the Blatant Beast. The cloud lifted early in 1594 with the lover's acceptance (Sonnets 62, 63), while the definite renunciation of ambition brought inward peace and serenity (see *Faerie Queene* 6. 9 and 10—Pastorella—, especially the contrast drawn by Meliboee and Calidore between the shepherd's life and the pursuit of " the worlds gay showes "—9. 18-25. Cf. Mackail, *Springs of Helicon*, pp. 129 f.). His sweetest and mellowest poetry belongs to the few remaining years of his life (*Epithalamion, Prothalamion, Hymns of Heavenly Love and Heavenly Beauty, Mutabilitie*), deepening to the prophetic vision of the

> stedfast rest of all things firmely stayd
> Upon the pillours of Eternity (7. 8. 2).

But in Book V, we note that the loss of the exuberant fancy, which is at once a source of strength and weakness in the earlier books, produces a new simplicity in the structure of the narrative. The persons are less numerous than in Books III and IV, and their actions are more clearly and firmly described. There are no digressions from the theme of justice, the idea of which plainly underlies all the incidents. Large sections (canto 4, stanza 21—canto 7, Radigund; cantos 8-11, stanza 35, Arthur and Mercilla) form connected narratives. There is little complexity or obscurity in the moral allegory, which indeed tends to merge into the direct presentation of a hero overthrowing unjust persons and performing other acts of justice, the story thus ceasing to be allegorical at all. Talus is the most striking allegorical figure in the Book. In him the physical force which executes the judicial decrees of the State is vividly symbolized as a subhuman being, 1. 12. 7:

> Immoveable, resistlesse, without end,

faithful as a watchdog (6. 26), terrible as a storm (7. 35), with no moral initiative, but constantly needing to be held in check (7. 35, 11. 65, 12. 7, 43).

The treatment in this Book of the virtue of justice is no doubt one-sided. For the most part its operations rather than its nature and conditions are dealt with. The treatment is not psychological. Of justice as an active principle in the human heart, regulating conduct and harmonizing the desires, we see but little. We learn, it is true, something of its nature in Artegall's argument with the giant,

especially in the saying that " in the mind the doome of right must bee " (2. 47. 6),
i. e. that justice is not a mechanical rule, but is a matter of moral judgment " according to the line of conscience " (1. 7. 4).   Again, it is highly significant that
Artegall's yielding to sentimental pity when his duty is to slay Radigund leads to
his downfall.   There is also an inner struggle when he has the opportunity of
escaping at the cost of violating his pledge (5. 5 ff.).   The final victory of justice
is seen when he submits meekly to the assaults of Envy, Detraction, and the
Blatant Beast, because his arms and his henchmen were lent him to maintain public
right, and not for his private ends.   Elsewhere, however, Artegall is seldom confronted with the temptation to act unjustly; the moral problem is hardly shown
presenting itself for solution in his breast.   His rôles are those of an arbiter, in
the cases of Sanglier, the two Florimells, Guyon's horse and the quarrelling brothers; of an exponent of the principles of social justice, in his argument with the
giant; and of an avenger of public wrongs in his remaining adventures.   Prince
Arthur also plays the last of these parts by quelling the Souldan, the Seneschal,
Geryoneo, and the fiend beneath the altar.   The trial of Duessa represents the
vindication of the State against multiform wrong.   There are but few traces of a
study of Aristotle's analysis of justice in the *Nicomachean Ethics,* Book V.   (Distributive justice: the giant with the scales, the rule of Radigund.   Corrective justice in voluntary transactions: the two brothers.   Corrective justice concerned
with secret crimes: Braggadochio, Dolon, Duessa, &c.   Among instances of injustice in the broader sense of vice, Aristotle mentions, *Nic. Eth.* 5. 11. 2, throwing away one's shield—cf. Burbon; and reviling—cf. Detraction and the Blatant
Beast.)

H. C. NOTCUTT (" The *Faerie Queene* and its Critics," pp. 70-8).   The third
misconception that has vitiated the criticism of the *Faerie Quene* can be touched
upon only in the briefest manner, though it deserves much fuller treatment.   It has
to do with the interpretation of what is often called the historical allegory underlying the poem, but which would be better described as allusion to contemporary
persons and events.   It is difficult to account for some of the statements that have
been made in regard to this matter by responsible critics.   Professor Courthope,
for instance, in his *History of English Poetry,* writes as follows: " The subject of
the fifth book is Justice; but this, so far from being the ' private virtue ' promised
by the poet, is almost entirely political; relating either to the government of Lord
Grey in Ireland, the attacks of Philip II on the Low Countries, or the religious
back-slidings of Henry IV of France " (2. 268).   But so far from this being the
case we find, when we turn to the poem itself, that these historical matters occupy
just one quarter of the book—three cantos out of twelve—and that many different
aspects of Justice in private life are dealt with in the other nine cantos.   Dean
Church is a little farther from the truth.   He says: " The adventures of Artegal
mainly preserve the memory of Lord Grey's terrible exploits against wrong and
rebellion in Ireland " (*Spenser,* p. 161).   A reference to the text of the poem
shows that the part of the adventures of Artegal which represents Lord Grey's
exploits in Ireland occupies one canto out of twelve.

This is not a promising start if we are looking for guidance as to the way in
which Spenser has managed the historical side of his allegory.   And there are

other misconceptions that have helped no less to set the reader on the wrong track for understanding the poem. It is obvious, for example, that, in the ninth and tenth cantos of Book V, the fate of Duessa is meant to call to mind the trial and execution of Mary Queen of Scots. This was recognized in Spenser's own day, and we are told that her son, who was then James VI of Scotland, so keenly resented the reference to his mother that he appealed to Elizabeth to punish the presumption of the poet. From this it was assumed that wherever Duessa appears in the poem she stands for Mary Queen of Scots, and a passage that did not square with this interpretation was put on the rack and stretched so that it might fit. Thus the references to Duessa in the First Book have been, though not without some difficulty, applied to various incidents in Mary Stuart's life, and it is only somewhat recently that Miss Winstanley has shown, with an almost mathematical completeness of demonstration, that the reference is really to Mary Tudor and not to the other Mary. Similarly in Book V, Artegal, so far as the incidents recorded in the twelfth canto are concerned, represent Lord Grey, but in the eleventh canto, where the allusion is to events in the career of Henry IV of France, Artegal cannot stand for Lord Grey, since he took no part in these affairs. He may perhaps represent the Earl of Essex. [See HEFFNER, pp. 324-330 below.] And other similar examples might be adduced.

Some of these changes of reference are too obvious to be overlooked. But instead of being regarded as clues that might lead to an understanding of Spenser's purpose in referring to contemporary events, they have usually been regarded as blemishes calling for such apology as could be offered. Church suggests that they are intended " to throw curious readers off the scent. . . . There is," he says, " an intentional dislocation of the parts of the story, when they might make it imprudently close in its reflection of facts or resemblance in portraiture. A feature is shown, a manifest allusion is made, and then the poet starts off in other directions, to confuse and perplex all attempts at interpretation, which might be too particular and too certain " (*op. cit.* p. 131). But it is an unlikely explanation. We shall probably get much nearer to the truth if we recognize that throughout the poem the moral allegory is the main concern of the poet, and that the allusions to contemporary events and persons are brought in merely by way of illustration. Artegal represents Justice or, perhaps we should say, the man who is striving to carry out the ideal of Justice in public and private life; and when Spenser makes use of some incidents in the career of Lord Grey, when he was trying to put into effect in Ireland the principles of Justice, then for the moment Artegal represents Lord Grey. But in other parts of the story, when other incidents are being used to illustrate the working of Justice, Artegal may be intended to remind us of some other person of note, or more frequently there will be no such allusion at all (this point has been well put by Professor E. A. Greenlaw, in *Modern Language Notes,* March 1920 [see above]). There are no standing personal equations in the *Faerie Queene,* and many of the attempted identifications need to be reduced to lower terms before they can be regarded as approximating to the intention of the poet.

If the views so far put forward come anywhere near the truth, it would appear that the critics have not succeeded in throwing much light on the difficulties of this great poem. They have, it would seem, given too little heed to the help that

Spenser himself has offered to his readers, and, having failed to recognize a coherent idea and purpose in the poem, they have too readily assumed that no such idea and purpose exist.

MOHINIMOHAN BHATTACHERJE (*Studies in Spenser*, pp. 1-18). In Plato Justice is but another name of Temperance. It is a state of harmony in the soul produced by the balance of the three principles, *viz.*, Reason, Passion and Appetite. This is its definition in the *Phaedrus* where it is figured in the image of the charioteer (Reason) and the winged horses (Appetite and Passion). In the *Republic* this virtue is explained by reference to the state and the activities of its different members. Spenser deals with this virtue under the name of Temperance in the Second Book of the *Faerie Queene* where a number of characters and episodes illustrates this doctrine of harmony. It was only to be expected, when Spenser came to deal with Justice in the Fifth Book, that having exhausted its inner content, *viz.*, the idea of harmony in the soul in Book II, he would treat of the external manifestation of it in the state and that Book V would allegorise the Platonic conceptions of perfect and imperfect forms of government. But this expectation is not realised except to a very slight extent. It has accordingly been said that Book V of the *Faerie Queene* has no moral significance, that it has only a historical meaning and that it is a colourless and mediocre production.

While these charges are true to a certain extent, Spenser had an excuse for not introducing ancient political speculations into his poem. This is to be found in his letter to Sir Walter Raleigh where, in unfolding the plan of the *Faerie Queene,* he undertakes to deal in it only with the twelve moral virtues of Aristotle and expressly excludes political virtues from the scope of his poem. "I labour to pourtraict in Arthure, before he was king, the image of a brave Knight, perfected in the twelve private morall virtues, as Aristotle hath devised; the which is the purpose of these first twelve books: which if I finde to be well accepted, I may be perhaps encoraged to frame the other part of *polliticke virtues* in his person, after that he came to be King." The Legend of Justice (Book V), however, is not merely a historical narrative in disguise. Ancient ideas on Justice are found scattered throughout the poem, though the story as a whole is not regulated by them—in fact, it is not a connected story at all but only a string of episodes. These ancient ideas are mostly drawn from Aristotle's and Plato's philosophy and lend colour to some of the characters. It must, however, be admitted that nowhere is the influence of Aristotle or Plato very marked.

Aristotle deals with Justice in Book V of his *Ethics* and he takes up the enquiry where Plato leaves it. Aristotle defines Justice as " a moral disposition," but the idea underlying this definition had been fully thought out and exhaustively analysed by Plato. According to Plato this disposition or temperance is the outcome of a balance of the three principles of the human soul. But Aristotle, without entering into the nature or the causes of this disposition, is content to believe that Justice is " a moral disposition such that in consequence of it men have the capacity of *doing* what is just, and *actually do it,* and wish it. Similarly also with respect to Injustice, it is a moral disposition such that in consequence of it men do unjustly, and wish what is unjust."

Aristotle is more concerned with the consideration of " what is Just " *in action.*

It is his idea of practical Justice that has left its traces in Spenser; but this idea of Aristotle also had its origin in Plato. Justice in Aristotle has two meanings but it is its restricted sense with which he is concerned in his *Ethics*. In this sense, a just man is satisfied with his own dues—his own share of wealth or property, while the unjust man wants more than this. "The Just will be the lawful and the *equal* and the unjust the unlawful and the *unequal*," "the equal" and "the unequal" standing for the contented and the grasping man respectively. This idea of the just man is present in Plato, though it is there only as a corollary to the theory of harmony in the soul. . . . But what has a subordinate place in Plato assumes great importance in Aristotle who fills his discourse on Justice with analyses and illustrations of the unjust action hinted at by Plato, *viz.*, misappropriation of other people's belongings.

Aristotle classifies Justice into two classes: Distributive and Corrective. Distributive Justice is concerned with the determination of the shares of partners in joint production, and these are proportionate to their respective contributions to the common or joint fund. Corrective Justice, on the other hand, comes in only when some grasping man has appropriated more than his share and the equilibrium has to be restored. This equilibrium is described by Aristotle as the "mean," "equal" or "just." The restoration of the equilibrium is effected by making over to the original owner the property of which he had been wrongfully deprived, *i. e.*, by restoring the *status quo ante*. . . . In the case of Corrective Justice there is no question of proportion, for whatever is wrongfully taken must be given back irrespective of the position or condition of the parties (*Ethics* 5. 7). . . .

From this conception of Justice Aristotle derives his view of the nature and function of the Judge. Since the Judge is to execute justice, he must himself be just. He is equally removed from the extremes and is the follower of the *via media*. "Going to the judge is in fact going to the Just. And men seek a judge as one in the mean which is expressed in a name given by some to Judges, *Mesidioi*, or middlemen, under the notion that, if they can hit on the mean, they shall hit on the Just. The just is then surely a mean, since the Judge is also."

Injustice caused by a "grasping man" which calls for the interference of Corrective Justice arises out of voluntary as well as involuntary transactions. Examples of the former class are selling, buying, use, bail, etc., and examples of the latter are theft, adultery, poisoning and false witness which "affect secrecy" and insult, death, bonds, plundering, maiming, foul language and slanderous abuse, which are "accompanied with open violence (*Ethics* 5. 5.)."

Spenser in Book V follows Aristotle in giving instances of injustice. Artegall is the personification of Justice and the persons punished by him typify some of the forms of injustice mentioned above. Thus, Braggadocchio who is punished in canto 3 is a thief, Pollente and Munera are plunderers, Radigund, the Amazon Queen, is guilty of causing "bonds" or captivity, Adicia to whom Queen Mercilla sends Samient for carrying on negotiations stands charged with "insulting" and using "foul language" against the messenger, Dolon attempts to assassinate Britomart, while Sanglier actually murders his own lady and tries to kidnap the wife of the Squire.

Illustrations of the Aristotelian conception of Justice "which is corrective in the various transactions between man and man" are also to be found in Spenser.

In Book V such justice is administered by the restoration of the portion of a man's property unlawfully seized by another, so as to bring back the original state of " equality."   In canto 4 the episode of the two brothers furnishes an example. The two islands bequeathed to them by their father were originally equal, but a portion of one, the heritage of Bracidas was washed off and deposited as an accretion on the island of Amidas.   The result was inequality or injustice, though here the author of the crime was the sea.   Artegall, as the impersonation of Justice, administered Corrective Justice or restored the *status quo ante* by decreeing that the chest of treasure should belong to Bracidas, it being assumed that it was equal in value to the accretion on Amidas' island, since both arose out of the sea.

In canto 2, the Giant poses to be the administrator of Corrective Justice and though he is found out to be an imposter, his method of work is Aristotelian. [The author reviews the Bracidas-Amidas and the Giant episodes (cantos 4 and 2) as cases in point.]

According to the Giant there is injustice in the relative conditions of the rich and the poor, the " Lordlings " and the " Commons," for the upper classes are, according to him, so many vampires sucking out the life-blood of the lower.   He, therefore, wants to make an equal division of wealth amongst the rich and the poor.   He says:—

> Tyrants that make men subject to their law,
> I will suppresse, that they no more may raine;
> And Lordlings curbe, that Commons overaw;
> And all the wealth of rich men to the poore will draw.

Some have read into this speech principles similar to those that underlay the French Revolution, while others have found its source in the Anabaptist Theory of Equality [see PADELFORD, pp. 336-341 below].   But Spenser's debt to the Aristotelian conception of Corrective Justice is clear from the arguments of the Giant on the equalisation of wealth and encroachment on other people's property and from his use of the word " Justice."

As pointed out above, Aristotle thinks that " upon a dispute arising, men have recourse to the Judge. . . . And men seek a Judge as one in the mean."   Such a Judge is Spenser's Artegall.   He had been asked to decide cases of dispute more than once, *e. g.,* between Amidas and Bracidas, Guyon and Braggadocchio, while he was the champion of Justice in a number of episodes.   He was trained up by Astraea to act as an umpire or a middleman and the whole of his youth was spent in receiving this training and demonstrating its practical usefulness amongst beasts of the forest.

Plato gives pre-eminence to Justice as the greatest of virtues which helps on the growth of other virtues.   Aristotle says of Justice, in a broad sense, " This Justice is, in fact, Perfect virtue.   Yet not simply so, but as exercised towards one's neighbour; and for this reason Justice is thought oftentimes to be the best of the virtues."   Spenser has the same notion about the superiority of Justice over other virtues.

> *Most sacred virtue* she of all the rest,
> Resembling God in his imperiall might;

He laments that the reign of this supreme virtue is a thing of the past, it having flourished on this earth only during the reign of Saturn.

Over and above Aristotle's practical applications of Platonic ideas, direct traces of Plato's conception of Justice are to be found in Book V of the *Faerie Queene*. Artegall is the impersonation of Justice and his adventure is undertaken to punish Grantorto who is described as a tyrant. Another antagonist of Artegall, whom he encounters in the course of his journey, is similarly described. Radigund is a tyranness. Prince Arthur represents in every book of the *Faerie Queene* the specific virtue allegorized in it and, therefore, in Book V he stands for Justice. His antagonist Gerioneo is also called a tyrant. Now it is Plato who in his *Republic* sets up Tyranny as the opposite of Justice. Platonic Justice is the consummation of virtue, while Tyranny in Plato is the worst vice.

Plato distinguishes tyranny in the temperament of man from tyranny in the state: the tyrannical man from the tyrannical ruler. The tyrannical ruler is the product of love of extreme liberty on the part of the people. The tyrant panders to their vices and, having thus gained power, satisfies his own hidden desire. The lovers of license or extreme liberty then become so many slaves ready to do anything at the bidding of the tyrant who " has a mob entirely at his disposal (*Republic* 8)." Tyranny in the state is thus the direct outcome of Democracy. In a Democracy people enjoy the utmost license and do away with vested rights. They kill or banish rich men and divide their wealth equally amongst themselves, grasp the sovereign power and use it recklessly." "Democracy comes into being after *the poor have conquered their opponents*, slaughtering some and banishing some, while to the remainder they give an *equal share of freedom* and power." The Democrats are led by demagogues who urge them on to *wreck* and *destroy* old institutions by holding up before them a glorious vision of equality and liberty. Referring to demagogues, Plato says, " In a democracy they are almost the entire ruling power, and while the keener sort speak and act, the rest keep buzzing about the bema and do not suffer a word to be said on the other side; hence in democracies almost everything is managed by the drones." Spenser has some episodes based on these ideas of Plato. Spoliation of the rich, equal distribution of wealth and emancipation of the people are the task to which the Giant, in canto 2, sets himself.

> Tyrants that make men subject to their law,
> I will suppresse, that they no more may raine;
> And Lordlings curbe, that Commons overaw;
> And all the wealth of rich men to the poore will draw.

But he was only the demagogue behind whom stood a great mob.

> Therefore the vulgar did about him flocke,
> And cluster thicke unto his leasings vaine,
> Like foolish flies about an hony crocke;
> In hope by him great benefite to gaine,
> *And uncontrolled freedome* to obtaine.

When the Giant was thrown into the sea, this mob, baulked of its hope of gain, tried to cause disorder in the state.

> They gan to gather in tumultuous rout,
> And mutining, to stirre up civill faction,
> For certaine losse of so great expectation;
> For well they hoped to have got great good,
> And *wondrous riches* by his innovation.

Spenser also notes the state of slavishness and stupidity to which a tyrant's rule reduces the citizens of a state. When Artegall killed Grantorto, some people who apparently felt the sting of tyranny hailed his victory with applause. But there were others who had sided with the tyrant and who " did late maintayne that Tyrant's part, with close or open ayde." These were punished by Artegall. Similarly there was a " warlike rout " which supported the tyranny of the Souldan and Adicia (8. 50). Spenser describes these people always as a vulgar, stupid lot, devoid of intelligence and a sense of decency. It is true that the Elizabethans always looked upon the Nobility as the sole repository of culture and sense and regarded the common people as boorish and dull. Spenser's ideas on this point might have been influenced by the current opinions to a certain extent; still in the legend of Justice the influence of Plato in these matters must not be lost sight of.

Plato says that the tyrant first poses to be the *protector of the people,* but when he is entrusted with power, he ruins those whom he had promised to protect against danger. "The people have always some champion whom they set over them and nurse into greatness. When he first appears above ground, he is a protector. He is not restrained from shedding the blood of kinsmen; by the favorite method of false accusation he brings them into Court and murders them, making the life of man to disappear, and with unholy tongue and lips tasting the blood of his fellow citizens; some he kills and others he banishes . . ."

The portrait of Gerioneo exactly fits in with this description. When Belge first became a widow, he offered himself as her guardian and protector and then usurped her kingdom and procured the death of her children.

The most important characteristic of Platonic Justice is harmony, while tumult is the mark of injustice. The tyrannical or the extremely unjust man is described in Book II of the *Republic.* Incontinence is the law of his being. He is ever passing through an orgy of lewdness and dissolute pleasure for which money is always necessary. And for money he is ready to " cheat and deceive," to " use force," to " plunder " and to commit the grossest " treachery." Most of these vices are to be noticed in the character of Duessa in canto 9 of the Fifth Book. She stands charged with all the offences mentioned by Plato—guile, treachery, deceit, adultery and incontinence of life and is the personification of the wildest and most tumultuous mental state darkened by passion and vice [st. 48 quoted].

This picture has to be contrasted with that of Mercilla who in opposition to Duessa is the personification of Justice. She is reserved and dignified, calm and peaceful. Her mind being unruffled by excitement or tumult of any kind, she can deal even-handed justice to all. Her court is only a visible reflection of her internal being. Awe and Order are the two guards who preserve order in it. The ladies that are in attendance upon her are Dice, Eunomie, Eirene, Reverence and, last but not least, Temperance.

Glaucon says in Book II of the *Republic* that Justice is the interest of the " strongest " and he means that immorality or wickedness can assert itself by means of sheer brute force against temperance and goodness. Socrates shows that an intemperate (*i. e.,* unjust) man is weak inwardly. His mental faculties being disobedient to reason, he cannot concentrate his powers and exert them effectively, just as a nation divided against itself cannot hold the field against a united enemy. Hence intemperate and undisciplined strength is represented in Plato by " a multitudinous, many-headed monster, having a ring of heads of all manner of beasts, tame and wild (*Republic* 9)." It has no real courage and no discretion.

Following Plato, Spenser makes his tyrants giants of physical strength. Gerioneo is actually a giant by descent and has "three double hands thrice multiplyde." Grantorto is also described as a giant "of stature huge." The Souldan, too, possesses inordinate strength. All of them fight recklessly and are defeated by the disciplined valour of men whose physical strength was decidedly inferior to theirs.

In Book II of the *Republic,* Glaucon describes in his own way what he believes to be the fate of the really just man. According to him, a prudent man ought to seem just and not to be just; for a show of justice will bring him honour and injustice in practice will yield him profit. But the truly just man who cannot make a parade of his sense of justice can have neither pecuniary gain nor the respect of his neighbors. On the contrary, "The Just man who is thought unjust will be scourged, racked, bound—will have his eyes burnt out; and at last, after suffering every kind of evil, he will be impaled." Spenser was impressed by the fate of the really just man as portrayed by Glaucon. Virtue is not always rewarded in this world and Spenser felt keenly the futility of human attempt to reward the meritorious and the deserving. This note of despondency is struck at the very beginning of the Fifth Book where Justice or Astraea is said to have left the world in disgust because the golden age had ended. Spenser's dissatisfaction is further symbolised in the fate of Artegall. The champion of Justice on his return from his adventure is assailed by the hags Envy and Detraction. Foul slander and threat of harm are his reward. His fate thus resembles that of the really Just man as depicted by Plato.

H. S. V. Jones (*A Spenser Handbook*, pp. 249-261). In Book V Spenser repeats certain details of narrative structure already noted in Books I and II. For example, early in the first canto is introduced the motif of a quest assigned by the Fairy Queen. Just as the Red Cross Knight was to rescue the land of Una from the dragon of sin, so Arthegall was assigned the task of recovering the heritage of the lady Eirena, wrongly withheld by Grantorto. The story, thus set in its course, proceeds to three *exempla* of justice, those of Sanglier, Pollente, and the giant with the scales. These, one should note as marking here a characteristic difference of structure, are, unlike the corresponding *exempla* of temperance in Book II, in no way connected with the objective or subsequent developments of the plot. Reverting to the Florimell story in canto 3 Spenser turns that very pointedly to the account of his ethical theme by giving prominence to the punishment of Braggadocchio; but here again, as in the following story of the two brethren, there is no effort to weave this thread of narrative interest into the subsequent action of the book. So far we have but a set of *exempla* connected only by the person of Arthegall and unified only by their common theme. Nor is there any attempt, as in Books III and IV, to pattern the story by studied parallelism and contrast.

This highly episodic arrangement of rather more than the first fourth of Book V gives way in canto 5 to the continuous narrative interest of the Arthegall-Radigund-Britomart story, which, like the Florimell episode, resumes an earlier theme. But so far as Book V is concerned it is quite independent of what precedes or follows. Occupying about the same space as the purely episodic section of the book, the poet's moral intention does not here encroach to an equal extent upon his art. After being introduced by the rescue of Terpine, the story passes to the defeat and rescue of Arthegall, developing a romantic interest in the Clarin incident and providing a complication in Dolon's plot against Britomart.   As emphasizing the independence of this part of Book V we should note further that Arthur, though very prominent in the last division of the book, does not here rescue the hero, and that Britomart's separation from Arthegall after she has liberated him from Radigund is very weakly motivated.

Rather more than half of the book having been thus divided into two distinct sections, the last five cantos are as sharply marked off for the exploits of Arthur and Arthegall.   More fully than in any previous book Arthur here coöperates with the titular hero.   Together they slay the Soudan and capture Guile in cantos 8 and 9.   Then, as in Book II, canto 9, Arthur and Guyon go together to the House of Temperance, so here in a corresponding canto Arthur and Arthegall accompany each other to Mercilla's palace; and Arthur champions Mercilla as in the earlier book he had championed Alma.   Such correspondences might suggest that Spenser had at one time in mind a structure for the fifth book similar to that which he has followed in Book II, but that the necessity of continuing the Britomart story and the exigencies of the political allegory resulted in more patchwork arrangement than we find in any other book of the *Faerie Queene*.

Spenser's account of Justice follows the main lines of Aristotle's analysis of the virtue in Book V of the *Nicomachean Ethics*.   In chapter 3 of this Book Aristotle defines Justice as complete virtue, not, to be sure, "in an absolute sense, but in relation to one's neighbours."   It is "more glorious than the star of eve or dawn."   Some such comprehensive sense, Spenser may have had in mind in the opening lines of the first stanza of canto 7.

> Nought is on earth more sacred or divine,
> That gods and men doe equally adore,
> Then this same vertue that doth right define.

In the Greek sense of the term any wrong action may be called unjust; e. g., acts of cowardice or anger.   It is interesting to note that Spenser shares with Aristotle one illustration of this point,—the cowardice of the man who throws away his shield in battle (Aristotle 5. 4 and *F. Q.* canto 9, st. 46).

But clearly the poet is particularly interested in justice understood as "a part of virtue"; and this, following Aristotle, he divides into distributive and corrective justice. . . .

While conceding (Chapter 6) that the standards of merit will vary with the government, the democrats setting up freedom as their standard, the oligarchs wealth or nobility, and the aristocrats virtue, Aristotle, and Spenser following him, sides with the aristocrats.   These were entitled by virtue of their native nobility to the wealth, powers, and privileges that churls would wrest from them.   Inimical to the existing social order, which Spenser believed was divinely appointed by God, were not only the forces of violence and corruption but also the misguided social idealists, who, like the Anabaptists of Munster, would create a society embodying subversive ideas of liberty, fraternity, and equality.   Dealing with the subject in the third chapter of the third book of his *Governour*, Sir Thomas Elyot

wrote: "The inferior persone or subjecte aught to consider, that all be it (as I
have spoken) he in the substance of soule and body be equall with his superior,
yet for als moche as the powars and qualities of the soule and body, with the disposition of reason, be not in every man equall, therfore God ordayned a diversitie
or preeminence in degrees to be amonge men for the necessary derection and
preservation of them in conformitie of livinge." If we think that the instinct of
beasts whereby they choose governors and leaders is reasonable, "how farre out
of reason shall we judge them to be that wolde exterminate all superiorietie,
extincte all governaunce and lawes, and under the coloure of holy scripture, whiche
they do violently wraste to their purpose, do endeavour them selves to bryng the
life of man in to a confusion inevitable." Quite similar views Spenser might
have met with in his master Chaucer, who has his Parson say: "But for-as-muche
as the estaat of hooly chirche ne myghte not hav be, ne the commune profit myghte
not hav be kept, ne pees and reste in erthe, but if God hadde ordeyned that some
men hadde hyer degre and som men lower, therfore was sovereyntee ordeyned to
kepe and mayntene and deffende hire underlynges or hire subgetz, in resoun, as
ferforth as it lith in hire power, and not to destroyen hem ne confounde."

These ideas of distributive justice Spenser has illustrated in the two episodes
that constitute the second canto of the fifth book. The story of Pollente and
Lady Munera deals with the acquisition of wealth by the wicked through deceit
and violence. As Pollente symbolizes power, his daughter Munera, like the Lady
Mede of *Piers Plowman,* represents bribery and the forces of corruption. In contrast with the true nobility founded upon virtue, Pollente is a *parvenu,* a *nouveau
riche,*

> Having great lordships got and goodly farmes,
> Through strong oppression of his power extort.

His daughter, too, has wrongfully amassed so much wealth that she is richer than
many princes and, a land grabber, she

> purchast all the countrey lying ny
> With the revenue of her plenteous meedes.

No doubt, as has been suggested, the prototype of such a family Spenser could
easily have found in Ireland. In the second episode of the Giant with the scales
the poet passes from a practical to a theoretical treatment of his subject. If the
economic doctrine which Spenser has here in mind is Communism, the doctrine
illustrated in Plato's *Republic,* Sir Thomas More's *Utopia,* and the social experiment of the Anabaptists in Munster, he evidently misunderstands that which he
undertakes to condemn. The giant on the rock argues for the equalization of
property, not for the ownership of all property by the state. Rejecting the Aristotelian principle of proportionate distribution, explained above, the giant, speaking for the many-headed multitude, would reduce all things "unto equality." As
in the former episode the poet attacked the newer aristocracy of wealth and power,
here he assails the "vulgar," the "rascall crew," who gather about the visionary
social reformer as do "foolish flies about an hony crocke." The only answers
made by Spenser to the advocates of democratic principles, such as the pamphle-
teer Robert Crowley, who lived in the poet's time, is that the established order
was divinely appointed and that the proposed reforms are contrary to the principle

of the golden mean.   Forgetting perhaps the July eclogue, Spenser can write in
stanza 41;

> The hils doe not the lowly dales disdaine;
> The dales doe not the lofty hils envy.

For his social philosophy, he would argue, he can find a divine sanction.   But
it is Aristotle of whom he is thinking when in stanza 49 he writes;—

> it was not the right which he did seeke;
> But rather strove extremities to way,
> Th'one to diminish, th'other for to eeke:
> For of the meane he greatly did misleeke.

The logic of this contention should be referred to the seventh chapter of the fifth
book of the *Nicomachean Ethics*.   "That which is proportionate," says Aristotle,
"is a mean, and that which is just is proportionate"; and, further on, we read,
"disproportion may take the form either of excess or defect; and this is actually
the case, for the author of the injustice has too much, and the victim has too little,
of the good."   Evidently for both Aristotle and Spenser equalization implies disproportion, and is therefore contrary to the golden mean.

If we turn now from distributive to corrective justice, we shall find that Spenser follows Aristotle in discriminating between the unjust and the unfair, or
between law and equity.   In the fourteenth chapter of the fifth book of the *Nicomachean Ethics*, Aristotle declares that justice and equity "are not absolutely the
same, nor generically different"; and, further on, that "while that which is equit-
able is just, it is not just in the eye of the law, but is a rectification of legal justice.
And the reason is that all law is couched in general terms, but there are some
cases upon which it is impossible to pronounce correctly in general terms."

To equity as to distributive justice Spenser gives both general and particular
treatment.   The particular case is the story of the two brothers in canto 4, to
whom the sea brings respectively land and treasure.   Here, again, as in the theory
of society set forth in canto 2, the case is referred to the tribunal of God.   That
which, acting through the forces of nature, God has brought about, must be right;
as it is right that there should be hills and valleys, princes and peasants.

The theoretical statement of the principle of equity here involved is implicit
in the symbolism of canto 7.   Here Isis stands for "that part of justice which is
equity" (7. 3), and, further, as we gather from stanzas 15 and 22, she represents
Britomart herself, while the crocodile, standing for Osiris, is also a symbol of
Arthegall.   The whole relationship, then, between Britomart and Arthegall is here
conceived in terms of that between equity and justice, and equity is understood
as involving clemency [st. 22 quoted].

The vice corresponding to this virtue of clemency, as Seneca pointed out in
the *De Clementia*, is *misericordia* or pity, and it is this infirmity which has brought
about the downfall of Arthegall in canto 5, as it was almost the undoing of Sir
Guyon during his journey to the Bower of Bliss.   Having overcome Radigund
and unlaced her helmet, he is astonished by her beauty [st. 13 quoted].

Just as the defect of clemency is pity, so the vice corresponding to the firmness,
the *severitas* of the upright judge, is *crudelitas* or barbarity.   *Misericordia* and
crudelitas Seneca describes as vices of the mind, a leaning, on the one hand, to

weak pity and, on the other, to savageness. True justice, then, as here understood, is what Aristotle calls a state, or as Spenser says in canto 2, stanza 47:

> But in the mind the doome of right must bee.

Such a view of equity, or of the relation between mercy and justice, Spenser
might have found expressed in the literature of his own time. It was, indeed,
often invoked to support a philosophy of tolerance. In England not only Lord
Bacon and Hooker but Gabriel Harvey, the poet's friend, reasoned against the
intolerance of extremists. Hooker's intention in his *Ecclesiastical Polity* was "not
to provoke any but rather to satisfy all tender consciences"; and Bacon recommended that every one in those troubled times should be "swift to hear, slow to
speak, slow to wrath." Writing in a similar vein in his *Pierces Supererogation*,
Harvey counseled a following of Aristotle's doctrine of the golden mean; for "it
is neither the Excess, nor the Defect, but the Meane, that edifyeth." In France
quite similar views were expressed by Michel de l'Hôpital, the author of the *Traité
de la Reformation de Justice*, and Jean Bodin, who wrote among other works the
Six Livres de la République. "Never," says de l'Hôpital, "under the pretext of
mercy should we work injustice, nor under the protection of a harsh and severe
justice should we be guilty of any cruelty." In the opinion of Bodin the proper
temper of the magistrate may be described as "gravité douce."

Evidently Spenser in his "Legend of Justice" has represented this doctrine as
the ideal of his Queen. The very name Mercilla, here assigned Elizabeth, makes
the matter clear; and among those attending upon her throne are wise Eunomie,
mild Eirene, and "goodly Temperance in garments clene." In the very act of
enforcing justice she was "ruing" the "wilful fall" of Duessa. In another
passage the queen, Mercilla, is described as holding in her royal hand a sceptre
which is

> The sacred pledge of peace and clemencie,
> With which High God had blest her happie land,
> Maugre so many foes which did withstand.
> But at her feet her sword was likewise layde,
> Whose long rest rusted the bright steely brand;
> Yet when as foes enforst, or friends sought ayde,
> She could it sternely draw, that all the world dismayde.

In his consideration of corrective justice Aristotle, as already noted, had distinguished voluntary from involuntary transactions. The former are voluntary
because "the origin of these transactions is voluntary"; i. e., "people enter upon
them of their own free will"; and the examples given by Aristotle are various
forms of business transactions that would be covered nowadays by business law.
An example of this type of justice is offered once more by the case of the two
brothers, whose story begins with the bequests contained in the will of their father.
On the other hand, Aristotle's so-called involuntary transactions, whether secret or
violent, are naturally not overlooked in Spenser's allegory. Theft, here listed by
Aristotle, is illustrated in the story of Guyon's horse stolen by Braggadocchio, and
false witness, another item in Aristotle's list, by

> That false Duessa, which had wrought great care
> And mickle mischiefe unto many a knight,
> By her beguyled and confounded quight;

and plots of assassination by the tale of Dolon and his trap-door in canto 6. Of the items in Aristotle's list of examples of violent injustice Spenser has illustrated murder in the story of Sanglier, both imprisonment and contumelious treatment in the episode of Arthegall and Radigund, and slander in the episode of the hags and the Blatant Beast in canto 12.

In the thought of Jean Bodin we may find a parallel not only for Spenser's philosophy of justice but also for those views on the "woman question" which occupy so considerable a part of the fifth book. Opposed to the idealism of the third book and contrary to the views expressed by Plato and Sir Thomas More, Spenser here takes a position with which John Knox, the author of the *First Blast of the Trumpet against the Monstrous Regiment of Women,* might have agreed. Like Knox, he must have had in mind such dominant women as Margaret of Parma, Catherine de' Medici, Mary Queen of Scots, and her mother, Mary of Lorraine. As representative of the class he sets up Radegund, opposing to her Britomart, in whom had been focussed the feminine idealism of the "Legend of Chastity." The poet comments upon the type in the twenty-fifth stanza of the fifth canto [quoted]. Taking a similar position, Bodin had written in the *Republic:* "There has never been either law or custom which has exempted women from the obedience and reverence which they owe to their husbands"; again, "there is nothing greater in this world, as Euripides says, nor more necessary for the conservation of republics, than obedience of the wife to her husband."

If, seeking further light upon Spenser's ideal of justice, we turn now, as we have done before, to Cicero's *De Officiis,* we may find grounds for disagreeing with Dr. Gough in his opinion that in canto 5 Arthegall's "symbolic rôle is so far forgotten that he seizes on a prospect of escape in spite of his parole, and encourages Clarinda's passion with ambiguous compliments and 'faire semblant.'" Cicero might have judged otherwise, since he writes in the tenth chapter of the first book of the *De Officiis:* "Justice is altered by an alteration of circumstances. Further, it is plain to any one's sense that such sort of promises can never be binding as are made by people overawed by fear, or overreached by deceit." Since Spenser gives much attention to the relation between justice and deceit, let us note, further, the following passage in the thirteenth chapter of the same treatise: "In fine to close up this discourse of justice, . . . there are two ways or methods whereby one may injure or oppress another; the one is fraud and subtlety, the other open force and violence; the former of which is esteemed the part of a fox, and the latter of a lion; both of them certainly very unworthy of a reasonable creature, though fraud, I think, is the more odious of the two. But of all injustice, theirs is certainly of the deepest dye, who make it their business to appear honest men, even whilst they are practising the greatest of villanies."

B. E. C. DAVIS (*Edmund Spenser,* pp. 122-4). The entry of Artegall is prepared at greater length and with more flourish than that of any other character. He is first mentioned by Guyon to Arthur just before they reach the House of Alma as one of the most famous of Gloriana's knights. His image inspires Britomart throughout her adventures and he appears in three out of the six completed books. Yet for all this, and partly because of it, the "salvage knight" of Britomart's young dreams is less convincing than any of his fellows. Whereas the latter are represented as human personalities distinguished by traits appropriate to the allegory, Artegall is either Lord Grey or simply abstract Justice personified. For exercise " in justice law " Astræa at first appointed him to arbitrate in disputes between the beasts of the forest; but this part of his career, which might have made a good story, is dismissed in a few stanzas, and we meet him already an accomplished justiciar, inspiring terror rather than affection [1. 8 quoted].

The part he plays is by no means so impressive as the brave words promise. At his first encounter with Britomart, after a preliminary success at Satyrane's tournament, he is badly worsted. He prefers preaching to action, leaving the heavier responsibilities to Talus whom on more than one occasion he most ungallantly sends in advance (2. 20).

> to invent
> Which way he enter might *without endangerment,*

and who is generally called off in the name of mercy when the field has already become a shambles. The achievement of his task—the rescue of Irena—is protracted beyond endurance. Deprived, for the first time, of the help of Talus he succumbs to Radigund, and after being ignominiously rescued from a woman by a woman he goes his way (7. 45),

> ne ever howre did cease
> Till he redeemed had that Lady thrall.

Yet he finds time to engage with Arthur, to play the lesser part in an intrigue for entrapping the Soldan, to stand by whilst Talus tackles Guile and at Samient's request to tarry for an indefinite period at the court of Mercilla. His self-reproach is indeed well founded (11. 41):

> "Too much am I to blame for that faire Maide,
> That have her drawne to all this troublous strife,
> Through promise to afford her timely aide,
> Which by default I have not yet defraide";

and we cannot but recognise a certain poetic justice in the fate that condemns him, after his long-delayed battle with Grantorto, to return to Gloriana with nothing but the insults of Envy and Detraction to reward him for his pains.

His supernatural endowments likewise ill became a champion of heroic virtue. It might have been supposed that Chrysaor, the traditional sword of justice which nothing can withstand, would have sufficed. But Chrysaor is almost negligible in comparison with the astounding " iron groom," Talus. The pseudo-Platonic *Minos* makes mention of one Talus appointed by Minos to travel thrice a year throughout Crete, bearing the brazen tables of the law and on this account surnamed " the Brazen." Apollonius Rhodius comes nearer Spenser in speaking of the same Talus as " made of brass and invulnerable." The tower of Dunother, in *Huon of Bordeaux,* is guarded by two men of brass, each holding an iron flail. But neither authority nor the demands of allegory can palliate the offence of admitting this grotesque automaton, Thor with his hammer but without his humour, upon the shores of old romance. Talus is a very affront to the hero's dignity, a lapse on the part of Spenser that can only be attributed to waning power.

APPENDIX II

HISTORICAL ALLEGORY

T. BIRCH (*Life of Mr. Edmund Spenser*, pp. xxxv-xxxvi). In this Poem are many Allusions to particular Characters and Actions in the Reign of Queen Elizabeth, which is figuratively represented in the Fifth Book under the Virtue of Justice. That Queen, who in other Parts of the Poem, appears under the Character of the Queen of Fairy Land, is there describ'd under the Name of Mercilla, sending Relief to Belge or the Netherlands, and reducing the tyrannical Power of Geryoneo, or Spain. The Tryal of the Queen of Scots is shadow'd in the Ninth Canto. Sir Philip Sidney is generally allow'd to be meant by Prince Arthur, as Sir Burbon was undoubtedly intended to characterise Henry IV. of France, the Genius of which Country is express'd by the Lady Flourdelis.

UPTON (*A Letter concerning a new Edition of Spenser's Faerie Queene*, pp. 6-9). The Lion attends on Mercilla (5. 9. 33. 3-4)

> Whylest underneath her feete, thereas she sate,
> An huge great Lyon lay.

Mercilla is plainly Queen Elizabeth, and the Lady brought to the bar, is Mary Queen of the Scots (st. 38). Her two paramours, faithlesse Blandamour and Paridell (st. 41) are the Earls of Northumberland and Westmorland. The poet tries to apologize for his Faery Queene's conduct towards this unfortunate prisoner; but his Faery Queene was—a Woman.

In some places of his poem Spenser has given us the names themselves, lest we might mistake him. Thus he mentions Sir Bourbon (5. 11. 52) meaning Henry King of Navarre, who was excluded the crown of France because a protestant, and hence (st. 44), " In dangerous distress of a rude rout."

The Lady Flourdelis is the Genius of France. Bourbon in the encounter with the rabble rout, i. e. his rebellious subjects, flings away his shield, and thus becomes a recreant Knight ("Relicta non bene parmula": this being the greatest mark of infamy in a warriour) i. e. He leaves the protestant religion, and in lieu of it gains the crown (5. 12. 2. 3-4),

> The love of lordships and of lands
> Made him become most faithless and unsound.

However the Genius of his country, the Lady Flourdelis, still looks on him as a recreant Knight; notwithstanding she is forced to admit him (5. 11. 64), " So bore her quite away, nor well nor ill apaid."

Nor less visible is the Episode of Belge (5. 10. 6):

> There came two Springals (The Marquess of Hauree and Adolph
>   Metherk) of full tender years,
> Farre thence from forrein land, where they did dwell,
> To seek for succour of her and her peares,

299

complaining of the afflicted state of the Netherlands, and desiring help from Queen Elizabeth against the Tyranny of the King of Spain. Prince Arthur, i. e. Sir Philip Sidney, undertakes this adventure. . . .

'Tis traditional (whether from the poet himself I never could learn) that Prince Arthur represents Sir Philip Sydney. But were it not for this tradition, I should be inclined to believe the Earl of Leicester imaged under this faery knight: 'twas the Earl of Leicester, who made that great figure in the Netherlands; 'twas he whom Queen Elizabeth even encouraged in his addresses to her: and if we judge too from his Character, he wanted this present from the Redcross Knight, much more than Sir Philip Sydney. . . .

In the fifth book of the *Faery Queene,* Irene becomes a suppliant for succour against an oppressive tyrant: and for this enterprise Arthegall is chosen. Is not Irene the same as Ierne, Ireland? And who can Arthegall be, but Arthur Lord Grey of Wilton, Lord Lieutenant of Ireland; who drove the Spaniards from thence, and was successful against the rebels? The detraction and envy he met with, is finely described by our poet at the end of the twelfth and last Canto. This tribute of praise Spenser could not well help paying him, as he was his Secretary. Lest too we should miss the application, his arms are blazoned in allusion to his name (*F. Q.* 3. 2. 25):

> His crest was covered with a couchant hownd,
> And all his armour seem'd of antique mould,
> But wond'rous massy and assured sownd,
> And round about yfretted all with gold,
> In which there written was with cyphers old,
> Achilles armes which Arthegall did win.
> And on his shield enveloped sevenfold
> He bore a crowned little Ermilin,
> That deckt the asure field with her fayre pouldred skin.

"Griseum," in the barbarous Latin age, signified fine furr, or "Ermin." "Griseum, Grisium, pellis animalis cujusdam, quod vulgo Vair Gelli appellant," etc., Car. du Fresne. Chaucer, picturing the dress of the Monk, in the Prologue to the *Canterbury Tales,* says (193-4)

> I see his sleves purfiled at the hand
> With grys, and that the finest in the land.

i. e. I see his sleeves at his handwrists fringed with the finest furr or ermin that could be procured. . . .

The Crest likewise of the Knight's helmet was a gray hound, ready to spring on his prey. His name too Arthegall corresponds with his Christian name Arthur; and means here "Arthur's peer."

JOHN UPTON (*Spenser's Faerie Queene,* 2. 633-5). The historical allusions in this book are so very apparent, that the most superficial readers of Spenser never could mistake them, because he mentions the very names. But I wonder that they stopped here, and did not pursue the hint, which the poet had given them. (2. Pr. 4):

Of Faery lond yet if he more inquire,
By certaine signes here set in sundry place,
He may it find; ne let him then admire,
But yield his sense to be too blunt and base,
That n'ote without an hound fine footing trace.

. . . Let us trace out the episode of Belge, "There came two springalls (viz. the Marquis of Hauree and Adelph Metkerk. See Cambden [*History of Elizabeth*], p. 221, anno 1577.) Farre thence from forrein land (from the Netherlands) where they did dwell, To seeke for succour of her (Q. Elizabeth) and her peeres." The Briton prince, in whom I think imaged the Earl of Leicester, undertakes to deliver Belge from the cruelties of Geryoneo, i. e. the K. of Spain. . . . Mercilla is plainly Q. Elizabeth; the lady brought to the bar, Mary Q. of Scots; "the sage old sire that had to name"

The kingdom's care with a white silver head,

means the lord treasurer Burleigh: Spenser by some former poems had brought himself into this mighty man's displeasure, 6. 12. 41. He now seems glad to curry favour; and methinks goes a little out of his way in making himself a party-man by abusing the memory of this unhappy Queen.—But this is foreign to my design; let us return to our history. The two paramours of Duessa, the Q. of Scots, are Blandamour and Paridell, i. e. the Earls of Northumberland and Westmorland. Blandamour is the Earl of Northumberland, because the poet calls him, The Hotspurre youth, 1. 35. This was the well-known name given to the young Percy in the reign of King Henry IV. And is not this speaking out, as plain as the nature of this kind of poetry admits? Paridell is the Earl of Northumberland: Arthegal, I am thoroughly persuaded, is Arthur Lord Grey of Wilton, Lord Deputy of Ireland, our poet's patron. His military and vigorous executions against the rebels in Ireland, brought upon him a load of envy and detraction, when he came back to England: and this is very plainly hinted at in the close of the 12th Canto. (Compare Cambden, pp. 243 and 257, anno 1580, and Lloyd's *State Worthies*, in the life of Arthur Grey Baron of Wilton.) These circumstances are a strong proof that Ireland, agreeable to this kind of prosopopoeia, is shadowed out to us by Irena. With this hint given, read and apply the following verses, 12. 40.

And that bright sword the sword of justice lent,
Had stained with reproachful crueltie,
In guiltlesse blood of many an innocent.

"The sword of justice," i. e. according to the fable, the sword of gold given him by Astraea; according to the moral, the sword he received as Lord Deputy of Ireland, and the ensign of his command.

But I have still farther proofs: for what is Irena, but Ierna, a kingdom or state that stands in need of succour, as much as Belge? See likewise how the situation of the Island is pointed out, 6. 7.

She to a window came that opened west
Towards which coast her love his way addrest.

i. e. (in the historical view) Arthegal was going towards Ireland, which lay west of England. See likewise 12. 3

> To the sea shore he gan his way apply.

And, 12. 26, he calls it a ragged common-weale; as certainly it was, distracted with civil wars, and torn in pieces with perpetual rebellions, fomented by the K. of Spain, and the Pope.

If any should think that Irena means Peace in general, his interpretation might seem to be countenanc'd by the old quarto; which in one place (viz. 1. 4.) spells it Eirena. But this is the same name with the fair lady that attends Mercilla's throne, in 9. 32. And in all other places 'tis spelt Irena, or Irene; and so perpetually in all the Folio editions.

Old Sir Sergis, I take to be Walsingham. The K. of Spain is imaged in the son of Geryon. 10. 8, in the soldan, 8. 28. and in Grandtorto. The seneschal in 10. 30 seems the Duke of Alva.

Will it appear too refining, if we suppose that the Sarazin Pollente, with his trap-falls, and his groome of evil guize, hence named Guizor (2. 6) alludes to Charles the IXth. K. of France, "who by sleights did underfong them?" If this is allowed, who can help applying the name of Guizor, to the head of the Popish league, and chief persecutor, the Duke of Guise? And to carry on still this allusion, what is all that plot laid in the dead of night, by the same sort of miscreants, to murder the British virgin (6. 27.) but a type of that plot laid against the chief of the British, as well as other protestant noblemen, "that being thus brought into the net, both they, and with them the evangelical religion, might with one stroke, if not have their throats cut, yet at least receive a mortal wound" (Cambden, p. 187) a plot, which though not fully accomplished, yet ended in a massacre, and was begun at midnight, at a certain signal given, on the eve of St. Bartholomew, anno 1572.

What shall we say of the tilts and tourneyments at the spousal of fair Florimel? Had the poet his eye on those tiltings, performed at a vast expence, by the Earl of Arundel, Lord Windsor, Sir Philip Sidney, and Sir Fulk Grevil, who challenged all comers; and which were intended to entertain the French nobility, and the ambassadors, who came to treat of Anjou's marriage with the queen? (See Cambden, p. 265.) Methinks I sometimes see a faint resemblance between Braggadochio and the Duke of Anjou, and their buffoon servants, Trompart and Simier.

In the 5th Canto Arthegal is imprisoned by an Amazonian dame, called by a French name Radigund; for Radegonda was a famous queen of France. Now as Spenser carries two faces under one hood, and means more always than in plain words he tells you; why, I say, does he who writes in a "continued allegory," give you this episode, if there is not more meant than what the dull letter contains? The story, I think, is partly moral, but chiefly historical, and alludes to Arthegal's father being taken prisoner in France; who almost ruin'd his patrimony to pay his ransom. (See Cambden, p. 68; and Lloyd's life of Arthur Grey, Baron of Wilton.) 'Tis not at all foreign to the nature of this poem to mix family histories, and unite them in one person.

In the 9th Canto we read of a wicked villain which "wonned in a rocke," and pilfered the country all around: he is named Malengine, from his mischievous disposition. Is not this robber a type of those rebels, who had taken their refuge in Glandilough, "beset round about with craggy rocks, and a steep downfal, and with trees and thickets of wood, the paths and crossways whereof are scarce known to the dwellers there abouts" (Cambden, p. 241. Compare 9. 6.) This villain is destroyed without mercy or remorse, as the rebels were with their accomplices, 9. 19:

> Crying in vain for help, when help was past.

But if the reader has a mind to see how far types and symbols may be carried, I refer him to my own note on 8. 45 [sts. 30-45 in the Commentary].

And upon a review of what is here offered relating to historical allusions, if the reader thinks my arguments too flimsy, and extended beyond their due limits, and should laugh

> To see their thrids so thin, as spyders frame,
> And eke so short, that seem'd their ends out shortly came,

I would desire him to consider what latitude of interpretation all typical and symbolical writings admit; and that this poem is full of historical allusions, as the poet hints in many places.

EDWIN GREENLAW ("Spenser and British Imperialism," pp. 351-370). In the fifth book we have no longer the personified virtues and vices of mediaeval allegory, everything being subordinated to the treatment of problems of government. The book as a whole bears on the three crucial events in the reign of Elizabeth prior to the collision with Spain in 1588: the suppression of the rebellion in Ireland, fomented as it was by the policy of Philip; the trial and execution of Mary, also a necessary step in repelling Spanish aggression; and the direct attack on Spain through intervention in the Netherlands. The theme of the book is the necessity for the exercise of imperial power to the utmost in putting down rebellion active and incipient, the right of a strong nation to aid an oppressed and suffering people, and, in some minor passages, the right of England to establish an empire beyond the seas. The method of the book is to tell, by means of incidents suitable to a metrical romance, the story of Grey's experience in Ireland; to present from two points of view a defense of Elizabeth's execution of her rival; and to relate the experience of Leicester in the Low Countries. But deeper than this allegorical treatment of contemporary events lies the exposition of a theory of government that makes the book one of the most remarkable productions of its time.

The greatest space is given to the Irish problem. Irena (Ireland) must be delivered from Grantorto (Spain) by that queen whose glory it was to aid all suppliants and to be the patron of all weak princes (1. 4). Artegall, who represents Justice united with sovereign Power, on this occasion personified by Lord Grey, is deputed for the task. Then follows a series of incidents by which Spenser gives a vivid picture of the wretchedness of the country. The Squire mourning over the headless trunk of his love is a symbol of the woe wrought by murder and lawlessness (1. 13-30). The story of the Saracen and his daughter Munera (2. 1-28) illustrates the evils of bribery and corruption in government. How directly this applied is revealed not only in Spenser's prose tract but in many of the letters and documents of the period. In the larger conception of the problem of government, it represents something more serious than lawlessness. Bragga-docchio, who claims the victory really won by Artegall (3. 14-15, 20-22), repre-sents those who by defamation of others and by self-seeking aim at securing credit not rightfully theirs. Here the historical reference seems to be to the quarrels among the English leaders in 1580; they plotted against each other, sought to thwart all plans for progress, and sent to England letters filled with petty jealousy and malice (*Carew Papers*, Feb., 1581). The larger significance of the story, including the account of the way in which all the people and even the knights themselves were unable to distinguish between the true Florimel and the false, is to show the danger to the government from men who are selfish and unscrupulous, a danger increased from the fact that the crowd does not accurately judge between merit and pretense. To enforce this distrust of the crowd (*vulgus*), Spenser introduces by way of parenthesis or interlude the story of the giant with scales (2. 30 ff.), showing that socialistic theories of property and democracy are vain.

Spenser now discusses the paramount right of the sovereign over all subjects (cantos 4 ff.). The historical material is drawn from the events in the north from the uprising of the earls to the execution of Mary. The incident of the two broth-ers who quarrel over the treasure chest cast on the shore by the waves is somewhat obscure (4. 4-20). At first sight, it is but another of the minor incidents scat-tered through the book to illustrate the simplicity of justice; other examples being the interesting modification of the judgment of Solomon, where Artegall discerns which of two knights truly loves a woman by proposing to cut her in half and give each a portion (1. 25-26); the decision as to the true and the false Florimel (3. 22-24); and the awarding of the horse to Guyon (3. 35). But the incident is apparently founded on fact, since it refers, I believe, to the story of Northum-berland's claim of treasure cast ashore in his jurisdiction in 1560, and possibly also to his claiming of the custody of Mary on the ground that she had landed in his territory (Pollard, *Polit. Hist. of Eng.*, 1547-1603, 278 ff.). In 1566 Parlia-ment refused to sanction the Queen's claim to minerals wherever they might be found, thus recognizing Northumberland's objections to the attempt of the Queen to mine copper at Keswick (*ibid.*, 282). Spenser probably means to assert the right of the Queen to lands, leavings of the sea, which had been discovered by her mariners, and the passage should be compared with his defense of Raleigh's projected expedition to Guiana (4. 11. 22) and with the references, in *Colin Clout*, to Elizabeth as the Queen and to Raleigh as the Shepherd of the Ocean.

In the episode of Radigund, the great rebellion of the earls is again made use of, this time through the fact that Grey was concerned in it in some degree. Apparently Spenser attributes Grey's sympathy for Mary to the influence on him of her personal beauty (5. 12, 6. 1, 8. 1). By far the most interesting aspect of the case, however, is the application to Ireland. It will be remembered that Arte-gall, disarmed by the beauty of Radigund, is made to assume the dress of a woman and to perform the menial tasks of a woman (5. 23-25; 7. 37-41). With this should be compared the sad state of Turpine, found by Artegall in the power of women, his hands tied behind his back (4. 22). Here we have an arraignment of womanish methods applied to the solution of the Irish problem; Artegall clad in woman's garments and with a distaff in his hand is a fit representative, says Spenser, of the course advised by some.

The story of Samient (8) introduces more specifically the attempts of Philip to undermine the power of Elizabeth. She represents Ireland, and serves Mercilla, who represents Elizabeth's gentleness and mercy as Britomart represents her might. Mercilla is in danger from the machinations of a mighty man [sts. 18-9]

> That with most fell despight and deadly hate
> Seekes to subvert her Crowne and dignity,
> And all his power doth thereunto apply. . . .
>
> Ne him sufficeth all the wrong and ill
> Which he unto her people does each day;
> But that he seekes by traytrous traines to spill
> Her person, and her sacred selfe to slay:
> That, O ye Heavens, defend! and turne away
> From her unto the miscreant himselfe;
> That neither hath religion nor fay,
> But makes his God of his ungodly pelfe,
> And Idols serves: so let his Idols serve the Elfe!

Here is a pretty accurate picture of Philip: his secret plotting against England; his trust in his riches, an allusion to the vast stores of gold secured from the American voyages; his idolatry. The Saracens sent to destroy Samient represent the Spanish expeditions designed to wrest Ireland from England, one of which Grey destroyed at Smerwick. The triumph of Arthur over the Soldan prophesies the end of Philip.

The allegory is continued in the next canto in the account of the capture of Guile, described like one of the wretched outcasts that continually warred on the English in Ireland (9. 8-11); his den, his flight, his many changes of form (9. 12-19) give a vivid picture of the difficulties encountered by those who tried to stamp out the rebellion of the natives. It is noticeable that neither here nor in the story of Irena, nor, indeed, in any of the tracts dealing with the subject do we find Ireland identified with these outcast natives. To Spenser and his contemporaries Ireland is the fair realm to be made fit for habitation as a part of the English domain; the "wild Irish" do not enter into the calculation except as they may benefit by the peace that is to follow the subjugation of the rebellious chiefs and the casting-out of Spain. But in England itself would the lower classes have received a whit the more consideration in Spenser's time? And what of Fielding's and Goldsmith's accounts of the miseries of the poor and the injustice which they found in the courts and prisons of the eighteenth century? And Dickens? Why pour vials of wrath on Spenser's head for not being two or three centuries in advance of his time in respect to the doctrine of the equality of men?

The object of this lengthy analysis of the political allegory in the fifth book has been to show how admirable is Spenser's method and how complete his interpretation of contemporary history. The remaining cantos, dealing for the most part with the execution of Mary and the intervention in the Netherlands, require no special treatment; their excellence is apparent to any reader. There is, for example, the brilliant apology for the execution of Mary. In the seventh canto,

Britomart, representing Elizabeth as the sovereign power of the nation, slays Radigund (Mary the seducer) without compunction; in the ninth, Mercilla, queenly but gentle and merciful, reluctantly passes judgment upon Duessa. Again, Prince Arthur, personifying the nation as distinct from the sovereign power, is at first inclined in Mary's favor, but is convinced by the evidence against her that no other course is possible. Artegall is no longer Lord Grey, but the Justice and Power that accompany sovereignty, unswayed by prejudice, and really sentences Duessa to death, because Mercilla

> Though plaine she saw, by all that she did heare,
> That she of death was guiltie found by right,
> Yet would not let just vengeance on her light;
> But rather let, instead thereof, to fall
> Few perling drops from her faire lampes of light;
> The which she covering with her purple pall
> Would have the passion hid, and up arose withall.

The Legend of Justice is a charming romance, and its moral allegory, less academic and symmetrical than that of the first book, answers to the fondness of the Renaissance for the epic of the perfect man. But it is much more. The most important events in the history of Elizabeth's development of a powerful government are treated, not badly and incoherently as in the chronicles, but in an allegory that unifies and interprets. It is not of our modern type of philosophical history any more than it is modern chronicle, but it illustrates in a high degree that Renaissance tendency to interpret life by means of symbols so apparent in its sonnet, pastoral, novel, and epic. Finally, it possesses a higher interest even than these. The Renaissance created the State; it also produced many treatises on the theory of the State. In England this new interest was manifested not only in such books as *Utopia* or the *Boke of the Governour,* or in the translations of Machiavelli and collections of similar political axioms, but also in romances like *Arcadia* and the fifth book of the *Faerie Queene.* Fulke Greville says of Sidney's purpose in writing his novel: "In all these creatures of his making his intent and scope was to turn the barren Philosophy precepts into pregnant Images of life . . . lively to represent the growth, state, and declination of Princes." This comes very near anticipating Bolingbroke's famous saying, "History is Philosophy teaching by example," and both these aphorisms apply with surprising accuracy to this Legend of Justice. The whole book treats of the danger to England from Spanish aggression; of the need of centralization of power in the sovereign coupled with the inflexible manifestation of that power in dealing with plot and rebellion; and of the right of the Queen to rule the seas and to interfere in behalf of the oppressed people of the Netherlands. Each minor adventure leads toward the climax in the triumph of authority, showing how lawlessness, bribery, selfish quarreling and jealousy among the leaders, the danger from womanish theories of mildness, all contribute to thwart the purposes of the ministers of the sovereign. The story of Ireland's thraldom is twice told, in the accounts of Samient and of Irena; the might of the Queen and the awakened spirit of England combine to free her. Again, the story of Mary's fall is twice told, with consummate skill in its representation of Elizabeth as the personification of English sovereignty and in that other trial scene wherein Elizabeth the woman weeps that she must doom a sister to death. The story of the relief of the Netherlands is also presented in two aspects: as another illustration of the all-embracing tyranny of the Spanish monarch, and as a proof of the dawning sense in the English nation of the duty to aid a weaker people in distress. At the end of the book, in the story of the hags Detraction and Envy and in the hint of the ravages of the blatant beast of Scandal, the theme descends from lofty philosophy to become intimate and tender in the story of how the faithful servant of the Queen returned unhonored, unthanked, and broken-hearted. Here in truth is a turning of the barren precepts of philosophy into pregnant images of life, a life not merely of men and measures, but also breathing the spirit of the new imperial England. [The next section treats the *Veue of the Present State of Ireland* from the same point of view.]

From her accession to the year 1588 Elizabeth's policy had of necessity been defensive. With the execution of Mary, however, and the humbling of Philip's pride, the party represented by Walsingham, Raleigh, and Drake became insistent that a bolder national course should be followed. With the great increase of interest in travel and the knowledge that rich territories might easily be brought within British dominion, to say nothing of the success Philip had attained in making his colonies pay the expenses of his wars, they found public opinion gradually coming to their views. But Elizabeth and Burghley still hesitated. The "forward school" urged that the victory over the Armada be followed up by increasing the navy and planting colonies in opposition to those of Spain. Had this course been followed, England would not have been so handicapped in her later attempts at colonization, and the terrible expense of the Irish campaigns of the nineties, due once more to Philip's plotting, would have been saved. The most that the Queen would allow, however, was piracy under government protection; one finds nearly all the projects presented to the Queen during this period stressing the possibilities of securing rich booty. Men like Walsingham and Raleigh saw the larger possibilities in founding a new empire beyond seas, but Burghley was not a statesman of that type. After the death of Burghley, his son Robert inherited his power and his policies; madly jealous of Raleigh and Essex, he blocked all plans for progress.

Throughout the most critical years of this period, from 1579, when the Alençon marriage was imminent and the active campaign of Rome and Spain in England, Scotland, and Ireland was beginning, to 1595, when Elizabeth, confronted by the results of Spain's plotting in Ireland and by the fact that her great rival was stronger than ever on the sea and in the possession of colonies that were rich sources of supplies, became convinced of the need of a more vigorous policy, the course of Spenser was absolutely consistent. In the earlier period he stood with Leicester and Sidney; later he gave the support of his literary genius to Walsingham and defended the memory of Grey; in the nineties he agreed with the colonial policy of Raleigh and Essex. I am well aware of the danger in thus comparing the visions of the bard of fairy-land with the deeds of men who, like him, saw visions of England's destiny but who risked their lives and fortunes to make these dreams realities. In the flush of youth, when he was received into the brilliant circle at Leicester House, I am convinced that Spenser meant to be a man of action as well as a writer of verse; no doubt in the later years when far distant from the court he wrote the epic that his friends were living he often felt the ineffective-ness of his life. Like Sordello, prevented from being a man of action, he sought through the imaginative interpretation of heroic deeds to realize, in some sort, his ideal. Drake, it has been finely said, was an ocean knight-errant, smiting and spoiling in knightly fashion and for a great cause; a scourge of the enemies of his country and of his faith. And Spenser, looking in his mirror of Shalott, saw, in reflection it is true, the deeds of these knights-errant and interpreted them. He who reads the records in the calendars of state papers, the letters dealing with the crises and the projects of these eventful years, the journals of returned travelers, can hardly fail of the impression that most of these men had little conception of the vast significance of their work; intrigue and chicane in dealing with Ireland, greed for gold in every charter granted Gilbert and Raleigh and Drake, marked the policy of Burghley. A few men conceived, perhaps prematurely, an England greater than any continental power, and to these men Spenser gave his genius and his pen.

Fulke Greville's account of Sidney is less a biography than a record of con-versations. From these we may get an idea of the topics that were discussed when Spenser was on intimate terms with his first idol. We are repeatedly told of his sense of the danger from Spain and the folly of temporizing; he saw that Philip's power rested largely upon the richness of his mines in America; he advised open attack on Philip himself and indirect attack by fetching away his golden fleece; to him Elizabeth was the Queen of the Seas, and should keep a strong fleet upon her ocean; as a natural consequence, England should herself establish colonies abroad. The revelation which these pages give of a man whose range of thought and knowledge and whose grasp of great problems of government were so remark-able helps to make clear how extraordinary must have been the contagion of his character. Every one of these leading ideas was reflected by Spenser. Every one of them was contrary to the settled policy of Burghley.

Next to Sidney, Raleigh had the greatest influence on Spenser's political opin-ions. When the company of shepherds asked Colin to tell the subjects of the songs exchanged between him and the Shepherd of the Ocean, he told a modest story of the loves of the Bregog and the Mulla, and then told of his friend's joy at being again in the good graces of that Cynthia who was Queen of the Seas:

> For land and sea my Cynthia doth deserve
> To have in her commandement at hand.

There is no need to outline Raleigh's great achievement, in action and in his writ-ings, toward the making of an imperial Britain; Spenser's name for him, the Shepherd of the Ocean, is at once a stroke of genius and a proof of understand-ing and sympathy that outweighs any tract on colonial expansion that the poet could have written. All these men were students of government. Gilbert early gave himself to "studies pertening to the state of government and to naviga-tions." In the *Arcadia* and in the conversations reported by Greville, Sidney gave proof of his interest in large problems. In the "Maxims of State" in which Raleigh summed up his conception of these same problems we have a work drawn, like Spenser's *Veue*, from *Il Principe* and laying down exactly the same principles which Spenser maintained should govern the course of England with respect to Ireland.

Besides the references in *Colin Clout*, Spenser gives other evidences of interest in the English vikings and in the development of colonies. The eloquent passage in the *Veue* has already been cited. The allegory of the two brothers and the dispute about the treasure chest, with the conclusion that lands set apart from other lands by the power of the sea belong to him who seizes them, seems to be a justification for the right of discovery. That Spenser read with interest the accounts of the journeys to lands formerly unknown is proved by the stanza about the "hardy enterprize" through which daily "many great regions are discovered." Moreover, he saw in his own epic the reflection of the journeys of these travelers through uncharted seas. [6. 12. 1 quoted.]

In all this mass of literature, written through the fifteen most eventful and critical years of Elizabeth's reign, is revealed a course as unswerving as it is lofty. I have elsewhere (*PMLA* 25. 560) alluded to the folly of supposing that *Mother Hubberds Tale* was called in because of Burghley's jealousy of a brilliant young poet who dared resent his failure to secure a good appointment. The present study, I think, throws further light on the reasons for Spenser's hatred of the great chancellor. To Spenser, Burghley represented Machiavellism according to Gentillet; the craft and temporizing and deceit of politicians of this school was abhorrent to his high-souled idealism as it was to Sidney's. This hatred was expressed not only in the *Tale* but throughout the *Faerie Queene* and in *Colin Clout*. In a time when references to political subjects were exceedingly dangerous, when certain passages in Holinshed alluding to Ireland were canceled and when even such a work as Drayton's metrical version of the Psalms was recalled, it required courage of a high order to write as Spenser wrote. Moreover, he did not hesitate to rebuke Burghley in a way impossible of misunderstanding, as the splendid defense of love in the proem to the fourth book of the *Faerie Queene* proves. Artegall's censure of Burbon refers directly, of course, to Henry of Navarre, but it is noticeable that the policy that he censures,

> To temporize is not from truth to swerve,
> Ne for advantage terme to entertaine,

represents also the very element in Burghley's political philosophy that Spenser detested (5. 11. 56). Even the sonnet addressed to the Lord Treasurer on the publication of the *Faerie Queene* contains no compliment, and is subtly defiant. Spenser's course was consistent and manly; he was not, like Dryden, ready to change his politics and his religion wherever there was hope of personal gain; his attack on Burghley was due to ideals of government and conduct which he held throughout his life, not to wounded self-love.

Taken as a whole, these writings of Spenser's present an interpretation of Elizabethan political idealism without parallel elsewhere. To regard him as a "functionary" of Leicester, of Essex, or of any other man, or to regard him as a morose and disappointed applicant for the favors of the great, is wholly unjust. Those who find in him the master of a sweetly flowing verse that has made him the "Warwick of poets" shall have their reward. But he was more than this. Dreamer of dreams, Galahad of the quest for Beauty, he was also of good right a member of that little group of men who saw beyond the welter of court intrigue and petty politics the glorious vision of an imperial England. He had his limitations, it is true; at first sight he seems to fail to realize the idea of the nation in the larger sense; one does not find in him the passionate love of native land that quivers through the lines attributed by Shakspere to the dying John of Gaunt. His loyalty is personal; he conceives the State as Machiavelli conceived it; to him the Prince is the State. Yet on the whole, the two great poets who were the glory of Elizabethan England are of one accord. The splendid lines of Faulconbridge defying a conqueror to set foot on British soil breathe the spirit that animates all Spenser's work, and the England of Gaunt's adoration was to the poet of allegory his sovereign lady queen.

EDWIN GREENLAW (Review of Cory's *Edmund Spenser: A Critical Study,* *MLN* 35. 168-9). Now, although it is quite possible that in the courtship of Gloriana by Prince Arthur Spenser may have had in mind, at times, Leicester's long ambition, there is no reason whatever to suppose that the poem had for one of its purposes either prophecy of a union between the two or poetical propaganda to bring such a union to pass. For one thing, Spenser's explanation of his general intention in the *Faerie Queene*, given in his letter to Raleigh (dated 23 January, 1589), could not have been written until after Leicester's death, after all thought of a marriage had been abandoned for many years, and after Spenser's bitter complaint about Leicester's abandonment of him had been expressed in *Virgils Gnat.* Mr. Cory's conjecture about the nature of the second twelve books is thus by a simple matter of chronology untenable. Furthermore, the only place in the *Faerie Queene* where Arthur may plausibly be identified as Leicester is in the fifth book, and even this identification is rendered uncertain by the fact that the Arthur of Book V frees Belge, while Leicester assuredly did not settle the problem at all, but rather was called ignominiously home. The pitfalls that lurk in the path of anyone who applies too rigidly any scheme of identification of the personages in the poem may be seen if we consider what the poet does with his personifications of Elizabeth. We know, for example, from the letter to Raleigh that he shadows forth the Queen not only in Gloriana but also in Belphoebe. We also know that Mercilla represents Elizabeth, and Britomart. Now Britomart and Artegal are lovers, and Artegal, part of the time at least, is Lord Grey. Does this prove that Spenser contemplated a marriage between Grey and his Queen? The fact is that the union between Artegal and Britomart symbolizes the union between British justice and the might of Britain in war. At a given moment the course of British justice is made concrete in the course of Lord Grey in Ireland. Artegal, *for this moment,* is Lord Grey. It is the same with the identifications of other major characters. The union of Arthur and Gloriana symbolizes the restoration of the old British line, through the Tudor family, to the supreme power in England (I have discussed this point at some length in an article on "Spenser's Fairy Mythology," *SP* 15. 105-122 [Book I, pp. 351-3]). A cardinal principle of Spenser's political philosophy was that this new Britain ought to crush the growing menace of Spain. To do this, not only must Ireland be freed from Philip's propaganda, but the Low Countries must be given their liberty. The Queen, half-heartedly, aided the Low Countries, and at one time Leicester was in command of an expeditionary force there. *For this moment,* therefore, Arthur, representing Britain, becomes concrete, personalized, in Leicester. It is no more necessary to believe that Arthur is *always* Leicester than it is to believe that Artegal is always Grey. It is not necessary, therefore, to anyone familiar with Spenser's methods in allegory, to suppose that the union between Arthur and Gloriana, the union between England and the old British line, meant to Spenser any actual marriage of the Queen to Leicester or to anyone else. And even if he had begun the composition of his poem with any such idea, it was obviously impossible at the time when the letter to Raleigh was written, and there are no traces of it remaining in the poem itself.

Finally, the dedicatory letter, far from suggesting that Spenser contemplated a second poem of twelve books celebrating the deeds of Leicester as king-consort or at least pointing out the path which the royal pair should follow, is in reality to be explained on quite other grounds. Spenser himself is explicit as to his intention. He says that Homer, in the persons of Agamemnon and Ulysses, had portrayed a good governor and a virtuous man; that Virgil had combined the private and public virtues in the person of Æneas, and Ariosto in his Orlando; Tasso, he says, separated the two sets of virtues, public and private, in his Rinaldo and Godfredo. Following these illustrious examples, Spenser proposes, in the first twelve books, to deal with the twelve private virtues; if these books are well received he will continue with an exposition of kingship. There is, therefore, no basis for any conjecture about an "epic of the future," devoted to Leicester's deeds as king-consort, just as it is impossible to construct out of the adventures of Arthur in the first six books, except for the expedition to the Low Countries, any history of Leicester as king-consort-elect. An epic of Britain, glorifying the reigning house, and containing, according to the poetical theory of the time, an exposition of perfect courtiership, was the object of Spenser's endeavor; herein lies the explanation of the structure of the poem.

ALFRED B. GOUGH (*Edmund Spenser's Faerie Queene, Book V*, pp. xlvii-xlix). Spenser's treatment of justice is thus not only external, but political. His earlier plan of dealing with the political virtues in a sequel is here abandoned, owing to his resolve to make the vindication of Lord Grey's Irish policy the main theme of the Fifth Book. This naturally led him on to other notable illustrations of public justice from the history of his own time. Perhaps the chief interest of the Book lies in the political thought underlying it. . . .

It would be absurd to judge the politicians of the sixteenth century by modern humanitarian standards. With all their greed, cruelty, and arrogance they were consciously battling against a double tyranny that threatened the roots of the national life not only of England, but of Western Europe at large. Spenser, who like all great poets combined true manliness with the delicate sympathy of a woman, had learnt his statecraft in a hard school. Strong, narrow, honest soldiers and administrators like Sir Henry Sidney and Lord Grey taught him the danger of half-measures. His head approved while his heart wavered, and he subordinated his instincts to arguments. His uneasiness is seen in those passages where contrary to the facts Talus is called off like a hound that has tasted blood.

In other ways Spenser's genius does not move freely in its political shackles. The hard facts did not always satisfy the demands of poetic justice. Prince Arthur retired with dishonour from the fight with the Seneschal, and Belge was glad to be rid of him. Geryoneo and Grantorto were scotched, not killed. Where Spenser's imagination has free range, as in the story of the two Florimells, or in the cantos which deal with Radigund and Britomart, he is far happier than in the quasi-historical narratives that fill the last five cantos. Very recent history is seldom a fit matter for poetry, especially when the poet's country is engaged in a fierce national and religious struggle. But whatever the faults of the Fifth Book of the *Faerie Queene* may be, it is, taken as a whole, a true reflection of the ardent patriotism, the adventurous temper, the steadfast energy, and the religious and moral zeal that animated the higher types of English warriors and statesmen of the time. It is an idealization of the Elizabethan spirit in action.

PAULINE HENLEY (*Spenser in Ireland,* pp. 130-145). From an Irish histori-cal point of view the fifth book is the most interesting, as it contains the Legend of Artegall or Justice, under which figure Spenser portrays his patron Lord Grey. While the identification of many of his characters is extremely difficult, if not impossible, he lays aside most of the vagueness of allegory in dealing with this statesman and paints him almost without disguise. He is the Salvage Knight—the adjective is equivalent to Irish in Spenser—come to rescue Irena, or Ierna, which was the name used for Ireland by some of the classical writers. (This is the name under which Ireland appears in the Greek writer Poseidonos, who flourished about 150 B. C. It represents the old name, Iverna—McNeill: *Phases of Irish History,* pp. 133-4. Claudian and Strabo use this same name, Ptolemy calls it Iuernia, Solinus has Iuerna.) . . .

The Ireland of Spenser's sympathies here is loyal Ireland—the natives and their rights do not enter into his consideration. The Lady Irena accordingly does not typify the Banba of the bards, but England's loyalists struggling in afflicted plight against somebody or something called Grantorto. This " strong tyrant " has been identified as either Philip II of Spain or Desmond's rebellion. . . .

But to return to Artegall and his mission—Spenser does not put any Spanish colouring into the picture of Grantorto, whereas there are many details pointing to an intended Irish figure, and consequently it is likely that the Poet intended to typify the Desmond rebellion rather than the King of Spain. This " strong Tyrant," moreover, does not occur in any of the previous Books of the *Faerie Queene,* and seems to be connected with the period when Grey was Deputy. Spain attacking England through Desmond's rebellion was the special problem that the Deputy was sent to deal with in Ireland. Grantorto is represented as a giant, owing to the formidable strength of the rebellion, and the possibilities that lay behind it. This redoubtable antagonist was accoutred in Irish fashion,

> And on his head a steele cap he did weare
> Of colour rustie-browne, but sure and strong;
> And in his hand an huge Polaxe did beare,
> Whose steale was yron-studded but not long,
> With which he wont to fight to justifie his wrong:

in short, a warrior of the period, who fought with an ancient weapon—probably the Catholic religion—but was vanquished by Chrysaor, the Sword of the Lord, with which Artegall strikes off the head of " the cursed felon." True to the policy of the English in asserting that they were saving the Irish from the cruel exactions of the Anglo-Irish lords, Spenser would represent the people as rejoicing in the overthrow of the Earl of Desmond.

> Which when the people round about him saw,
> They shouted all for joy of his successe,
> Glad to be quit from that proud Tyrants awe,
> Which with strong powre did them long time oppresse.

Grantorto being dead, Artegall with the help of Talus the "yron man" with the flail, who typifies the strong arm of justice, puts his ruthless policy into force. [12. 25-26 quoted.]

Envy and slander prevent this "good Lord" from finishing the work, and having been recalled to England,

> His course of Justice he was forst to stay,
> And Talus to revoke from the right way
> In which he was that Realme for to redresse:
> But envies cloud still dimmeth vertues ray.
> So, having freed Irena from distresse,
> He took his leave of her there left in heavinesse.

It was only a poet turned politician who could have conceived the victim as mourning the departure of that "most gentell, affable, loving and temperate" governor, who had reduced her to a gaunt spectre of famine. . . .

One cannot but admire Spenser's warm championship of his discredited patron, in face of the anger of Elizabeth and the attacks of the Court factions, though his intemperate zeal leads him to support what even his contemporaries considered an exceptionally cruel policy. As a poet he would have wished to close the adventure in true fairy-tale style, but "the times were out of joint," poetry and politics would not blend, and so he ends with an outburst of bitterness and scarcely veiled contempt for the government policy. Lord Grey died about the time when Spenser started the sixth book, and he drops the subject after introducing Sir Calidore's meeting with Sir Artegall, and reiterating his defiant admiration. . . .

Though the enfranchisement of Irena was the special mission of Artegall, he meets with other adventures before he goes to her rescue, and many of these also have reference to Ireland, and deal with persons or incidents connected with the Grey administration, for the whole book is intended to portray him as the instrument of Elizabeth's justice. A fanciful but sinister legend attached to Strangcally Castle, on the Blackwater, is said to have supplied the details of Pollente's Bridge. Whatever allegorical meaning Spenser intended to attach to the Sarazin, dead he bears a resemblance to Sir John of Desmond, who accompanied by his cousin James FitzJohn Fitzgerald, last Geraldine owner of Strangcally Castle, was ambushed by Colonel Zouche, near Castlelyons. He was wounded in the throat, but Zouche hoped to bring him to Cork alive to stand his trial. He expired on the way. The corpse was brought to the city, where his head was cut off and sent to Grey as a New Year's gift in 1582. It was spiked on Dublin Castle, and the mutilated trunk was hung in chains on the North Gate of Cork, where it remained for nearly three years, till a high wind blew it into the river one stormy night. The grisly present to the Lord Deputy probably came to the Secretary's hands.

The fight between Artegall and Pollente takes place on a bridge with trapdoors, which, on being let down, precipitate the enemy into the water beneath. Locked in a fierce grip both fall into the river, and the struggle continues till Artegall strikes off the head of the other. [2. 19 quoted.] Here we have another alleged oppressor of the people, like Grantorto.

Pollente begins as the power of Spain, and ends as Sir John of Desmond; his daughter the Lady Munera begins as the wealth of Spain, and as some of the Spanish treasure was used to finance the expedition to Smerwick, she seems to end up as that unlucky garrison, and is slain. The assault on the Fort of Gold (Dunanoir or Fort del Ore), the defenders begging for terms and being refused, Artegall's alleged pity for them, his unwillingness to interfere with the course of Justice which lay in the hands of Talus, the corpses thrown over the walls to the sands beneath to be washed out on the tide, are all incidents of that siege. In this second allegory of Spain fomenting rebellion in Ireland, his wife, Adicia, is representative of the Papacy.

The trap-door device appears again in the sixth canto in connection with the sleeping apartment of the unsuspecting Britomart, and the Bridge of Pollente appears too in the same canto, when Dolon the deceiver plans with his sons the destruction of the Briton Maid, mistaking her for Artegall. If Dolon be taken as representative of the House of Desmond, then Guizor, the Groom of Pollente, slain in the first plot would be Fitzmaurice, though that event took place before Grey's coming to Ireland. The remaining two sons (Sir James and Sir John) are slain in connection with this second conspiracy, and again there is the reference to Sir John's body going over the Bridge and being swept away in the river. Dolon, the head of the House, is made their father, and his death, which occurred after Grey's recall, is not referred to here.

Just as Elizabeth, Spain, Rome, and the other chief interests of the day appear under different figures—so does Ireland. The fifth book contains a new female figure—Radigund the Amazon, who is hostile to all the Knights of Maydenhead. Under this guise Spenser must have intended to represent the Ireland that was in arms against England, and who was eventually killed by Britomart. She is quite a different figure to the sweet and gentle Florimell, or to the sorrowful Lady Irena. Here we have

> A Princesse of great power and greater pride
> And Queene of Amazons, in armes well tride.

Engaging in single combat with Artegall, this haughty warrior queen, so reminiscent in her splendour of that other Amazon Maev, is overcome, but her wonderful beauty causes the victor to weaken, she takes advantage of his admiration and pity, conquers him by guile, and his fame and honour suffer at her hands. What was involved in the struggle between them is clear from the compact she makes with him:

> But these conditions doe to him propound:
> That if I vanquishe him, he shall obay
> My law, and ever to my lore be bound;
> And so will I, if me he vanquish may,
> What ever he shall like to doe or say.

From this passage it is evident that Spenser realized that however much the issue might be obscured by the vacillation of some of the Irish, for the truly Gaelic Ireland it was victory and independence or else subservience for evermore to an alien government and tradition. Such views he never utters in his political tract, and it is the Poet too and not the politician who is seized " with pittiful regard " at the sight of the fair face of the country blood-stained and marred by combat, but still " A miracle of nature's goodly grace."

More than once Spenser finds this outlet in his poetry for feelings that politically would be out of place, and hence some of his most blood-thirsty sentiments of the *View* have their contradiction in the *Faerie Queene,* and this makes it doubtful as to which is his real opinion. Whatever license he might claim in poetry, a political tract, if it was to serve his interest, could embody nothing contrary to accepted English policy, and hence the poet who wrote " For blood can nought but sin, and wars but sorrows yield," has his name for ever linked in Ireland with exceptional cruelty. But it was the struggle in him of the poet against the politician, the effort to deal justly with what he was forced to admire, and at the same time bound to hate, that led him to make an appeal for the Salvage Man in Book VI. May it not be that the Poet in one of his softer moods was dreaming of a peace that he typifies under the allegory of Serena, a gentle lady wounded on both sides by the Blatant Beast? She tries to establish friendly relations between the Salvage Man, or the ordinary people of Ireland, and Timias and Arthur, representative of the English Government in Ireland. The slanderous propaganda of both sides, tending to fan the flames of racial hatred, produces the wounds in Serena's sides.

But if Spenser the Poet had any such ideas, they were cast aside by Spenser the Politician, when on going over to England to publish this second part of his poem he again found himself in the atmosphere of imperialism, and becoming the opportunist once more, he presented to the Queen his *View of the Present State of Ireland.* Yet even in this tract intended to advocate an uncompromisingly stern policy, Serena lays her hand on him and he brings in again, most inconsistently, this idea of a rapprochement.

The presentation of this apology for officialdom was his last bid for advancement. He was, in acknowledgment, recommended for the shrievalty of Co. Cork.

When one thinks of this struggle of two warring personalities in Spenser one is not surprised at the increasing querulousness that arose from his failure to mould this world in which he found himself, nearer to his heart's desire, or rather to the heart's desire of Elizabeth and her Council. It is a pity, as Mr. Yeats puts it, that he did not come merely as a poet to this land " where the mouths that have spoken all the fables of the poets had not yet become silent. All about him were shepherds and shepherdesses still loving the life that made Theocritus and Virgil think of shepherd and poet as the one thing; but though he dreamed of Virgil's shepherds he wrote a book to advise, among many like things, the harrying of all that followed flocks upon the hills, and of all ' the wandering companies that keep the wood.' "

H. S. V. JONES (*A Spenser Handbook,* pp. 261-271). The political allegory of the fifth book is more transparent than that of any other in the *Faerie Queene.*

Touched lightly in the earlier cantos, it develops in great detail from canto 6 to the end. Its main themes present different aspects of the Catholic danger in England, France, the Low Countries, and Ireland. In canto 6 Dolon's plot against Britomart clearly reflects Catholic attempts against the life of the Queen. If we recall the rôle that Philip II here played, we shall be disposed to identify the character of Dolon with the Spanish king. Beneath a surface of friendly relations, represented by the treaty of 1573 and suggested in the allegory by Dolon's hospitality, Philip lent his support to the schemes of Mendoza, the Spanish ambassador, and the Jesuit mission. He seems also to have had a hand in the Throckmorton plot of 1583, that had as its purpose the assassination of Elizabeth. It has been further suggested that the two knights who seek to murder Britomart in her chamber may be identified with the Duke of Guise and his brother, the Duke of Mayenne, who had planned in 1583 to coöperate with Philip in an invasion of England.

In canto 7 the Radigund-Britomart duel is obviously to be interpreted as the conflict between Mary Queen of Scots and Elizabeth. The allegory is so far true to the historical situation that the two queens may be said to have contended not only for the advantage of their respective religions but for their lives. If the Queen of Scots had been victorious, Elizabeth would no doubt have met the fate of Mary. Furthermore, the slaughter of the Amazons by Talus will suggest the punishment of English Catholics; for example, the hundreds that were hanged after the Rising of the Northern Earls had failed.

Leaving in canto 7 the theme of Mary's political duel with Elizabeth, Spenser returns to the subject of Anglo-Spanish relations. In the rôle of Samient, who acts as a messenger between Mercilla and the Souldan, the poet glances at the efforts of Elizabeth to adjust by diplomacy the differences between the two countries. It is significant that the hero of this episode in Spenser's story is not Arthegall but Arthur. The distortion of history in this case is noteworthy. Leicester, with whom Arthur is here as elsewhere to be identified, was, indeed, appointed by Elizabeth as the commander-in-chief of her land forces when the Spanish invasion threatened; but the great victory was of course by sea, and with that Leicester had nothing to do. Nevertheless, details of the Pagan's warlike equipment and of his fighting have been referred to the Spanish Armada; for example, the effect of Arthur's unveiled shield to that of the English fireships sent against the Spanish galleons, and Arthur's attack of the Souldan from behind, explained in stanzas 31-6, to the plan of the English leaders to make a rear attack upon the Spanish ships in the Thames. If ingenuity seems here to overshoot the mark, we might accept as significant the parallel between the Souldan's chariot furnished with hooks and Parma's ships held in reserve at Antwerp, which were similarly equipped with iron spikes and hooks.

In canto 9 the allegory shifts to Ireland. Malengin in his unkempt appearance and in the deceit which his name declares represents certainly the wild and elusive Irish against whom Lord Grey had to contend. The agility and trickery which he uses in making his escape are suggestive of the methods of guerilla warfare employed by the Irish; and the poet's introduction of the episode at this point might be interpreted as meaning that the Lord Deputy's policy was to destroy the roving bands of the wild Irish before proceeding to restore Ireland to its true allegiance and save it from Roman dominion. The trial of Duessa, which is a further episode in this canto, points so clearly to the trial and condemnation of Mary, Queen of Scots, that it called forth a well-known protest from her son, James VI. We should not expect here historical accuracy in detail. Elizabeth was of course not present in person at Mary's trial, and no doubt Spenser was misleading in writing:

> Yet in that wretched semblant, she did sure
> The peoples great compassion unto her allure.

On the other hand Arthegall's presence is supported by the historical fact that Lord Grey was a member of the commission that tried the case against the unhappy queen and later passed upon her the sentence of death. In stanza 40 Spenser has no basis in history for saying that mention was made at the trial of the many knights that Mary had "beguyled and confounded quight," but he is correct in pointing out that the sole charge brought against her was that of

> vyld treasons, and outrageous shame,
> Which she against the dred Mercilla oft did frame.

In the concluding stanza of the canto Spenser interprets the well-known indecision of Queen Elizabeth in a way to suggest that it was prompted more by sympathy than policy. However, it should be noted that among those who pleaded for Duessa was

> Daunger threatning hidden dread,
> And high alliance unto forren powre.

In compact form canto 10 deals with the conflict between England and Spain in the Netherlands. As in the poet's account of the trial of Mary, Queen of Scots, Elizabeth is here represented as the merciful queen. She goes into the Netherlands as into Ireland because of her sympathy for the oppressed population. "It is greater prayse," says the poet, "to save, then spill." It is on this key that the tenth canto opens. The story proper begins with the arrival at Mercilla's court of "two springals" of the widow Belge. Of her seventeen sons all but five had been devoured by the fell tyrant Geryoneo. No allegory could be more transparent than this. The name of the distressed lady and the exact correspondence between the number of her sons and the number of the provinces which constituted the Netherlands, puts the meaning of the passage beyond the shadow of a doubt. In all probability the "two springals" who wait upon Mercilla are to be equated with the provinces that took the lead in the revolt of the Netherlands, namely, Holland and Zealand, although Upton was of the opinion that they represented the Marquess of Havre and Adolf Meetkercke, whom the states sent as special envoys to England in 1577.

The story told by the messengers lends itself almost as easily to interpretation as the above details of the allegory. Some question might arise as to whether Geryoneo should be identified with Philip II or with the Hapsburg dynasty, which in the person of the emperor Charles V fell heir to the Netherlands on the death of Charles the Bold, Duke of Burgundy. If the latter is the husband of the Lady Belge, Charles V is the "bold tyrant" whom in her widowhood she accepted as her champion. In accord with this, the more likely interpretation, is the description of the policy of the champion in the following lines [st. 12. 6-9 and st. 13 quoted]. This is true to history in that the tyranny of Philip II was preceded by the wise policy of Charles V. The latter, indeed, showed " careful diligence " in unifying the Netherlands and in freeing them from the Empire. In this way he might be said to have inaugurated their independence. But later, like Spenser's champion, he " spoiled his own work," in the words of Mr. Armstrong, " by granting the Netherlands to Philip." If we accept the more common identification of the husband of Lady Belge with William, Prince of Orange, the quoted passage is less easy of explanation. . . .

The continuation of the Arthur-Geryoneo story in the first thirty-five stanzas of canto 11, departing still farther from history, seem to take on the character of hopeful prophecy. Though Leicester was dead, England might some day conquer Philip on land. as she had done on the sea; and, in destroying Spanish rule in the Netherlands, might eradicate at the same time the Catholic power in that country. In the meantime, more or less successful campaigns were being conducted against different parts of that unwieldy Spanish empire not inappropriately symbolized in the giant of the three bodies and the six hands; for example, the expedition to Portugal in 1589, that to the Azores in 1590-2, and the raid of the West Indies by Drake and Hawkins in 1595-6. . . .

The theme of Arthegall's rescue of Irena, which had been introduced in canto 9, is brought to a term in the final canto of the fifth book. Dr. Gough's identification of Grantorto (Great Wrong) with the Pope would be preferred to the traditional identification with Philip II; because it was the Pope rather than Philip that took an active part in Irish affairs. It was he who in 1577 gave James Fitzmaurice a commission to conquer the country, who in 1579 bestowed a consecrated banner upon the small expedition headed by Fitz-maurice and his own legate Dr. Saunders; and who in 1580 despatched the 800 Italians and Spaniards, most of whom were put to the sword by Grey in the well-known massacre at Fort del Oro. To this inconclusive event of the Irish campaign Spenser gives an air of finality in his account of the rescue of Irena through the defeat and death of Grantorto. The subsequent policy of the Lord Deputy he describes in the twenty-sixth stanza [quoted].

Whatever we might think of Grey's " true Justice," the stern measures which he took in order to subdue Ireland are here clearly stated. That, however, the suspicion of undue severity was unwarranted the poet suggests in representing Arthegall in stanza 8 as staying the fury of Talus. Nevertheless, it was feared from the beginning that the Deputy's anti-Catholic zeal might carry him to extremes; as is clear from the instructions which he took to Ireland. He was warned against being too strict in religious matters and " to have an especial care that by the oppression and insolencies of the soldiers our good subjects may not be alienated from us." The tone of these instructions is in accord with the characterization of Elizabeth by the Master of the Rolls as the " Amor Hiberniae." In the very opening stanzas of the twelfth canto, Spenser, the champion of Grey, protects himself against the imputation of criticizing the queen by praising her clemency; but Grey doubtless would have agreed with Waterhouse's remark to Walsingham: " If the Queen will use mildness with the traitors, she would do better to discharge her army at once." Whatever differences existed between the Queen and her Lord Deputy, Grey's enemies made the most of them. At Smerwick, it was said, he was guilty of bad faith as well as cruelty because he had obtained the surrender of Fort del Oro only by promising clemency to the garrison. Burghley, Grey himself complained, lent an ear to the slanderous reports in circulation; and such an act as his execution on insufficient evidence of guilt of Nicholas Nugent, former Chief Justice of the Common Pleas in Ireland, certainly did him no good.

To the slander and detraction that led to the Lord Deputy's recall, Spenser pays his respects in the concluding stanzas of the twelfth canto. In his description of the two hags, Envy and Detraction, and of the Blatant Beast, he expresses the full measure of his contempt for Grey's enemies. They have been actuated by no high motives; it is simply their nature to " grieve and grudge " at all that they see done " prays-worthy." They sorrow over the good and rejoice over the evil of which they hear; and while concealing the good, they publish the evil far and wide. What is well meant, they misconstrue; and in common haunts they are active in gossip and slander. In stanza 37 the poet makes a good point when he argues that the very agencies of Envy and Detraction which are hostile to Grey are at the root of the Irish question. They were hostile to him because he had freed Irena from their own snares,—a suggestion that the Roman Catholics had inspired the attack on the Lord Deputy.

IVAN L. SCHULZE (" Spenser's Belge Episode and the Pageants for Leicester in the Low Countries, 1585-6," pp. 235-240). It is my purpose to show that the pageants presented in honor of Leicester in Holland, in 1585-86 [Holinshed, *Chronicles*, ed. 1807, 4. 640-651], profoundly influenced Spenser's allegory in one of the most important episodes in *F. Q.*

In the fall of 1585 Queen Elizabeth finally decided to aid the Low Countries in their struggle against Spain. Leicester was placed in command of the English forces in September. On December 8, the expedition sailed for Flushing. The earl's arrival at Flushing was the signal for a series of triumphal receptions that would have graced the return of an ancient Roman conqueror. His entry into city after city was greeted with the wildest enthusiasm. In these receptions pageantry played a conspicuous part. [He quotes extracts from the descriptions of the pageants at Dort, Dec. 21, 1585; Donhage, Dec. 27, 1585; and at Haarlem, March 3, 1586.] . . .

In summary, there is more than sufficient evidence to show that Spenser was familiar with these Leicester pageants. In the very first verses addressed to the earl, upon his entry into Dort, Spenser's Belge occurs in the line—" The widow countrie wailing in hir losse." In the Donhage pageants the provinces are symbolized by young virgins, and in the Utrecht pageants by young men; and Leicester is compared with Arthur of Britain. The Haarlem pageants are closely linked with Spenser through the Mulciber and Lerna incidents. As a whole, in addition to these detailed similarities, the Pageants in tone and intention are a counterpart to Spenser's treatment of the Belge episode.

KERBY NEILL (" The Faerie Queene and the Mary Stuart Controversy," pp. 207-214). [This paper places Spenser's allegorical description of the trial of

Mary Stuart against the background of the controversial literature—books, tracts, and poems—on the subject. Mr. Neill recognizes four rather well-defined stages in this "battle of the books," and devotes the first two of the three sections of his paper to a review of the literature.]

This brief sketch indicates the major works that appeared in the long controversy over Mary Stuart's claim to the English throne. The original issue was her right to succeed Elizabeth. John Hale's *Declaration of the Succession,* answered by Morgan's *Allegations,* which in turn was answered by the *Allegations against the Surmised Title,* marked the first phase of the struggle. After the Darnley murder and Mary Stuart's flight into England, the main issue was her guilt or innocence. The writings of the Bishop of Ross, of Buchanan, and the Norfolk pamphlet were the main works dealing with the second phase. The third stage, which was closely linked to the second, was the assertion of her title in preference to Elizabeth's at the time of the Northern Rebellion. The fourth and final issue was openly the religious one. Did Mary fall a victim to the cruel persecutions of the heretic Queen or was she justly condemned for her manifold treasons against the life and country of the Queen who had stood mercifully between her and the execution of justice for nearly sixteen years? The pamphlets following the executions of Campion, Somerville, Throckmorton, and Parry were merely preliminaries to the outburst that inevitably followed the execution of the leader of the Catholic cause in England. From the very beginning of the religious persecutions, Elizabeth made every effort to avoid the charge of cruelty that was made time and again by the Catholics and which became the keynote of the final attack upon her. The English writers parried with broadside, pamphlet, and even epic. The Mary Stuart passages in the *Faerie Queene* must be viewed essentially as part of this controversy.

Spenser grew up in the atmosphere created by the uncertain succession. During his most formative years he saw the fall of Mary Stuart in Scotland, her flight into England, and the ensuing discord that followed her like a handmaid. His patron Leicester was closely linked with the problem of Mary Stuart and the succession through the possibility of a marriage with either Elizabeth or Mary. (Leicester was supposed to have been raised to the earldom and created Baron of Denbigh in order to make him a more suitable match for Mary. Elizabeth is said to have promised her the succession if she would marry him—Camden, *Hist.,* pp. 67-8. In 1574 he was said to have contemplated making her an offer of marriage—J. D. Leader, *Mary Queen of Scots in Captivity,* London, 1880, pp. 340-1. In the early part of Elizabeth's reign, his brother-in-law, the Earl of Huntingdon, was advanced as a possible heir to the throne through his descent from the Duke of Clarence. *Leycester's Commonwealth,* 1584, accused him of designs to seize the throne for himself, and there was gossip that he would " obtrude some Bastard-son of his for the Queen's *natural* Issue "—Camden, *Hist.,* pp. 166-7.) Problems such as these were discussed at Leicester House, probably very cautiously, and possibly Spenser exchanged views with other politically minded young men such as Sidney. Miss Albright has suggested a relationship between Spenser and the Davisons, and the possibility of an exchange of books. In Davison's library were the *Allegations* and the Norfolk pamphlet. (" *The Faerie Queene* in Masque at the Gray's Inn Revels," *PMLA* 41, 497-516. See especially p. 512. I cannot agree with Miss Albright, p. 508, that Spenser's attitude toward Mary Stuart needs any special explanation such as his personal feeling toward Davison, p. 516. Her interpretation of Spenser's handling of the Mercilla episode fails to consider the contemporary attitude toward Mary's trial. As the present study will show, Spenser's attitude toward the entire problem is in no way original, but it is merely the poetic expression of the commonplace views of the Protestant English party.) Spenser's treatment of Mary Stuart in the characters of Duessa and Radigund shows that he was well acquainted with the problem of her claim to the succession.

An analysis of Spenser's attitude toward Mary Stuart in the trial of Duessa (5. 9. 25-50), furnishes a basis for the interpretation of less obvious passages. (The identity of Duessa furnishes a separate problem in each half of the *Faerie Queene*. I have not found sufficient evidence to contribute anything to the interpretation of Frederick M. Padelford, and of Ray Heffner, " Spenser's Allegory in Book I of the Faerie Queene," *SP* 27. 142-61 [see Appendix VI to Book I]. The discussion here is limited to Books 4 and 5.) King James's complaint over the way his mother is handled is a commonplace of Spenser criticism, and the identity of most of the other characters was suggested long ago by Upton and Todd, but the episode has not been related to the written controversy over Mary's execution. Spenser appropriately introduces his defense of the government by alluding to the attacks on Elizabeth. When Arthur and Artegall approach the palace of Mercilla where the trial is about to be held, they see a poet whose tongue is nailed to a post for his foul blasphemies, bold speeches, and lewd poems against the Queen. Over the head of the offender is the title BONFONT with " bon " crossed out and " mal " substituted for it, making the name " Malfont." A. B. Gough has attempted to identify this poet as Ulpian Fulwell, but his evidence is extremely slight. " Bonfont " might be a translation of " Fulwell," but the satires by this poet on the court of Lady Fortune which apply to Elizabeth and possibly to Leicester have only a remote connection to the subject Spenser is about to discuss, the trial of Mary Stuart. There is nothing in the passages cited by Gough to suggest any relation whatever to Mary or to Elizabeth's treatment of her. Fulwell attacks court life in the conventional way and with a touch of bitterness that is the mark of failure. Gough offers no evidence that Fulwell was punished for his writings, and the work cited is dated long before the last phase of the battle of the books. A far stronger case could be made out for Richard Verstegan, also known as Rowlands. He was at Oxford while Spenser was at Cambridge. Both young men were interested in antiquities. Verstegan studied English history and Anglo-Saxon, and in 1576 he published a translation of a German antiquarian work, *The Post of the World*. Soon afterwards he moved to Antwerp where he set up as a printer and engraver. Both as a source of antiquarian knowledge and as a printer he might have been " bonfont " to Spenser. Moreover, he was later punished for reviling Elizabeth in the *Theatrum Crudelitatum Hereticorum Nostri Temporis* (1587). Since this work contained a life of Mary which expressly accused Elizabeth of cruelty, a reference to it would be particularly appropriate as an introduction to an account of Elizabeth's mercy in dealing with her rival. I am inclined to believe, however, that Spenser is referring to all the attacks on his Queen rather than to any specific work or person.

After alluding to the writings against Elizabeth, which almost universally

accused her of cruelty, Spenser hastens to the defense by portraying her as Mercilla presiding over a court of strict justice. This is the essence of his argument:
pity must not prevent the execution of justice. He emphasizes the theme by
repeating it twice. In 5. 9. 38 he describes Duessa as "a Ladie of great countenance
and place" whose nobility is "blotted with condition vile and base," but
nevertheless,

> Yet in that wretched semblant, she did sure
> The peoples great compassion unto her allure.

(H. S. V. Jones, *A Spenser Handbook,* N. Y., 1930, p. 263, says that "no doubt
Spenser was misleading in writing" these two lines. I do not agree with him.
Most of the later works in Mary's defense appealed to pity, and the replies to
them tried to show that her crimes were beyond forgiveness. This is exactly what
Spenser attempts. I believe that his lines are a true indication of public opinion.
See *Hatfield MSS* 1. 433.) But the prosecuting attorney accuses her of such
heinous crimes that the people are moved rather to loathe than to pity her.
Although he makes a general reference to the many knights she has "confounded,"
the specific charge is treason against Mercilla (5. 9. 41):

> For she whylome (as ye mote yet right well
> Remember) had her counsels false conspyred,
> With faithlesse *Blandamour* and *Paridell,*
> (Both two her paramours, both by her hyred,
> And both with hope of shadowes vaine inspyred,)
> And with them practiz'd, how for to depryue
> *Mercilla* of her crowne, by her aspyred,
> That she might it unto her selfe deryve.

The reference to these two lovers, who are Duessa's companions in Book 4, definitely links her trial with her former appearance in the preceding book. Her fellow conspirators were "hyred" as well as led by "shadows vaine"; but the plot
was discovered before it could be put into execution, and the actors were punished. These phrases seem to indicate that Blandamour and Paridell represent
the men involved in the Babington Plot, if they were not its leaders. Duessa is
being tried for her complicity. She has transgressed against Authority, the law
of Nations, Religion, the cause of the people, and Justice charges her with breach
of laws. All these offenses are against Concord, the virtue of Book 4. The wit-
nesses for the defense bring forth Pity, Womanhood, Noble Birth, Grief, and
Danger from Foreign Power. The force of these arguments touches Prince
Arthur, and he is inclined to take her part. Here Spenser is referring to the
defenders of Mary. He makes their arguments very similar to the appeal made
by the Bishop of Ross which is cited above. But the prosecution brings forward
Ate, the mother of debate and all dissension, who exposes all of Duessa's plots
and treasons. This is another definite link with Book 4 where Ate and Duessa are
companions: it is Justice that condemns her, but the sins are against Concord.
Then follow the accusations of Murder, Sedition, Incontinence, Adultery, and
Impiety, which are all sins against Temperance. (In *F. Q.* 5. 10. 4, Duessa's fall
is described as "wilful"; *i. e.* against reason.) It was thus that the Commons
argued against Mary as early as 1572:

The late Scottish Queen hath heaped up together all the Sins of the Licentious Sons of *David,* Adulteries, Murders, Conspiracies, Treasons and Blasphemies against God. . . . (D'Ewes, p. 209).

These charges sufficiently establish Duessa's dangerous character, and Mercilla sorrowfully condemns her.

Spenser expressed himself with great clearness. To him Mary Stuart was a woman whose former nobility was sullied with the very worst crimes. She threatened the country with both civil war and foreign invasion; she had plotted against Elizabeth's life and the Protestant religion; she had seduced subjects from their allegiance; and her private life was unspeakably vile; in short, she constituted a national danger, and it was necessary that the claims of justice should supersede Elizabeth's policy of mercy. Thus stated, free from the ornaments of poetry, Spenser's view appears as merely the accepted defense of the English government. It was the argument advanced by the Commons in 1572, and was restated with greater emphasis after Mary's condemnation. The same view can be found in nearly all of the writings against Mary in the last phase of the battle of the books. George Whetstone's *The Censure of a Loyal Subject* furnishes an example that is so apt that it might pass for a comment on the passages in Spenser:

In very truth necessitie hath made the bloody devices of the Scottish Q. so common, as no good subject may justly be forbidden to derive the cause both of foraigne and domestike conspiracies, from her princely heart. Our Sacred Q. Elizabeth's mercy hath many years contended . . . to preserve both the life and honor of this most unkinde queen . . . some zealous members of the church of God, in publique writings did set downe, the danger of her Majesties mercye in Christian policy shewed by many waightie reasons, that God delivered the Scottish Queen unto the sword of her justice. . . . (Egerton Brydges, *British Bibliographer,* London, 1810-14, 4. 141-2.)

This analysis establishes certain facts and gives leads for further investigation:

1) The trial of Duessa (Mary Stuart) is definitely linked with her appearance in Book 4.
2) One group of her sins, though previous to the specific charge with which she is accused, is against temperance, the virtue of Book 2.
3) Spenser's view of Mary's character is in accord with that taken by her enemies.

Duessa's only important appearance in Book 4 is in the first canto, stanzas 17-54. She has "chang'd her former wonted hew," which may signify that falsehood now appears in a new guise in the person of Mary Stuart. (The reference to her as daughter of the Emperor of the West is limited to Book 1. There seems to be practically no connection between Duessa's appearance in the first and second parts of the *Faerie Queene.*) Duessa has brought her companion, Ate, from Hell because she knows her

> To be most fit to trouble noble knights,
> Which hunt for honor. . . .

This apparition is a political vice who has overthrown "many a public state," and her dwelling at the gates of Hell is decorated with the memorials of ruined

countries. Among these is Alexander's empire which, as both the Commons and
the Lords had pointed out to Elizabeth (D'Ewes, pp. 81, 106), was destroyed
because of uncertainty about the succession. Her ears are filled with "false
rumors" and "seditious troubles." Furthermore,

> . . . All her studie was and all her thought,
> How she might overthrow the things that Concord wrought.

Blandamour and Paridell make up the rest of the ungodly crew, and the latter
soon raises his spear against Britomart but is discomfited. The whole picture is
very similar to a political allegory written in the form of a masque for the projected meeting of Mary and Elizabeth in 1562. Its purpose was to bring about
peace between the two Queens, and the abstract characters Discord and False
Rumor are driven back to Hell. (Paul Reyher, *Les Masques Anglais,* 1512-1640,
Paris, 1909, pp. 125-8. See comment by Greenlaw, *Studies,* p. 91. It is also indicated in the masque that Mary Stuart must have the virtue of temperance if she is
to gain the succession.) Between the time of the masque and the second part of
the *Faerie Queene,* Mary Stuart had been outstanding as a source of discord:
Scotland had fallen into the worst kind of civil anarchy during her reign, and
when she fled into England trouble followed her as Ate followed Duessa; the
Northern Rebellion, the Norfolk Conspiracy, the Ridolfi Plot, the treasons that
centered in Mendoza, the Spanish Ambassador, such as Throckmorton's plan
for an invasion of England, the negotiations with France, the attempts on Elizabeth's life by Somerville and Parry, and finally the Babington Plot, all these were
the result of her position as a rival for Elizabeth's throne, so that Whetstone
could say in 1587 that all foreign and domestic conspiracies were derived from
her "princely heart." With this historical background, Spenser reverses the
process of the masque and portrays Mary Stuart (Duessa) as summoning Discord
(Ate) from Hell to trouble the works of Concord, the archetype of government.
He emphasizes Ate's political significance by showing the public ruin she has
wrought in the past. She is bawd to Duessa, just as civil strife encouraged men
to follow Mary Stuart, whose only hope rested upon overthrowing the then established order. The preceding section has indicated the attitude toward the succession as the root of English discord. Elizabeth's own poem, written on the situation at the time of the Norfolk Conspiracy, calls Mary the "daughter of debate,
that eke Discord doth sow," (Strype, *Annals* 2. 89) and Spenser characterizes her
in the same way. Further evidence for this interpretation is furnished by the
trial of Duessa in Book 5, which definitely refers back to her appearance in Book
4, where, with her companions Blandamour, Paridell, and Ate, she is sowing the
discord for which she is punished. Ate even appears as a witness against her. I
conclude, therefore, that this is "continued allegory," that in both Books 4 and 5
Duessa represents Mary Stuart. (Paridell's attack on Britomart, then, represents
one of Mary's followers vainly trying to overthrow Elizabeth.)

RAY HEFFNER ("Essex and Book Five of the *Faerie Queene,*" pp. 67-82).
That Essex was Spenser's patron in the last years of the poet's life is indicated by
the well established tradition that the generous Earl sent the dying poet twenty
pounds, which he refused, and that Spenser's funeral expenses were paid by Essex.

(Ben Jonson's statement in his *Conversations with Drummond* is supported by a MS poem in the British Museum, *Triton's Trumpet*, written by John Lane in 1621, and by Peacham in *The Truth of Our Times*, 1638, pp. 37-8. The *Conversations* were not printed until the Eighteenth century. See my article, "Did Spenser Die in Poverty?," *MLN* 48. 221-6. Camden, *Annals*, ed. 1631, Bk. 4, p. 134, is one authority for the payment of Spenser's funeral expenses by Essex.) The dedicatory sonnet to Essex, published with the *Faerie Queene* (1590), indicates that Spenser was looking to that nobleman to continue the patronage of Leicester and Sidney. It is certain evidence, too, that he intended to place Essex in his great epic, though it seems equally certain that it says that Essex has no place in the first three books of the *Faerie Queene*. (I suggest on this point, however, that Spenser does not include Essex in the first three books because the events described there are those with which Essex was not associated. In other words, the events in these books are too early in the reign for Essex to have had any part in them. On the other hand, Spenser predicts that Essex will play an important part in the last years of Elizabeth's reign. It is well to note in this connection that the closing year for Spenser would be the year in which he completed his writing, not necessarily the last year of Elizabeth. Therefore, since Spenser's hopes seem to have been high at the time of this sonnet's writing, "the last praises" of the Faery Queene would probably have covered the years from about 1590 to 1600. It is worth pointing out, too, that Spenser's reserving of Essex, a young man, for his "last praises" would indicate that chronology entered into his conception of "continued allegory.")

In the dedicatory sonnet Spenser tells Essex:

> But when My Muse, whose fethers nothing flitt
> Doe yet but flagg, and lowly learne to fly
> With bolder wing shall dare alofte to sty
> To the last praises of this Faery Queene,
> Then shall it make more famous memory
> Of thine Heroicke Parts.

Here Spenser promises Essex, in no uncertain terms, that he shall have a part in some future installment of the *Faerie Queene*. Whether he is to be in the second three books or in the last six, we cannot ascertain from this sonnet. I shall, of necessity, limit myself to a study of the second three books. It will be my purpose, then, in this paper to discover Essex's part in one of these books—Book 5.

If we examine the political affiliations of Spenser, we see that he was naturally a member of the Progressive Puritan Party, of which Essex was the leader from 1590 until his death. In the early days Spenser had supported Leicester and Sidney, then Grey; and around 1590 he supported Raleigh in his progressive policies. In other words, Spenser was constant in his allegiance to the principles of this "forward school." Professor E. Greenlaw in his article, "Spenser and British Imperialism," points out that Spenser expounds his political views in Book 5 of the *Faerie Queene*. These views are those of the leaders of this "forward school." The cardinal principles of the party, according to Professor Greenlaw, were: (1) an attempt to force Elizabeth into an open break with Spain; (2) Elizabeth's duty to assume the leadership of the Protestant nations of Europe and to render them effective aid against Spain; (3) Elizabeth's right to seize and colonize lands beyond the seas. In addition, Spenser justifies the execution of Mary Stuart, and defends the character and policies in Ireland of Lord Grey, in the person of

Artegall, the chosen instrument of Justice. In this connection, Professor Greenlaw finds the *Veue of the Present State of Ireland* to be a prose counterpart of Book 5 of the *Faerie Queene*.

An examination of the book itself, however, will show that at least one incident does not belong to the period of Grey and Leicester. The episode of Burbon, in the eleventh canto, belongs rather to the 1590-94 period. Here, there can be no doubt, Artegall represents my Lord of Essex. In this canto Artegall sees a knight beset by a " rude rout chasing him to and fro," while his lady is left " all succorless." Artegall and Talus rescue the knight and learn that his name is Burbon and his lady's Flourdelis. Burbon is, of course, Henry IV of France; the " rude rout chasing him to and fro " is a good description of his affair with the League. Flourdelis is France.

In October 1590, Henry sent Viscount Turenne to England to solicit aid from Elizabeth. His instructions contained the following: " Après le dernier devoir rendu, il visitera M. Le Comte d'Essex." (Quoted by W. B. Devereux, *Lives of the Devereux, Earls of Essex* 1. 212-3.) Turenne was commanded to procure Essex's aid to the furtherance of Henry's cause. Henry himself wrote to Essex in the same year (*ibid.* 1. 213), addressing him as " Mon Cousin " and asking his aid with Elizabeth.

Essex needed very little urging to give his aid to so chivalrous a prince as Henry. So, on February 4, 1591, M. Veauvoir La Nocle wrote to his king: " Le Comte d'Essex fait toujours compte de passer en France." (*Ibid.* 1. 214.) And on June 20, 1591, Essex wrote to Richard Bagot: " Mr. Bagot, I am commanded into France for the establishment of that brave King in possession of Normandy. . . ." (*Ibid.* 1. 215-6.) His commission to command the forces in Normandy was issued at Greenwich July 21, 1591. (*Ibid.* 1. 217-8, abstract of the Commission.) Shortly after the reception of his commission, Essex left Dover for Dieppe at the head of four thousand regular troops and a host of gentlemen adventurers. While in France he took part in the siege of Rouen and himself besieged Gournay, which fell September 27, 1591. During the siege of Rouen his brother Walter was slain. Essex distinguished himself both on the field of battle and in camp. (For details see Cayet, *Chronologie Nouvemaire*, and Coningsby, *The Siege of Rouen*.) In September 1591 he was recalled by Elizabeth, but after a few weeks spent in feasting with the Queen, she, with tears admonishing him not to put himself in harm's way, allowed him to return (Oct. 17). He was, over his own protest, recalled January 8, 1591-2, and Sir Roger Williams succeeded him in command. It was Essex, however, who received the praise for having aided Henry Burbon—no praise of him was complete without a mention of his French wars. In the ballads on his life and death we find the following:

> Then Into ffrance this lorde was sente,
> And Walter Deverox, his brother dere;
> Ten thousand men with hym there wente
> Taccompanye this gallante peere.
> At Gurnaye hee greate fame did wynne;
> That towne by valor hee tooke in.
>
> To-wardes brave [Rouen] then marched hee,
> His brother leadinge his brave trayne
> Whoe was shott by the enemye . . .

> The frenche kinge did his furye staye
> whoe with great multitudes came there;
> But withe Honor Hee Marcht awaye,
> ffor hee there forches [forces?] did not feare
> Then Deverox in esteme was heilde,
> Whoe gott renowne in Towne and feilde.
>
> (Richard Williams, " The Life and Death of Essex,"
> lines 60-78, *Ballads from MSS* 2. 26.)

And in another ballad of about the same time (" A Lamentable Ditty composed upon the death of Robert Lord Devereux, late Earle of Essex, who was beheaded in the Tower of London on Ash Wednesday in the morning, 1600," *Roxburghe Ballads* 1. 564-570, lines 33-40) :

> Abroad, and eke at home
> *gallantly, gallantly,*
> For valour there was none
> like him before.
> In Ireland, France, and Spaine,
> they fear'd great Essex name—
> And England lov'd the same
> in every place.

In this same period is a third similar ballad (" Elegy on the E[arl] of Essex," printed in *Ballads from MSS* 2. 245-9) :

> His Cullers he hath spred in france
> in honor of our Royall queene;
> Where death has sat vpon his lance,
> Wher as in battaile he hath bin:
> the Papish posts he sent to hell
> that did against their king rebell.
>
> Rebellious townes he taught to know
> allegance due vnto their king,
> As quene Rene, and other more,
> With [Which?] to subiection he did bring:
> All france admird this english gere
> & king therof held him full dere.

Thomas Campion, who seems to have been one of the gentlemen adventurers under Essex in France (Percival Vivian, ed. *Works*, Oxford, 1909, pp. xxxiii, xxxiv), has two poems on the French wars. The first is a Latin epigram, *In Obitum Gual. Deuoreux fratis clariss. Comitis Essexiae.* The second concerns Essex himself, and, as Vivian points out, seems to have been written at the time of Elizabeth's reconciliation with the young Earl in April, 1592. It is addressed *Ad Daphnin* and was published in the volume entitled *Poemata* in 1595. In a marginal note Campion explains the title thus: *Clarissimus Essexiae comes sub Daphnidis persona adumbratur.* The occasion was Essex's return from France in 1592. In 1598 Essex is praised in a long Latin poem by W. Vaughan for his deeds of valour in Portugal, the Low Countries, and France. (*Poematum Libellus continens 1., Encomium illustrissimi Herios, D. Roberti Comitis Essexiæ authore Guilielmo Vaughanno Mardunensi in Artibus Magistro Londini 1598.* Cited by Richard Schiedermair in *Der Graf von Essex in der Literatur*, München, 1908.)

In 1595 " W. C.," an unknown writer, in *A Letter from England to her three daughters, Cambridge, Oxford, Innes of the Court* admonishes Cambridge to sing of her beloved son:

And if this or such like be not matter, wherein your deare cherished muse may justly delite it selfe, and sweetely please others, then sing of Warres, and of learned Valour: of *Mineruas* foe-danting shield: of *Mars*—conquering honor: of the courts leadstarre: of Englands *Scipio*: of *France* his ayde: of fames glorie . . . of thrise honorable & worthilie-worthie-honored-noble Essex. (*Polimanteia . . . Whereunto is Added A Letter from England to her three daughters . . . 1595.* Account and full text of the "letter" in Sir Egerton Brydges's *British Bibliographer* 1. 274-85, p. 282.)

Spenser, it should be remembered, was a Cambridge man, and might well have taken this advice to be addressed particularly to him. He is, moreover, mentioned earlier in the letter: ". . . for in your children shall the loue-writing muse of divine *Sydnay*, and the pure flowing streame of Chrystallin *Spenser* suruiue onely: write then of Eliza's raigne, a task onely meete for so rare a pen" (p. 281).

Gabriel Harvey, Spenser's friend and correspondent, advised Barnaby Barnes: ". . . be thou Barnaby, the gallant Poet, like Spenser, ere the valiant souldiour, like Baskerville; and ever remember thy French service under the brave Earle of Essex." (*Pierces Supererogation* in *Works*, ed. Grosart, p. 15.) In a published letter to Christopher Bird in 1592, Harvey mentions French affairs in the following passage (*Foure Letters and Certaine Sonnets, Especially touching Robert Greene, and other parties by him abused . . .* 1592, Bodley Head Quarto reprint, Second Letter, pp. 25-6):

The next weeke you may happily haue a letter of such French occurrences, and other intelligences, as the credible relation of inquisitive frendes, or imployed straungers shall acquaint me withall. That most valorous, and braue king wanteth no honourable prayses, or zealous prayers. Redoubted Parma was neuer so matched: and in so many woorthy histories, aswell new, as olde; how few comparable either for Vertue, or Fortune? The Spanyard, politique inough, and not ouer-rashly audatious, will bee aduised before he entangle himselfe with more warres attonce: knowing how the braue Earle of Essex, woorthy Sir John Norrice, and their valiant knightes, haue fought for the honour of England: and for the right of Fraunce, of the Low countries, and of Portugall. Thrise happy Fraunce: though how vnhappy Fraunce that hath a Soueraine Head, such resolute Hartes, and such inuincible Handes to fight for thee; that will either recouer thee most mightily, or die for thee most honourably. Were I of sufficient discourse, to record the valiauntest, and memorablest actes of the world; I would count it a felicity to haue the oportunity of so egregious, and heroicall an argument: not pleasurably deuised in counterfaite names, but admirably represented to the eie of France, and the eare of the World, in the persons of royall, and most puissaunt knightes; how singularlie worthy of most glorious, and immortal fame. Gallant wits and brave pennes may honorably bethinke themselves: and even ambitiouslye frame their stile to a noble emulation of Liuy, Homer, and the divinest spirits of all ages. . . .

Spenser and Harvey were in constant correspondence. Through such accounts as Harvey proposed to send to Bird, Spenser got the greater part of his information of what was going on in England and on the continent. Now, if I read Harvey correctly, he promises to send Bird an account of the affairs in France—but he would like to write "an heroicall argument." By "heroicall argument" he means,

I think, a poetic account. Because of the lustre of the names concerned, he would use real, rather than feigned names. Harvey was accustomed to write poetical exercises for his friend Spenser, some of which are preserved, but by no means all. It is not too much then to suppose that Harvey, if he wrote any such account, would have sent it to Spenser. At least, we may be reasonably sure that he wrote Spenser somewhat the same sentiments as he here sends to Bird. In this same volume is Harvey's sonnet entitled " L'enuoy: or an Answere to the Gentleman, that drunke to Chaucer, vpon view of the former Sonnets, and other Cantos, in honour of certaine braue men." That one of these " other cantos " concerned Essex is most likely, and that Spenser saw it is indicated by the opening lines of the sonnet:

> Some Tales to tell, would I a Chaucer were:
> Yet would I not euen now an Homer be:
> Though Spencer me hath often Homer term'd.

The volume is closed by a sonnet by Spenser addressed to Harvey, and throughout the letters Harvey is lavish in his praise of the *Faerie Queene*.

With these things in mind, let us examine Spenser's account of the French affairs. In stanzas 43-65 of Canto 11 of the *Faerie Queene* is found the story of Burbon. Here, Spenser, contrary to his usual practice, uses real names. We notice in this Canto *Belge, Burbon, Irena, Flourdelis*, and in another connection *Guizor*. So, I think it quite probable that Spenser's account of Burbon may have owed something to a Harvey communication.

Stanzas 43-5 describe the condition of Henry IV of France in his fight with the League. Henry had been brought up a Calvinist and was the leader of the Huguenots in the French Wars of religion. He was, on his ascension to the throne in 1589, recognized by the Protestants and moderate Catholics, but was resisted by the League, which, with the aid of Philip II of Spain, dominated North-eastern France. At one time Henry was so nearly overcome by the League that he held only one city. In 1589, Elizabeth sent him 4,000 men under Lord Willoughby, and in 1591 the Earl of Essex was dispatched to his aid. Therefore, as I have pointed out before, Artegall cannot represent Lord Grey in this incident. As the quotations from Spenser's contemporaries show, Essex was credited with having rescued Henry from the League. So, Spenser in this incident keeps his promise of the dedicatory sonnet to make " more famous memory " of Essex's " heroicke parts."

This is recognized by Richard Niccols, a contemporary of Spenser and Essex, in his *Englands Eliza*, printed in the *Mirrour for Magistrates* in 1610. Niccols borrows from Spenser throughout the poem. His account of Elizabeth's aid to Henry reads:

> Witness great *Burbon*, when that house of Guise
> Did counterchecke thee in thy lawful claime,
> In thy defence what prince did then arise,
> Or with strong hand, who in fights bloodie frame
> Did ioyne to wound thy rebell foes with shame?
>   But England's queene, who still with fresh supplie
>   Did send her forces gainst thine enemie:
>
>   (stanza 365)
>
> When noble *Deuoreux*, that heroicke knight,
> To shew his loue to armes and cheualarie,
> Ingag'd his person in that furious fight
> Before that towne, hight Roan in Normandie.
>
>   (stanza 368)

The incident of Burbon's throwing away his shield (sts. 52-6) refers to Henry's joining the Catholic church in July 1593. Henry, as I have said before, was bred a Protestant and was the recognized leader of the Huguenots in the French Wars of Religion. The Catholic League, which had opposed him on his coming to throne, could not produce a claimant with a good title. The country itself was exhausted by the long civil conflict and longed for peace. Henry's religion seemed the only bar to a general pacification. Since he had no very deep religious convictions, he consented to " receive instruction," and was admitted to the Church in July 1593. The " conversion " of Henry did not have at once the desired effect. Although Paris received him about a year after, the country as a whole was not pacified until 1595.

When Elizabeth was informed of Henry's change of religion, she was, to quote Camden (*Annals*, Bk. 4, pp. 50-51), " full of sorrow, and much disquieted in mind, suddenly tooke her penne, and soone after sent this letter vnto him:

' Alas, what great sorrow, what inward griefe, what sighs haue I felt at my heart for these things. . . . It is a matter full of danger to doe euill, that good may come of it . . . certainly, from henceforth I cannot be your sister by the father: . . . God . . . bring you backe againe to a better mind.

Subscribed

Your sister, if it be after the old
manner, as for the new I haue
nothing to doe with it.' "

Both Elizabeth and Lord Burghley were in favour of abandoning Henry entirely. Essex, who was at the time virtually Foreign Secretary, alone supported Henry, and it was his influence which kept Elizabeth from deserting the King. Essex argued that Elizabeth should continue her support, for otherwise Henry would make a separate peace with Spain. In 1595, Essex sent Antonio Perez to France in order that he might send back to England alarming reports relative to Henry's intentions. The purpose, of course, was to frighten Elizabeth into an alliance with Henry, in order to prevent him from joining her enemies against her. When Perez failed to carry out the plans, Essex upbraided him in the following manner: " I am doing what I can to push on war in England; but you; you! Antonio, what are you doing on that side." (Quoted in Martin A. S. Hume's *The Great Lord Burghley*, p. 475.)

In Spenser's version, Artegall rebukes Burbon for his faithlessness and subsequent excuse that he is merely temporizing and means to resume his shield (Protestantism) at the first opportune time (st. 56),

> Fie on such forgerie (said *Artegall*)
> Vnder one hood to shadow faces twaine.
> Knights ought be true, and truth is one in all.

Yet, later on (st. 57),

> Sir *Artegall*, albe he earst did wyte
> His wauering mind, yet to his aide agreed.

Therefore, it seems to me quite evident that Spenser's contemporaries would have interpreted the Burbon incident as referring to Essex's aid to Henry IV, for that Earl was generally recognized as the French King's champion in England.

It is, I think, significant that in one of the few open allusions in the *Faerie Queene* to contemporary events Spenser refers to Essex as Artegall, the chosen instrument of Justice. The Burbon incident, however, is represented as taking place before the liberation of Irena. In stanza 36 of the eleventh canto, Artegall sets out on his quest, the rescue of Irena (Ireland). But on his way he meets Burbon, and the last part of the canto is taken up with this incident. In Canto 12 the story of Irena is resumed. But the verses by way of argument read:

> Artegall doth Sir Burbon aide,
> And blames for changing shield:
> He with the great Grantorto fights,
> And slaieth him in field.

Gough explains the fact that Burbon is mentioned in the argument to Canto 12 instead of Canto 11 by suggesting that Spenser intended to include him in the last canto. He further suggests that the incident was added as an after-thought when the book was already complete. Although Gough is perhaps correct in his supposition that stanzas 43-65 were inserted after the rest of the book had been written, he fails to see the real significance of the insertion. He fails to account for Spenser's placing of the story in the middle of the Irena episode and for the fact that the writer of the argument seems to have wanted to play up the Burbon story. The explanation of the latter point is, I think, fairly simple. Spenser had promised Essex in 1590 to include him in a later installment of his epic. Therefore, in 1596 when he was making a stronger bid for that Earl's favour and patronage, this record of one of Essex's adventures would be played up. Naturally, he would want to catch the eye of his patron—he would make it perfectly obvious that he meant to fulfill his promise of the dedicatory sonnet. [See HEFFNER in Appendix to Book VI, and GOUGH's note on 11. 43-5.]

It is of more interest, however, that an incident in which Essex plainly figures should be related by Spenser to the question of Ireland. Not only is Ireland freed by "Burbon's ayde," Artegall, but that hero proceeds directly from his rescue of the French King to the liberation of Ireland. Therefore, if Artegall is Essex in the Burbon incident, Spenser either disregards altogether the time element in the two episodes or wishes to connect Essex with the Irish question. What, then, was the situation in Ireland at this time (1596), and what connection had Essex with it?

In 1594 Sir Henry Duke wrote to the Lord Deputy and Council: "I am informed by those who came out of Tirone, that all Ulster doth daily prepare themselves for rebellion, and do stay but for their appointed time." (*Cal. S. P. Ireland*, 1592-6, p. 234.) In 1595 Essex drew up for Elizabeth a "Memorial against Invasion." In the second part of which, under the heading "Designs of the Enemy" we find: "2. In Ireland, where they have a part already in rebellion." And later on: "Against Ireland your majesty must send supply of men, money, victuals, and ship. . . ." (T. Birch, *Memoirs of the Reign of Queen Elizabeth* 1. 292-3, reprinted in full.) In a letter to Sir Robert Sidney on February 28, 1596, Rowland Whyte says: "Here it is reported, that the English troopes in France will be cashiered at the six months end, or recalled to be sent to Ireland." (*Sidney Papers*, ed. Collins, 2. 22.) Then, too, it was reported early in 1596 that the Spaniards were preparing to send further assistance to Ireland. Spanish troops were expected to embark for Ireland at any time (*DNB*, "Essex." *Cal. S. P. Dom.*, *passim*).

So, from 1594 to 1596 affairs in Ireland were the principal concern of Elizabeth and her Foreign Secretary. Ireland had always been the chief threat of Spain. Spanish troops and propaganda in Ireland had done much to keep the spirit of rebellion alive. Grey's massacre of the Spanish garrison at Smerwick is evidence of the deep hatred of the English for the Spanish troops in Ireland. Naturally, when it was rumoured in 1596 that Spanish assistance was expected in Ireland, those interested in Irish affairs regarded the situation as exceedingly grave, and began to cast about for some leader who could once and for all reduce the Irish to submission and thereby do away with the Spanish Menace in that direction.

There was no person in England or Ireland better informed or more interested in Irish affairs than Edmund Spenser. It was in 1596 that he wrote his *Veue of the Present State of Ireland*. Spenser's purpose in this writing was to point out to the authorities the causes of the failure of previous commanders in Ireland and to suggest ways and means through which that country might be finally conquered. As a final point, he urges the creation of a Lord Lieutenantship for Ireland; " and in suggesting for the office that man on whom the eye of England is fixed, and our last hopes now rest, he points clearly to Essex as the only person equal to coping with the situation." Mr. William Cliff Martin in a recent article, " The Date and Purpose of Spenser's *Veue*" (*PMLA* 47. 137-143), argues plausibly that Spenser referred to Essex not only as the proper person to settle the Irish question but also as that " noble person, who . . . coasting upon the South Sea stoppeth the ingate of all that evil which is looked for . . . " (Globe ed., p. 650) in Ireland. Reference is to Essex's Cadiz expedition, and the expected evil is the Spaniard. Mr. Martin says further (p. 140) :

The letters cited above show conclusively that the eye of all England is indeed fixed on Essex at this time and that the hope of breaking the power of Spain is the last hope upon which the retaining of Ireland as an English possession may rest.

Essex, then, is more bound up in the *Veue* than surface considerations would indicate. Undoubtedly, the *Veue* is for the final ear of the Queen, but the channel for the message is very important. There is no one more talked of throughout the spring and summer of 1596 than Essex. And when one concedes the identity of the proposed Principal Officer, it is but a logical step to suppose it is Essex whom Spenser has in mind, when he says that what he has set down in the *Veue* is for his own good and the satisfaction of Eudoxus, and that " who so list to overlook them . . . may perhaps better his own judgment." (*Veue*, p. 638b.)

Spenser considers Essex the logical man for Principal Officer. But Spenser is not alone in proposing Essex for Ireland. Although Essex did not go to Ireland until 1599, he was aware as soon as he returned to England in August, 1596, that the proposal of Ireland was in the air. Almost within the month he wrote to Antonio Perez, September 14, 1596, stating that he was being charged with certain failings in the last expedition, that all honor was being stripped from him; that it was thought proper to banish him to Ireland under the show of governing that Kingdom; that he had determined, however, to stay at court unless he should be permitted to go to Ireland with such a fleet and for... he should choose on his own terms. (Birch, 2. 140-141.)

In the light of this evidence, then, Spenser's insertion of the Burbon incident in the story of Irena indicates that he sought in that place to point to Essex as the person who could solve the Irish problem.

This interpretation does not conflict with that of Professor Greenlaw, who sees in the Irena episode a defense of the policies of Lord Grey. Spenser, by pointing to Essex in this connection, is merely giving to an old story a more timely and significant meaning. No doubt, in the first writing of this story Spenser had Grey in mind, but at the time of its publication its special reference was to Essex. With this in mind, let us examine the other progressive policies in the book. As Professor Greenlaw has pointed out, Book 5 is primarily a statement of the principles of the " forward" school, men who had caught the vision of a " new imperial Britain." The first principle of this school was the forcing of Elizabeth into an open break with Spain. Leicester and the other leaders of the Progressives were never able to commit Elizabeth to a determined war against Philip. The only aggressive action that she would ever consent to was war through her " sea dogs," but even then she always insisted that their exploits be under the cloak of private enterprise. Drake's voyage to the coast of Spain in 1586 was rendered futile by the restraining orders devised by her and her peace-loving Lord Treasurer. Had Drake been given a free hand, he would have destroyed Philip's invincible armada before it ever got out of its home port. The armada victory itself was forced on her, and the follow-up expedition of Drake in 1589 was defeated in England at the Council table. Drake remained idle at home until 1596. Elizabeth's temporizing and Lord Burghley's love of negotiation completely blocked any effort of the Progressives to follow up the advantage gained in the defeat of the armada. For the same reasons the Protestant nations in Europe could get no consistent aid from England. Leicester felt her anger because he definitely tied her to the protection of the Estates. In fact, Burghley and his party consistently blocked all efforts of the Progressives to commit Elizabeth to an imperial policy. And it was not until my Lord of Essex assumed the leadership of the party that " the old fox was made to crouch and whine."

The aid of Henry IV in 1591 was the first of Essex's achievements toward a liberal policy. When he returned from France, however, he " determined on a domestical greatness," was appointed a privy councillor, and immediately began his championship of the progressive policies and his opposition to Lord Burghley. By 1593 he was handling all foreign correspondence; he was virtually foreign secretary. Open, impulsive, and absolutely fearless, he began a campaign for the principles of his predecessors. He advocated the same principles as Leicester and Sidney, but with a difference: he put the principle above his own advantage and declined to admit defeat. So successful was he in his efforts, aided by his great popularity, that by 1593 he had not only Burghley but Elizabeth herself hard put to defend the policy of peace so long in vogue. In that year Elizabeth in a speech to Parliament remarked:

It may be thought Simplicity in me, that, all this Time of my Reign, I have not sought to advance my Territories, and enlarge my Dominions; for Opportunity hath served me to do it . . . I am contented to reign over my own, and to rule as a just Princesse.

Yet the King of Spain doth challenge me to be the Quarreller, and Beginner of these wars. . . . (*A Collection of Scarce and Interesting Tracts from the Sommers Collection*, London, 1795, p. 64.)

That Essex was the spirited leader of the War Party at this time is seen in every one of his acts. In a debate about peace in 1598, he gave a summary of his principles. (Camden, *Annals*, pp. 493-4.) An examination of this speech against peace will show it to be a concise statement of the cardinal principles of the "forward school."

That he stood strongly for the Protestant nations is evident from the letters preserved in the *Cecil MSS* (Vol. 5). A few of them will suffice:

August 20, 1595, the Governor of Dieppe wrote to Essex to advise him of conditions in that place and to beg him to continue his good graces.
August 12/22, 1595, M. du Montmartin:
Sending him M. de La Haye, one of the oldest and best of Huguenots, to represent to him the misery of Brittany, which has no hope of deliverance from the servitude of Spain except at the hand of the Queen of England.

In the same year many letters from George Gilpin to Essex show that he had taken the Estates under his protection. On Nov. 13, 1596, at a great entertainment to Bouillon, Henry IV's envoy, Essex promised to dispatch another expedition to Henry's aid.

His interest in the voyages of the seamen is evidenced not only by his own adventures on the sea, but also by his support of Drake and the other sea-dogs. Julian S. Corbett (*The Successors of Drake*, London, 1900, p. 24) names Essex as Drake's successor as the embodiment of the war spirit in England. He it was who obtained the Queen's sanction for the last voyage of Drake and Hawkins. One of their letters to him shows that they depended on him to avert the disaster that had defeated so many of their projects—Elizabeth's change of mind. On August 13, 1595, they wrote to Essex: "and for our own particulars, we humbly beseech your good lordship that if her Majesty do alter our first agreement that you stand strongly for us" (*Cecil MSS* 5. 319).

So, in 1596 it seemed that Essex had finally accomplished what Leicester and Walsingham had failed to do—he had beaten Burghley and had, it seemed, committed Elizabeth to an open break with Spain. His Cadiz expedition in that year has been called the most brilliant single success of English arms between the battles of Agincourt and Blenheim. Spenser celebrates it and Essex in his *Prothalamion* (st. 9):

Yet therein now doth lodge a noble Peer,
Great *Englands* glory and the Worlds wide wonder,
Whose dreadfull name, late through all *Spaine* did thunder,
And Hercules two pillors standing neere,
Did make to quake and feare:
Faire branch of Honor, flower of Cheualrie,
That fillest *England* with thy triumphs fame,
Joy haue thou of thy noble victorie,
And endlesse happinesse of thine owne name
That promiseth the same:
That through thy prowesse and victorious armes,
Thy country may be freed from forraine harmes:
And great *Elisaes* glorious name may ring
Through al the world, fil'd with thy wide Alarmes,
Which some brave muse may sing
To ages following.

I suggest that Spenser here names his own muse. Spenser sees, then, in the Cadiz voyage a realization of the principles advocated in Book 5 of the *Faerie Queene.* It is Essex who will complete the work started by Leicester, Sidney, Walsingham, and Grey. Not only is he the only man in England who can settle affairs in Ireland, but to Spenser he is the man who will make possible the "New Imperial Britain." And although Book 5 relates the deeds of Leicester and Grey, it has a more significant and timely purpose: it is a support of Essex in his attempt to force a progressive policy on Elizabeth and Burghley. By pointing to Essex so plainly in the Burbon and Irena episodes, Spenser is again using old material for a new pointed purpose. He has fulfilled his promise of the dedicatory sonnet, by presenting to us Essex as the leader of the forward school, and the hope of England for a great imperial policy.

APPENDIX III

THE POLITICAL ALLEGORY OF CANTO II

FREDERICK M. PADELFORD ("Spenser's Arraignment of the Anabaptists," pp. 434-448). The theme of the canto is the subject of property rights, and the canto falls into two parts,—the first twenty-eight stanzas dealing with extortion and the remaining twenty-six with communism. . . .

Whatever specific abuse, if any, Spenser may have in mind in this first episode, it is evident that he is here condemning the injustice of ill-gotten gains. The counterpart occupies the latter half of the canto, in which those who deny all property rights are as roundly scored. . . .

In briefest terms, in the second episode a loud-mouthed, muddle-headed agitator, a demagogue parading under the banner of justice, by shouting communism and denouncing property rights, and by denying the validity of law and authority, attracts a rabble of shallow-pated malcontents drawn from different nations. He is challenged by Artegall, the personification of justice, who declares that sovereignty and property are divinely-ordained institutions, created and supported by the mysterious providence of God, that in human life as in nature there are compensations for every loss, and that the true and the false, the right and the wrong—in other words, good and evil—cannot be placed in the balance and weighed against each other. Finally, the monstrous mischief-maker is forcibly dumped into the sea, and his disciples, who cannot be appeased by gentler means, are quieted by force. . . .

It must be evident that the allegory of Artegall and the Gyant is no mere academic handling of the subject of communism; it is a scathing denunciation of it, in which the personal feeling of the author is sufficiently evident. Spenser here throws down his gage. If the subject had been regarded as merely theoretical, an answer to such speculative and idealistic exercises as Plato's *Republic* and More's *Utopia*, Spenser would have replied in the traditional vein of Aristotle (*Politics* 2. 5), who held that the sense of possession is necessary to thrift and enterprise, is a source of keen pleasure, furnishes opportunities for the practice of temperance and liberality, and makes for harmony and real unity in the state.

Was there, then, a party or sect, in the England of Spenser's day, who were regarded as obstreperous advocates of communism, and who were sternly suppressed? Assuredly there was; a sect whose contentions were generally supposed to be those stated in the allegory, against whom the very arguments were used that are employed in the poem, whose followers were drawn from different nations, who were thought to arouse the ignorant and the designing, and to check whom the English government was forced to expel the leaders across seas without ceremony and to threaten the residue with force. This sect was the Anabaptists.

I shall now present the proofs in detail, and try to substantiate the thesis that the latter part of this canto is an arraignment of the Anabaptists.

Citations without number might be given to show that it was generally believed

336

that the Anabaptists, like the giant, though pretending to be reformers, were, in reality, stubborn sowers of dissension, distorting the Scriptures and tending to alienate the minds of men from each other and to dissolve the bonds of society through their denial of property rights, social distinctions, and civil and ecclesiastical authority. Two citations, however, may be taken as representative.

The first is from the pen of Bishop Hooper and was written in the time of King Edward VI (*Later Writings of Bishop Hooper,* Parker Society, p. 76):

For many times, as well heretofore as in our days, have been superstitious hypocrites and fanatical spirits, that have neglected and condemned the office of magistrates, judgments, laws, punishments of evil, lawful dominion, rule, lawful wars, and such like, without which a commonwealth may not endure. They have condemned also the ministry and ministers of Christ's church; and as for Christian society and charitable love, they confound. They use the ministry of the church so that it is out of all estimation, supposing themselves to be of such perfection, that they need neither the ministry of the word, neither use of Christ his holy sacraments, baptism and the supper of the Lord. And the other they use with such devilish disorder, that they would by a law make theirs their neighbours', and their neighbours' theirs, confounding all propriety and dominion of goods. . . .

And now in our time, to the great trouble and unquietness of many commonwealths in Europe, the Anabaptists have resuscitated and revived the same errors: which is an argument and token of the devil's great indignation against civil policy and order. For he knoweth, where such errors and false doctrines of political orders be planted, two great evils necessarily must needs follow: the one is sedition, that bringeth murders, blood-shedding, and dissipations of realms; the other is blasphemy against Christ's precious blood; for these sects think they be able to save themselves of and by themselves.

[A second citation to the same effect is given from Whitgift's "Answer to the Admonition," Strype, *Life and Acts of Archbishop Whitgift* 1. 71.]

Again, the arguments employed by Artegall to refute the contentions of the giant are precisely those commonly employed against the teachings of the Anabaptists. Artegall refutes the communistic doctrines of the giant by declaring them opposed to God's purpose and authority. This is the universal argument employed by Churchmen against this doctrine of the Anabaptists.

Thomas Rogers, in his *Exposition of the XXXIX Articles* (Thomas Rogers, *The Catholic Doctrine of the Church of England,* Parker Society, p. 352), presents the view of the Church in the following condensed form:

ARTICLE XXXVIII

Of Christian men's Goods, which are not common.

The riches and goods of Christians (1) are not common, as touching the right, title, and possession of the same, as certain Anabaptists do falsely boast. Notwithstanding (2) every man ought, of such things as he possesseth, liberally to give alms to the poor, according to his ability.

PROPOSITION I

The riches and goods of Christians, as touching the right, title, and possession of the same, are not common.

THE PROOF FROM GOD'S WORD

Against community of goods and riches be all those places (which are infinite) of holy scripture, that either condemn the unlawful getting, keeping, or desiring of riches, which, by covetousness, thievery, extortion, and the like wicked means, many do attain; or do commend liberality, frugality, free and friendly lending, honest labour, and lawful vocations to live and thrive by. All which do shew that Christians are to have goods of their own, and that riches ought not to be common.

Of this judgment be the reformed churches.

Henry Bullinger in his *Decades* (Parker Society 2. 18), a work of great vogue in England, in discussing the eighth commandment maintains that the holding of property is supported by both the Old Testament and the New, though " There is no small number of that furious sect of Anabaptists, which deny this property of several possessions." Bullinger's evidence is in brief as follows: God gave Abraham property; God apportioned the promised land among the children of Israel; Jesus commanded works of mercy and liberality, impossible under communism; Paul commanded laying up of alms; the early Christians sometimes sold their lands to relieve the necessity of their fellows, which could not have been done if they had not owned property; they broke bread from house to house, which implies that they had not renounced their possessions.

As the Anabaptists based their doctrine of communism upon the supposed practice of the Apostolic Church, the discussion naturally centered upon the early chapters of Acts. The orthodox contention is thus succinctly expressed by Thomas Cartwright (quoted in *The Works of John Whitgift*, Parker Society, 1. 352. Cf. also *The Works of Bishop Hooper,* Parker Society, 2. 42):

For, I pray you, what community is spoken of either in the two, or three, or fourth of the Acts, which ought not to be in the church as long as the world standeth? Was there any community but as touching the use, and so far forth as the poor brethren had need of, and not to take every man alike? Was it not in any man his power to sell his houses, or lands, or not to sell them? When he had sold them, were they not in every man his liberty to keep the money to himself at his pleasure? And all they that were of the church did not sell their possessions, but those whose hearts the Lord touched singularly with the compassion of the need of others, and whom God had blessed with abundance, that they had to serve themselves and help others; and therefore it is reckoned as a rare example that Barnabas the Cyprian and Levite did sell his possession and brought the price to the feet of the apostles.

The communistic doctrine was thus shown to be opposed to the social conditions allowed God's chosen people under the Old Dispensation, and the members of his inspired Church under the New. As Artegall declares,

> He gives to this, from that he takes away,
> For all we have is his: what he list doe, he may.

Again, the denial of temporal authority by the giant and by the fox [*Mother Hubberds Tale* 129-149], the boast of the giant that he would suppress tyrants and curb the nobility, are part and parcel of the supposed Anabaptist program and were condemned by Artegall on the same grounds as by the Churchmen. In a sermon preached at St. Paul's on November seventeenth, 1583, the anniversary of Queen Elizabeth's coming to the throne, Archbishop Whitgift speaks as follows (*Life and Acts of John Whitgift*, Parker Society, 3. 75): "The second sort (of the disloyal) are the Anabaptists; who wil have no government at al. And they ground their heresy upon the fifth to the Galathians, ' Stand fast in the liberty wherewith Christ hath made you free.' And again, ' You are called unto liberty.' " The fox was arguing from these very passages when he said,

> For why should he that is at libertie
> Make himself bond? sith then we are free borne,
> Let us all servile base subjection scorne.

The words of Artegall,

> He maketh kings to sit in soveraranty;
> He maketh subjects to their powre obay;

voice the attitude of the English Church, as of the Reformation in general. They correspond exactly to the first two divisions of this sermon, that obedience to magistrates is the express commandment of God, and that sovereignty exists by the ordinance of God. To quote again (*ibid.* 71):

(1) The commandment of God is evident; by the first commandment of the second table: " Honour thy father and thy mother."
Christ himself paid tribute; and left it as a perpetual rule to al, " Give unto Caesar," &c. " Let every soul be subject unto the higher powers": and, " Obey those that are set over you," saith his Apostle. And S. Peter, " Be subject to every humane ordinance for the Lord's sake."
" Yee must needs be subject," saith S. Paul. " Oportet subjici." Obedience is nothing indifferent: to be taken or shaken off at our own pleasure: but " for fear," and for " conscience sake " also, as the same Apostle adds.
If this charge were made by the Apostles when the magistrate was an infidel, and in the time of Nero, a cruel persecutor, how much more ought obedience be commanded now by us, and yielded by you, to a Christian magistrate, that saveth you from persecution.
(2) It is the ordinance of God. The magistrate is appointed by God. He is his Vicar and Vicegerent. He giveth him his name; and title: " Vos dii estis." " I said, Ye are gods."
" Dominus dat sceptrum, cui vult, et aufert ": i. e. " God gives the sceptre to whom he wil, and takes it away."
" Per me reges regnant ": i. e. " By me Kings reign."
" Promotion cometh neither from the east, nor from the west. God setteth up and pulleth down whom it pleaseth him."

The words of Artegall to the giant,

> He pulleth downe, he setteth up on hy,

are the very words of the Proverb here employed in refuting the teachings of the Anabaptists.
Can there longer be any question that the giant represents the Anabaptists, and his noisy declarations, the Anabaptist cult?

The vain efforts of the giant to balance good and evil, I take to be a criticism of the supposed Anabaptist doctrine of salvation by works, the doctrine that close account is kept of a man's deeds and that his chance of salvation depends upon having a snug balance on the right side of the ledger. The English Churchmen did not believe in any such system of divine bookkeeping. I think Spenser is saying, in terms of allegory, that we are justified by faith alone, and that it is idle to try to determine any man's claim upon God by balancing his good deeds over against his evil deeds. So dreadful is sin in the sight of God, so impotent is man by nature, that nothing but faith in Christ can be to him of any avail. Bishop Bale classed the Anabaptists with the Papists because of this doctrine, and Thomas Rogers classed them with the Turks.

It now remains to explain the action of Talus in shouldering the giant off the land into the sea. As a result of the persecutions in the Netherlands under Alva, a great many Anabaptists took shelter in England, and in the year 1568 their presence was considered so grave a menace that the following proclamation was issued against them (Strype, *Life and Acts of Archbishop Grindal*, 181):

The Queen's Majesty understanding that of late time sundry persons, being infected with certain dangerous and pernicious opinions, in matters of religion, contrary to the faith of the Church of Christ, as Anabaptists, and such lyke, are come from sundry parts beyond the seas into this her realme, and speciallye into the citie of London, and other maritime townes, under the colour and pretence of flying from persecution against the professors of the Gospel of Chryst: whereby if remedy be not speedily provided, the Church of God in this realme shall susteyne great daunger of corruption, and sects to increase contrary to the unitie of Chryst's Church here established.

For redresse whereof, her Majestie, by advice of her Counsayle, having commanded the Archbishop of Canterbury, Byshop of London, and other Byshops to see the parishes in London, and other places herewith suspected, to be severely visited, and all persons suspected to be openly tried and examined, touching such phanatical and heretical opinions; willeth and chargeth all manner of persons born eyther in forreigne parts, or in her Majesties dominions, that have conceaved any manner of such heretical opinion as the Anabaptists do hold, and meaneth not by charitable teaching to be reconciled, to depart out of this realme within twenty days after this proclamation upon payne of forfeiture of all their goods and cattelles, and to be imprisoned, and further punyshed, as by the laws eyther ecclesiastical or temporal in such case is provided.

I suggest that it was this harsh removal across seas of these troublesome sectarians that is figured forth in the precipitation of the giant into the sea. Twice before in Elizabeth's reign had like measures been taken, but they were not carried through so vigorously.

Such, then, do I take to be the allegory of Sir Artegall and the giant.

The canto as a whole is a definition of the correct theory of property by the elimination of wrong theories, and an exposition of the office of the true nobleman, the man of virtue ($\dot{\alpha}\rho\epsilon\tau\dot{\eta}$), in upholding economic justice. Extortion and communism are in equal violation of that divine law upon which justice is based, and it is the duty of the true knight, on the one hand to defend the poor against the greed of the plutocrat, and on the other, to defend property against the revo-

lutionary folly of the communist.   As succinctly expressed in the opening lines of
the canto:

> Nought is more honorable to a knight,
> Ne better doth beseeme brave chevalry,
> Than to defend the feeble in their right,
> And wrong redresse in such as wend awry.

In Book Two, Spenser had already condemned the greed for gold on the grounds
of temperance, and had defined the attitude which the virtuous man should take
toward riches.   Sir Guyon, the knight of Temperance, in response to the tempta-
tions of Mammon, rejoins:

> But I in armes, and in atchievements brave,
> Do rather choose my flitting houres to spend,
> And to be Lord of those, that riches have,
> Then them to have my selfe, and be their servile sclave.
>
> [2. 7. 3. 6-9]
>
> All that I need I have; what needeth mee
> To covet more, than I have cause to use?   [2. 7. 39. 3-4]

I have elsewhere tried to show that in matters ecclesiastical Spenser chose the
golden mean; I think it is evident from the present study that he likewise inclined
to the golden mean in the matter of riches.

It remains to be observed that this attitude is precisely that advocated by the
Elizabethan divines.   The condemnation of concupiscence in the first part of the
canto, like the condemnation of communism in the second, runs parallel to the
prevailing ecclesiastical thought.   In the sermon on the eighth commandment,
quoted above, Bullinger condemns extortion and the inordinate love of money
with as much warmth as he condemns the communism of the Anabaptists.   The
prevailing attitude of the English Churchmen is succinctly expressed in the words
of the articles agreed upon in the convocation of 1552, and published by King
Edward VI (*Liturgies of King Edward VI*, Parker Society, p. 536): " The riches
and the goods of Christians are not common, as touching the right, title, and possession of the same, (as certain Anabaptists do falsely boast:) notwithstanding
every man ought of such things, as he possesseth, to give alms to the poor, according to his ability."   Thus in this canto, as in the first book, Spenser identifies himself with current ecclesiastical thought.

MERRITT Y. HUGHES (" Spenser and Utopia," pp. 133-146, abstracted).
" The sixteenth century had its democracy, but it was not of our kind.   It was
more thoroughgoing than ours.   It recognized that men are all subject to the law
of their nature and consequently owe each other a certain mutual respect which
transcends all differences of rank.   Spenser has plenty of glimpses of the humor
and wisdom of this kind of democracy even in his aristocratic *Faerie Queene*.   In
Book III, canto 11:

> Kings, queenes, lords, ladies, knights, and damsels gent
> Are heaped together with the vulgar sort
> And mingled with the raskall rabblement,
> Without respect of person or of port,
> To show Dan Cupid's power and great effort.

The sixteenth century never lost sight of the common destiny of men, nor failed
to recognize the obligation

　　　　　. . . to love our brethren that were made
　　　　　Of that selfe mould and that selfe Maker's hand,
　　　　　That we, and to the same again shall fade,
　　　　　Where they shall have like heritage of land,
　　　　　However here on higher steps we stand,
　　　　　Which also were with selfe same price redeemed
　　　　　That we, however of us light esteemed.　(H. H. L. 198-204)

The political and religious ideas of the Renaissance fixed a gulf between gentlemen and commons and denied the latter a share in the management of the society
of which they were a part and forbade them to try or even to wish to better their
state.　Over against these restrictions it put a code of corresponding obligations
upon the rulers.　There was one law for people and another for king and nobles,
but both were brought under the higher laws, political and religious, which were
embodied in the ideas of the Commonwealth and the Church.　To those laws all
were alike slaves. . . ."

" In the scene between Artegall, Talus, and the Giant in Book V of the *Faerie
Queene* (2. 29-54), Spenser expressed the sixteenth century's sense of the separation of the classes and summed up the bitterness of the more than fifty years of
struggle into which the religious and industrial changes of the time had thrown
them, both in England and on the Continent."

The episode is improperly construed by Miss Winstanley (*MLQ* 3. 11) as
evidence of Spenser's Calvinistic fatalism, for it reflects a traditional social attitude.　Instance North's translation of the Bishop of Guevara's handbook of politics, published in 1557 under the title *The Diall of Princes*, Elyot's *Booke of the
Governour*, John Tyndall's *Book of the Obedience of a Christian Man*, and
casual observations by such historians as Holinshed.

Spenser shared in the recognition of a past age of gold, which both Christian
belief and the newly explored mythology encouraged, and " Artegall is Astraea's
emissary to restore the age of Saturn, from which the Book takes its departure,"
but the poet did not countenance the theory that this restoration should be accomplished through a communistic leveling of society.　Like other Elizabethan gentlemen he shuddered at the thought of the Peasants' War in Germany and Ket's
revolt in 1549.

" *Mother Hubberds Tale* and the second canto of Book V of the *Faerie Queene*
are at the hither end of a line of political tracts issued against the seditionists of
Edward VI's reign and their doctrines.　The most important of these was Sir John
Cheke's ' The Hurt of Sedition, how grievous it is to a Commonwealth ' or ' The
True Subject to the Rebel,' which appeared about 1550 and is preserved entire on
the pages of Holinshed and in part in Strype's *Memorials*.　The disturbances died
down with Elizabeth's accession and the subject passed from pamphlets into literature.　Sidney introduces us to it in the fifth chapter of the *Arcadia,* when Kalendar
hears that his son has been captured in battle by the Helots and

that the hate of those paysaunts conceaved against all Gentlemen was suche, that
everye houre hee was to looke for nothing but some cruell death:　which hether-
unto had onely beene delayed by the Captaines vehement dealing for him.

Presently the rebels make their captive, Pyrochles, their captain, 'God wott, little prowde of that dignitie,' for noble blood and noble rank cannot remain long separated with Sidney. In Book II of the *Arcadia* he resumes the subject of the peasant revolt and tells a story which resembles Spenser's account in the fifth book of the *Faerie Queene* in the contempt he shows for the common people, and in their easy defeat by Zelmane, Basilius, and Dorus, who makes a great slaughter among them with a sheep-hook, as Talus does with his flail in the later version of the story. There is more realism in Sidney's fight than there is in Spenser's, and the savage joke of the painter who lost his hands in the fray is unlike the spirit of Spenser in the *Faerie Queene* although it has parallels enough in the 'Present State of Ireland.'

" Sidney's cynical account of the confused objects of his rebel peasants shows that he was thinking of recent events in England and on the Continent, and also that his mind was full of classical treatments of such scenes as he was painting. Homer's mobs like swarms of bees and Agrippa's Fable were in his thoughts. He wrote (*Arcadia*, p. 217):

. . . when they began to talke of their grieves, never Bees made such a confused humming: the towne dwellers demanding putting downe of imposts: the country felowes laying out of common . . . Al cried out to have new councellors: but when they should think of any new, they liked them as well as any other, that they could remember, especially they would have the treasure so looked unto, as that he should never neede to take any more subsidies. At length they fell to direct contrarities. For the Artisans, they would have Corne and Wine set at a lower price, and bound to be kept so still: the plowmen, vine-laborers, and farmers would none of that. The countrimen demanded that every man might be free in the chief townes: that could not the Burgesses like of. The peasants would have the Gentlemen destroied, the Citizens (especially such as Cookes, Barbers, and those that lived most on Gentlemen) would but have them reformed.

Spenser was only following suit when he wrote:

> Therefore the vulgar did about him flocke,
> And cluster thicke unto his leasing vaine,
> Like foolish flies about an hony crocke,
> In hope by him great benefite to gaine,
> And uncontrolled freedome to obtaine.

" The relation between Spenser's ideas in Book Five of the *Faerie Queene* and the mass of floating conservative opinion about the social order which is reflected in the books of Elyot, Tyndall, North, Cheke, and Sidney which have been mentioned, illustrates the extent to which he was indebted in this passage, as he was in all that he wrote, to the spirit of his time and to literary traditions of the past. He was not speaking merely as a Calvinist, although it happened that Calvin, and, for that matter, Luther too, professed the same political principles and exerted themselves in their defence. At heart in this, as in some other passages, Spenser was really closer to the Roman faith which he abhorred than he was to the Protestantism which he professed.

" The second canto of Book Five is a partisan pamphlet. It tells only one side of the dispute between gentles and commons. For the other side we must

turn to the old historians and divines. Spenser's choice of sides, and his introduction of this material into the poem, leaves no doubt of his feeling toward
democracy as we understand it today. Whitman's ' dignity of the common people,' would have been unthinkable to him. The modern conception of the better-
ment and self-expression of the people collectively would have aroused his scorn
and the idea that they should participate in government would have stirred his
laughter. His mind was, as Mr. Cory has put it, conservative and ' institutional.'
He was an aristocrat, and he reserved the worst vials of his wrath, as Shakspere
did for the demagogues, Brutus and Sicinius, in *Coriolanus,* for Utopian ideals
and idealists. Spenser showed himself democratic in recognizing that gentle virtues sometimes spring in vulgar soil; and in keeping his eyes steadily upon the
essential human equality from which differences in blood and rank cannot emanci-
pate; but for democracy and for socialism in any of its varieties he took more
particular pains than any other Elizabethan writer to let us know that he entertained no sympathy at all.

"With this conclusion the paper properly ends, but it may be of interest to
suggest a possible definite historical allegory in the story of the Giant whom Artegall overthrows. It lies in the rebellion already mentioned which had its centre
in Norwich in 1549. The parallel between the events at Norwich and those at
Münster, which have been pointed to as likely to have been in Spenser's eye, is
close enough in a general way to let either serve as inspiration for the passage.
Probably Spenser was writing without a very definite slant on history. The rebels
in 1549, like those in the *Faerie Queene,* were led by a specious man of straw,
John Ket, who promised a Utopian reformation. Ket, like the Giant, was overthrown at the very beginning of the armed struggle, but only after a long and
formal debate with the representative of authority, and his people were cut to
pieces in a terrible slaughter by a large force of Swiss and Italians. Holinshed
writes that ' Norreie, king at armes,' offered the Marquis of Northampton's pardon
to the rebels in the city and pleaded with them to adopt sane counsels. A man
named Flotman came forward as their herald and

utterlie refused the kings pardon, and told Norreie certeinely that they would either
restore the Common-wealth from decaie, into which it was fallen, being oppressed
through the covetousnesse and tyrannie of the gentlemen: either else would they
like men die in the quarrell.

Then the mercenaries were set upon them and they died, but hardly like men, if
the chronicler is to be trusted.

"The parallel between the foreign troops and Talus is on the surface. The
Iron Man embodied Spenser's memories of the little bands of English men-at-arms
in Ireland but he also represented the avengers of lawlessness universally. Ulti-
mately, perhaps, he typifies the violence with which nature rights the gross wrongs
of history. In a passage discussing the fancy and the imagination Coleridge mentions Talus as an example of Spenser's poetic powers at their best. He writes:

He has an imaginative fancy, but he has not imagination, in kind or degree,
as Shakspere or Marlowe have; the boldest effort of his powers in this way is the
character of Talus.

De Vere and De Selincourt have written of Talus in a similar spirit of praise. De Selincourt says:

> By his [Artegall's] side he sets Talus, the iron man, the most powerful embodiment of Justice in the abstract. In Sir Artegall and his remorseless squire the different types of allegory are seen at once in their best contrast and in perfect harmony.

Talus is undoubtedly one of the most satisfactory inventions in the whole allegory. He is more convincing and significant than any of the other companions of the Knights errant except Una, and he probably stood very definitely for the iron soldiers who avenged the cause of Justice in Spenser's time and for the principle which lay behind their existence in society. He answered also to a sense of fitness which we still feel in these matters and which North phrased definitely for his age in a passage in the *Diall*:

> We ordeine and commaund, that the prince do not onely not kill with his hands, but also that he doo not see them do justice with his eyes. For how muche noble and worthie a thing it is, before the presence of a prince, that all should receive honour: so sclaunderous a thing it is that any in his presence should loose their lyves."

M. BEER (*A History of British Socialism,* London, 1929, pp. 46-7). On the whole, with the rise of Protestantism the clear Scriptural text of the Ten Commandments prevailed over the communistic traditions of Primitive Christianity, monastic orders, and scholastic *ius naturale*. The work begun by the author of *Piers Plowman* was accomplished by Bishop Latimer. Communism lost its sanction in Church and State, and took refuge with the extreme wing of nonconformity, revolutionary rationalism, and working class organisations, while society at large moved toward individualism, whose first manifestation was the Elizabethan Age—an age of pioneers, men of keen initiative. Its great interpreters, Spenser and Shakespeare, were both anti-communist and anti-democratic. Spenser, in his *Faery Queene*, matches Artegall, the champion of true justice and skilled in righteous lore, against the communist Giant, who, standing on a rock near the sea, is telling the vast crowd that, with the huge pair of scales held in his hands, he would weigh equally all the world, for he saw that all was unequal and that the elements of Nature as well as the men in society were encroaching upon each other's share. [Development of the episode briefly outlined.]

MERLIN L. NEFF ("Spenser's Allegory of the Toll Bridge," pp. 159-167; condensed). The second canto of the fifth book presents the two extremes of distributive justice in the episodes of Artegall's conflict with Pollente and Lady Munera, and his struggle with the Gyant by the sea. If Mr. Padelford is correct, the second episode is a specific thrust at communism as promulgated by the Anabaptists. I believe that the first episode, although suggested in plot by the *Orlando Furioso,* is equally specific. Although Greenlaw (*MLN* 35. 174) interpreted it as " an exemplum showing the evils of bribery," bribery is merely incidental. Rather, I take it, Spenser is attacking monopolies—the very opposite of communism— through one of its most flagrant forms, the extortionate tolls. It was " the evil fashion, and wicked customes of that bridge " (28. 7-8) that Artegall was called upon to reform, and it was the powerful and iniquitous Pollente, keeper of the bridge, whose head was pitched on a pole as a warning to like offenders.

Although monopolies had long existed as a source of revenue for the crown, or for private individuals who enjoyed royal favor, grants of monopolies increased to such an extent under Elizabeth that, if Hume is correct (*History of England* 4. 44), they were more iniquitous than in any other period of English history. These monopolies were of two types, external and internal. External grants of monopoly were made on many imported articles, such as salt, soap, glass and metals; internal, on control of highways, fishing rights, dam sites, bridges and ferries. The patentee secured high and arbitrary power from the Council and was protected in his extortion. Dekker (*The Non-Dramatic Works of Thomas Dekker,* Huth Library, 3. 366-7) defines such an individual as a catch-poll:

A *Catch-poll* is one that doth both catch and poll: who is not content onely to haue the sheepe, but must sheare it too; and not sheare it, but to draw bloud too. So then by this *Etymology* of the word, any one that sinisterly wrests and scrues *Monopolies* into his hands, to fill his Coffers, (though his owne conscience whispers in his eare, that hee beggers the Common-wealth) and his Prince neuer the better for it: but the poore Subjects much the worse: Hee is a *Grand Catchpoll.*

Pollente was obviously a catch-poll, for Spenser (8. 8) states that he "pols and pils the poore in piteous wize."

The specific monopoly on bridges, ferries and roads had developed over a long period of time. During the feudal period roads and bridges were kept in repair by the "trinoda necessitas" acts, which threw the responsibility upon the landed proprietors. With the decline of feudalism, which terminated many of the services hitherto required of serfs, roads and bridges deteriorated, and the responsibility for upkeep was then either placed upon communities or counties, or was granted to individuals upon the toll basis. The *Statutes of the Realm* and the *Calendar of Patent Rolls* [frequently quoted] tell the story of the demands in this connection that were made upon towns, parishes or counties, of the graft that crept in, of the grants in patent to favored individuals, even including members of the royal household, and of the commissions appointed to remedy the extortion and bribery that constantly attended these grants.

The public protest at the abuses of monopoly, though discouraged by those in high place, steadily increased during Elizabeth's reign until in her last Parliament (1601) specific steps were taken by the commoners to break the prerogative power (Sidney Lee, "The Last Years of Elizabeth," *Cambridge Modern History,* 3. 357):

An Act was introduced by a private member, Lawrence Hyde, declaring monopolies illegal and extortionate. Great frankness characterized the debate; the grants of monopolies were declared to be derogatory to her Majesty, odious to the subject, and dangerous to the commonwealth; the grantees were denounced as bloodsuckers of the commonwealth. The Queen perceived at once the seriousness of the situation, and showed infinite resource in her method of meeting the crisis. . . . She understood, she declared, that the patents which she had granted were grievous to her people; they should be looked to immediately, and none be put into execution but such as should first have a trial according to the law, for the good of the people; she was resolved to defend her people from all aggression, and would take immediate order for the reformation of the grievance. . . . Three days later the Queen by proclamation suspended all patents of monopoly, until their legality should have been tested by the law officers of the Crown.

Similar abuses existed in Ireland, and these must frequently have come to Spenser's attention. Thus Auditor Jenyson, reporting to Lord Burghley on January 26, 1587 (*Calendar of State Papers of Ireland* 1586-8, pp. 246-7), specifically cites the extortion practiced at the bridge of Athlone:

Sir Henry Sidney was of great credit, and also famous in this government as by divers his erections appeareth, and most chiefly by the bridge at Athlone, which is one of the best acts done for the commonwealth in this land during man's memory, and doth now grow into some ruin, by reason of the strong stream that runneth there, and in process of time will overthrow it, which repairing betimes and so from year to year when need should require would maintain it forever. And that were easily to be done with the toll there taken, and would also be some increase to Her Majesty's revenue, the same being now turnd to private use, and nothing thereof either answered to Her Majesty or yet bestowed on the bridge. And the toll Sir Richard Byngham informeth me is well worth 100 £. sterling per annum, which is levied in this sort, viz., of every twenty cows or beeves that come over the bridge, one cow or beef out of every score, and if the number be under 20 for every cow 4d. sterling, and so of horsepacks, mares, colts, swine, and sheep ratably, and is thought there is five or six thousand kine yearly, at the least, driven over that bridge.

Through the specific monopoly of toll bridges Spenser may have symbolized the general evil of monopolies and patents that choked the commonwealth. The trap door may possibly set forth the methods of bribery and fraud that allowed the unskilled and unwary to be trapped by fierce Pollente. It is worthy of note that Talus takes no actual part in endeavoring to overcome the taker of toll, perhaps because the patents protected individuals legally in their nefarious business. Talus does take an active part, however, against Lady Munera, the keeper of the gold hoard, who endeavors to bribe justice.

If this view of the episode is correct, it is important to point out that Spenser is bold in his presentation of the monopolistic evil and its necessary reform. He was in advance of the main body of reform legislation. As late as 1571 a member of the House of Commons had been severely reprimanded by the Council for venturing to complain against licenses and monopolies. (William Hyde Price, *The English Patents of Monopoly*, p. 20.) Book V, appearing in 1596, presented the need for justice in the economic system and the reform measures necessary at the time when the public was strongly remonstrating against patents of privilege. Such a historical view of this canto reveals Spenser's attitude toward social justice when the nobility were thriving on unjust grants from the English sovereign.

APPENDIX IV

THE ITALIAN ROMANCES

Susannah Jane McMurphy (*Spenser's Use of Ariosto for Allegory*, pp. 35-6). There remains the love story of Britomart and Artegall. The first encounter, wherein Chastity overcomes an unknown Justice, and the second, in which she is attacked for having defrauded Love, but, being seen, enchants her assailant, whom she in turn recognizes as the masculine virtue long since conceived in dreams, contain but a trait or two of Bradamante's duel with Ruggiero. The exact situations which Spenser creates nowhere appear in Ariosto. Bradamante overthrows many with the lance of gold but Ariosto skillfully avoids having her encounter Ruggiero with this weapon. There is a long duel in the lists at Paris, all a summer's day, between Bradamante, in her own behalf, to secure herself from an unwelcome marriage, and Ruggiero, as Leo's champion, unknown to his betrothed. From this Spenser draws Britomart's failing strength at one point in the struggle beside the fountain. But the contract between Chaste Love and Justice is not derived from Ariosto, for not even the most ingenious allegorizer could interpret Ruggiero as justice. (Toscanella makes a sorry attempt to identify Ruggiero with marital fidelity in spite of his two serious defections, and several delays.)

The only important act of Ruggiero's which Spenser adopts is his leaving Bradamante after a brief interview, on each of two occasions, to hasten to the relief of his King, Agramante. Ariosto praises in this his recognition of the superior claims of public over private duty, honor over love. On one of these occasions, Ruggiero is seriously wounded, and so unable to keep his day with Bradamante. In like manner, Artegall breaks his compact with Britomart by reason of his imprisonment by Radigund. Britomart's fight with Dolon's sons at Pollente's bridge may be an imitation of Bradamante's encounter with Rodomonte on the narrow bridge over the Rhone, which he holds against all comers in order to avenge the death of Isabella. This princess he himself slew, for she entrapped him into the murder to save her honor. It is not quite clear that there is a necessity for this exploit at the bridge in Spenser's tale of Chastity and Justice. In the House of Dolon, she is resisting a new evil, Guile, by armed and sleepless watch, but on the narrow way across the flood, what moral principle is illustrated except that which we have had before, the prowess of the golden spear? Though this is now the Book of Justice, we have nothing here like Bradamante's pointed accusation that Rodomonte is punishing the innocent for his own crimes of lust and murder. Spenser may have some idea of symbolizing the dangers of the path to virtue, but on the whole, he cannot be said to have developed the material he adopts or endowed it with richer significance. As to the Golden Lance, Toscanella, at last, after this exploit, tells us that it meant the hidden virtue which none may resist. Of course Spenser has his lance from Ariosto, and he may have its meaning from Toscanella, but he could equally well have seen its possibilities for himself.

348

Britomart's jealousy in the interim between Artegall's failure to reappear and Talus' arrival with the news of his capture, is exactly modeled upon Bradamante's like passion—the watching of the road, the counting of the days, the varying imaginations of accident and disloyalty, even the passionate weeping and throes of grief upon her bed. Spenser is probably correct in counting Chastity a jealous virtue. But in casting about for a suitable object of the jealousy, he seems to have rejected Ariosto's device of the long lost sister of Ruggiero, the Amazon Marfisa.—If he had lived in the twentieth century, he might have seen unrealized allegorical possibilities in it.—He chooses rather the pride of the—shall we say female adventurer, or new woman?—who has abandoned her "sphere" to shine more brilliantly in another, to vindicate her self-sufficiency by equal force, or, if out-shone, to conquer still—by being out-shone. There is a radically modern suggestion in Britomart's sallying forth to her lover's rescue through competition with Radigund in arms. Bradamante's corresponding victory over Marfisa in several encounters, Fornari and Toscanella interpret as the victory of virtue over pride. Radigund has in common with Marfisa a fierce, almost termagant arrogance of strength. Marfisa is always triumphant. At the one moment when she is about to be conquered by Ruggiero, the shade of Atlante intervenes to reveal their kinship, to reconcile the pair, and to appease Bradamante. In place of this incident, Spenser has Artegall overcome by Radigund's beauty, just as on an earlier occasion by Britomart's. He adds the whole fiction of Radigund's Amazon kingdom and Britomart's repeal of the liberties of women. Although he may have obtained a suggestion from the lascivious kingdom of the women of Laiazzo, yet there are no details to connect Radigund with these, and closer parallels can be found in classical literature.

APPENDIX V

INDEX OF SOURCES AND ANALOGUES

Greek

AESCHYLUS. Commentary: 7. 2; 10. 8. 8; 11. 1. 1-6.

ANTHOLOGIA PALATINA. Commentary: 4. 20. 2-3.

APOLLODORUS. Commentary: 1. 2. 1-5; 1. 2. 6-9; 1. 12; 4. 31. 4; 5. 24. 2-9; 7. 10. 5; 10. 9-10; 10. 10. 1-2; 11. 23-25.

APOLLONIUS RHODIUS. Appendix I: Davis; Commentary: 1. 12; 4. 31; 7. 2 ff.; 10. 9-10.

ARISTOPHANES. Commentary: 7. 12. 2.

ARISTOTLE. Appendix I: Bhattacherje, Davis, DeMoss, Gough, Jones; III: Padelford; Commentary: 2. 29 ff.; 2. 48-49; 3. 15. 5; 12. 32. 8.

AXIOCHUS. Commentary: 11. 59. 6-8.

CLEMENT OF ALEXANDRIA. Commentary: 11. 17. 9.

DIODORUS SICULUS. Commentary: 1. 2. 1-5; 1. 2. 6-9; 4. 29 ff.; 4. 31. 6; 4. 33. 5; 7. 2 ff.; 7. 3. 1; 7. 4. 7-8; 7. 8. 9; 7. 10. 5.

EURIPIDES. Commentary: 2. 4 ff.; 3. 10. 4; 3. 24; 5. 49. 1-4; 8. 43. 1-7; 8. 47. 8; 8. 49. 9; 12. 1. 4-6.

EUSTATHIUS. Commentary: 1. 12.

HERODOTUS. Appendix I: Upton; Commentary: Pr. 8; 7. 4. 1-5; 7. 22. 2.

HESIOD. Commentary: Pr. 9; Pr. 9. 7; 1. 9-10; 3. 25. 1; 5. 49. 3-4; 7. 2; 9. 31-32; 10. 8. 8; 10. 9-10; 10. 10. 6-8.

HOMER. Commentary: 1. 5-11; 1. 15. 2; 2. 4 ff.; 2. 30 ff.; 2. 44. 9; 3. 4. 1-2; 3. 24. 9; 4. 31. 4; 5. 2-3; 5. 3. 6-9; 6. 32; 6. 32. 1; 7. 9. 1-3; 7. 22. 2; 7. 28. 5-9; 7. 39; 8. 35. 5-9; 8. 36. 4-5; 8. 42. 4-5; 8. 45. 1; 9. 12. 6-7; 9. 17-19; 9. 31-32; 10. 35. 8-9; 11. 58. 1-2; 11. 59. 6-8.

IBYCUS. Commentary: 1. 12.

LUCIAN. Commentary: 1. 12.

ORPHEUS OR ONOMACRITUS. Commentary: 1. 12.

PAUSANIUS. Commentary: 1. 12.

PHOTIUS. Commentary: 1. 12.

PINDAR. Commentary: 9. 31-32.

PLATO. Appendix I: Bhattacherje, Davis, Jones; Commentary: 1. 12; 3. 17 ff.; 3. 24; 4. 31 ff.; 5. 49. 3-4; 7. 1; 7. 2 ff.; 7. 2; 9. 12. 6-7.

PLUTARCH. Commentary: 2. 4 ff.; 7. 2 ff.; 7. 4. 7-8; 7. 9. 7; 7. 10. 1-2; 7. 10. 3— 11. 6; 11. 6; 12. 32. 8.

POSEIDONOS. Appendix II: Henley.

PTOLOMAEUS. Appendix II: Henley; Commentary: Pr. 7. 6.

QUINTUS SMYRNAEUS. Commentary: 5. 2-3.

SOPHOCLES. Commentary: 1. 12.

SUIDAS. Commentary: 1. 12.

XENOPHON. Commentary: 3. 22. 3; 8. 41. 6.

ZENOBIUS. Commentary: 1. 12.

Latin

Bible

Commentary: Pr. gen; Pr. 10. 2-5; Pr. 10. 6; Pr. 11; Pr. 11. 2; 1. 5-11; 1. 15. 7;
1. 26. 1-5; 2. 27. 6-9; 2. 29 ff.; 2. 35. 1-4; 2. 40; 2. 41; 2. 41. 5; 2. 41. 5-6;
2. 41. 7; 2. 41. 8; 2. 41. 9; 2. 42. 1; 2. 42. 5—43; 2. 42. 5-9; 2. 43. 2; 3. 37.
5; 3. 40. 1-3; 4. 11. 2; 4. 22. 9; 4. 25. 6; 5. 39. 3; 6. 1. 7; 6. 22. 1; 6. 27. 2;
7. 1. 6; 7. 1. 9; 7. 4. 1-5; 7. 10. 2; 7. 12. 2; 7. 22. 2; 8. 2. 1-3; 8. 4. 8; 8. 19.
5-6; 8. 28. 4-6; 8. 30-40; 9. 29. 4-5; 10. 1. 7-8; 10. 11. 5-9; 10. 24. 6; 10.
28. 7; 11. 19. 5-7; 11. 34. 4; 11. 46. 3; 11. 47. 9; 12. 1. 3; 12. 36. 2-5;
12. 42. 9.

Italian

ALCIATI.   Commentary: 12. 30. 6.
ARIOSTO.   Appendix I: Warren; III: Neff; IV: McMurphy; Commentary: 1. 3;
1. 9-10; 2. 3. 1-4; 2. 4 ff.; 2. 11-19; 2. 18; 2. 54; 2. 54. 1-5; 3. 2. 5-9; 3. 5;
3. 10-15; 3. 15. 4; 3. 19. 1-7; 3. 23. 5; 3. 33-34; 3. 34. 3; 3. 37; 3. 40;
4. 2-3; 4. 11; 4. 21 ff.; 4. 29 ff.; 4. 30. 1; 4. 31; 4. 42. 3; 5. 12; 5. 57;
6. 3 ff.; 6. 7. 4; 6. 8; 6. 36-39; 7. 3. 5; 7. 26 ff.; 7. 45; 8. 36. 4-5; 8. 37;
8. 51; 9. 1; 9. 11. 6-8; 9. 12. 6-7; 9. 13. 1-7; 10; 11. 36; 11. 58. 1-2; 12. 13;
12. 43.
FRA BELLO.   Commentary: 12. 13.
BERNI.   Commentary: Pr. 2. 5-6; 11. 6. 9; 11. 23-25.
BOCCACCIO.   Commentary: 2. 1. 5-7; 3. 25. 1; 5. 24. 2-9; 5. 24. 3-4; 6. 32; 6. 32.
1; 7. 10. 3—11. 6; 8. 31. 1-4; 8. 43. 1-7; 8. 47. 5-6; 9. 6. 5; 10. 13. 8-9; 12.
13; 12. 29-32.
BOIARDO.   Commentary: 2. 44. 9; 2. 54. 1-5; 3. 2. 5-9; 3. 5; 3. 14. 8-9; 3. 23. 5;
8. 36. 4-5; 8. 50. 7-8; 9. 13. 1-7; 9. 14. 2-3; 11. 58. 1-2; 12. 13.
CASTIGLIONE.   Commentary: 3. 17 ff.
DANTE.   Commentary: 2. 54. 1-5; 3. 19. 1-7; 4. 36. 7; 10. 13. 8-9; 12. 13.
MACHIAVELLI.   Appendix II: Greenlaw.
NATALIS COMES.   Commentary: Pr. 2. 6. 7; 1. 2. 1-5; 1. 5-11; 1. 12; 2. 4 ff.;
2. 7 ff.; 5. 23. 1-5; 6. 32. 1; 7. 2 ff.; 7. 4. 5; 7. 10. 3—11. 6; 8. 39 ff.; 8. 40;
8. 47. 1-2; 9. 31-32; 10. 9-10; 10. 10. 1-2; 10. 10. 7-8; 10. 20. 7-8; 11. 6;
11. 23-25; 11. 32. 4.
PETRARCH.   Commentary: 5. 53. 7-8.
PULCI.   Commentary: 8. 9. 9; 8. 36. 4-5; 11. 58. 7-9.
SERVIUS.   Commentary: 7. 8. 9; 10. 9-10.
TASSO.   Commentary: 3. 1. 1-4; 3. 4. 1-2; 3. 19. 1-7; 3. 23. 5; 4. 48. 3; 5. 12-14;
5. 24. 2-9; 5. 40. 5-6; 8. 2. 4-9; 8. 24. 7; 8. 36. 4-5; 11. 58. 7-9; 12. 13.

French

ALANUS DE INSULIS.   Commentary: 1. 5-10; 7. 2 ff.
BODIN.   Appendix I: Jones; Commentary: Pr. 1; 2. 34 ff.; 5. 25.
CAYET.   Appendix II: Heffner.
ANDREAS CAPELLANUS.   Commentary: 6. 3-4.
FROISSART.   Commentary: 3. 34. 3; 6. 3-4.
DE L'HÔPITAL.   Appendix I: Jones; Commentary: 7; 12. 8.
MONTAIGNE.   Commentary: 3. 33-34.

MATTHEW PARIS. Commentary: 4. 38. 4.
JAUFRE RUDEL. Commentary: 5. 53. 7-8.
BERNARD DE VENTADORN. Commentary: 6. 24. 5-9.
DE VENUS LA DEESSE D'AMOR. Commentary: 9. 32. 6-9.
JOHANNES DE SACRO BOSCO. Commentary: 2. 35. 7-9.

Romances

AMADIS DE GAUL. Commentary: 1. 9-10.

English

ADLINGTON. Commentary: 7. 2 ff.
ALLEGATIONS AGAINST THE SURMISED TITLE. Appendix II: Neill.
ARDEN OF FEVERSHAM. Commentary: 9. 10.
ASSEMBLY OF LADIES. Commentary: 9. 27 ff.
BATMAN UPPON BARTHOLOME. Commentary: 5. 53. 1-4.
BEDINGFIELD. Commentary: 9. 20 ff.
BULLINGER. Appendix III: Padelford.
CAMDEN. Appendix II: Heffner, Neill, Upton; Commentary: 8. 30-45.
CAMPION. Appendix II: Heffner.
CAREY, ROBERT. Commentary: 3. 4. 1-5.
CARTWRIGHT. Appendix III: Padelford.
CAXTON. Commentary: 4. 29 ff.
CHAUCER. Appendix II: Upton; Commentary: Pr. 9. 5; 1. 9-10; 1. 25. 1-3;
    2. 4 ff.; 2. 33. 3; 3. 3; 3. 9. 7; 4. 36. 7; 5. 36. 2; 5. 42. 6-9; 5. 53. 7-8; 6. 24.
    5-9; 7; 7. 30; 8. 40. 9; 9. 23. 7-9; 10. 3. 6-7; 12. 1. 7-9.
CHEKE. Appendix III: Hughes.
CONINGSBY. Appendix II: Heffner.
COURT OF LOVE. Commentary: 5. 53. 7-8; 6. 17-18.
CROMPTON. Commentary: 9. 43-45.
DEE, JOHN. Commentary: 2. 35. 5.
A DEFENCE OF THE HONORABLE SENTENCE AND EXECUTION OF THE QUEENE OF
    SCOTS. Commentary: 9. 43-45.
DIGGES, THOMAS. Commentary: 2. 35. 5.
DYMNOCK. Commentary: 12. 8-9.
ELYOT. Appendix I: Jones; II: Greenlaw; III: Hughes.
FIELD, JOHN. Commentary: 2. 35. 5.
FULWELL, ULPIAN. Appendix II: Neill; Commentary: 9 25-26.
GEOFFREY OF MONMOUTH. Commentary: Pr. 11. 9; 7. 12 ff.; 9. 33. 4.
GOWER. Commentary: 2. 9-10; 8. 40. 9.
GROVE. Commentary: 3. 2. 8.
HALES, JOHN. Appendix II: Neill.
HALL. Commentary: 3. 37. 5-9.
HARDYING. Commentary: Pr. 11. 9.
HARINGTON. Commentary: 4. 42. 3; 9. 11. 6-8; 9. 29. 9.
HARLEIAN MS 7368. Commentary: 2. 41. 5-6.
HARVEY. Appendix I: Jones; II: Heffner; Commentary: Pr. gen.

HAWES. Commentary: 2. 27. 8; 5. 42. 6-9; 7; 9. 23. 8; 11. 23. 7.

HOLINSHED. Appendix II: Schulze; III: Hughes; Commentary: 2. 19.

HOOKER. Appendix I: Jones; Commentary: 2. 19.

HOOPER. Appendix III: Padelford.

HUON OF BORDEAUX. Appendix I: Davis.

KNOX. Appendix I: Jones, Padelford; Commentary: 4. 31 ff.

LANGLAND. Appendix III: Hughes; Commentary: 2. 9-10; 9. 29. 9.

LEGH, GERARD. Commentary: 5. 21. 3-7.

LESLIE, JOHN. Commentary: 9. 20 ff.

LEYCESTER'S COMMONWEALTH. Appendix II: Neill.

LITURGIES OF KING EDWARD VI. Appendix III: Padelford.

LLOYD. Appendix II: Upton.

LYNDSAY, DAVID. Commentary: 9. 1. 2.

MACHYN, HENRY. Commentary: 3. 4. 6—6. 3.

MALORY. Commentary: 1. 12. 6; 1. 26. 6-9; 2. 4 ff.; 3. 2. 5-9; 3. 5. 6; 3. 10. 9;
      3. 34. 3; 4. 7. 3; 4. 25. 4; 5. 22. 9; 5. 36 ff.; 6. 27. 6-9; 6. 32. 1; 8. 14. 7;
      11. 22. 1-2; 11. 40.

MANDEVILLE. Commentary: 4. 29 ff.

MORE. Appendix I: Jones; Commentary: 4. 31 ff.

MORGAN. Appendix II: Neill.

NICCOLS. Appendix II: Heffner.

NORTH. Appendix III: Hughes.

THE PEARL. Commentary: 1. 8. 9—9. 1.

POLIMANTEIA. Appendix II: Heffner.

PUTTENHAM. Commentary: 3. 3. 1-2.

RALEIGH. Appendix II: Greenlaw; Commentary: 4. 29 ff.; 4. 36. 1.

RECORDE, ROBERT. Commentary: 2. 35. 5.

RICHE. Commentary: 2. 27. 8.

ROGERS, THOMAS. Appendix III: Padelford.

ROLLAND. Commentary: 9. 36 ff.

ROXBURGHE BALLADS. Appendix II: Heffner.

SACKVILLE. Commentary: 8. 45. 1.

SEGAR. Commentary: 3. 4. 8-9.

SIDNEY. Appendix II: Greenlaw; III: Hughes; Commentary: 3. 2. 8; 3. 23. 5;
      5. 24. 2-9.

SKELTON. Commentary: 2. 9-10; 2. 27. 8.

SPEED. Commentary: 12. 8-9.

STOWE. Commentary: 3. 4. 8-9; 9. 23. 7-9.

STRIFE OF LOVE IN A DREAM. Commentary: 9. 27 ff.

STRYPE. Appendix I: Padelford; II: Neill; III: Padelford, Hughes.

TURPIN. Commentary: 3. 34. 3.

TYNDALL. Appendix III: Hughes.

VAUGHAN. Appendix II: Heffner.

VERSTEGAN. Appendix II: Neill.

WARNER. Commentary: 8. 31. 1-4.

THE WARS OF ALEXANDER. Commentary: 4. 24. 3.

WHETSTONE. Appendix II: Neill.

WHITGIFT. Appendix III: Padelford.

23

TEXTUAL APPENDIX

The list of variants includes (1) verbal differences in *1609* and *1611*; (2) the readings of *1596* altered in our text; (3) changes in spelling in early editions which involve a possible change in pronunciation, the adding or dropping of a syllable, or any apparently significant peculiarity; and (4) examples of the readings of later editions. Unless it is involved in the change, punctuation is not given in recording a variant. Minor variations in spelling, such as the adding or dropping of a final e, the use of v and u, capitalization, and use of the hyphen, are not distinguished in the variants given from the editions later than *1596*. Inconsistencies in the use of ligatures are ignored in all the editions. Our usage in regard to typographical conventions is explained in the general note in Book I, p. 516.

The following symbols are used for reference to the editions and commentaries cited:

b	1596 (three copies)	*U*	Upton, 1758
c	1609	*C*	Church, 1758
d	1611-12-13	*T*	Todd, 1805
E	1679 [second title-page dated 1678]	*Ch*	Child, 1855
H₁	Hughes, 1715	*Co*	Collier, 1862
J	Jortin, 1734	*M*	Morris and Hales, 1869
H₂	Reprint of Hughes, 1750	*G*	Grosart, 1882-4
B	Birch, 1751	*D*	Dodge, 1908
W	Warton, 1762 [first ed. 1754]	*S*	Smith, 1909-10

TITLE

line 1.   FIFTH] FIFT   *cd*
     5.   ARTEGALL] ARTHEGAL(L)   *cd EHC (and so usually)*

PROEM

  i. 3.   prime,] prime.   *b*
     9.   wourse . . . wourse] worse . . . worse   *cd EH*
 ii. 2.   at] as   *d EHBG*
     9.   degendered] degenered   *d EHC*
iii. 4.   corrupted] corrrupted   *c*
 iv. 7.   farre from,] farre, from   *d ET*   farre from   *H₂UCChCoMDS*
vii. 4.   the] *om. B*
 ix. 1.   ancient] ancicnt   *d*
     4.   ne] no   *d E*
     9.   dred] drad   *cd EH₁*   dread   *H₂*
 xi. 1.   Dread] Drad   *cd EH₁*
     2.   stead] place   *b*
     8.   great] grcat   *c*

CANTO I

Arg. 3.   *doeth*] *doth*   *cd EHCoM*
     4.   *his*] *His*   *c HBUCTChMD*
 ii. 5.   There] Their   *H₂*

356

9. dread] drad *cd EH*
iii. 2. *Artegall.*] *Art(h)egal(l)* : *HUCTChCoMD Artegall,* S
iv. 1. *Irena*] *Eirena b BCD*
vi. 5. gifts] giftes *c*
ix. 1. dreaded] dradded *cd EH₁*
x. 7. came] cam e *d*
xi. 2. lenger] longer *E*
8. sixt] fixt *E* sixth *H (Co reads* fixt *in T; not so our copy)*
xiii. 4. misdeede] misdced *d*
xiv. 3. An] And *T*
7. inwardly,] inwardly: *c* inwardly; *HB* inwardly *UCT*
xv. 1. well away] weal-away *cd EH*
xvi. 2. why?] why, *b*
xvii. 3. I] *om. T*
4. knowne] knowen *cd*
7. downe throwne,] downe-throwne. *c*
8. Fro] From *HB*
xix. 7. it's] its *cd E*
xx. 9. of] off *H₂*
xxii. 4. selfe vnwist,] selfe, vnwist, *HChDS* selfe vnwist *UCTCoM*
xxiii. 2. then] them *EH*
xxiv. 9. the] thc *b (broken e)*
xxv. 1. Now] now *b G*
xxvi. 3. and] and the *B*
9. is] his *cd E*
xxx. 5. aduenture] adueuture *b*

CANTO II

Arg. 3. *Munera*] *Momera bcd E*
4. *race*] *rase cd EH*
ii. 7. As] And *b*
9. spousde] spouse *d E*
iv. 1. he] she *b*
5. way] wav *d*
vi. 2. way,] way; *b* way *HCCoM*
vii. 9. ouersight.] ouersight *b*
xi. 4. Who] When *M*
8. Loe] loe *bcd EG*
9. expire.] expire *d*
xiii. 3. whot] hot *cd EH*
xiv. 9. wold] would *cd EHC*
xv. 2. champian] champain *d E*
xvii. 5. But] *spaced to left b*
Artegall] *Art egall b (correctly spaced in some copies)*
xviii. 9. dight.] dight *b*
xxii. 2. Castle] *The initial* C *is probably a filed* G *in b*
xxiii. 2. piteous] pittious *c* pititious *d*
6. ouer] upon *B*
xxvi. 2. lye;] lye, *b (copy 3 and U. of Washington copy; corr. in some copies)* B
6. he] *om. d E*
7. trye] Dye *H*
xxviii. 1. raced] rased *cd* ras'd *EH*

xxix. 6.   admire.] admire, *cd EHCCoMG* admire; *UTChD*
xxxii. 4.   earth] eare *b*
xxxiv. 9.   to trow] I trow *HU*
xxxv. 4.   right.] right, *b S* right: *UTChCoMD*
xxxvii. 6. its] it's *cd EHC*
       7.   be?] be. *b* (*S reads* be *in b*) be: *CCoM*
xxxviii. 1. these] those *cd EH₁*
xxxix. 9.   that] but *G*
   xli. 5. sit] fit *b* (*copy 3 and U. of Washington copy; corr. in some copies*)
  xlvi. 1. *Artegale*] *Arthegal* *E*
       9.   way] lay *cd EHG*
 xlvii. 4. Be] be *bd ECG*
    l. 5.   make] makes *b BU*
   li. 6.   good,] good; *b B*
 liii. 3.   stroke] strook(e) *cd EH*
  liv. 2.   foreby] soreby *d EH₁*

CANTO III

    v. 7.   fift] fifth *H*
       8.   sixt] sixth *H*
   ix. 6.   prisoner] Pris'ner *HC*
       8.   thence] hence *T*
   xi. 7.   Th'other] The other *d EH₂CTChCoMDS*
       9.   th'other] the other *d EHCTChCoMDS*
  xiv. 1.   thether] thither *cd EH*
  xix. 1.   the azure] th' azure *cd EHBUCT*
   xx. 2.   aduewed] adviewed *cd* adview'd *E* had view'd *H* had vewed *U*
  xxii. 7. fere] Fear *H*
 xxiv. 2.   image] imagc *b*
  xxv. 8.   this] his *d E*
       9.   bewray] betray· *B*
 xxvi. 7.   *Braggadochio* selfe] *Braggadochio*'s self *H*
xxxii. 4.   should him the field denie] the Field should him deny *H*
xxxiv. 2.   *Guyon* selfe] *Guyon*'s self *H*
 xxxv. 3.   steed] Seed *H₂*
xxxvi. 8.   hee:] hee *b*
xxxix. 6.   can] 'gan *H*
   xl. 1.   *Flush with lines 2-8 in b*
       6.   we] were *b BU*

CANTO IV

  Title.   IIII.] IIII *b*
    i. 3.   haue] of *d E*
   ii. 6.   president] precedent *cd EHC*
   iv. 5.   fires] fircs *b* (*broken e*)
       9.   threats] threat *d E*
            mood.] mood *d* moo *U* (*corr. in some copies*)
   vi. 5.   readinesse: thereby] readinesse thereby, *cd EHS* readinesse, thereby *BCCoD*
                 readinesse thereby *UTChM*
   ix. 5.   be hight] behight *H*
   xv. 8.   espiall] especiall *B*
  xvi. 5.   what] that *d ETChCoM*
 xvii. 3.   the] *om.* *H₁*

xix. 7. randon] random(e)   *d EH*

xx. 3. *Bracidas*] *Bracidas* *b*

6. Then] then *U*

xxii. 2. pinnoed] pinniond *d E* pinion'd *H*

xxvi. 1. *Terpine*] *Turpine* *b BUTCbCoMGD*

xxvii. 7. Knighthod] Knighthood *cd EHUTCb*

xxviii. 4. *Terpine*] *Terpin* *b UCTCbCoMGDS* *Turpine* *B*

xxix. 1. woont] wont *cd EH*

xxxi. 4. cloth] clothe *cd H*

And then] and then *cd EHUCTCbD*

xxxiii. 1. *Artegall*)?] *Artegall?*) *b* *Arthegall*) *C* *Artegall,* *D*

4. and] aud *c*

xxxiv. 5. *Terpine*] *Terpin* *bc UCTCbCoMGDS* *Tirpin* *d* *Tirpen* *E* *Turpine* *B*

9. would] wold *d*

xxxvi. 1. watchmen] watchman *cd EHCbMD*

8. her selfe, halfe] her selfe halfe, *b* her self(e), arm'd like *cd EHBC* herself arm'd like *U*

xxxvii. 6. there] their *d E*

xxxix. 3. doale] doile *b G*

diuide,] dauide, *b B (who corrects to* divide *in Errata)* *G* diuide. *d E*

xlvi. 8. times] time *E*

xlvii. 9. disauenterous] disauentrous *c H* disaduentrous *d E* disadventerous *BUT*

xlviii. 3. *Clarin*] *Clarind'* *cd EH*

7. yeester day] yesterday *cd EUTS*

xlix. 1. propound,] propound; *CTCb* propound: *CoMD* propound. *S*

li. 4. accepting well,] accepting, well *CT*

CANTO V

Arg. 3. *her*] *bcr (broken h)* *b*

4. *Clarins*] *Clarind's* *cd EH*

v. 3. fell] full *T*

vii. 5. fayling] faylng *d*

viii. 2. anduile] anvile *d E* Anvil *H*

3. sunny] suuny *d*

7. dread] drad *cd EH₁*

ix. 9. drew.] drew *c*

xii. 8. winters] winter *d E*

xv. 2. an] a *d E*

xvi. 1. dred] drad *cd EH₁*

xviii. 4. to'a] to a *cd EHBU*

xx. 8. a napron] an apron *cd EHBUCTG*

xxxi. 1. faithfull] fearefull *T*

xxxii. 1. *Clarin*] *Clarind'* *cd EH*

7. cast] ca *[blurred]* *d*

xxxvii. 4. weaue] wear *E*

xxxviii. 2. beseeming well,] beseeming, well *cd EHC* beseeming well *UTCbCoM*

8. though vnlike,] though (vnlike) *cd EHUTCbMS* though unlike *Co*

xl. 5. borne] *S reads* borne, *in b; not so our copies, which show only the mark of a lead*

xli. 2. he] she *c*

xliv. 4. shold] should *cd EHC*

xlviii. 7. this] his *E*

liii. 1. fayning] fauning *E*

2. her owne] hcr owne   *b* (*broken e*)
3. doeth] doth   *cd EH*
lv. 7. maladie,] maladie;   *b BG*
9. wold] would   *c*
lvi. 4. *Clarin*] *Clarind'*   *cd EH*
lvii. 8. gayned,] gayned.   *d E*

CANTO VI

iv. 1. Sometime] Sometimes   *d E*
2. aduenturous] aduentrous   *cd EHB*
3. Sometime] Sometimes   *H*
7. from] for   *cd EH*
vii. 9. vnto her loue] vnto loue   *E*
ix. 2. where] wherc   *b* (*broken* e)
3. at once] attonce   *cd E*
xi. 4. newes-man] newes-men   *B*
xii. 4. honour] Honours   *H₂*
xiii. 9. singulfs] singults   *cd EHCMS*
xvi. 1. wellaway] weal-away   *cd EH*
7. things] thinge   *B* (*in his Errata*) *D* thing *ChCo*
xvii. 5. Heard] Here   *b* (*corr. in U. of Washington copy*)
xix. 3. th'euen-tide] the euen-tide   *cd EHUCTChCoMDS*
7. constraine,] constraine.   *b GS* constraine;   *UTChD*
xx. 1. salute] salute.   *b*   salute,   *S*
xxi. 9. empeach.] empeach   *b*
xxiv. 1. their] her   *cd EHU*
4. of her] ofher   *b*
7. suffering] suffring   *cd EH₁* suff'ring   *H₂*
xxv. 4. wellaway] weal-away   *cd EH*
9. nights] [k]nights   *G*
should] shold   *d E*
xxvi. 6. continually] continuallly   *c*
xxvii. 2. of his] ofhis   *b*
xxix. 2. arm'd] armed   *cd EHBUCTChCoMDS*
5. glims] glimse   *cd*   glimpse   *EH*
xxx. 5. euer] eucr   *b* (*e broken in some copies*)
6. scattred] scattered   *cd EC* scatter'd   *H*
xxxi. 3. to abide] t'abide   *cd EHUT*
xxxiii. 5. owne] one   *E*
7. auenge] reuenge   *d E* (*M and G read* reuenge *in c*)
xxxiv. 6. heedinesse] heedinsse   *d*   Heedliness   *H₁*
7. their] that   *cd EHU*
xxxv. 5. vilde] vile   *cd EH*
family.] family   *b*   family;   *UM* family: *TChD*
9. nether] neither   *cd EHBC*
xxxvi. 9. ouer] o'er   *T*
xxxvii. 9. slight] flight   *d E*
xl. 7. his rootes] the roots   *d*   the rots   *E*

CANTO VII

Arg. 1. *comes*] *come*   *c*
iii. 6. *Britomart*] *Britomart*   *b*

iv. 3.   sacrifize] sacrifice   *cd EH*
  7.   portend;] portend: *c*
vi. 5.   twine] twinc   *b* (*broken e*)
  9.   with her] with his   *CbD*
vii. 5.   sclender] slender   *cd EH*
viii. 3.   desining] defining   *EH₁*
x. 8.   Had] Has   *H*
xii. 6.   sencelesse] sensely   *E*
xiii. 1.   seem'd, as] seem', das   *b*
  5.   to robe] to be   *d EH₁*
     red,] red.   *b* (*S reads* red *in b*)
xvii. 9.   resaluted] resaluten   *E*
xx. 7.   vp-standing, stifly] up-standing stifly,   *UCTCo*
xxi. 4.   couldst] coulst   *b BU*   coul[d]st   *G*
xxiii. 6.   realme:] realme;   *CoM*   realme.   *S*
  7.   shalt] shall   *H₁*
xxv. 9.   hold.] hold   *b*
xxviii. 7.   lenger] longer   *d EH*
  8.   tie,] tie.   *b B*   tie (*followed by a blur—a badly printed comma?*)   *c*   tie
     d EHUCTChCoMS
xxix. 2.   smot] smote   *cd EHB*
  3.   strokes] stroke   *B*
  9.   hackt] backt   *E*
xxxiv. 1.   wrothfull] wrathfnll   *E*
  4.   though] through   *E*
xxxv. 1.   retrate] retreat(e)   *d EH*
xxxviii. 5.   bad] sad   *cd EHU*
  8.   nourishing] flourishing   *d*   flowrishing   *E*
xlii. 3.   Princess] Princes   *b UChCoG*
xlv. 4.   ease] cease   *d E*

CANTO VIII

Arg. 3.   *Soudan*] *Souldan*   *cd EHC*
ii. 9.   the] th_e (*e is slipping out*)   *b*   (*copies 2 and 3*)
iv. 8.   to] too   *H₂*
viii. 1.   him] hm   *b*
  7.   dispiteous] despiteous   *cd EH*
xiii. 1.   Sir] sir   *bcd G*
xiv. 3.   Since] Sith   *cd EH*
xvi. 1.   them] then   *b B*
xxii. 4.   brust] burst   *H₂*
xxiv. 2.   complained] complained.   *b G*
xxv. 4.   First] First,   *cd EHCTChCoMDS*
  6.   sad] said   *EB*
xxvi. 4.   right] Right   *H*
xxix. 2.   the] a   *H₁*
xxx. 2.   meanings] meaning   *B*
  3.   presumpteous] presumptuous   *cd EHBCT*
xxxiv. 8.   curat] curas   *EHB*
xl. 6.   knowen] knowne   *b G*
  9.   *Flush with lines 2-8 in b*
xlii. 7.   wound] wouud   *d*

xliii. 3.   loues] loue   *cd EHUCT*
xliv. 2.   to] so   *H₁*
xlv. 2.   caused] causcd   *b*
xlviii. 6.   whether] whither   *cd EH*
xlix. 1.   mad] bad   *c*
     8.   outrage] courage   *E*
l. 6.   nigh] by   *B*
     8.   cowheard] coward   *cd EH*
li. 9.   Marcht] Match'd   *H₂*

CANTO IX

Arg. 1.   *Arthur] Arthure*   *B*
i. 8.   dreadded] dradded   *cd EH₁*
ii. 3.   let her euer] euer let her   *B*
     6.   Prince] Princ   *d*
vii. 1.   earne] yearn(e)   *cd EH*
viii. 2.   villains] villain(e)   *d E*
ix. 6.   straight] straght   *d*
x. 9.   vnderneath] vnderneath,   *cd EHChM*
xviii. 4.   hard] hart   *b*
xxi. 1.   knights] Knight   *d E*
xxii. 8.   oftimes] oft-times   *cd EHUCT*
xxiii. 9.   *Flush with line 8 in b*
xxvi. 4.   FONT] FONS   *bcd EHBUCT*
     6.   *Malfont] Malfons*   *EH*
     9.   sclaunders] slanders   *cd EH*
xxix. 2.   purpled] purple   *d E*
xxxi. 4.   hight] hight,   *b G*
     5.   *Litæ,] Litæ*   *b G*
xxxiii. 4.   mote] might   *B*
     8.   rebellions] rebellious   *cd EHUCTChCoMGDS*
xxxiv. 1.   dreaded] dradded   *cd E*
xxxvi. 6.   heard] *om. H₁ (recorded by C; corr. in our copy)*
xl. 8.   vyld] vile   *cd EH*
     9.   dred] drad   *cd EH₁*
xli. 1.   ye] they   *B*
     5.   inspyred,)] inspyred.)   *b G*   inspyred)   *cd EHBUCCoM*
xlii. 1.   fauour] favours   *H*
xliii. 6.   pled] plead   *cd EH*
     8.   hed] head   *cd EH*
     9.   red] read   *cd EH*
xliv. 1.   appose] oppose   *cd EHUCT*
xlv. 7.   *Nobilitie]* Nobilitie   *b*
     9.   *Griefe]* Griefe   *b*
xlvi. 2.   empassionate] compassionate   *E*
     8.   his] in   *E*
xlviii. 3.   detect,] detect.   *cd E*

CANTO X

Arg. 2.   *Belge] Belgee*   *b BUTChCoMGD*
i. 3.   *Mercie,] Mercie*   *b*
iii. 2.   doest] do'st   *cd E*   dost   *H*

6. *Armericke*] *Armoricke* C Americke *ChD*
iv. 1. it praysed was] it praysed it was B
5. tempred] tempted E
v. 9. doe still] dost ill *H₂*
vi. 4. and of her] and her *cd EHCTCoMG*
vii. 1. *Belge*] *Belgæ* *bc ChCoMGD*
viii. 4. Idols] idol *Ch* (*in later issues only*) idole *D*
ix. 1. bred] brad *cd EH₁*
3. dred] drad *cd EH₁*
8. food] good E
x. 2. cowheard] cow heard *c* cow-heard *d EH*
Eurytion,] *Eurytion.* *c* *Eurytion;* *d E*
5. walkt] walk *H₁*
xi. 1. this,] this *H₂UTChCoM*
6. flourish] florisht *d E* flourish't *H₁*
7. new made] a new-made *H₁*
8. decesse] decease *cd EH*
xv. 5. cowheard] coward *cd EH*
xvi. 8. to] on *H*
mount,] mount; *b G*
xvii. 4. care,] care; *bcd EHBG*
8. *Artegall*] *Artigall* *b CoMGD*
xviii. 8. fastnesse] safeness *d EH*
xxii. 7. where] wherc *b*
xxiii. 1. whether] whither *d EHUT*
4. sky-threating] sky-threatning *d EHUT*
xxiv. 3. your] you *d E*
5. farewell] farwell *E*
xxviii. 6. sacrifice] sacrifize *cd E*
xxix. 2. stone,] stone; *bcd EG* stone *BUCTChCoMDS*
xxx. 2. dreaded] dradded *cd EH₁*
xxxii. 4. wold] would *cd EHUCTCo*
xxxiv. 6. battrie] battery *cd EHUT*
7. one] some *E*
xxxvii. 3. past,] past; *b BG*
6. hard] had *cd EH*
preased] preaced *cd E* pressed *H*

CANTO XI

Cant. XI.] *Cant. XI* *b*
i. 5. dome] doom(e) *d EHC*
v. 5. it] in *E* him *H₁*
7. his first] this first *B*
9. could haue riue] could not riue *d E* he could rive *H* (*G reads* could not riue *in c*)
x. 3. can] 'gan *H*
xii. 4. to] on *EH*
8. And] Ane *c*
gnasht] gnash *d E* gnash'd *H*
xiii. 9. with] wirh *c*
throgh] through *cd EHBUCTChM*
xiv. 9. dole] dool(e) *cd EH₁*

xvi. 2. sight,] sight; *b G*

   3. some . . . some] som . . . som *c*

xvii. 6. That] The *C*

xviii. 7. vilde] vile *cd EH*

   8. rout] root(e) *d E*

xix. 3. hie] hic *b* (*broken e?*)

   7. flame;] flame *CTChCoM* flame, *UD*

xx. 4. sacrifize] sacrifice *cd EH*

xxi. 1. earne] yearn(e) *cd EH*

   3. her] his *U*

xxiv. 7. And] An *cd EHU*

xxv. 8. vnto] into *d E*

xxix. 5. as stonisht] astonish'd *H₁*

   6. he] she *E*

       stound] stonn'd *cd E* stunn'd *H*

xxx. 3. stonied] stonned *H₁*

xxxi. 4. brust] burst *d E*

xxxiii. 1. she] he *E*

   3. renowmed] rowned *E* renowned *H*

xxxv. 1. *Belge*] *Belgæ* *bc*

   6. *Belge*] *Belgæ* *bc*

xxxvii. 7. *Irene*] *Irena* *H*

xxxix. 5. vnrighteous] vnrigteous *b G*

xl. 5. reare,] reare *b UG*

   6. by] sure aby *d EHUCTChCoMGD*

xli. 2. too] to *EHUTCoS*

   6. know] knew *bcd EH₁*

xlii. 2. prouide:] prouide. *BUCTChD* prouide? *CoMS*

xliii. 9. tumultuous] tumultous *cd E*

xlvi. 4. Fro] From *H*

xlix. 6. caytiues] captives *E*

l. 3. *Grandtorto*] *Grantorto* *cd EHC*

li. 1. this] his *c H₁B*

lii. 2. dismay?] dismay; *d E*

   5. loose] lose *cd EH*

   8. mote] more *E*

liii. 8. *Grandtorto*] *Grantorto* *cd EHC*

liv. 9. corruptfull] corrupted *d E* (*M and G seem to read* corrupted *in c*)

lv. 4. you] ye *E*

   8. disauentrous] disaduentrous *cd EH*

lvi. 9. dissemble] disscmble *b*

lvii. 9. with all] withall *b*

lx. 2. had] haue *cd EH*

lxi. 1. *Burbon*] *Bourbon* *H₁*

   7. hyre] meed *bcd EHBUCTChCoMGDS*

   8. froward] forward *b B*

lxii. 1. What] what *b CG*

lxiii. 9. hold.] hold; *b U*

lxiv. 7. his] him *E*

CANTO XII

i. 3. deuils] diuels *cd E*

   9. endure] enduren *cd EHUCTChCoMGDS*

iii. 5. hethertoo] hether too   *b* (*copy 2; corr. in some copies*)   hithertoo   *cd E*
  hitherto   *H*

  v. 9. the Eagle] th' Eagle   *cd EHBUCTCo*

  vi. 5. those,] those   *UCTChCoMD*
  feare] feare,   *CTChCoMD*

viii. 8. thether] thither   *cd EH*

  xi. 6. *Artegalls*] *Artegals*   *b*

  xii. 3. countenance] count'nance   *cd EH*

xiv. 1. presumpteous] presumptuous   *cd EHB*
  4. to ward] toward   *cd EH*

  xv. 8. gerne] gcrne   *b*

xvi. 6. sight] fight   *b BG*

xvii. 5. such] sure   *cd EH*

xix. 2. oft] oft,   *cd EHD*
  9. burdenous] burdenons   *c*

xxiii. 2. stroke] strook(e)   *cd EH*

xxvii. 4. stay,] *possibly a broken semicolon in b; all copies examined show a trace of a dot*

xxix. 3. mis-shape] mishap   *d E*
  7. blew] blee   *H₁*

  xxx. 6. hungrily] hungerly   *cd EH*

xxxi. 2. and] or   *d E*

xxxiii. 9. good] goods   *d*
  bereaued] be. reaued-   *d*

  xl. 5. sword, the sword] sword the sword,   *b*
  8. *Grandtorto*] *Grantorto*   *HC*

xlii. 1. among] among,   *cd EHCTChD*
  5. sclaunders] slaunders   *cd*   slanders   *EH*

CRITICAL NOTES ON THE TEXT

By James G. McManaway

PROEM

ii. 2.   at earst] as earst   *d EHBG*   Upton cites 6. 3. 39. 1, " as now at earst " in support of *b*. Collier: " ' At last ' for ' at earst ' would not have been an unprecedented misprint; but the meaning is nearly the same. ' As earst ' would be, ' as formerly.' "   Smith cites particularly *Sh. Cal.*, December 103 and 105, " where there is the same contrast between ' first ' and ' at earst.' "

9.   degendered] degenered   *d EHC*   Collier cites *Hymn of Heavenly Love* 94, " degendering," which *d* changes also to " degenering."

iv. 7.   farre from,] farre, from   *d ET*   farre from   *H₂UCChCoMDS*   Noun clauses are frequently set off by commas.

vii. 8.   thirtie] thirteen   conj. Hillard, Child, Morris.   Smith: " Child's [!] ' thirteen ' is said to be astronomically correct, or nearly so, for Spenser's date."

xi. 2.   stead] place   *b*   See Critical Notes on the Text, Book II, p. 507.

CANTO I

i. 5.   their] her   conj. Church, who takes " vice " as the antecedent here and also in line 9; he also alludes to the Chaucerian spelling " her " = " their," and suggests that the compositor may have modernized the MS spelling " her."

iii. 2.   *Artegall.*]   *Art(h)egal(l)*:   *HUCTChCoMD*   Artegall, *S 1596* frequently uses a period before a relative clause; cf. 1. 12. 7, etc.

Irena] *Eirena*   *b BCD*   Most editors accept the spelling of *c* to avoid ambiguity with Mercilla's attendant Eirene (9. 32. 6).   The spelling of *b* may well be Spenser's, who may have in mind the Greek word for peace.

xxiv. 9.   The inner forme of the outer gathering of sig. N (pp. 194, 195, 206, 207) is in two states.   The first state is represented by copy 3 of *1596*, which reads " fit " at 2. 41. 5.   The corrected state, found in copies 2 and 3, reads " sit."

Page 199 of the inner forme of the inner gathering has another correction, but it seems incidental.   The signature, " N₄," is found in copy 3 (the uncorrected state) as follows:

he his backe
N 4

By the time the sheet of copy 1 was in the press, the signature had slipped so that the position of N was changed and the 4 was turned ninety degrees in a counter-clockwise direction:

he his backe
N ⤙

Copy 2 has N in the second position and the 4 turned upright:

he his backe
N 4

xxvi. 9.   is] his   *cd E*   Collier records the marginal correction of this misprint in Drayton's copy of *1611*.

CANTO II

ii. 7.   As] And   *b*   Probably the compositor repeated the word from the preceding line.

366

iii. 3.   the scattred] her scattred   conj. Upton, regarding the second " the " as a printer's error.

xi. 4.   Who] When   *M*   Tho   conj. Church.   Collier notes the marginal emendation " When " in Drayton's copy of *1611*; this is paleographically acceptable, if we suppose the MS read " Whē."   No emendation is required, however, for, as Smith observes, " such changes of construction are not uncommon when a clause intervenes as here."

xxiv. 9.   to trow] I trow   *HU*   This emendation, which is conjectured by Birch and Church, is recorded by Collier as being in Drayton's copy of *1611*.   Though he adopts it, Upton remarks that " ' to trow ' seems right " in spite of 3. 5. 5. 9.

xli. 5.   sit] fit   *b* (*copy 3 and U. of Washington copy*)   See note on 1. 24. 9.

xlv. 8.   weight] scale   conj. Church.   Collier cites the marginal correction " launce " in Drayton's copy of *1611*.

xlvi. 9.   way] lay   *cd EHG*   The emendation was made because, as Collier suggests, " the preceding line ends with ' way ' "; " but," says Smith, " identical rhymes, especially of homonyms, are not uncommon in this part of the stanza."   As in the case of 3. 11. 47. 9, however, Smith thinks the authority of the quarto is lowered because of the possibility of parablepsy: " The printers would be peculiarly liable to this error in this place if, in Spenser's manuscript, the Alexandrine overflowed into the eighth line of the stanza."

xlvii. 5.   but] 'bout   conj.   *BC*

CANTO III

xi. 7.   Th'other] The other   *d EH₂CTChCoMDS*   See 5. 18. 4 and 6. 19. 3 for other instances of questionable apostrophation.   Emendation is not, however, compulsory.

9.   th'other] the other   *d EHCTChCoMDS*   See note preceding.

xx. 2.   aduewed] adviewed   *cd*   had view'd   *H*   had vewed   *U*   has view'd   Dryden's emendation in his copy of *1679*.   Grosart equates " aduewed " with " 'ad vewed," the equivalent of Hughes' and Upton's readings.

xxxii. 9.   to] may   conj. Church.

xl. 5.   such Ladies and such louely knights] such lovely ladies, and such knights conj. Jortin.   See Upton's note in the Commentary, p. 193.   Collier: " The commentators, forgetting how often Spenser uses the epithet ' lovely ' for ' loving,' would deprive the knights of it and give it to the ladies."   Cf. 1. 1. 49. 8; 1. 3. 30. 1; 1. 10. 4. 8, etc.

6.   we here] were here   *b BU*   Collier thinks the compositor confused " we " and " here," producing " were here."

CANTO IV

i. 7.   And makes] And't makes   Marginal emendation in Drayton's copy of *1611*, recorded by Collier.

xxii. 2.   pinnoed]   No other use of this spelling is noted in the *N. E. D.*   Did the compositor misread " pinnõed " or " piniõed "?

xxxv. 1.   repry'ud] repri(y)u'd   *cd BCChDS*   repriev'd   *EH*   In contemporary MSS, the apostrophe is so frequently placed as in *b* that change is unnecessary.

xxxvi. 8.   halfe like a man] arm'd like a man   *cd EHBUC*   Todd defends the quarto reading by pointing out that Radigund is " an heroine, a virago, that is, a manlike female." He quotes H. Peacham, of Melpomene: " Melpomene is represented like a virago or manly lady."   Smith: " *1609* may be right; ' halfe ' in *1596* may have been repeated by parablepsy from ' selfe ': the punctuation of *1596* points to that."

xxxvii. 1, 3.   neare . . . so few] new . . . so few   conj. Birch, Church   neare . . . to feare   conj. Collier, who quotes this emendation in Drayton's copy of *1611* and argues that " to feare " might easily be misprinted " so few."   Smith: " Imperfect rhymes are not rare in *F. Q.*, but scarcely in this form; here there is no assonance.   Nor does this seem to be one of the 'substitutions' discussed in [Book II, p. 507]. Of conjectures, Church's [!] is the best." Grosart: "All very ingenious tinkering; but it must be repeated Spenser shews repeatedly such neglects, and was no Purist."

xxxix. 3. doale . . . diuide] doile . . . dauide *b* Smith: "There are two words 'dole' in Spenser, (a) portion, (b), mourning. This is (a)." Cf. *2 Henry IV* 1. 1. 169. "Spenser does not elsewhere use 'dole' in sense (a); in sense (b) it is common in *F. Q.*, and is spelt 'dole' or 'doole.' The spelling 'doile' (Fr. 'deuil') belonged rather to sense (b), but no sixteenth century instance is quoted in *NED*. It is not impossible that Spenser wrote 'doile' in sense (a), intending a play upon the two meanings. But more probably 'a' and 'i' have simply been interchanged, as *1609* takes it. (*1596* generally has 'deuide'; but 'diuide' also occurs.)"

xlviii. 7. yeester day] yesterday *cd EHUGS* Smith thinks this another misprint; "the latter part of this canto . . . is unusually full of such difficulties."

xlix. 5. say:] Probably a bad impression in the quarto of a turned italic colon. *BCCoMGD* read a period.

CANTO V

x. 4. fitting] sitting conj. Upton, who cites 1. 1. 30. 9.

xviii. 4. to' a] to a *cd EHBU* Smith: "The apostrophation shows synezesis, though the vowel is not omitted."

xx. 8. a napron] an apron *cd EBHUCTG* Collier thinks the compositor joined the consonant of the article to the next word; "thus we often find 'an awl' printed 'a nawl.'" "Napron" is so much like its French root that no emendation is required.

xxv. 8. base] grace marginal emendation noted by Collier in Drayton's copy of *1611*; "Spenser's word may have been misheard—'base' for 'grace'; but his meaning is very perspicuous as the text stands, and it ought not to be disturbed."

xxxvii. 4. weaue] wear *E* corr. by Dryden in his copy of *1679*.

xxxviii. 8. though vnlike,] though (vnlike) *cd EHUT'ChMS* though unlike *Co* Smith: "The meaning is, 'And even if (as is unlikely) they should last, etc.'" The quarto punctuation gives the intended sense if we read And = If. This usage, though common enough in Spenser's time, does not, according to the *NED* or Brendel's study, occur elsewhere in Spenser's works.

they] it conj. Church, who takes "cloud" as the antecedent; "or else we must read 'these clouds.'"

xlix. 6. mightie] witching marginal emendation cited by Collier from Drayton's copy of *1611*, with this comment: "Recollecting that 'm' and 'w' were not infrequently confounded by old printers, and that the termination of 'mighty,' if written with 'y,' could easily be mistaken, we think the change plausible, though by no means necessary: as a matter of taste, we might prefer, 'even womens witty trade, The art of *witching* words'; but we are by no means warranted in rejecting what Spenser perhaps wrote, for what Drayton, for aught we know, may have considered an improvement."

liii. 1. fayning] fauning *E* corr. by Dryden in his copy of *1679*.

CANTO VI

v. 6-7. Church thinks the printer caused the obscurity of the passage by transposing words; he suggests:

> For days but houres; for months that passed were,
> She told but weekes, to make them seeme more fewe.

He notes a like transposition at 6. 2. 3. 3. Collier thinks this proposal "in some respects warranted." Smith: "Spenser may have meant that she reckoned in months instead of weeks to make the time look shorter; e. g. said three months instead of twelve weeks, dwelling on the numeral and wilfully ignoring the noun. But this is one of those subtleties in which we feel the difference between Spenser and Shakespeare." He groups these lines with 2. 5. 12. 8-9 and 5. 6. 26. 5-6 and remarks: " To me these passages appear incorrigible." Gough calls the lines " a characteristic, if somewhat puerile example of a ' concetto ' in the artificial Italian manner." For a somewhat similar conceit, see *Romeo and Juliet* 3. 5. 44-5.

 vii. 9. vnto her loue] vnto loue *E* corr. by Dryden in his copy of *1679*.

 xiii. 9. singulfs] singults *cd EHCMS* See Critical Notes on the Text, Book III, p. 426. That " singulfs " is to be preferred finds confirmation in *The Lamentation of Melpomene, for the death of Belphoebe our late Queene. With a Ioy to England for our blessed King. By T. W. Gentleman*, a copy of which, apparently unique, is in the Huntington Library. See B$_{iii}$ recto and verso:

> The Fates (quoth they) in priuate so decreed,
> That she for whom thou weep'st, by death should bleed,
> And they which by deaths cruell hand are slaine,
> Nor sightes, nor singulfes can reduce againe.

 xii. 4. honour] Honours *H₂* Todd considers the emendation the better reading, but does not adopt it.

 xvi. 7. things] thinge *B* (*in his errata*) *D* thing *ChCo* Church, not noticing Birch's emendation, suggests that " Spenser, no doubt, gave ' thing ' or ' thinge.' " Collier notes that in Drayton's copy of *1611* the " s " is erased. Morris: " But the clause may stand if we look upon ' things ' as in the genitive case." Smith prefers " thinge " or " thing," if the passage must be emended, but sees " no real objection to taking ' things ' as nominative plural."

 xvii. 5. Heard] Here *b* (*corr. in University of Washington copy*) The catchword on R₂^v is correctly given " Heard," but the first word on R₃ was incorrectly set " Here " by the compositor, who probably mistook Spenser's " d " for final " e." The correction was made during the course of printing.

 xix. 3. th'euen-tide] the euen-tide *cd EHUCTChCoMDS* Smith considers this a case of erroneous apostrophation, but giving a strong accent to the first syllable of " toward " (cf. 6. 1. 19. 2) produces a smooth line without emendation.

 xx. 6. so him requite] him to requite conj. Church.

 xxv. 9. nights] [k]nights *G* This emendation was first proposed by Church, who would put a period after " want." Smith considers this, like many other of Church's conjectures, " rather plausible to common sense than convincingly Spenserian." May not Spenser have intended a pun—your want at night, i. e. your knight, who should ye waking keep?

 xxvi. 5. Ne lesse] This passage appears to Smith incorrigible, for the " sense requires ' ne more.' " In the one-volume edition, he suggests that " Spenser probably meant at first to turn the sentence differently."

 xxix. 2. arm'd] armed *cd EHBUCTChCoMDS* Smith calls this another case of erroneous apostrophation. But the " m " is syllabic; cf. Elizabethan " alarm " = " alarum."

 5. night] Collier: " Drayton altered . . . to ' light ' (but, as appears to us, without sufficient necessity) in his folio *1611*."

 xxxi. 5. proceede] succeede marginal emendation in Drayton's *1611*, recorded by Collier, who did not adopt it.

 xxxii. 7. did vnderminde] had vnderminde conj. Collier, Morris Upton: " As [Spenser] claims the liberty of taking away a letter by a rhetorical figure, the more easily to introduce his jingling terminations, as I have already shown in a note on 4. 11. 46. [9]. So by another rhetorical figure he claims the license of adding a supernumerary letter." He cites 2. 6. 10. 7, " Joue," which he thinks must be pronounced " Jowe " to rhyme with " blow, slow."

 xxxvi. 9. ouer] o'er *T* Collier agrees that the word must be pronounced " in the time of a monosyllable."

 xxxvii. 2. Who] Tho conj. Church.

 9. slight] flight *d E* corr. by Dryden in his copy of *1679*.

CANTO VII

vi. 9. with her] with his *ChD* This was first proposed as a conjecture by Church, who referred to stanzas 15, 16. Smith thinks the mistake may have been Spenser's. Collier rejects the emendation, since " ' her ' and ' his ' were frequently confounded by the old printers, owing to the fact that ' her ' was then often spelt ' hir.' " Grosart objects that " all such finicalness is antithetic to Spenser's use and wont."

viii. 3. desining] defining *EH*₁ query Grosart.

ix. 3. bake] bare conj. Church.

xii. 6. sencelesse] sensely *E* underlined by Dryden in his copy of *1679*.

xxiii. 6. realme] Smith notes the spelling " reames " for " realmes " in *1590* at 3. 5. 53. 3. To this may be added 4. 8. 45. 9, where " reame " rhymes with " streame." *NED s. v.* " realme ": " The earliest form adopted in Eng. was ' reaume,' which subsequently appears also in the reduced forms ' reame ' or ' reme ' and ' reume.' The more etymological spelling ' realm ' appears somewhat later, and did not finally become the standard form till about 1600."

8. extreame] Upton prefers " supreme " as being more in keeping with the nature of British sovereignty.

xlv. 9. for] in Drayton's marginal emendation in his *1611*, recorded by Collier, who thinks " call " for " fall " a more reasonable emendation.

CANTO VIII

ii. 2. Each of whose lockes did match a man in might] With Judges 16. 17, 19 in mind, Upton thinks the quarto reading was supplied by a corrector of the press to replace a blotted reading as follows: " Each of whose lockes did keep his matchless might."

viii. 1. misfortune him mistooke] Upton objects to the repetition of " mis- " and suggests " misfortune him o'ertook." Collier explains that " mistooke " means " took amiss."

ix. 3. ready prest . . . ready speare] Upton thinks the compositor's recollection of the first " ready " may have led him to substitute the second for " steady."

xxii. 6. lastly] hast'ly conj. Church, who points out the illogicality of the original in view of 23. 1.

xxvi. 4. right] Right *H* Church, rightly taking this word as an adverb, objects to Hughes' reading of it as a noun.

xxviii. 4. straight] light conj. Church, to avoid repeating the word, which occurs in the preceding line.

xxxi. 8. haue borne] t'haue borne Drayton's marginal emendation in his *1611*; recorded by Collier, who thinks it more correct but hardly more intelligible.

xl. 6. knowen] knowne *b G* Collier supposes that " the places of the ' n ' and ' e ' were accidentally changed." Smith: " *1596* might be upheld by comparison with 6. 4. 36, where ' vnknowne ' = ' showen ' = ' blowen ' = ' sowen.' But these are at the end of lines, where the number of syllables is indifferent."

xliv. 8. did] should conj. Church, wrongly.

xlvii. 5. owne] sons conj. Upton (*Letter . . . to Gabriel West*, p. 20). Warton (1. 101): " But surely the poet, and with no great impropriety of expression, might mean her *Son's* flesh, by her *owne* flesh."

CANTO IX

xxvi. 4. FONT] FONS *bcd EHBUCT* Although Upton and Church thought Spenser wrote " FONT," Child first made the change.

xxxiii. 8. rebellions] rebellious *cd EHUCTChCoMGDS* The letter is " n " and not a turned " u," as the reading of all the later editions would suggest. The passage does not call for emendation.

xliv. 1.   appose] oppose   *cd EHUCT*   Smith cites the use of "appose" in this sense by Drayton (Oxford ed., p. 44, line 4).   The spelling was current in Spenser's day, cf. *NED, s. v.* "appose, v¹," = "oppose, *v*, I. 1."

CANTO X

iii. 6.   *Armericke*] *Armoricke   C*   Americke   *ChD   Armoric*   conj. Jortin   *Americke* conj. Todd, which is in Smith's opinion highly probable.   "Otherwise we must take 'Armericke' to mean Armoric, i. e. of Brittany."   See the notes in the Commentary on 10. 3. 6-7, from the last of which it is evident that "Armerica" was a current spelling of the name of the New World.

vi. 4.   and of her] and her   *cd EHCTCoMG*   Collier doubts the wisdom of the omission, and Smith finds the second part of *F. Q.* less shy of trisyllabic feet than the first part.

viii. 4.   Idols] idol   *Ch* (in later issues only)   idole   *D*   Idol   conj. Church, referring to 10. 13. 8; 10. 27. 9; 10. 30.   Collier believes that Church is probably right: " 'Idols' appears here in the plural because, the next word beginning with the letter 's,' the old printer carried on the sound from one word to another."   This may have happened, but it is quite as likely that the compositor misread the final letter, as Dodge's reading suggests.

ix. 1, 3.   bred . . . dred] brad . . . drad   *1609* shows a decided preference for the spelling "drad"; here the corrector anticipated the change in line 3 and altered the last word in line 1 to secure an exact rhyme.   Cf. 5. 10. 28. 6, 8, 9 for another case of anticipation.

xi. 8.   decesse] decease   *cd EH*   Collier compares the spelling with "cesse" for "cease" in *All's Well* 5. 3. 72, "in both places in distress of the rhyme."

xv. 5.   for cowheard] far driving   conj. Upton, who objects to the use of the indecorous "cowheard."   He believes the copy was blotted and the reading made up by the corrector of the press.   But cf. 10. 10. 2; the emendation spoils the humor of Spenser's punning reference to the "cowheard" Eurytion, fear of whose prowess restrained all but Arthur.   Cf. his pun on "kyne" "kynd," 10. 9. 9.

xxiv. 5.   farewell] farwell   *E*   fare well   conj. Jortin   well fare   conj. Upton   wellfare conj. Church, referring to 3. 2. 10. 8 and 3. 2. 42. 1.   He thinks Spenser meant "welcome," "well may it fare."   Smith, thinking emendation needless, accepts Church's gloss.

xxvi. 3.   so now] now so   conj. Church.

xxix. 6.   him]   Todd first noted that the monster is female in 11. 22 ff.

xxxiii. 4.   tombling downe vpon the senselesse ground] tumbling senselesse downe vpon the ground   conj. Warton (2. 221), who points out another metathetical form at 6. 7. 26. 3.

5.   vnto his ghost from thraldome bound] t'his ghost, from thraldome now unbound conj. Upton   Collier rejects the emendation as needless.

CANTO XI

v. 8.   The whilest] The whil'st   *cd*   The whilst   *EH*   The whiles   conj. Upton.

dreadfully he driue]   Upton assumes that driue = driues; Church, with whom Todd agrees, that it is used for "drove," as in 1. 9. 38. 5, where the rhyme word is "giue." Warton (2. 222) would emend: "dreadfully he did drive," with the "y" slurred or cut off as in 1. 10. 61. 9.

9.   That seem'd a marble rocke asunder could haue riue] . . . could not riue   *d E* . . . he could rive   *H*   Warton (2. 222): "In this verse . . . there is an elleipsis of 'it' before 'seem'd,' and of 'he' before 'could'; and 'rive' should have been 'riv'd,' unless he wrote it 'rive' for 'riven.'"

ii. 3.   his Champion] his champions   conj. Upton, i. e. his three knights; cf. 10. 34.

xvi. 3.   some . . . some] som . . . som   *c*   The spellings result from the attempt to compensate the line.

xix. 5.   of] and   conj. Collier: "The sign for 'and' was not unfrequently of old mistaken and misprinted ' of.' However, we do not upon mere conjecture alter the text of all editions."

       xxi. 3.   her] his   *U*   Todd points out that Upton failed to normalize for sex in sts. 22 ff.

      xxix. 5.   as stonisht] astonish'd   *H*₁   Collier remarks that in *England's Parnassus,* 1600 (p. 462), " a very ill printed book," " as stonisht " is altered to " astonisht."

         6.   he] she   *E*   corr. by Dryden in his copy of *1679.*

      xxxiii. 1.   she] he   *E*   corr. by Dryden in his copy of *1679.*

         3.   renowmed] rowned   *E*   corr. by Dryden in his copy of *1679.*

    xxxvi-lxv.   These stanzas relate the Bourbon episode and, from the argument to Canto 12, seem to have been intended originally for the last canto. (See Commentary.) That Canto 11 originally ended with stanza 35 (the last but one on the page) is indicated by the catchword " *Canto.*" on page 332 (misnumbered 342) though the first word on page 333 is " There." " *Canto,*" or " *Cant.,*" is used as a catchword elsewhere in *1596* only when a canto ends on a verso and a new canto begins on the next page. The catchword never refers to the heading of the next page. The misnumbering of the page seems to have no significance, for according to Johnson's *Critical Bibliography of Spenser,* p. 30, two copies have this page numbered correctly.

    It may be that Gough is right (see his note on 11. 43-5 in the Commentary, pp. 259-60, and Heffner in Appendix II, p. 331), and that these stanzas were inserted after the printing had begun, having been intended originally for Canto 12 but for some reason having been transferred to Canto 11 after page 332 had already been set up. Gough implies that the shift was effected to avoid making Canto 12 too long, but with the addition of these it would have contained only seventy-three stanzas. There are other cantos in the *Faerie Queene* longer, e. g., Canto 12 of Book II (87).

    Obviously the author of the Argument to Canto 12 expected the canto to begin with this episode. Stanza 36 might be a suitable beginning; cf. *F. Q.* 6. 9 for a transitional sentence much like that which opens stanza 36: " But turne we now to noble Artegall." Could the misplacing of a sheet of paper containing this Argument have caused the mistake? Almost certainly not, because chance would not insert the misplaced leaf at the first point thereafter where a canto could logically begin. Besides, there would then have been no reason for the compositor to use the catchword " *Canto.*"

    Did someone consider the rhetoric of 12. 1 a better introduction to the final canto than the mechanical " turne we now " of 11. 36? The rhetorical introduction is, it is true, used more frequently than the other; see *F. Q.* 3. 3, 3. 11, and 4. 7 for close parallels. But this explanation is inadequate. Furthermore, it forces us to suppose that, after the text of Canto 11 had been set through stanza 35, with the catchword following as usual close after the text, stanza 36 was inserted between stanza 35 and the catchword, and that this was moved, still unchanged, to its present position at the bottom of the page. Another explanation may be the correct one. It is probable that the compositor, as well as the author of the Argument, expected Canto 12 to begin with the stanza now numbered 11. 36. He was composing by page galleys and possibly leaving to the stoneman the insertion of canto headings, boxes, and arguments. When he finished stanza 11. 35, there may have been a shortage of galleys (a large number would be required in the printing of a quarto in eights). He, we may suppose, set the catchword " *Canto.*" as usual at the foot of the text. Then, while waiting for a galley to be released by distribution of type, he started the composition of the text of the next stanza. What happened next is difficult to guess. The net result was that the canto division was forgotten, together with the need to insert the canto heading, the box and the argument. Someone did notice the misplaced catchword and shift it to the bottom of the page. Then the machining began. Too late to remedy the situation, someone noticed the mistake. The best solution, short of reprinting, was to introduce the canto division and argument where we now find it.

    [The strongest objection to this explanation is that the present beginning of Canto 12 is the usual general, moralizing, or reflective, stanza with which all other cantos begin. 6. 9. 1

is not a close parallel to 5. 11. 36, for it is general and reflective and not a review of previous action. The evidence seems to point to an editorial revision after page 332 had been set up and the catchword placed after stanza 35. When stanza 36 was added to the page the catchword was moved to the bottom of the page, the compositor neglecting to change it.—R. H.]

xl. 6. by] sure aby *d EHUCTChCoMGD* Collier: "The sense is precisely the same, while the measure is amended." But Smith: "A very effective tetrameter as it stands. The reading of *16(11)-12-13* is not, I think, authentic."

xli. 2. too] to *EHUTCoS* "Too" and "to" are frequently interchanged in books of this period. In this case, the compositor may have been influenced by the occurrence of "Too" at the beginning of the line.

6. know] knew *bcd EH₁* It is very easy to mistake secretarial "ow" for "ew." The present tense is preferable; but possibly Spenser intended to end line 8 with "threw" and changed to "did throw" only to fill out the measure.

xlii. 2. prouide:] prouide. *BUCTChD* prouide? *CoMS* This is indirect question, and the quarto punctuation is perfectly acceptable.

lvi. 9. To clarify, Church sets off "to dissemble" with commas, giving the equivalent of "May shame attend particularly on those who dissemble."

lix. 8. they] he   conj. Birch, Church; i. e. Talus, cf. line 9.

lxi. 7. hyre] meed *bcd EHBUCTChCoMGDS* Church first conjectured "hyre," which we read for the reasons assigned in the Critical Notes on the Text, Book II, p. 507. Collier approves the conjecture, and Grosart seems to do so. Todd, on the contrary, defends the quarto reading: "Spenser perhaps intended 'meed.' The stanza exhibits three triads of rhymes; and no alteration seems requisite." He cites Chaucer's use of the word in exactly the same way, *Miller's Tale* 3380. To this Collier rejoins that to accept the original rhyme scheme "is to make this stanza differ from every other in the poem."

8. froward] forward *b B* Smith: "The sense requires 'froward.'" Todd points out a similar confusion of the words at 6. 10. 24. 7, and Smith cites 2. 2. 38 for the distinction between the two.

CANTO XII

i. 9. endure] enduren *cd EHUCTChCoMGDS* Collier thinks the final "n" dropped out in the press. Upton remarks that if the quarto reading is correct, the word is trisyllabic. And so it is; cf. Spenser's frequent use of "fire" as illustrating the contemporary practice of inserting an extra vowel sound before "r." See Critical Notes on the Text, Book II, p. 510.

viii. 1. Till] When   conj. Church.

5. Till] Then   conj. Church, who would also put a colon after "slake" at the end of line 4.

xvi. 6. sight] fight *b BG* Collier supposes the compositor of *1596* made the easy mistake of "f" for long "s."

xvii. 5. such] sure *cd EH* According to Collier, Drayton restored "such" in the margin of his copy of *1611*.

xix. 2. shame] harme   marginal emendation in Drayton's *1611*, recorded by Collier, who suggests that the compositor's eye caught the word "shame" from line 3.

xxviii. 6. and to that] add to that   conj. Upton.

xxxiii. 5. her owne] in her   conj. Church. Todd correctly argues for the original reading; Envie did murder, did destroy the peace of, her owne mind; cf. 35. 8, "for her selfe she only vext."

xliii. 7. nought would swerve] nothing swerved   conj. Church, to perfect the rhyme.

BIBLIOGRAPHY

(Supplementary to Bibliographies of Preceding Volumes)

EDITIONS

Blakeney, E. H. The Faery Queene, Book V. London, 1914.

Gough, Alfred B. The Faerie Queene, Book V. Oxford, 1918.

Hillard, G. S. The Poetical Works of Edmund Spenser. Boston, 1839.

MISCELLANEOUS

Beer, M. A History of British Socialism. London, 1929.

Bhattacherje, Mohinimohan. Studies in Spenser. Calcutta, 1929.

Cook, Albert S. Notes on Milton's Ode on the Morning of Christ's Nativity. Transactions of the Connecticut Academy of Arts and Sciences 15 (1909). 307-368.

Cornish, F. Warre. Chivalry. London, 1908.

Craik, G. L. Spenser and His Poetry. 3 vols. London, 1845.

DeMoss, William Fenn. The Influence of Aristotle's "Politics" and "Ethics" on Spenser. Chicago, 1920.

Draper, J. W. Spenser's Use of the Perfective Prefix. MLN 48 (1933). 226-228.

————. Spenser's Talus Again. PQ 15 (1936). 215-217.

Grubb, Marion. A Brace of Villains. MLN 50 (1935). 168-169.

Harman, E. G. Edmund Spenser and the Impersonations of Francis Bacon. London, 1914.

Heffner, Ray. Essex and Book Five of the Faerie Queene. ELH 3 (1936). 67-82.

Hughes, Merritt. Spenser and Utopia. SP 17 (1920). 132-146.

Jones, H. S. V. Spenser's Defense of Lord Grey. University of Illinois Studies in Language and Literature 5 (1919). No. 3.

Jones, Richard F. Ancients and Moderns. Washington University Studies, N. S. (1936). No. 6.

Mustard, W. P. Note on Spenser, Faerie Queene 5. 5. 24. MLN 20 (1905). 127.

Neff, Merlin L. Spenser's Allegory of the Toll-Bridge. PQ 13 (1933). 159-167.

Neill, Kerby. The Faerie Queene and the Mary Stuart Controversy. ELH 2 (1935). 192-214.

Notcutt, H. C. The Faerie Queene and its Critics. Essays and Studies by Members of the English Association 12 (1926). 63-85.

Owst, C. R. Literature and Pulpit in Mediaeval England. Cambridge, 1933.

Padelford, Frederick M. Spenser's Arraignment of the Anabaptists. JEGP 12 (1913). 434-448.

————. Talus: The Law. SP 15 (1918). 97-104.

Root, R. K. The Book of Troilus and Criseyde. Princeton, 1926.

Schulze, Ivan L. Spenser's Belge Episode and the Pageants for Leicester in the Low Countries, 1585-6. SP 28 (1931). 235-240.

————. Notes on Elizabethan Chivalry and the Faerie Queene. SP 30 (1933). 155-159.

————. Reflections of Elizabethan Tournaments in the Faerie Queene 4. 4 and 5. 3. ELH 5 (1938). 278-84.

Warton, Thomas. Poems upon Several Occasions . . . By John Milton. 2nd edition, London, 1791.